AI-Driven Cybersecurity Systems, Applications, and Resilient Infrastructure

Eduard Babulak
https://orcid.org/0000-0003-2450-090X
US National Science Foundation, USA

IGI Global
Scientific Publishing
Publishing Tomorrow's Research Today

Published in the United States of America by
IGI Global Scientific Publishing
701 East Chocolate Avenue
Hershey, PA, 17033, USA
Tel: 717-533-8845 | Fax: 717-533-7115
Website: https://www.igi-global.com E-mail: cust@igi-global.com

Library of Congress Cataloging-in-Publication Data

CIP Data Pending
ISBN13: 9798260016084
Isbn13Softcover: 9798260016091
EISBN13: 9798260016107

British Cataloguing in Publication Data
A Cataloguing in Publication record for this book is available from the British Library.

I would like to dedicate this Book to my family and friends who provided me with their kind support and encouragement during the Book project.

Editorial Advisory Board

Table of Contents

Preface xiv

Acknowledgment xvii

Introduction xviii

Chapter 1
Smart Cyber Defense Systems AI Approaches for Threat Detection and Incident Management 1
Shaista Ashraf Farooqi, Asia e University, Pakistan

Chapter 2
Automated Threats: Understanding and Mitigating AI-Generated Cyber Attacks 39
Muhammad Virga Mulia, Universitas Esa Unggul, Indonesia
Binastya Anggara Sekti, Universitas Esa Unggul, Indonesia
Anisah Sri Utami, Universitas Esa Unggul, Indonesia

Chapter 3
From Black Boxes to Cyber Sentinels: Interpretable Generative AI for Threat Intelligence and Digital Forensics 69
Syed Ibad Ali, Parul Institute of Engineering and Technology, Parul University, Vadodara, India

Chapter 4
Lightweight Cryptography-Based Generative Explainable AI With Multi-Factor Authentication Methods for Safe Cyber Transactions in Oil Sector 101
Mishall Hammed Al-Zubaidie, University of Thi-Qar, Iraq & University of Southern Queensland, Australia
Amal Khaleel Hamad, University of Thi-Qar, Iraq

Chapter 5
Cognitive Adversarial Security Neuro: Symbolic and Generative AI Defense Ecosystems for Self-Evolving Cyber Resilience.. 139
Syed Ibad Ali, Parul Institute of Engineering and Technology, Parul University, Vadodara, India

Chapter 6
Explainable and Generative AI in Cybersecurity: Global Implementation Analysis 163
A. R. Deepti, Acharya Institute of Graduate Studies, India
Farzeen Basith, Acharya Institute of Graduate Studies, India
B. Manimekala, Christ University, India

Chapter 7
Defending Against AI-Generated Cyber Threats: Frameworks, Models, and Real-Time Generative AI Security Defenses 195
Muhammad Usman Tariq, Abu Dhabi University, UAE & University College Cork, Ireland

Chapter 8
Securing the Future: Enhancing Cybersecurity and Resilience in Digital and Software Supply Chains 221
Md. Owafeeuzzaman Patwary, American International University-Bangladesh, Bangladesh
Raisa Jarin, American International University-Bangladesh, Bangladesh
Apurbo Biswas, American International University-Bangladesh, Bangladesh
Md. Mobashir Tajuare Partho, American International University-Bangladesh, Bangladesh
Dipta Gomes, American International University-Bangladesh, Bangladesh
Md. Reazul Islam, University at Albany, State University of New York, USA

Chapter 9
Ensuring Safety of Financial Institutions in the Modern Era Through Quantum Computing and Cybersecurity 273
P. Ashok, Symbiosis Institute of Digital and Telecom Management, India
S. Lakshmi Sridevi, Chennai Institute of Technology, India
Sarala Patchala, KKR and KSR Institute of Technology and Sciences, India
Sidharth Sahoo, Symbiosis Institute of Digital and Telecom Management, India

Chapter 10
Quantum Resilient Trust Fabric: Human-Aligned Generative AI and Blockchain Fusion for Next-Generation Cybersecurity Governance................. 301
Syed Ibad Ali, Parul Institute of Engineering and Technology, Parul University, Vadodara, India

Conclusion 333

Compilation of References 335

About the Contributors 373

Index 377

Detailed Table of Contents

Preface xiv

Acknowledgment xvii

Introduction xviii

Chapter 1
Smart Cyber Defense Systems AI Approaches for Threat Detection and Incident Management 1
Shaista Ashraf Farooqi, Asia e University, Pakistan

AI-powered cyber defense systems have become essential as modern threats surpass the capabilities of traditional security methods. This chapter examines how machine learning, deep learning, NLP, and reinforcement learning enhance intrusion analytics, anomaly detection, malware and ransomware identification, and phishing prevention. It also explores AI-driven automation—including SOAR workflows, intelligent IDPS, digital forensics, and continuous authentication within Zero Trust models. Key challenges such as adversarial attacks, data privacy risks, model bias, and computational constraints are discussed, alongside emerging solutions like federated learning, differential privacy, generative threat simulation, and quantum-secure AI. Sector-specific applications across healthcare, finance, smart cities, industrial systems, and cloud–enterprise SOCs are highlighted. The chapter concludes with an architectural blueprint for unified smart cyber defense and insights into future trajectories for adaptive, resilient, and autonomous security systems.

Chapter 2
Automated Threats: Understanding and Mitigating AI-Generated Cyber Attacks 39
Muhammad Virga Mulia, Universitas Esa Unggul, Indonesia
Binastya Anggara Sekti, Universitas Esa Unggul, Indonesia
Anisah Sri Utami, Universitas Esa Unggul, Indonesia

This chapter explores the evolving landscape of AI-generated cyber threats and the corresponding defense mechanisms required to counter them. It examines how Generative AI (GenAI) is increasingly used to automate phishing, malware creation, and social engineering, while Explainable AI (XAI) enhances transparency and accountability in automated defense systems. The chapter develops a framework for understanding AI-automated attacks through the lens of the cyber kill chain, detailing how autonomy, adaptability, and hyper personalization redefine modern threats. It further proposes a multi-layered defense architecture that integrates behavioral analytics, adversarial training, and explainable automation to ensure ethical and interpretable cybersecurity operations. By analyzing case studies and ethical considerations, this chapter positions explainability as the cornerstone of future cyber resilience, where automation must remain accountable, transparent, and aligned with human oversight.

Chapter 3
From Black Boxes to Cyber Sentinels: Interpretable Generative AI for Threat Intelligence and Digital Forensics 69
Syed Ibad Ali, Parul Institute of Engineering and Technology, Parul University, Vadodara, India

The increasing sophistication of cyberattacks—driven by automation, deepfake data, and polymorphic malware—has rendered traditional opaque artificial intelligence (AI) models insufficient for maintaining security resilience. This book chapter introduces a transformative framework that reimagines cybersecurity through interpretable generative AI, uniting the transparency of Explainable AI (XAI) with the creative adaptability of generative modeling. The chapter positions these hybrid architectures as cyber sentinels—autonomous, self-learning systems capable of generating, detecting, and explaining complex threat scenarios in real time. By merging Generative Adversarial Networks (GANs), Variational Autoencoders (VAEs), and Transformer-based threat intelligence models with interpretability layers, the proposed system achieves both predictive accuracy and forensic accountability.

Chapter 4
Lightweight Cryptography-Based Generative Explainable AI With Multi-Factor Authentication Methods for Safe Cyber Transactions in Oil Sector 101
Mishall Hammed Al-Zubaidie, University of Thi-Qar, Iraq & University of Southern Queensland, Australia
Amal Khaleel Hamad, University of Thi-Qar, Iraq

This chapter proposes a novel multi-factor authentication (MFA) with six schemes, namely password salting/hashing, non-interactive zero-knowledge (NIZK) proofs, GPS-based validation, time-based one-time passwords (TOTP), DNA cryptography, and lightweight SPECK ciphers. Taken together, these elements address the deficiencies in prior authentication and achieve a tradeoff between security and computational efficiency. The system is verified by theoretical and experimental methods. Furthermore, it is theoretically examined under the Real-or-Random model (RoR) with generative/explainable Artificial Intelligence (AI)-driven cybersecurity and provides strong security guarantees in terms of unpredictability (even if reduced in certain security parameters) and defends against replay, insider misuse, brute-force key search attacks, as well as spoofing ones. The solution is developed in Java, and the system is empirically evaluated by performing 100 runs to examine essential performance features: randomness, determinism, stability, and scalability.

Chapter 5
Cognitive Adversarial Security Neuro: Symbolic and Generative AI Defense Ecosystems for Self-Evolving Cyber Resilience.. 139
Syed Ibad Ali, Parul Institute of Engineering and Technology, Parul University, Vadodara, India

The rapid evolution of cyber threats, driven by autonomous malware, generative adversaries, and large-scale AI-driven attack vectors, has outpaced the capabilities of conventional security frameworks. This paper proposes a Cognitive Adversarial Security Ecosystem that integrates neuro-symbolic intelligence, generative AI models, and self-evolving cyber-defense mechanisms to establish a resilient, adaptive, and explainable security paradigm. The proposed ecosystem leverages the complementary strengths of symbolic reasoning and neural learning to achieve high-fidelity threat detection, contextual decision-making, and automated mitigation against zero-day and polymorphic attacks. Generative adversarial models are employed to simulate sophisticated threat landscapes, enabling proactive vulnerability assessment and red-team intelligence at scale.

Chapter 6
Explainable and Generative AI in Cybersecurity: Global Implementation Analysis.. 163
A. R. Deepti, Acharya Institute of Graduate Studies, India
Farzeen Basith, Acharya Institute of Graduate Studies, India
B. Manimekala, Christ University, India

This chapter examines global implementation of explainable and generative AI in cybersecurity across diverse frameworks. Through comprehensive analysis across multiple countries and sectors, the study demonstrates AI-enhanced systems deliver considerable improvements in threat detection while reducing costs and response times. The key contributions include implementation frameworks, cross-cultural adaptation strategies, bias mitigation, and ROI methodologies. The critical challenges addressed include integration complexity, skills gaps, and ethical considerations.

Chapter 7
Defending Against AI-Generated Cyber Threats: Frameworks, Models, and Real-Time Generative AI Security Defenses 195
Muhammad Usman Tariq, Abu Dhabi University, UAE & University College Cork, Ireland

The emergence and rapid development of generative technologies have changed the nature of cyber threats, enabling enemies to use complex attacks in a more automated manner, create convincing deception using digital tools, and act more quickly owing to the availability of security gaps. The ability to defend against machine-generated attacks is at the heart of operational resilience and safeguarding sensitive data as organizations continue to expand their digital footprint. This chapter examines some of the emerging frameworks and defense models related to the risk of automated threat generation, with an emphasis on real-time security controls that are meant to detect, prevent, and adapt to new patterns of attacks. The results highlight the need for proactive design principles in the construction of security systems that will be effective in mitigating contemporary generative cyber threats. The integration of behavioral analysis, dynamic threat intelligence, deception systems, and automated defensive orchestration in security systems is important.

Chapter 8
Securing the Future: Enhancing Cybersecurity and Resilience in Digital and Software Supply Chains 221
Md. Owafeeuzzaman Patwary, American International University-Bangladesh, Bangladesh
Raisa Jarin, American International University-Bangladesh, Bangladesh
Apurbo Biswas, American International University-Bangladesh, Bangladesh
Md. Mobashir Tajuare Partho, American International University-Bangladesh, Bangladesh
Dipta Gomes, American International University-Bangladesh, Bangladesh
Md. Reazul Islam, University at Albany, State University of New York, USA

This chapter critically examines the cybersecurity and resilience challenges inherent in digital and software supply chains, where hyper-connectivity enlarges the attack surface and sophisticated adversaries exploit dependencies, as demonstrated by the SolarWinds, Log4Shell, and XZ Utils incidents. Our analysis identifies systemic security issues, ranging from significant visibility gaps to inadequate authentication mechanisms, and traces their direct impact on operational disruption and reputation damage. We explore the distinct security implications associated with foundational technologies, including cloud computing, Internet of Things (IoT), and blockchain, and propose specific hardening strategies tailored to each technology. The central argument presents a layered countermeasure strategy: adopting frameworks such as NIST CSF, embedding rigorous risk assessment, and evolving human factors through targeted training.

Chapter 9
Ensuring Safety of Financial Institutions in the Modern Era Through Quantum Computing and Cybersecurity 273
P. Ashok, Symbiosis Institute of Digital and Telecom Management, India
S. Lakshmi Sridevi, Chennai Institute of Technology, India
Sarala Patchala, KKR and KSR Institute of Technology and Sciences, India
Sidharth Sahoo, Symbiosis Institute of Digital and Telecom Management, India

Quantum computing imperils cybersecurity by utilizing superposition and entanglement—via algorithms like Grover's and Shor's—to breach classical RSA and ECC encryption. To secure critical economic data, particularly within European banks, the adoption of lattice-based, hash-based, and code-based cryptography, along with Quantum Key Distribution (QKD), is essential. This paper outlines a future "Architecture of Quantum Banking" (AQB) rooted in post-quantum cryptography. Beyond defense, the study explores how financial institutions can leverage QAOA and Quantum Monte Carlo simulations to optimize portfolios, accelerate derivative pricing, and enhance fraud detection. Additionally, quantum-enhanced machine learning and blockchain integration promise superior anomaly detection and transaction security. To navigate scaling challenges, the research emphasizes the necessity of collaboration between banks, technology firms, and research institutes to balance innovation with robust risk management.

Chapter 10
Quantum Resilient Trust Fabric: Human-Aligned Generative AI and Blockchain Fusion for Next-Generation Cybersecurity Governance................ 301
Syed Ibad Ali, Parul Institute of Engineering and Technology, Parul University, Vadodara, India

This chapter presents a quantum-resilient trust fabric that integrates human-aligned generative AI with blockchain-based governance to build secure, transparent, and future-proof cybersecurity ecosystems. By combining post-quantum cryptography, decentralized trust mechanisms, and interpretable generative intelligence, the framework offers strong resistance to quantum-era threats while ensuring ethical decision alignment. The fusion of AI-driven threat prediction, immutable ledger integrity, and automated smart-contract enforcement establishes an adaptive, scalable, and governance-ready cybersecurity architecture suitable for next-generation digital infrastructures.

Conclusion 333

Compilation of References 335

About the Contributors 373

Index 377

Preface

The accelerating convergence of artificial intelligence (AI) and cybersecurity is fundamentally reshaping how digital systems are protected, governed, and sustained. As cyber threats grow in scale, sophistication, and autonomy, traditional rule-based and reactive defense mechanisms are no longer sufficient to ensure resilience across modern infrastructures. The emergence of AI-driven cybersecurity systems capable of learning, adapting, and responding in real time, marks a transformative shift toward proactive and intelligent security paradigms.

AI-Driven Cybersecurity Systems, Applications, and Resilient Infrastructure brings together cutting-edge research and practical insights from global scholars and practitioners to explore this evolving landscape. The volume examines how advanced AI techniques including machine learning, deep learning, generative AI, explainable AI (XAI), and neuro-symbolic intelligence are redefining threat detection, incident response, digital forensics, authentication, and cyber resilience.

Beyond technological innovation, this book critically engages with the ethical, operational, and governance challenges associated with AI adoption in cybersecurity. Issues such as adversarial manipulation, model transparency, data privacy, bias, and computational constraints are addressed alongside emerging solutions including federated learning, differential privacy, and quantum-resilient architectures. The chapters collectively highlight the necessity of integrating human oversight, explainability, and accountability into increasingly autonomous defense systems.

Spanning diverse sectors including cyber security, computer hardware and software, healthcare, finance, industrial systems, smart cities, and global supply chains, this volume provides a comprehensive perspective on how AI can be leveraged to build secure, adaptive, and future-ready infrastructures. It serves as a valuable resource for researchers, practitioners, policymakers, and students seeking to understand and advance the next generation of cybersecurity systems.

CHAPTER OVERVIEW

Chapter 1: Introduces smart cyber defense systems powered by AI, focusing on advanced techniques such as machine learning, deep learning, natural language processing, and reinforcement learning for threat detection and incident management. It explores AI-driven automation in intrusion detection and prevention systems, SOAR platforms, and Zero Trust architectures, while addressing challenges like adversarial attacks and data privacy concerns. The chapter concludes with a unified architectural blueprint for resilient cyber defense.

Chapter 2: Examines the rise of AI-generated cyber threats, including automated phishing, malware, and social engineering attacks. It presents a structured framework based on the cyber kill chain and emphasizes the role of Explainable AI (XAI) in ensuring transparency and accountability. A multi-layered defense architecture integrating behavioral analytics and adversarial training is proposed.

Chapter 3: Explores the transition from opaque AI models to interpretable generative AI systems for cybersecurity. It introduces hybrid frameworks combining GANs, VAEs, and transformer-based models with explainability layers to enhance threat intelligence and digital forensics, enabling real-time detection and transparent decision-making.

Chapter 4: Proposes a secure multi-factor authentication framework incorporating lightweight cryptography and AI-driven mechanisms. The chapter details innovative techniques such as non-interactive zero-knowledge proofs, DNA cryptography, and SPECK ciphers, validated through theoretical models and experimental evaluation to ensure robust and efficient security in critical sectors.

Chapter 5: Presents a cognitive adversarial security ecosystem that integrates neuro-symbolic AI and generative models to enable self-evolving cyber defense. The framework emphasizes contextual reasoning, automated mitigation, and proactive threat simulation for combating advanced and zero-day attacks.

Chapter 6: Provides a global analysis of implementing explainable and generative AI in cybersecurity across different sectors and regions. It highlights improvements in detection accuracy, cost efficiency, and response times, while addressing challenges such as integration complexity, workforce skill gaps, and ethical considerations.

Chapter 7: Focuses on defense frameworks against AI-generated cyber threats, emphasizing real-time detection and adaptive response mechanisms. It discusses the integration of behavioral analytics, dynamic threat intelligence, and automated orchestration to enhance operational resilience in rapidly evolving threat environments.

Chapter 8: Investigates cybersecurity challenges in digital and software supply chains, analyzing vulnerabilities exposed by major cyber incidents. It proposes layered defense strategies incorporating established frameworks, risk assessment methodologies, and human-centered approaches to strengthen resilience across interconnected systems.

Chapter 9: Examines the implications of quantum computing on cybersecurity, particularly in financial systems. It discusses post-quantum cryptographic techniques, quantum key distribution, and quantum-enhanced analytics, while outlining strategies for secure and efficient financial operations in the quantum era.

Chapter 10: Introduces a quantum-resilient trust framework that integrates generative AI with blockchain technologies. The chapter emphasizes secure governance, ethical alignment, and decentralized trust mechanisms to support scalable and future-proof cybersecurity infrastructures.

The chapters in this volume collectively demonstrate that the future of cybersecurity lies in the seamless integration of intelligent, adaptive, and explainable systems. AI-driven approaches are not only enhancing the speed and accuracy of threat detection but are also enabling predictive, autonomous, and resilient defense mechanisms capable of addressing the complexities of modern digital ecosystems.

At the same time, the adoption of these technologies introduces new challenges that must be carefully managed. Ensuring transparency, mitigating bias, safeguarding privacy, and maintaining human oversight are critical to building trustworthy AI-driven cybersecurity systems. Furthermore, the emergence of quantum computing and increasingly sophisticated adversarial techniques underscores the need for continuous innovation and interdisciplinary collaboration.

This book highlights a clear trajectory toward unified, AI-enabled security architectures that combine advanced analytics, automation, and governance frameworks. By bridging theoretical advancements with practical applications, it provides a foundation for developing secure, ethical, and resilient infrastructures capable of withstanding both current and future cyber threats.

Eduard Babulak
US National Science Foundation, USA

Acknowledgment

I would like to use this opportunity to express my sincere gratitude to contributors, reviewers, to Mrs. Hessler, Ms Walter, Ms Long, Ms Eddinger, Ms Wagner, Ms Barrantes, Ms Travers, Ms McLouglin, Ms Wertman, the IGI Global Book Development Team, and all IGI Colleagues and Friends for their excellent support, kind guidance and good counsel during the course of this and my earlier projects. I would like to say great thank you to my family and friends for their kind support and encouragement during the Book project.

Introduction

The Third Millennium rapid advances in the field of Applied AI, Fast Internet, and Ultra-Smart Computing Software and Hardware, are opening new horizons in the Fully Automated Cyberspace and present new challenges in the AI driven Cyber Security Systems. The Ubiquitous access to Fast Internet facilitates unlimited access to information resources 24/7 to anyone and anywhere.

The pervasive and secure access to internet information resource via smart cyberspace has become essential to the government, business industry, health, transport, education, and all sectors in society worldwide.

The rise of Applied AI brought numerous benefits in smart technologies, but at the same time has opened a new Pandora Box for Cyber Crime and unethical use and manipulation of cyberspace resources. The Cyber Security researchers, innovators, engineer and decision makers are driven to learn, to develop future cutting edge Cyber Security technologies that will be provide 27/7 guarantees of Confidentiality, Availability and Integrity of information resource far beyond our imagination today.

The Book presents collection of selected peer reviewed papers bringing to light the state-of-the-art, the latest and future developments in the field of Applied AI, Smart Computing, Fast Internet and Cyber Security Software and Hardware

The book will be most valuable text for the cyber security researchers, industry innovators, technology developers, professionals, government and business decision makers as well as to academic community and general public.

The Book presents new perspectives on the Next Generation of AI inspired Cyber Security and Critical Cyber Security Infrastructure hardening and securing its reliability and availability 24/7 for the betterment of Mankind.

Eduard Babulak

US National Science Foundation, USA

Chapter 1
Smart Cyber Defense Systems AI Approaches for Threat Detection and Incident Management

Shaista Ashraf Farooqi
http://orcid.org/0009-0001-2066-5013
Asia e University, Pakistan

ABSTRACT

AI-powered cyber defense systems have become essential as modern threats surpass the capabilities of traditional security methods. This chapter examines how machine learning, deep learning, NLP, and reinforcement learning enhance intrusion analytics, anomaly detection, malware and ransomware identification, and phishing prevention. It also explores AI-driven automation—including SOAR workflows, intelligent IDPS, digital forensics, and continuous authentication within Zero Trust models. Key challenges such as adversarial attacks, data privacy risks, model bias, and computational constraints are discussed, alongside emerging solutions like federated learning, differential privacy, generative threat simulation, and quantum-secure AI. Sector-specific applications across healthcare, finance, smart cities, industrial systems, and cloud–enterprise SOCs are highlighted. The chapter concludes with an architectural blueprint for unified smart cyber defense and insights into future trajectories for adaptive, resilient, and autonomous security systems.

DOI: 10.4018/979-8-2600-1608-4.ch001

1. INTRODUCTION AND CONCEPTUAL BACKGROUND

The accelerated growth of cyber attacks is now surpassing the operational limits of conventional defense mechanisms, especially those dependent on static rule sets and signature-based detection workflows. Modern attackers now employ sophisticated techniques—including zero-day exploits, polymorphic ransomware, large-scale automated intrusions and AI-driven attack tools—that adapt quickly to evade conventional defenses. These evolving threats demand smart, adaptive, and autonomous cyber defense systems capable of continuous learning and real-time decision-making (George, 2024; Alanezi & AL-Azzawi, 2024).

Artificial Intelligence (AI) serves as a foundational pillar of modern security systems, enabling intelligent threat identification, proactive risk assessment, and autonomous incident response. Smart defense techniques utilize machine learning (ML), deep learning (DL), natural language processing (NLP) and reinforcement learning (RL) to analyze massive volumes of security telemetry, identify anomalous behaviors and predict emerging attack patterns with high accuracy (Chen et al., 2024). These capabilities support early threat discovery by monitoring network traffic, detecting behavioral deviations and uncovering latent indicators of compromise before such activities can escalate into major data breaches. Furthermore, AI-enabled automation enhances incident management by accelerating response actions, containing threats and reducing overall attack impact (Verma, 2024).

This chapter examines how AI is reshaping cyber defense into a smarter and more autonomous security paradigm, with a focus on AI-based threat detection models, intelligent analytics and automated incident response systems. The discussion further covers the operational and ethical complexities of deploying AI-driven security solutions. The chapter also explores emerging innovations—such as federated learning, quantum-assisted cybersecurity and self-healing autonomous networks—that will shape the future landscape of smart cyber defense.

1.1. Rationale for AI-Enabled Cyber Defense

The modern cybersecurity landscape is characterized by rapidly evolving, highly sophisticated threats that traditional defense mechanisms struggle to detect or mitigate. Attackers now employ zero-day attacks, polymorphic malware, advanced persistent threats (APTs) and AI-powered attack tools. These adaptive techniques enable them to bypass conventional signature-based antivirus software and rule-driven intrusion detection systems (IDS). As a result, organizations relying solely on static, predefined detection rules face significant blind spots when confronting novel or fast-changing threat vectors (Ilieva & Stoilova, 2024).

A major driver behind the shift toward AI-enabled cyber defense is the increased use of automation and artificial intelligence by cybercriminals themselves. Adversaries leverage AI to craft convincingly deceptive phishing campaigns, generate deepfake-based social engineering content, evade anomaly-based detection and orchestrate large-scale automated attacks with minimal human effort. Ransomware variants now incorporate advanced encryption, autonomous propagation and obfuscation techniques to enable them to infiltrate networks and escalate damage before traditional tools can respond. Similarly, zero-day attacks on unknown vulnerabilities—pose significant risks because signature-based defenses cannot recognize previously unseen attack patterns (Kinyua & Awuah, 2021).

The growth of virtualization, cloud computing, mobile ecosystems and the Internet of Things (IoT) has significantly expanded the organizational attack surface. Millions of interconnected devices, distributed services, APIs, supply chain integrations and remote-access points create numerous opportunities for malicious exploitation. Threats such as DDoS attacks, supply chain compromise and insider misuse have become increasingly common and more difficult to detect using traditional technologies (Rizky et al., 2024).

Given this complex and dynamic threat environment, AI-enabled cyber defense has become an operational necessity. AI systems can process massive, diverse data streams, learn from evolving adversarial behaviors and detect subtle anomalies that traditional systems consistently overlook. Furthermore, AI enables predictive risk modeling, intelligent incident response, and malicious activity analysis—capabilities essential for countering the speed, scale, and sophistication of modern cyberattacks (Salem et al., 2024). By integrating machine learning, deep learning and behavioral analytics, AI-driven defense mechanisms provide a more adaptive, proactive and intelligent approach to safeguarding digital ecosystems.

1.2. Evolutionary Trends in Cyber Threat Landscapes

The cyber threat landscape has rapidly evolved, driven by sophisticated attack techniques and the expansion of digital ecosystems. Traditional defenses—built on static rules and reactive mechanisms—can no longer match the speed and complexity of modern attacks. Adversaries now rely on zero-day exploits, AI-driven malware and large-scale automated phishing capable of bypassing conventional controls. In this context, Artificial Intelligence (AI) has emerged as a critical enabler of modern cyber defense, providing real-time detection, adaptive decision-making and predictive capabilities to protect digital environments (Sarker, 2024).

AI for Fast and Adaptive Threat Detection

AI-powered security systems can process large amounts of data in real time and spot patterns that suggest malicious activity. Unlike traditional tools, AI can recognize new attack behaviors and adapt as threats evolve. For example, AI-driven IDS can flag unusual spikes in outbound traffic or abnormal access attempts that may indicate a breach. AI-based firewalls also update their filtering rules automatically, blocking emerging threats without the need for manual action.

AI for Automated and Rapid Incident Response

A major strength of AI in cybersecurity is its ability to trigger immediate response actions. Modern attacks unfold in seconds, far faster than human analysts can react. AI-driven Security Orchestration, Automation and Response (SOAR) platforms streamline containment and remediation by isolating compromised devices, blocking malicious traffic and stopping ransomware encryption before major damage occurs. Similarly, AI-enhanced Endpoint Detection and Response (EDR) solutions continuously monitor endpoint behavior and can automatically interrupt suspicious encryption attempts during ransomware attacks (Kaur et al., 2024).

AI for Phishing and Fraud Prevention

Phishing campaigns have become increasingly sophisticated, often leveraging AI to craft highly realistic emails, deepfake content and automated social engineering messages. AI-powered security tools enhance phishing detection by analyzing email structure, linguistic features, sender behavior and embedded URLs. Modern email security systems, such as Google's ML-driven spam filters, can recognize fraudulent messages even when attackers modify content or attempt to mimic trusted communication styles (Eze & Shamir, 2024). These capabilities significantly improve protection against credential theft and financial fraud.

AI for Predictive and Proactive Defense

AI also plays a critical role in anticipating emerging cyber threats by analyzing global threat intelligence, historical attack trends, and dark web activity. Machine learning models and cognitive analytics platforms— such as IBM Watson for Cybersecurity. It scans vast quantities of threat reports, indicators of compromise (IOCs) and hacker discussions to identify early warning signs of potential attacks (Meduri et al., 2024). AI-driven threat hunting tools proactively search for vulnerabilities and misconfigurations by enabling organizations to strengthen defenses before attackers can exploit them.

1.3. Problem Definition and Theoretical Gaps

As cyber threats grow in scale and complexity, AI-driven detection has become central to modern cybersecurity. These systems aim to improve the speed, accuracy and efficiency of detecting and responding to attacks. By using machine learning, deep learning, and automation, AI enhances real-time threat identification, reduces reliance on manual analysis and strengthens overall IT resilience. This section outlines the core objectives and scope of AI-driven threat detection and highlights the remaining theoretical gaps.

Enhancing Threat Detection Accuracy

Traditional security tools rely heavily on predefined rules, which often leads to too many false alarms or missed detections when dealing with new or advanced attacks. AI improves detection accuracy by analyzing large amounts of data and learning from changing threat patterns. AI-based Intrusion Detection and Prevention Systems (IDS/IPS) use behavioral analysis to separate normal activity from malicious actions, reducing false alerts and improving overall threat visibility (Gunavathie et al., 2023).

Automating Incident Response and Mitigation

AI-driven threat detection not only identifies malicious activity but also automates key parts of the incident response process, helping reduce reaction times and minimize potential damage. Security Orchestration, Automation and Response (SOAR) platforms use AI to assess security alerts, isolate compromised systems and suggest remediation steps with little or no human input (Vast et al., 2021). For example, when ransomware is detected, AI-powered Endpoint Detection and Response (EDR) tools can stop the encryption process, quarantine the affected device and begin recovery actions to prevent the attack from spreading further.

Predicting and Preventing Cyber Threats

AI strengthens cybersecurity by applying predictive analytics to identify potential threats before they can cause damage. By examining patterns from past attacks and global threat intelligence, AI models can anticipate vulnerabilities and suggest proactive defense strategies. For instance, AI-driven Threat Intelligence Platforms (TIPs) collect data from multiple sources, including dark web forums, to detect indicators of compromise (IOCs) and alert organizations about possible cyberattacks in advance (Manda, 2024; Babulak, 2023).

Expanding Cybersecurity Across Multiple Environments

The scope of AI-driven threat detection extends beyond traditional IT infrastructures. AI is now integrated into cloud security, IoT security, mobile device security and network security, providing a multi-layered approach to cyber defense. For example, AI-powered Cloud Security Posture Management (CSPM) tools continuously scan cloud environments for misconfigurations, malicious activities and policy breaches ensuring secure cloud infrastructure. AI-based anomaly detection systems also support IoT networks by identifying malicious activity in connected devices and protecting critical systems from cyberattacks.

Figure 1 presents a Venn diagram showing the main cybersecurity domains enhanced by AI, including cloud security, network security, IoT and edge security, endpoint protection, and threat intelligence. The overlap highlights AI's shared role in real-time detection, predictive analysis, and automated response across these environments.

Figure 1. AI-enabled cyber defense domains and their intersections

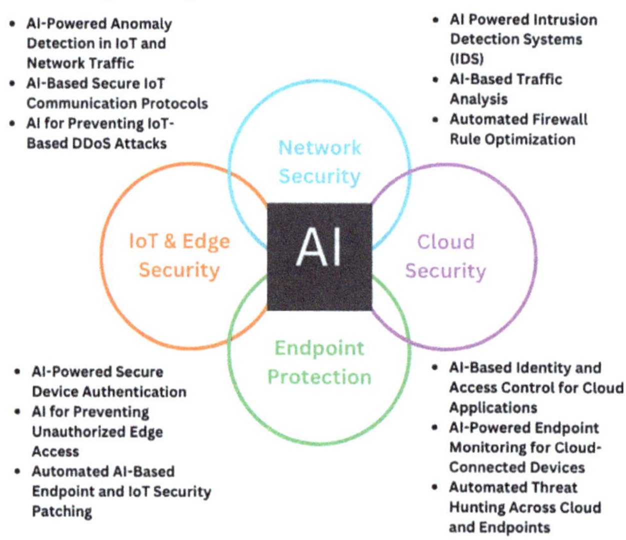

1.4. Objectives and Chapter Schema

This chapter provides a structured overview of how Artificial Intelligence (AI) strengthens modern cyber defense through intelligent threat detection, automated incident response and integration across diverse security environments. Its key objectives are to:

- outline the evolution of cyber threats and explain the limitations of traditional security mechanisms;
- justify the need for AI-enabled defense by emphasizing adaptive, predictive and automated security capabilities;
- identify major challenges and theoretical gaps in current AI-driven models, including adversarial risks, interpretability issues and scalability constraints;
- examine core AI techniques that support advanced detection and response;
- discuss technical, ethical and operational challenges in deploying AI for cybersecurity.

To achieve these objectives, the chapter is organized as follows. **Section 1** introduces the background, motivation, evolving threat landscape, and key theoretical gaps driving the need for AI-enabled cyber defense. **Section 2** outlines foundational AI methodologies and core cyber defense paradigms. **Section 3** examines intelligent threat analytics and advanced AI-based detection models. **Section 4** discusses AI-driven automated security operations and incident response mechanisms. **Section 5** presents the architectural framework underpinning smart cyber defense systems. **Section 6** explores domain-driven implementations of AI across healthcare, finance, smart cities, industrial CPS, and national security environments. **Section 7** addresses the ethical, adversarial, and governance challenges surrounding AI-driven cyber defense. **Section 8** concludes the chapter by summarizing key insights and identifying future research directions.

This schema ensures a coherent progression from foundational concepts to technical mechanisms, challenges, and future trends, offering a comprehensive view of smart cyber defense systems powered by AI.

2. Cyber Defense Paradigms and AI Foundations

As cyber threats grow more sophisticated, traditional defenses struggle to keep pace with evolving attack methods. Modern security demands intelligent, adaptive and data-driven approaches that can detect anomalies, anticipate emerging risks and automate mitigation. Artificial Intelligence (AI) is central to this shift. Using machine learning, deep learning and behavioral analytics, AI enables security systems to process large data volumes, uncover complex patterns and respond far faster and more accurately than conventional methods (Mavikumbure et al., 2024).

2.1. Threat Taxonomies and Adversarial Models

Modern cyber defense depends on understanding threat categories and the adversarial models that shape attacker behavior. Threat taxonomies classify attacks into structured groups—such as opportunistic, targeted, and adaptive threats. While adversarial models describe attacker capabilities, motivations and tactics. Together, these frameworks guide the design of AI-enabled defense systems capable of detecting and mitigating diverse threat vectors (Fakhouri et al., 2024).

Common threat categories include malware, phishing and social engineering, zero-day exploits, insider threats, DDoS attacks, and advanced persistent threats (APTs). These vary in sophistication and intent. APT campaigns involve long-term, stealthy intrusions by skilled adversaries, whereas ransomware seeks rapid impact through system encryption (Almeida & Vasconcelos, 2023). AI-driven defense systems use such taxonomies to build behavioral profiles and anomaly baselines that improve detection accuracy.

Adversarial models further characterize attackers by defining what they know, what they can modify, and how they attempt to subvert security systems. In cybersecurity, adversaries are often modeled as white-box, gray-box or black-box attackers.

- **White-box adversaries** understand the internal workings of a security model, enabling them to craft highly targeted evasion strategies.
- **Black-box adversaries** have limited information but still exploit observable system behavior to bypass defenses.
- **Gray-box adversaries** possess partial system knowledge, allowing moderately sophisticated attacks such as adaptive phishing or API probing.

With the rise of AI-enabled cyberattacks, adversarial models have expanded to include AI-driven attackers, where machine learning is used to automate reconnaissance, optimize attack paths and generate adversarial manipulations. These attackers can modify malware signatures, generate deceptive phishing content or alter network traffic patterns to evade detection (Chennam et al., 2022).

Threat taxonomies and adversarial models are essential precursors to AI-driven cyber defense. They inform model design, guide feature engineering, and enable security systems to anticipate attacker behavior. By embedding these foundational classifications into AI architectures, modern cyber defense frameworks gain the ability to reason about threat diversity, predict adversarial intent, and resist adaptive attack strategies (Tanikonda et al., 2022).

2.2. Limitations of Traditional Defense Mechanisms

Traditional cybersecurity defenses were built for static and predictable threat environments. These mechanisms struggle against today's rapidly evolving, automated and adaptive cyberattacks. A key limitation is their dependence on predefined signatures and rules, which prevents them from detecting zero-day exploits, polymorphic malware and novel attack strategies. Because updates are manual and reactive, attackers can move faster than traditional defenses can respond (Sontan & Samuel, 2024).

Traditional security tools also struggle to analyze large-scale, high-dimensional data, allowing subtle anomalies and early attack indicators to pass undetected. Their limited contextual and behavioral awareness further reduces effectiveness against insider threats, stealthy intrusions and advanced persistent threats (APTs) that closely resemble normal user activity. Furthermore, legacy perimeter-based defenses are unsuitable for distributed cloud, IoT and remote environments, where attack surfaces are broader and lateral movement is easier.

These shortcomings illustrate why modern cybersecurity requires adaptive, intelligence-drive, and automated defense mechanisms, particularly those enabled by AI.

2.3. AI Methodologies for Cyber Defense

AI methodologies form the analytical core of modern cyber defense, enabling more adaptive and accurate threat identification than traditional tools. By processing large-scale, high-dimensional security data, AI systems uncover attack patterns that conventional methods often miss.

Computational learning techniques provide the foundation:

- Supervised learning enables precise malware and phishing classification.
- Unsupervised learning detects zero-day threats, insider misuse, and emerging attack patterns.
- Reinforcement learning adds autonomous adaptability by evolving defensive strategies in response to changing attacker behavior.

Deep learning architectures further strengthen detection by analyzing complex and unstructured data. DNNs identify malicious behavior in unseen malware variants (Kok et al., 2020), RNNs and LSTMs detect deviations in sequential traffic associated with exfiltration or lateral movement (Vikram et al., 2024), and CNNs or

Transformer models enhance phishing and fraud detection even under adversarial obfuscation (Majgave & Gavankar, 2024).

Together, these AI methodologies shift cyber defense from static, reactive approaches to adaptive, predictive, and automated security operations, forming the basis for the advanced models discussed in the following subsections.

2.3.1. Computational Learning Models

Computational learning models form the foundation of AI-driven cyber defense, enabling the detection of known and unknown threats across complex environments. These models learn from historical data, real-time telemetry, and evolving attack patterns to classify malicious behavior, detect anomalies, and generalize to unseen threats.

- **Supervised learning** supports high-precision classification of malware, phishing, and spam by training on labeled samples, enabling signature-independent detection of threats resembling previously observed patterns (Mvula et al., 2024).
- **Unsupervised learning** is essential for zero-day and behavioral threat detection—anomaly-based IDS use it to model normal activity and flag deviations indicative of insider misuse or stealthy intrusions (Mvula et al., 2024).
- **Reinforcement learning (RL)** adds adaptability by learning optimal defensive actions through continuous interaction with hostile environments, supporting dynamic and automated threat mitigation (Fard et al., 2023).

Together, these learning approaches provide scalable and behavior-aware defenses necessary for modern cyber threat landscapes.

2.3.2. Deep and Reinforcement Architectures

Deep learning architectures significantly strengthen cyber defense by processing high-dimensional, unstructured, and behavior-rich data that traditional models cannot analyze. Their multilayered representations enable detection of subtle and evolving threats.

- **DNNs** enhance malware detection by analyzing execution behavior and system interactions, enabling identification of polymorphic and previously unseen variants.

- **RNN and LSTM** models capture temporal dependencies in network traffic, detecting patterns linked to data exfiltration, DDoS staging, and lateral movement that static rules often miss.
- **CNNs and Transformer-based models** support phishing and fraud detection by analyzing linguistic cues, metadata, and visual features, providing strong resilience against adversarial obfuscation.
- **Reinforcement Learning** further complements these architectures by enabling adaptive defensive strategies that adjust controls and thresholds in real time based on attacker behavior.

Collectively, deep and reinforcement architectures provide the representational strength and adaptive intelligence required for next-generation cyber defense, supporting scalable threat detection, behavioral monitoring and autonomous response across complex digital ecosystems.

2.4. Security Data Acquisition and Feature Abstraction

AI-driven cyber defense relies on acquiring and processing large volumes of security data from network logs, system events, user activity, emails, and file metadata. Effective data pipelines ensure these heterogeneous streams are captured in real time across cloud, IoT, and enterprise environments.

Feature abstraction then transforms raw data into usable representations. Supervised models use labeled features from known malware or phishing indicators, while unsupervised models extract statistical and behavioral features to detect anomalies and zero-day threats, common in modern anomaly-based IDS (Mvula et al., 2024).

Deep learning further automates feature extraction from high-dimensional, unstructured data. DNNs learn malware behavior, RNNs and LSTMs capture temporal network patterns linked to lateral movement and CNNs or Transformers identify linguistic cues in phishing content even under obfuscation.

Together, scalable data acquisition and advanced feature abstraction provide the foundational layer for accurate, adaptive AI-driven threat detection across diverse operational environments.

2.5. Systemic Limitations and Model Vulnerabilities

AI-driven cyber defense systems still face systemic limitations that affect their reliability and resilience. These challenges stem from their dependence on large datasets, vulnerability to adversarial manipulation, and the computational demands of real-time analytics.

Data poisoning remains a major risk, adversaries can introduce mislabeled or manipulated samples into training sets, corrupting models and creating exploitable blind spots—for example, malware mislabeled as benign reducing detection accuracy. At inference time, evasion attacks further threaten AI classifiers. Small perturbations to malware binaries, network flows, or phishing content can mislead deep models while preserving malicious intent, exposing the fragility of neural architectures (Ichetovkin & Kotenko, 2025).

Bias, lack of explainability, and trust issues also limit operational effectiveness. Models trained on imbalanced datasets may misclassify legitimate behavior as malicious, while opaque deep-learning decisions complicate verification, compliance, and analyst confidence (Chamola et al., 2023).

Scalability challenges persist as deep-learning IDS and behavioral analytics require substantial computational power, often causing latency and resource bottlenecks in large or resource-constrained environments.

These limitations underscore the need for adversarial training, continuous model monitoring, fairness-aware design, and optimized architectures. With these foundations established in Section 2, the next section examines how AI models operate in practice to profile threats, predict attacks, and support intelligent detection workflows.

AI learning techniques differ significantly in their ability to detect known and unknown threats, as summarized in Table 1.

Table 1. Comparative overview of AI methodologies

Threat Type	Description	Challenges
Advanced Persistent Threats (APTs)	Extended, targeted attacks, often state-sponsored, aimed at system infiltration, data theft, or operational disruption.	Difficult to detect due to stealthy, low-and-slow behavior; requires continuous monitoring and advanced analytics.
Zero-Day Vulnerabilities	Exploitation of previously unknown or unpatched software vulnerabilities.	No existing signatures or threat intelligence; signature-based tools cannot detect new exploits.
Ransomware	Malicious software that locks or encrypts files and systems and demands payment for their restoration.	Rapid propagation and strong encryption make early detection difficult; often linked to cryptocurrency-based payments.
AI-Powered Attacks	Attacks leveraging AI to automate exploitation, craft adaptive malware, or evade detection.	AI-driven malware evolves in real time, bypassing static and behavioral defenses.
Phishing and Social Engineering	Deceptive emails, messages, or interactions engineered to steal credentials or sensitive information.	Highly realistic attacks using deepfakes, AI chatbots, and linguistic mimicry evade traditional filters.

continued on following page

Table 1. Continued

Threat Type	Description	Challenges
Distributed Denial-of-Service (DDoS)	Overwhelming a target server or network with massive traffic using botnets.	Requires scalable protection and sophisticated traffic analysis to detect attack patterns in real time.
Insider Threats	Malicious or negligent activities by users with legitimate access rights.	Hard to detect because actions appear legitimate; requires behavioral analytics.
Supply Chain Attacks	Exploiting vulnerabilities in third-party vendors or software supply chains to penetrate numerous organizations.	Expands organizational exposure beyond internal controls; difficult to monitor external partners.
IoT and Cloud Security Risks	Exploitation of vulnerabilities in connected devices, cloud platforms, and virtualized environments.	Large, heterogeneous ecosystems are hard to secure; patches are delayed or inconsistent across devices.

3. Intelligent Threat Analytics and Detection Models

Building on the foundations of Section 2, Section 3 examines how AI techniques operate as active detection engines. The focus shifts from model mechanics to their applied roles in intrusion analytics, threat profiling, adaptive defense, and phishing detection. AI-driven threat analytics enhance defensive capabilities by identifying complex attack behaviors, adapting to adversarial changes, and enabling earlier intrusion detection than conventional tools.

3.1. Statistical and Predictive Intrusion Analytics

Statistical and predictive analytics form the first layer of intelligent threat detection by modeling normal behavior and flagging deviations linked to potential intrusions. Supervised learning classifies known threats with high accuracy using labeled attack data, detecting malware variants, brute-force attempts, and common phishing patterns (Babulak et al., 2025).

Unsupervised anomaly detection is crucial for identifying zero-day attacks, insider misuse, and long-dwell threats where labeled data is scarce. Anomaly-based IDS rely on clustering and density estimation to spot behaviors that deviate from baseline norms (Mvula et al., 2024).

Predictive intrusion analytics extend this capability by forecasting emerging threats through longitudinal trend analysis and correlated anomalies, enabling SOCs to anticipate ransomware campaigns, lateral movement, and exploit propagation paths, significantly reducing time-to-detection.

3.2. Deep Neural Threat Profiling

Deep neural architectures provide high-fidelity threat profiling by extracting complex patterns from high-dimensional security telemetry, enabling the detection of latent behaviors that rule-based systems cannot identify.

- **Deep Neural Networks (DNNs)** classify malware based on structural and behavioral attributes rather than static signatures, enabling the detection of polymorphic malware and obfuscated variants.
- **Recurrent Neural Networks (RNNs)** and **Long Short-Term Memory (LSTM) models** capture temporal patterns in traffic sequences, alert logs, authentication flows and API-call traces. These models detect multi-stage intrusions and stealthy lateral movement by recognizing subtle deviations in usage cycles.
- **Convolutional Neural Networks (CNNs)** and **Transformer-based models** enhance phishing detection by analyzing text semantics, sender profiles, formatting inconsistencies and embedded visual cues. These models remain accurate even when adversaries employ adversarial obfuscation, spoofed content, or AI-generated emails.

Deep neural profiling thus provides precise, multi-dimensional threat insights, greatly improving detection accuracy in complex, high-volume environments.

3.3. Reinforcement-Driven Adaptive Defense Agents

Reinforcement learning (RL) brings adaptiveness and autonomy to cyber defense by enabling agents to learn optimal defensive actions through interaction with evolving threat landscapes. Unlike static intrusion detection systems, RL-based agents continuously refine policies based on reward signals derived from the effectiveness of their responses (Sewak et al., 2023).

These agents dynamically adjust access controls, tune detection thresholds, isolate compromised assets, redirect traffic or reconfigure firewall policies—all without requiring predefined rules.

Because RL models evolve by observing attacker strategies, they are particularly suited for environments characterized by rapidly shifting threat dynamics, such as cloud platforms, IoT networks and hybrid enterprise systems.

RL-driven defense agents provide a pathway toward future autonomous SOCs capable of orchestrating real-time mitigation workflows with minimal human intervention.

3.4. AI-Enhanced Malware, Ransomware, and Zero-Day Detection

AI-based models significantly advance detection capabilities across sophisticated and emerging attack categories:

Malware Detection

AI models analyze memory behavior, execution patterns, system calls and API interactions to identify malicious activity even in previously unseen malware specimens. Behavioral detection surpasses signature-based tools by recognizing intent rather than relying on known patterns.

Ransomware Detection

Early detection is essential in ransomware response. AI monitors:

abnormal file encryption frequencies,
unexpected privilege escalations,
suspicious registry modifications, and
rapid file I/O bursts.
AI-driven EDR can halt encryption in progress and isolate devices to prevent propagation.

Zero-Day Detection

Zero-day attacks are difficult to detect because they exploit unknown vulnerabilities. AI models address this gap by:

using unsupervised anomaly detection to highlight abnormal system behaviors
clustering novel traffic patterns, and
identifying deviations from expected application behavior.

AI thus strengthens enterprise resilience against rapidly evolving threat classes that bypass traditional controls.

3.5. Cognitive Phishing and Social Pattern Analysis

Phishing attacks increasingly rely on AI-generated content, deepfakes and personalized manipulation strategies. Cognitive phishing detection leverages NLP,

Transformer models and contextual reasoning to combat such tactics. AI systems analyze message tone, linguistic structure, metadata, sender anomalies and behavioral context to identify spear-phishing and impersonation attempts.

Deep models examine:

urgency cues,
persuasion patterns,
abnormal communication sequences, and
hidden or obfuscated links.

By detecting both surface-level and latent semantic cues, cognitive phishing analysis significantly enhances protection against socially engineered threats, including BEC, CEO fraud, and multi-layer phishing chains.

3.6. Fidelity, Generalization, and Model Performance

For AI threat analytics to be operationally effective, models must maintain reliability and robustness across varying environments, device types and data distributions.

Key challenges include:

- **Generalization:** ensuring model accuracy on unseen threats, datasets, and network contexts.
- **Fidelity:** preserving precision and low false-positive rates in real-world deployment.
- **Environmental Drift:** adapting to shifts in user behavior and traffic patterns.
- **Adversarial Robustness:** maintaining stability against evasion and perturbation attacks.

Model performance is assessed through precision, recall, F1 score, false-positive/false-negative rates, latency and throughput—metrics that inform retraining schedules and guide operational tuning. Continuous model optimization is essential for sustaining detection quality as adversarial techniques evolve.

AI techniques supporting modern cyber defense—including ML, DL, NLP, RL, and behavioral analytics are mentioned in Table 2.

Table 2. Overview of AI techniques in cyber threat detection

AI Techniques	Core Functions	Use Cases
Machine Learning (ML)	Identifies and classifies threats using supervised and unsupervised data-driven models.	Spam filtering, malware classification, intrusion detection.
Deep Learning (DL)	Detects complex, non-linear attack patterns using multi-layer neural networks.	Advanced malware detection, real-time fraud detection, anomaly-based IDS.
Natural Language Processing (NLP)	Analyzes textual and linguistic data to detect phishing, social engineering, and dark web threat signals.	Phishing email detection, dark web monitoring, chatbot security.
Reinforcement Learning (RL)	Learns optimal defense strategies through continuous interaction with attack environments.	Adaptive firewalls, autonomous security agents, fraud prevention.
Anomaly Detection Models	Identifies deviations from established baselines to uncover unknown or zero-day attacks.	Zero-day exploit detection, network anomaly monitoring.
Behavioral Analysis Models	Analyzes behavioral patterns across users and systems to uncover insider threats and malicious actions.	Insider threat detection and unauthorized access prevention.
Automated Response Systems	Executes mitigation actions automatically to contain threats in real-time.	AI-powered EDR, SOAR-based automated incident response.
AI-Enabled Policy Optimization	Continuously updates security policies based on risk levels and changing behavior patterns.	Adaptive access control, AI-driven firewall rule optimization.

4. Automated Incident Intelligence and Response Mechanisms

AI has become a central enabler of automated security operations by integrating real-time threat detection with adaptive response mechanisms. Traditional SOC workflows are limited by manual analysis and high alert volumes, whereas AI-driven automation accelerates incident response, improves decision accuracy, and enhances operational resilience. This section examines how AI strengthens orchestration platforms, intrusion detection systems, threat hunting, digital forensics, and Zero Trust authentication frameworks.

4.1. AI-Driven Security Orchestration and Automated Threat Mitigation

AI-driven orchestration technologies consolidate security alerts, automate workflows, and coordinate rapid mitigation actions across distributed environments.

Automation reduces analyst workload, shortens response cycles, and provides consistent handling of recurring threats.

Security Orchestration, Automation, and Response (SOAR) Platforms

SOAR platforms leverage AI to integrate threat intelligence sources, correlate alerts, and trigger automated response playbooks. Traditional SOCs struggle with alert fatigue and delayed response times—SOAR systems address this challenge by centralizing logs from IDS, EDR, firewalls, and SIEM platforms into a unified operational dashboard.

AI-enhanced SOAR engines dynamically assess incident severity and initiate mitigation steps such as isolating compromised hosts, blocking malicious IPs, adjusting authentication policies, or enforcing network segmentation. Over time, SOAR systems refine their playbooks through machine learning, improving the speed, precision, and appropriateness of automated responses (Bartwal et al., 2022). This capability significantly reduces mean time to detect (MTTD) and mean time to respond (MTTR), enabling security teams to focus on complex analytical tasks.

AI-Enhanced Intrusion Detection and Prevention Systems (IDPS)

AI-driven IDPS platforms combine machine learning and deep learning to detect anomalies, identify unknown threats, and automate firewall or network policy adjustments. Unlike signature-based IDS/IPS tools, AI-enhanced systems learn evolving attacker behaviors—including insider threats, APTs, and zero-day exploits and respond dynamically.

For example, an AI-based IDPS can detect unusual lateral movement or a sudden surge of outbound traffic and immediately block the source while alerting analysts. Reinforcement learning further enhances intrusion prevention by enabling adaptive rule updates based on observed attack patterns. This transforms IDPS from passive monitors into active, intelligent defense components.

4.2. AI for Threat Hunting and Incident Investigation

AI expands the scope of proactive threat hunting and accelerates investigation of complex incidents. By automating correlation, anomaly detection, and attack-path reconstruction, AI significantly enhances forensic depth and investigative efficiency.

Figure 2 illustrates the five-phase incident response cycle, starting with preparation and concluding with the lessons-learned stage.

Figure 2. Incident response system

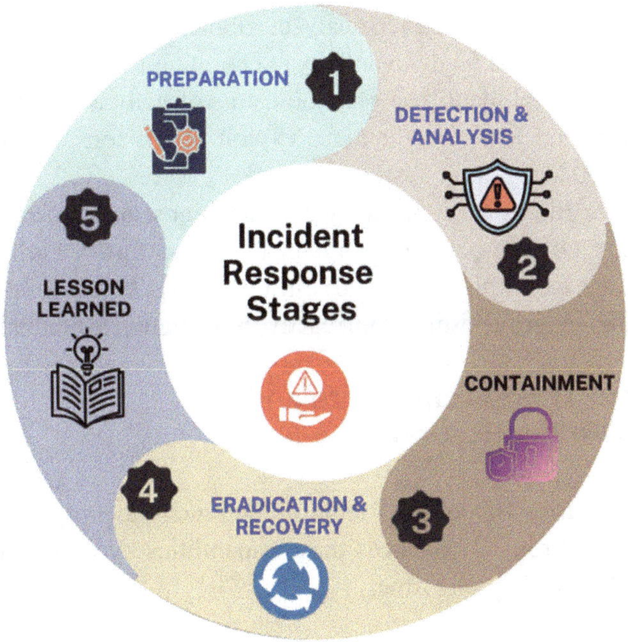

AI-Assisted Digital Forensics and Cyber Investigations

Traditional digital forensics is manual and time-intensive, requiring analysts to sift through large volumes of logs, memory dumps, and network records. AI streamlines this process by automatically correlating events, identifying suspicious artifacts, and reconstructing attack sequences.

Machine learning models detect unusual file modifications, unauthorized credential use, or anomalous access paths—patterns indicative of stealthy intrusions. Deep learning techniques recognize behaviors consistent with known attack techniques, even when obfuscation is used. NLP models further enhance investigations by extracting insights from threat reports, intelligence feeds, and dark web discussions. Together, these capabilities reduce investigation time while improving accuracy in threat attribution.

AI for Predictive Threat Intelligence

AI-driven predictive intelligence analyzes global attack data, network telemetry, and threat intelligence feeds to anticipate emerging threats. Unlike traditional reactive intelligence, AI identifies early indicators of malicious activity—such as coordinated scanning, leaked credentials, exploit discussions, or unusual botnet activity (Sarker, 2024).

By forecasting high-risk attack vectors, campaigns, or vulnerable assets, AI enables proactive defense planning. Organizations can fortify high-risk systems, deploy patches ahead of exploitation, and adjust firewall policies to address predicted threats. This shifts security posture from reactive remediation to predictive resilience.

4.3. AI in Zero Trust Architecture and Continuous Authentication

Zero Trust security frameworks require continuous identity verification and dynamic access control. AI enhances these capabilities by monitoring behavior, context, and risk signals in real time.

AI-Powered User Behavior Analytics (UBA)

AI-powered UBA models build behavioral baselines for each user and detect anomalies that may suggest compromised accounts, insider threats, or privilege abuse. Deviations such as unusual login locations, irregular access times, or anomalous file interactions trigger immediate security actions (Mohanty et al., 2024). UBA integrates seamlessly into Zero Trust frameworks by assigning dynamic risk scores and enforcing adaptive responses, including MFA prompts, session termination, or temporary access restrictions.

AI-Driven Identity and Access Management (IAM)

AI-driven IAM solutions continuously validate identity using contextual signals—geolocation, device reputation, authentication patterns, and network trust levels. When behavior deviates from expected norms, AI adjusts access rights or blocks attempts entirely.

These systems automate privilege auditing, detect orphaned accounts, and identify unauthorized access attempts (Hasan, 2024; Verma, 2024). By integrating adaptive access control with behavioral analytics, AI-driven IAM reinforces the Zero Trust mandate: never trust, always verify.

5. Architectural Framework for Smart Cyber Defense Systems

The emergence of AI-driven cybersecurity has shifted defensive strategies from reactive monitoring to proactive, autonomous, and multi-layered security architectures. Building a Smart Cyber Defense System requires a holistic integration of AI analytics, automated orchestration, real-time telemetry, and privacy-preserving intelligence. This section presents the architectural foundations, system integration principles, and unified blueprint necessary to operationalize intelligent cyber defense at scale.

5.1. Architectural Abstractions and Design Heuristics

A modern smart defense architecture must be adaptive, resilient, and secure-by-design. Key abstractions include distributed intelligence, modular AI components, and layered detection models grounded in privacy-preserving computation. Techniques such as adversarial training strengthen model robustness against manipulation (Shahana et al., 2024), while federated learning and differential privacy reduce exposure to centralized data leakage (Ameen et al., 2023; Kaur, 2024; Farooqi et al., 2025).

Scalability is achieved through hybrid cloud–edge deployments, enabling AI-driven intrusion detection and behavioral analytics to operate close to data sources while leveraging cloud scalability for model updates. Resource-efficient architectures incorporate pruning, quantization, and adaptive inference pipelines to support real-time decision-making.

Figure 3. illustrates layered AI-driven defense components, including data acquisition pipelines, SIEM–SOAR integration, threat analytics layers, automated response mechanisms, and continuous monitoring loops.

Figure 3. Architectural view of smart cyber defense system

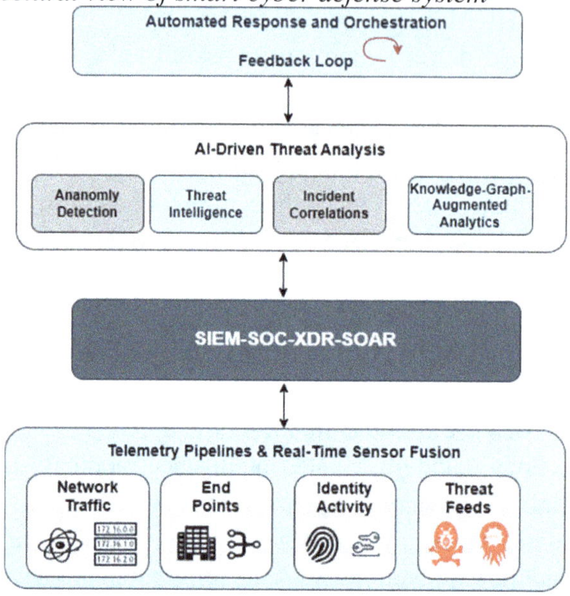

5.2. Integration Across SIEM–SOAR–SOC–XDR Ecosystems

AI transforms traditional SOC environments by tightly integrating SIEM, SOAR, XDR, and IDPS systems into a unified operational fabric. SOAR platforms automate triage, correlate threat intelligence, and execute response playbooks with minimal analyst intervention (Batewela et al., 2025). AI-enhanced IDPS models support real-time anomaly detection and dynamic firewall adjustments, while XDR consolidates endpoint, network, and cloud signals for unified detection.

User Behavior Analytics (UBA) and AI-driven IAM introduce continuous authentication and dynamic access control into SOC architectures, enabling Zero Trust enforcement across distributed environments (Wairagade & Ranjan, 2025). Together, these components form the operational backbone of an intelligent cyber defense ecosystem.

5.3. Telemetry Pipelines and Real-Time Sensor Fusion

An effective smart defense system requires high-fidelity, multi-domain telemetry streams. Data sources include endpoint logs, network flow data, cloud infrastructure events, dark web intelligence feeds, and user activity patterns. AI models fuse these heterogeneous signals in real-time to detect anomalies, malicious behaviors, and coordinated attacks.

Machine learning–driven IDS/IPS solutions process network telemetry continuously, while EDR agents capture file behavior, system calls, and encryption patterns indicative of emerging ransomware campaigns. NLP-enabled systems analyze threat intelligence reports and dark web chatter to augment telemetry with external signals (Rajendran & Tulasi, 2025).

Sensor fusion enhances situational awareness by correlating weak signals across layers—such as linking anomalous login behavior with external threat indicators—to identify sophisticated attacks that bypass traditional controls.

5.4. Knowledge-Graph Augmented Threat Intelligence

Knowledge graphs enrich threat intelligence by modeling cyber entities, relationships, and temporal attack patterns. AI-driven platforms extract IOCs, malware signatures, actor profiles, and TTPs from structured and unstructured intelligence sources, including dark web forums and security logs.

Graph-based reasoning supports link prediction, threat clustering, and context-aware prioritization, enabling analysts to understand attack campaigns holistically. Knowledge-graph augmentation enhances predictive threat intelligence, allowing organizations to anticipate ransomware trends, emerging exploits, and cross-domain infiltration strategies (Loevenich et al., 2025).

5.5. Unified Smart Defense System Blueprint

The integrated architecture synthesizes AI-driven analytics, automated orchestration, knowledge graphs, and self-healing mechanisms into a cohesive smart defense blueprint. Key components include:

- Distributed AI inference layer for endpoint, network, and cloud detection
- SOAR-driven automation fabric for rapid incident response
- XDR correlation engine for cross-domain analytics
- Zero Trust access enforcement through UBA + IAM
- Self-healing orchestration for automated containment and recovery
- Privacy-preserving AI modules using FL + DP
- Quantum-ready cryptographic layer for future-proof security

This unified blueprint provides end-to-end intelligent defense, enabling organizations to detect, predict, and autonomously mitigate complex cyberattacks. Key challenges in AI-driven threat detection are summarized in Table 3.

Table 3. Key challenges in AI-driven threat detection and representative use cases

Challenge Area	Concise Description	Representative Use Cases
Data Privacy and Compliance	AI systems require sensitive data, raising privacy and regulatory concerns (GDPR, HIPAA).	Healthcare threat detection must protect patient data while analyzing EHR and IoMT logs.
Adversarial Machine Learning Attacks	AI models can be manipulated through poisoning, evasion, and model extraction.	Malware authors craft adversarial samples to bypass DL-based antivirus systems.
Bias, Explainability, and Trust	Biased data leads to unfair decisions; black-box models reduce transparency.	Financial fraud detection must be explainable for regulatory audits.
Scalability and Computational Load	Real-time AI analysis demands high computing power and efficient scaling.	Cloud IDS must inspect large traffic volumes with low latency.
Model Drift and Evolving Threats	AI models degrade as attacker tactics change, requiring frequent updates.	Phishing models must be retrained as attackers modify templates and behaviors.
Integration and Operational Complexity	Integrating AI with SIEM, SOAR, EDR, and cloud systems is technically challenging.	Enterprises require complex pipelines to connect AI-driven EDR with SOAR workflows.

6. Domain-Driven Implementations of AI-Enabled Cyber Defense

AI-driven cyber defense systems are deployed across sectors with distinct regulatory, operational, and threat environments. Their design must adapt to the specific risks of healthcare, finance, and cyber-physical infrastructures, where attacks can cause service disruption, financial instability, or harm to human safety. This section outlines how autonomous and adaptive AI defenses are applied in key domains, highlighting sector-specific challenges and deployment considerations.

Figure 4 illustrates the major sectors where smart cyber defense frameworks are deployed, highlighting healthcare, finance, smart cities, and cloud-enterprise SOC environments.

Figure 4. Sector-Specific Applications of Smart Cyber Defense Systems

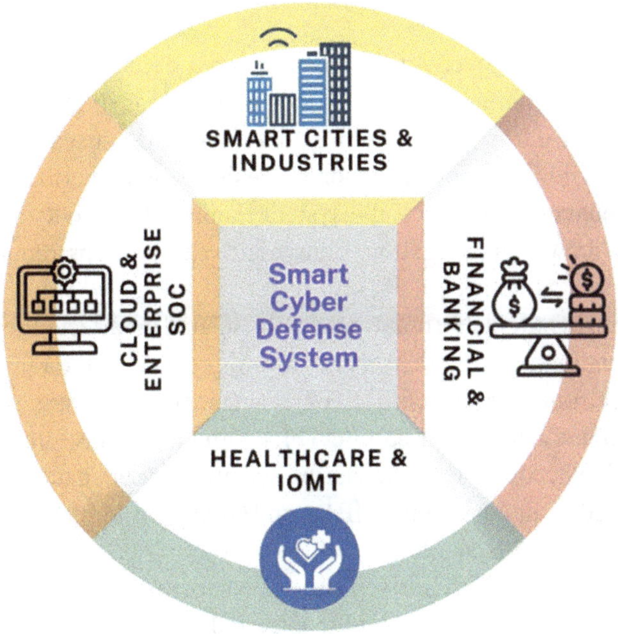

6.1. Healthcare Security and IoMT Threat Resilience

Healthcare and IoMT environments face high cyber risk due to interconnected medical devices, legacy systems, and sensitive patient data. AI strengthens resilience through predictive analytics, anomaly detection, and automated response (Ameen et al., 2023). AI-driven intrusion detection models flag abnormal device behavior—such as unexpected traffic from infusion pumps or monitors—revealing possible compromise or lateral movement.

Predictive threat intelligence helps anticipate ransomware activity targeting hospitals, while Federated Learning (FL) and Differential Privacy (DP) enable institutions to improve threat models without sharing medical data, supporting HIPAA and GDPR compliance (Farooqi et al., 2024). AI-powered SOAR workflows further automate containment of compromised endpoints, and UBA-based continuous authentication reduces insider-driven risks.

Case Study: AI-Driven Ransomware Prevention in a Smart Hospital Network

A major hospital deployed an AI-enabled cyber defense system to protect its IoMT ecosystem, including infusion pumps and patient monitors. Shortly after deployment, the AI intrusion detection model identified unusual outbound traffic from several infusion pumps—behavior inconsistent with normal clinical workflows. Using behavioral analytics, the system flagged the activity as indicative of early-stage ransomware propagation, consistent with patterns reported in recent healthcare attacks (Almotiri, 2025).

The integrated SOAR platform automatically isolated the affected devices, blocked lateral movement, and alerted the security team, preventing the ransomware from reaching the electronic health record (EHR) servers. To further strengthen defenses, the hospital adopted Federated Learning (FL) with partner institutions, improving anomaly detection accuracy without sharing sensitive patient data. Differential Privacy (DP) ensured compliance with HIPAA and GDPR while enabling collaborative model training (Farooqi et al., 2024).

This case highlights how AI-driven anomaly detection, automated containment, and privacy-preserving learning significantly reduce IoMT attack impact while maintaining clinical continuity.

6.2. Financial Cybersecurity and Transactional Threat Defense

Financial institutions operate in high-risk environments defined by high-volume transactions, strict regulatory mandates, and sophisticated adversaries. AI-driven cyber defense is critical for mitigating fraud, account compromise, and targeted attacks against transactional systems. Machine learning and deep learning models detect subtle anomalies in transaction patterns, enabling real-time fraud identification, while reinforcement learning supports adaptive countermeasures against evolving attacker behaviors (Sayeed et al., 2025).

AI-enhanced IAM and behavioral biometrics strengthen identity verification and reduce account takeover risks. Within Security Operations Centers (SOCs), AI-augmented SOAR workflows correlate alerts across SIEM, XDR, fraud analytics, and AML systems to accelerate investigation and response. NLP techniques further analyze regulatory advisories and dark-web activity to identify emerging financial threats (Singh, 2025).

Given the need for low-latency, high-accuracy decisioning, financial AI defenses depend on optimized telemetry pipelines and predictive analytics, alongside growing adoption of quantum-resistant cryptographic research to protect long-term transactional integrity.

Case Study: AI-Driven Fraud Detection in Real-Time Payment Networks

A leading digital banking platform integrated an AI-enabled fraud detection engine to secure its high-volume real-time payment network. The system employed deep learning models trained on historical transaction patterns to identify subtle anomalies, such as micro-transaction bursts and atypical cross-border transfers—patterns commonly associated with coordinated fraud operations (Sarana et al., 2025).

During deployment, the AI engine detected a sequence of low-value transfers routed through multiple newly created accounts. Reinforcement learning algorithms flagged the behavior as a synthetic identity fraud attempt, triggering the SOAR module to automatically freeze the accounts, block further transactions, and notify the fraud investigation team. NLP-based threat intelligence further revealed dark-web discussions promoting the same fraud technique, enabling the bank to update its risk models and educate partner institutions. The bank later adopted quantum-resistant encryption pilots to safeguard long-term confidentiality of transactional data.

This case demonstrates how AI-driven analytics, adaptive fraud detection, and automated incident response enhance security in fast-moving financial ecosystems.

6.3. Smart Cities, IoT, and Industrial Cyber-Physical Domains

Smart cities and industrial cyber-physical systems (CPS) integrate transportation networks, energy grids, automation systems, and large-scale urban IoT, creating broad attack surfaces that demand adaptive, real-time defense. AI-driven anomaly detection identifies malicious changes in sensor telemetry, PLC behavior, and industrial protocols, while deep learning models detect process manipulation such as abnormal actuator commands or voltage shifts (Demertzi et al., 2023).

Sensor-fusion architectures combine data from IoT sensors, CCTV, SCADA, and network logs to enhance situational awareness. AI-enabled predictive maintenance and self-healing mechanisms help identify vulnerabilities in machinery before exploitation, reducing downtime and safety risks.

Zero Trust deployments in smart city environments rely on AI-based UBA and continuous authentication to secure vast device ecosystems. Knowledge-graph threat intelligence further links cross-domain events, such as correlating an IoT device compromise with suspicious traffic targeting critical infrastructure. AI-automated response also supports rapid isolation of compromised components to prevent cascading failures across CPS networks.

Case Study: AI-Based Intrusion Detection in a Smart City Energy Grid

A regional smart city deployed an AI-enabled cyber defense platform to protect its energy distribution grid, which integrated IoT sensors, smart meters, and SCADA-controlled substations. Shortly after deployment, the anomaly detection model identified irregular voltage fluctuations and unexpected actuator commands issued to a substation's circuit breakers. These patterns matched known cyber-physical intrusion behaviors documented in recent smart grid attacks (Chen et al., 2021).

The AI-driven sensor-fusion engine correlated data from smart meters, network logs, and SCADA telemetry, confirming coordinated manipulation rather than a mechanical fault. The automated response module immediately isolated the affected segment, preventing further propagation toward critical load centers. A follow-up analysis revealed that attackers attempted to exploit vulnerable IoT meters as an entry point for lateral movement. To strengthen resilience, the city implemented knowledge-graph threat intelligence and AI-based UBA for continuous device authentication. These measures significantly reduced risk of cascading grid failures, aligning with best practices for CPS protection (Bishwas & Sen, 2024).

6.4. Defense, National Security, and Critical Infrastructure Protection

Defense and national security environments face state-sponsored intrusions, cyber-espionage, and targeted attacks on critical infrastructure. AI provides essential capabilities for rapid detection, situational awareness, and autonomous response across high-risk defense systems. AI-driven intrusion detection models process high-volume telemetry from military networks, satellite channels, and command-and-control systems to identify covert reconnaissance and stealthy lateral movement (Alauthman et al., 2025).

Reinforcement learning enables adaptive cyber defense by dynamically adjusting countermeasures as attacker strategies evolve, while knowledge-graph intelligence enhances threat attribution by linking indicators across cyber, physical, and communication layers. AI-augmented SOAR workflows support military SOCs by automating triage and incident containment for attacks on communication, logistics, and mission-critical systems.

AI-enhanced IAM and UBA models strengthen insider-threat detection in classified environments through continuous behavioral verification. Privacy-preserving approaches such as Federated Learning and Differential Privacy allow secure intelligence sharing among allied partners without exposing operational data. In cyber-physical defense assets—such as autonomous drones, military sensors, and critical power grids—AI detects anomalous control commands and supports automated containment to maintain operational integrity.

Case Study: AI-Enabled Intrusion Detection in a National Defense Command Network

A national defense agency deployed an AI-driven cyber defense framework to secure its command-and-control (C2) network, which integrates satellite communication channels, military sensors, and battlefield information systems. Soon after deployment, the AI intrusion detection engine detected a pattern of low-frequency, distributed reconnaissance traffic—behavior consistent with state-sponsored lateral movement techniques observed in recent defense-sector attacks (Patel & Patel, 2025).

The system's knowledge-graph threat intelligence correlated anomalies across satellite telemetry, encrypted communication logs, and endpoint events, confirming a coordinated infiltration attempt rather than benign network noise. The SOAR platform automatically initiated containment by segmenting the affected nodes, revoking compromised credentials, and isolating command channels without interrupting ongoing operations. Further analysis indicated that the adversary attempted to exploit a misconfigured authentication gateway. To strengthen resilience, the agency implemented Federated Learning (FL) with allied partners to collaboratively refine detection models while preserving operational secrecy. Differential Privacy (DP) ensured that no sensitive mission data was exposed during the shared learning process (Sharma & Bairwa, 2025).

This case demonstrates how AI-enabled threat detection, automated containment, and privacy-preserving intelligence sharing enhance national defense readiness against sophisticated, state-sponsored cyber threats.

Overall, AI enhances the speed, precision, and autonomy of defense-grade cybersecurity, making it integral to protecting national security and critical infrastructure from advanced multi-vector cyber threats.

7. Ethical, Adversarial, and Governance Dimensions with Future Trajectories

AI-driven cyber defense introduces powerful detection and response capabilities, but also raises critical ethical, adversarial, and governance considerations. As AI models are increasingly embedded into national infrastructures, healthcare systems, financial institutions, and autonomous cyber-physical environments, ensuring safe, transparent, and accountable deployment becomes central to long-term trust and security. This section outlines the key ethical principles, adversarial risks, regulatory imperatives, and open research challenges shaping the future trajectory of smart cyber defense (Thangamani et al., 2025).

7.1. Ethical and Trustworthy AI in Cyber Defense

The use of AI for security operations must balance effectiveness with ethical responsibility. Trustworthy AI requires fairness, privacy protection, and responsible data governance, especially when AI systems process sensitive organizational logs or personal behavioral patterns. Ethical deployment emphasizes privacy-by-design practices, bias mitigation, and federated or decentralized learning frameworks that minimize unnecessary data exposure. Ensuring ethical AI also requires safeguarding against misuse—preventing AI cyber defense tools from being repurposed for offensive or coercive digital operations (Bello, 2025).

7.2. Adversarial Machine Learning Threat Vectors

Despite its strengths, AI introduces new attack surfaces. Adversarial machine learning enables attackers to compromise models through poisoning, evasion, and model extraction attacks. Poisoning attacks corrupt training datasets, degrading detection accuracy, while evasion attacks manipulate inputs—such as malware samples or network packets—to bypass classifiers. Model inversion and extraction can reveal sensitive internal patterns, threatening privacy and intellectual property (Abomakhelbet al., 2025). These adversarial vectors highlight the need for continuous model hardening, adversarial training, and robust monitoring of AI-driven security pipelines.

7.3. Explainability, Transparency, and Accountability

Cyber defense decisions—especially automated responses affecting critical assets—require traceable and explainable reasoning. Traditional deep learning models often function as "black boxes," creating challenges for analysts who must validate alerts, audit decision-making, or meet regulatory disclosure requirements (Agarwal, 2025). Explainable AI (XAI) techniques improve trust by revealing why a model classified an event as malicious, how risk levels were assigned, or which features influenced a response action. Transparency further supports accountable governance, enabling SOC teams to review automated decisions, detect bias, and calibrate system behavior.

7.4. Regulatory Compliance and Global Security Standards

AI-based cyber defense must align with international frameworks governing privacy, digital security, and responsible AI. Regulations such as GDPR, HIPAA, NIST AI Risk Management Framework, ISO/IEC cybersecurity standards, and emerging AI governance laws outline requirements for data protection, fairness, auditability, and secure model deployment (Hundeyin et al., 2025). Global harmonization is critical, as cyber threats often span borders while regulation remains jurisdiction-specific. Compliance-driven architectures increasingly rely on differential privacy, secure federated learning, audit logs, and explainable model components to meet legal expectations without compromising security performance.

7.5. Open Challenges and Future Cyber Defense Directions

Despite rapid progress, several unresolved challenges shape the future of AI-enabled cybersecurity. Ensuring robustness against adversarial manipulation, maintaining high accuracy across diverse environments, and reducing over-reliance on opaque models remain pressing issues. Scalability is another concern, as real-time AI analytics must operate efficiently across massive distributed infrastructures. The future will also demand stronger quantum-resilient defenses, self-healing networks capable of autonomous recovery, and global collaboration frameworks for threat intelligence sharing. Continued advances in privacy-preserving learning, explainable security models, and adaptive reinforcement-based defenses will define the next generation of smart cyber defense systems (Beltrán-López et al., 2025; Zhang et al., 2022).

8. Chapter Conclusion

The accelerating sophistication of cyber threats has rendered traditional, rule-based defense mechanisms insufficient for protecting modern digital ecosystems. This chapter demonstrated how Artificial Intelligence fundamentally reshapes cyber defense by enabling predictive, adaptive, and autonomous security capabilities. Through machine learning, deep learning, reinforcement learning, NLP-driven intelligence, and behavior-based detection, AI enhances the precision, speed, and situational awareness required to counter advanced attacks, including zero-day exploits, ransomware, insider threats, and large-scale coordinated intrusions.

At the architectural level, AI supports integrated SIEM–SOAR–SOC–XDR ecosystems, real-time telemetry pipelines, knowledge-graph threat intelligence, and self-healing networks, enabling end-to-end intelligent defense. Sector-specific analyses further showed how AI strengthens cybersecurity across healthcare, finance, industrial IoT, smart cities, and national security environments.

Despite its transformative potential, AI-enabled cybersecurity introduces notable risks. Adversarial machine learning, model bias, opacity in decision-making, and compliance challenges require continuous attention. Ethical and governance frameworks—emphasizing transparency, accountability, and privacy-preserving learning—are essential for building trust and ensuring responsible deployment.

Looking ahead, future cyber defense will increasingly rely on quantum-resilient models, generative threat simulation, federated intelligence sharing, and fully autonomous defense agents. As cyber threats evolve, AI will remain central to developing resilient, intelligent, and future-ready security infrastructures.

REFERENCES

Abomakhelb, A., Jalil, K. A., Buja, A. G., Alhammadi, A., & Alenezi, A. M. (2025). A Comprehensive Review of Adversarial Attacks and Defense Strategies in Deep Neural Networks. *Technologies, 13*(5), 202. DOI: 10.3390/technologies13050202

Agarwal, G. (2025). Explainable AI (XAI) for Cyber Defense: Enhancing Transparency and Trust in AI-Driven Security Solutions. *International Journal of Advanced Research in Science. Tongxin Jishu, 5*(1), 132–138. DOI: 10.48175/IJARSCT-23624

Alanezi, M., & AL-Azzawi, R. M. A. (2024). AI-Powered Cyber Threats: A Systematic Review. *Mesopotamian Journal of Cybersecurity, 4*(3), 166–188. DOI: 10.58496/MJCS/2024/021

Alauthman, M., Mashaleh, A., Aslam, N., Alkasassbeh, M., & Almomani, A. (2025, April). Next-Generation Critical Infrastructure Security: A Framework for Autonomous Defense Systems. In *2025 1st International Conference on Computational Intelligence Approaches and Applications (ICCIAA)* (pp. 1-6). IEEE. DOI: 10.1109/ICCIAA65327.2025.11013052

Almeida, G., & Vasconcelos, F. (2023). Self-healing networks: Adaptive responses to ransomware attacks. DOI: 10.20944/preprints202312.1538.v1

Almotiri, S. H. (2025). AI driven IOMT security framework for advanced malware and ransomware detection in SDN. *Journal of Cloud Computing (Heidelberg, Germany), 14*(1), 19. DOI: 10.1186/s13677-025-00745-w

Ameen, A. H., Mohammed, M. A., & Rashid, A. N. (2023). Dimensions of artificial intelligence techniques, blockchain, and cyber security in the Internet of medical things: Opportunities, challenges, and future directions. *Journal of Intelligent Systems, 32*(1), 20220267. DOI: 10.1515/jisys-2022-0267

Babulak, E. (Ed.). (2023). *AI Tools for Protecting and Preventing Sophisticated Cyber Attacks*. IGI Global., DOI: 10.4018/978-1-6684-7110-4

Babulak, E., Al_Dabass, D., & Tomar, G. (2025). Cyber Security Prevention, Defenses Driven by AI and Mathematical Modelling and Simulation Tools. *Frontiers of Computer Science, 7*, 1685873. DOI: 10.3389/fcomp.2025.1685873

Bartwal, U., Mukhopadhyay, S., Negi, R., & Shukla, S. (2022, June). Security orchestration, automation, and response engine for deployment of behavioral honeypots. In *2022 IEEE Conference on Dependable and Secure Computing (DSC)* (pp. 1-8). IEEE. DOI: 10.1109/DSC54232.2022.9888808

Batewela, S., Ranaweera, P., Liyanage, M., Zeydan, E., & Ylianttila, M. (2025). Addressing Security Orchestration Challenges in Next-Generation Networks: A Comprehensive Overview. *IEEE Open Journal of the Computer Society*, *6*, 669–687. Advance online publication. DOI: 10.1109/OJCS.2025.3564788

Bello, A. (2025, September). Ethical Risk Modeling for Trustworthy ML-Based Cyber Defense. In *2025 IEEE International Conference on eScience (eScience)* (pp. 333-334). IEEE. DOI: 10.1109/eScience65000.2025.00057

Beltrán-López, P., Pérez, M. G., & Nespoli, P. (2025). Cyber Deception: Taxonomy, State of the Art, Frameworks, Trends, and Open Challenges. *IEEE Communications Surveys and Tutorials*. Advance online publication. DOI: 10.1109/COMST.2025.3594788

Bishwas, A. K., & Sen, M. (2024). Strategic Roadmap for Quantum-Resistant Security: A Framework for Preparing Industries for the Quantum Threat. *arXiv preprint arXiv:2411.09995*. /arXiv.2411.09995DOI: 10.48550

Chamola, V., Hassija, V., Sulthana, A. R., Ghosh, D., Dhingra, D., & Sikdar, B. (2023). A review of trustworthy and explainable artificial intelligence (xai). *IEEE Access : Practical Innovations, Open Solutions*, *11*, 78994–79015. DOI: 10.1109/ACCESS.2023.3294569

Chen, D., Wawrzynski, P., & Lv, Z. (2021). Cyber security in smart cities: A review of deep learning-based applications and case studies. *Sustainable Cities and Society*, *66*, 102655. DOI: 10.1016/j.scs.2020.102655

Chen, Q., Li, D., & Wang, L. (2024). The Role of Artificial Intelligence in Predicting and Preventing Cyber Attacks. *Journal of Industrial Engineering and Applied Science*, *2*(4), 29–35. DOI: 10.5281/zenodo.12786734

Chennam, K. K., Mudrakola, S., Maheswari, V. U., Aluvalu, R., & Rao, K. G. (2022). Black box models for eXplainable artificial intelligence. In *Explainable AI: foundations, methodologies and applications* (pp. 1–24). Springer International Publishing., DOI: 10.1007/978-3-031-12807-3_1

Demertzi, V., Demertzis, S., & Demertzis, K. (2023). An overview of cyber threats, attacks and countermeasures on the primary domains of smart cities. *Applied Sciences (Basel, Switzerland)*, *13*(2), 790. DOI: 10.3390/app13020790

Eze, C. S., & Shamir, L. (2024). Analysis and prevention of AI-based phishing email attacks. *Electronics (Basel)*, *13*(10), 1839. DOI: 10.3390/electronics13101839

Fakhouri, H. N., Alhadidi, B., Omar, K., Makhadmeh, S. N., Hamad, F., & Halalsheh, N. Z. (2024, February). Ai-driven solutions for social engineering attacks: Detection, prevention, and response. In *2024 2nd international conference on cyber resilience (ICCR)* (pp. 1-8). IEEE. DOI: 10.1109/ICCR61006.2024.10533010

Fard, N. E., Selmic, R. R., & Khorasani, K. (2023). A review of techniques and policies on cybersecurity using artificial intelligence and reinforcement learning algorithms. *IEEE Technology and Society Magazine*, *42*(3), 57–68. DOI: 10.1109/MTS.2023.3306540

Farooqi, S. A., Abd Rahman, A., & Saad, A. (2025, January). A theoretical comparison of federated learning with differential privacy and blockchain for security and privacy in iomt. In *2025 19th International Conference on Ubiquitous Information Management and Communication (IMCOM)* (pp. 1-8). IEEE. DOI: 10.1109/IMCOM64595.2025.10857505

George, A. S. (2024). Emerging Trends in AI-Driven Cybersecurity: An In-Depth Analysis. *Partners Universal Innovative Research Publication*, *2*(4), 15–28. DOI: 10.5281/zenodo.13333202

Gunavathie, M. A., Sneha, P. D., Yuvarani, K., & Swathyshree, P. (2023, July). An Exploration of Real-Time Intrusion Detection and Prevention Systems for Next Generation Networks. In *2023 World Conference on Communication & Computing (WCONF)* (pp. 1-5). IEEE. DOI: 10.1109/WCONF58270.2023.10235147

Hasan, M. (2024). Enhancing Enterprise Security with Zero Trust Architecture. *arXiv preprint arXiv:2410.18291*. /arXiv.2410.18291DOI: 10.48550

Hundeyin, W. O., Adegbenro, S. A., Rindap, Y. P., & Adaba, C. A. (2025). Integrating Privacy-Preserving AI Models into AI Governance Frameworks. DOI: 10.38124/ijisrt/25oct209

Ichetovkin, E., & Kotenko, I. (2025, March). A Technique for Protecting Machine Learning Components of Intrusion Detection Systems from Evasion Attacks. In *2025 International Russian Smart Industry Conference (SmartIndustryCon)* (pp. 735-740). IEEE. DOI: 10.1109/SmartIndustryCon65166.2025.10986131

Ilieva, R., & Stoilova, G. (2024, September). Challenges of AI-Driven Cybersecurity. In *2024 XXXIII International Scientific Conference Electronics (ET)* (pp. 1-4). IEEE. DOI: 10.1109/ET63133.2024.10721572

Kaur, H. SL, D. S., Paul, T., Thakur, R. K., Reddy, K. V. K., Mahato, J., & Naveen, K. (2024). Evolution of endpoint detection and response (EDR) in cyber security: A comprehensive review. In *E3S Web of Conferences* (Vol. 556, p. 01006). EDP Sciences. DOI: 10.1051/e3sconf/202455601006

Kinyua, J., & Awuah, L. (2021). AI/ML in Security Orchestration, Automation and Response: Future Research Directions. *Intelligent Automation & Soft Computing, 28*(2), 527–545. Advance online publication. DOI: 10.32604/iasc.2021.016240

Loevenich, J. F., Adler, E., Hürten, T., Spelter, F., Roncevic, D., & Lopes, R. R. F. (2025, May). Automating Cyber Threat Intelligence and Attack Chain Generation using Cyber Security Knowledge Graphs and Large Language Models. In *2025 International Conference on Military Communication and Information Systems (ICMCIS)* (pp. 1-10). IEEE. DOI: 10.1109/ICMCIS64378.2025.11047951

Majgave, A. B., & Gavankar, N. L. (2024). Automatic phishing website detection and prevention model using transformer deep belief network. *Computers & Security, 147*, 104071. DOI: 10.1016/j.cose.2024.104071

Manda, J. K. (2024). AI-powered Threat Intelligence Platforms in Telecom: Leveraging AI for Real-time Threat Detection and Intelligence Gathering in Telecom Network Security Operations. Available at *SSRN* 5003638. http://dx.doi.org/DOI: 10.2139/ssrn.5003638

Mavikumbure, H. S., Cobilean, V., Wickramasinghe, C. S., Drake, D., & Manic, M. (2024, July). Generative AI in cyber security of cyber physical systems: Benefits and threats. In *2024 16th International Conference on Human System Interaction (HSI)* (pp. 1-8). IEEE. DOI: 10.1109/HSI61632.2024.10613562

Meduri, K., Gonaygunt, H., & Nadella, G. S. (2024). Evaluating the effectiveness of AI-Driven frameworks in predicting and preventing cyber-attacks. *International Journal of Research Publication and Reviews, 5*(3), 6591–6595. DOI: 10.55248/gengpi.5.0324.0875

Mohanty, R. K., Kumar, A. P., Padmaja, R., & Prashanthi, V. (2024). Deep Learning for Analyzing User and Entity Behaviors: Techniques and Applications. In *Consumer and Organizational Behavior in the Age of AI* (pp. 219-250). IGI Global. DOI: 10.4018/979-8-3693-6864-0.ch006

Mvula, P. K., Branco, P., Jourdan, G. V., & Viktor, H. L. (2024). A Survey on the Applications of Semi-supervised Learning to Cyber-security. *ACM Computing Surveys, 56*(10), 1–41. DOI: 10.1145/3657647

Patel, P., & Patel, R. (2025). Reinforcement Learning for Cyber Defense: AI Architectures for Securing US Critical Infrastructure. http://dx.doi.org/DOI: 10.2139/ssrn.5360107

Rajendran, R. K., & Tulasi, B. (2025). Natural Language Processing (NLP) for Threat Intelligence. In *Analyzing Privacy and Security Difficulties in Social Media: New Challenges and Solutions* (pp. 247-262). IGI Global Scientific Publishing. http://doi.org/DOI: 10.4018/979-8-3693-9491-5.ch011

Rizky, A., Firli, M. Z., Lindzani, N. A., Audiah, S., & Pasha, L. (2024). Advanced cyber threat detection: Big data-driven ai solutions in complex networks. *Journal of Computer Science and Technology Application*, *1*(2), 136–143. DOI: 10.33050/corisinta.v1i2.42

Salem, A. H., Azzam, S. M., Emam, O. E., & Abohany, A. A. (2024). Advancing cybersecurity: A comprehensive review of AI-driven detection techniques. *Journal of Big Data*, *11*(1), 105. DOI: 10.1186/s40537-024-00957-y

Sarker, I. H. (2024). *AI-driven cybersecurity and threat intelligence: cyber automation, intelligent decision-making and explainability*. Springer Nature., DOI: 10.1007/978-3-031-54497-2

Sayeed, S. A., Rahman, M. M., Alam, S., & Kshetri, N. (2025, April). FSCsec: Collaboration in Financial Sector Cybersecurity-Exploring the Impact of Resource Sharing on IT Security. In *2025 13th International Symposium on Digital Forensics and Security (ISDFS)* (pp. 1-6). IEEE. DOI: 10.1109/ISDFS65363.2025.11012024

Sewak, M., Sahay, S. K., & Rathore, H. (2023). Deep reinforcement learning in the advanced cybersecurity threat detection and protection. *Information Systems Frontiers*, *25*(2), 589–611. DOI: 10.1007/s10796-022-10333-x

Shahana, A., Hasan, R., Farabi, S. F., Akter, J., Mahmud, M. A. A., Johora, F. T., & Suzer, G. (2024). AI-driven cybersecurity: Balancing advancements and safeguards. *Journal of Computer Science and Technology Studies*, *6*(2), 76–85. DOI: 10.32996/jcsts.2024.6.2.9

Sharma, S. B., & Bairwa, A. K. (2025). *Leveraging AI for Intrusion Detection in IoT Ecosystems: A Comprehensive Study*. IEEE., DOI: 10.1109/ACCESS.2025.3550392

Singh, H. (2025). Securing High-Stakes Digital Transactions: A Comprehensive Study on Cybersecurity and Data Privacy in Financial Institutions. *SSRN*, *5267850*, •••. https://ssrn.com/abstract=5267850. DOI: 10.2139/ssrn.5267850

Sontan, A. D., & Samuel, S. V.Adewale Daniel SontanSegun Victor Samuel. (2024). The intersection of Artificial Intelligence and cybersecurity: Challenges and opportunities. *World Journal of Advanced Research and Reviews, 21*(2), 1720–1736. DOI: 10.30574/wjarr.2024.21.2.0607

Tanikonda, A., Pandey, B. K., Peddinti, S. R., & Katragadda, S. R. (2022). Advanced AI-Driven Cybersecurity Solutions for Proactive Threat Detection and Response in Complex Ecosystems. *SSRN, 3*(1). Advance online publication. DOI: 10.2139/ssrn.5102358

Thangamani, R., Vimaladevi, M., Kamalam, G. K., & Subramanian, K. M. (2025). Securing the Future: Quantum Computing in Cybersecurity. In *Quantum Computing, Cyber Security and Cryptography: Issues, Technologies, Algorithms, Programming and Strategies* (pp. 441-487). Singapore: Springer Nature Singapore. DOI: 10.1007/978-981-96-4948-8_17

Vast, R., Sawant, S., Thorbole, A., & Badgujar, V. (2021, April). Artificial intelligence-based security orchestration, automation and response system. In *2021 6th International Conference for Convergence in Technology (I2CT)* (pp. 1-5). IEEE DOI: 10.1109/I2CT51068.2021.9418109

Verma, D. (2024). Enhancing Cybersecurity Through Adaptive Anomaly Detection Using Modern AI. https://urn.fi/URN:NBN:fi:jyu-202405273981

Vikram, A., Shnain, A. H., Jeet, R., Vennila, C., Sahu, P., & Krishnakumar, K. (2024, September). AI-Powered Network Intrusion Detection Systems. In *2024 IEEE International Conference on Communication, Computing and Signal Processing (IICCCS)* (pp. 1-6). IEEE. DOI: 10.1109/IICCCS61609.2024.10763627

Wairagade, A., & Ranjan, S. (2025, April). User Behavior Analysis for Cyber Threat Detection: A Comparative Study of Machine Learning Algorithms. In *2025 13th International Symposium on Digital Forensics and Security (ISDFS)* (pp. 1-6). IEEE. DOI: 10.1109/ISDFS65363.2025.11011949

Zhang, Z., Ning, H., Shi, F., Farha, F., Xu, Y., Xu, J., Zhang, F., & Choo, K. K. R. (2022). Artificial intelligence in cyber security: Research advances, challenges, and opportunities. *Artificial Intelligence Review, 55*(2), 1–25. DOI: 10.1007/s10462-021-09976-0

Chapter 2
Automated Threats: Understanding and Mitigating AI-Generated Cyber Attacks

Muhammad Virga Mulia
http://orcid.org/0009-0003-5626-163X
Universitas Esa Unggul, Indonesia

Binastya Anggara Sekti
http://orcid.org/0000-0001-5489-4888
Universitas Esa Unggul, Indonesia

Anisah Sri Utami
http://orcid.org/0009-0001-4348-5736
Universitas Esa Unggul, Indonesia

ABSTRACT

This chapter explores the evolving landscape of AI-generated cyber threats and the corresponding defense mechanisms required to counter them. It examines how Generative AI (GenAI) is increasingly used to automate phishing, malware creation, and social engineering, while Explainable AI (XAI) enhances transparency and accountability in automated defense systems. The chapter develops a framework for understanding AI-automated attacks through the lens of the cyber kill chain, detailing how autonomy, adaptability, and hyper personalization redefine modern threats. It further proposes a multi-layered defense architecture that integrates behavioral analytics, adversarial training, and explainable automation to ensure ethical and interpretable cybersecurity operations. By analyzing case studies and ethical considerations, this chapter positions explainability as the cornerstone of future cyber resilience, where automation must remain accountable, transparent, and aligned with human oversight.

DOI: 10.4018/979-8-2600-1608-4.ch002

1. INTRODUCTION

The evolution of Artificial Intelligence (AI) has fundamentally reshaped the digital security landscape. Once regarded primarily as a defensive technology, AI now exists in a dual role both as a guardian of digital systems and as a potential weapon for adversaries. The emergence of Generative AI (GenAI) and Explainable AI (XAI) represents two sides of this transformation. On one hand, GenAI offers the capacity to create new data, generate code, simulate human behavior, and automate complex decision-making. On the other, XAI introduces interpretability and accountability into automated systems, ensuring that their decisions are not opaque or arbitrary. Together, these technologies redefine the balance between security and vulnerability in cyberspace. In recent years, AI-generated cyber threats have demonstrated how machine learning and generative models can be exploited to create intelligent, adaptive, and scalable attacks. Malicious actors increasingly leverage AI to automate processes that previously required human creativity and expertise such as generating phishing messages, crafting malware, or mimicking human voices. The ability of GenAI to synthesize human-like content at scale enables attackers to deceive both individuals and automated security systems. Unlike traditional attacks, these new threats evolve dynamically, adapting to their environment in real time and often bypassing conventional detection mechanisms. The automation of cyber attacks represents a paradigm shift in how digital threats are conceptualized and executed. Traditional malware or phishing schemes followed predictable patterns that could be identified and countered with static signatures or rule-based defenses. In contrast, AI-generated threats exhibit characteristics of autonomy, adaptability, and self-improvement. For example, a generative model trained on malicious code can create new variants that evade antivirus detection, while large language models can produce socially engineered emails that mirror a target's linguistic style. This ability to combine contextual awareness with speed and scalability creates a new class of cyber threats intelligent, evolving, and highly personalized. As the offensive use of AI accelerates, defensive strategies must evolve in parallel. Organizations can no longer rely solely on traditional rule-based systems or human analysts to counter AI-driven attacks. Instead, cybersecurity must embrace the same level of intelligence and automation to remain effective.

Figure 1. Dual role of artificial intelligence in cybersecurity: The balance between generative AI and explainable AI

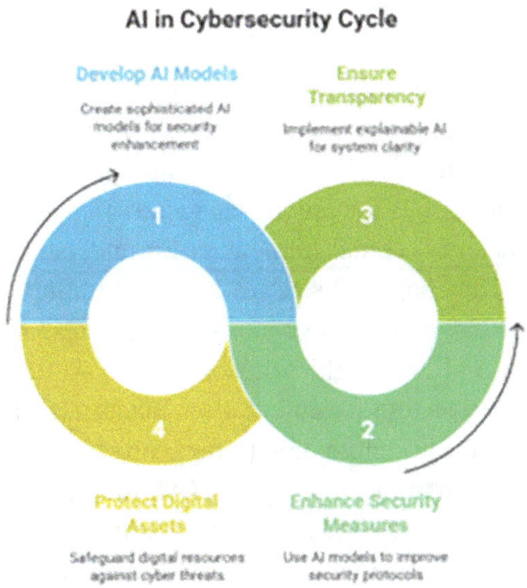

Defensive AI systems must be capable of detecting, responding to, and explaining their decisions in real time. This last capability *explainability* is critical for ensuring that automated systems maintain human oversight, transparency, and trustworthiness. Without explainability, even the most advanced defensive AI could act as a "black box," making decisions that are efficient but not accountable. Explainable AI (XAI) thus serves as a bridge between technological efficiency and ethical responsibility. It enables human operators to understand the reasoning behind an AI's conclusions, identify potential biases, and validate that security decisions align with organizational policies and legal frameworks. In cybersecurity contexts, XAI is not merely a theoretical concept but a practical necessity. Security analysts must comprehend why an AI model flags a specific email as malicious, why a network segment is quarantined, or why a user account is locked. Transparent AI-driven defense systems enhance trust, facilitate auditing, and ensure compliance with standards such as GDPR, ISO 27001, and the NIST AI Risk Management Framework. The increasing sophistication of AI-driven threats also raises questions about the ethics and governance of artificial intelligence. As attackers exploit generative models for malicious purposes, defenders must establish clear boundaries for AI use, ensuring that defensive automation remains aligned with ethical norms. The dual-use nature of AI means that the same algorithms capable of detecting anomalies can also be weaponized to conceal them. Consequently, cybersecurity professionals face the dual challenge of defending against AI-generated threats while also preventing misuse of defensive AI tools themselves. With the emergence of a new generation of sophisticated cyberattacks, the integration of Artificial Intelligence (AI) and Mathematical Modeling and Simulation tools has become a crucial component of the cybersecurity toolkit, ensuring that counter-cyber measures remain effective and reliable in real-time, around the clock (Babulak et al., 2025). This chapter aims to provide a comprehensive exploration of AI-generated cyber threats and the strategies required to mitigate them effectively. It examines how generative models contribute to automated attacks, identifies the unique characteristics of AI-driven adversarial behavior, and presents a conceptual framework for understanding these emerging threats. Furthermore, the chapter discusses how integrating Explainable AI into cybersecurity systems can enhance decision-making transparency, foster human-machine collaboration, and ensure ethical accountability. Ultimately, this discussion positions AI not merely as a tool for automation, but as a transformative force that demands a rethinking of the principles governing both offensive and defensive cyber operations. As generative artificial intelligence (AI) tools and large language model (LLM)-based applications continue to advance rapidly in the algorithmic era, their integration into English as a Foreign Language (EFL) teaching and learning should be approached carefully to support, rather than replace, learners' critical thinking (CT) skills (Liu et al., 2025).

2. EVOLUTION AND CHARACTERISTICS OF AI-GENERATED THREATS

The rise of AI-generated cyber threats represents not merely an incremental evolution in cybercrime but a fundamental transformation in how attacks are designed, executed, and sustained. Traditional cyber threats relied on manual configuration, signature-based evasion, and human creativity for deception. In contrast, modern attacks increasingly draw upon Generative Artificial Intelligence (GenAI), enabling adversaries to automate decision-making, craft content that mimics human authenticity, and dynamically adapt to defensive countermeasures. This evolution has blurred the boundaries between machine-generated deception and human ingenuity, leading to what scholars and practitioners now refer to as *algorithmic adversaries*. Understanding this evolution is essential to developing defenses that are not only intelligent but also transparent, interpretable, and ethically grounded. Generative Artificial Intelligence Appropriation (GAIA) refers to the process through which users embrace Generative AI tools, modify them to suit their specific purposes, and incorporate them into their professional or creative practices (Khatri et al., 2026).

Figure 2. Evolution and characteristics of AI-generated cyber threats

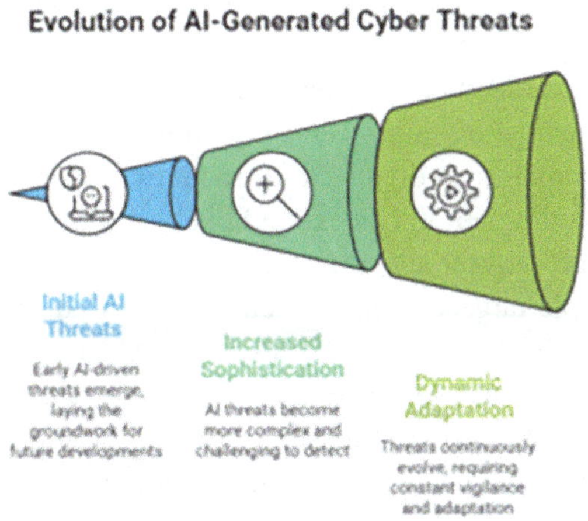

2.1 Generative AI as an Offensive Tool

Generative AI technologies ranging from Large Language Models (LLMs) such as GPT and Claude to image, video, and audio synthesis systems like Stable Diffusion and VALL-E have dramatically lowered the technical barriers to conducting sophisticated cyber attacks. Attackers can now leverage these tools to automate processes that once required significant skill and time, turning AI into a potent offensive instrument. For instance, automated phishing generation allows adversaries to use LLMs to compose highly convincing emails that emulate a target's communication style. By analyzing publicly available data such as social media posts or professional correspondence AI can craft messages that appear authentic and contextually relevant, substantially increasing the likelihood of victim engagement. Similarly, AI-driven malware creation enables the rapid synthesis of new and unique malware variants. Code-generation models, when misused, can assist in developing polymorphic code, ransomware, and exploit payloads that mutate faster than traditional antivirus systems can identify them. This democratization of cyber weapon development lowers the skill threshold for entry, empowering not only state-sponsored groups but also independent threat actors with limited technical backgrounds. A particularly concerning dimension of GenAI misuse lies in deepfake manipulation. Using advanced generative models, adversaries can fabricate realistic audio, video, or image content to impersonate individuals, spread disinformation, or conduct high-impact social engineering. In corporate or governmental contexts, this could mean impersonating executives or public officials to authorize fraudulent transactions or influence decision-making. When combined with social media automation and bot amplification, such AI-generated content can destabilize trust in information ecosystems, contributing to broader societal and political risks. Beyond content generation, autonomous reconnaissance and exploitation has emerged as a new capability enabled by reinforcement learning and adaptive algorithms. AI agents can continuously scan digital infrastructures, identify vulnerabilities, and prioritize exploitation based on context and likelihood of success. Unlike human hackers who operate sequentially, AI systems can perform simultaneous assessments across multiple targets, refining their tactics based on real-time defensive responses. Collectively, these offensive uses of GenAI have redefined the nature of cyber attacks making them more scalable, context-aware, and resistant to traditional countermeasures. Large Language Models (LLMs), which possess the ability to store information over extended periods and process both visual and textual inputs, are increasingly recognized as valuable tools for understanding the intricate dynamics of virtual reality (VR) interface development (Qi et al., 2026).

2.2 Key Characteristics of AI-Driven Cyber Attacks

AI-generated cyber attacks differ from conventional ones in both form and function, exhibiting a series of characteristics that fundamentally reshape the concept of threat automation. First, speed and scale are unprecedented. Generative systems can produce thousands of unique phishing messages, malicious scripts, or synthetic identities in seconds, overwhelming conventional defense systems that rely on human review or manual detection. This acceleration compresses the time window available for defenders to detect, analyze, and respond to incidents. Second, adaptability defines the new generation of threats. AI-driven attacks exhibit polymorphic and adversarial behaviors modifying their structure, content, or code when encountering resistance. For example, a machine learning-based malware can analyze the security environment it infiltrates and adjust its operations to evade detection, much like an organism adapting to immune responses. This adaptability transforms cyber attacks into living systems that continuously evolve rather than static entities with predictable signatures. Third, hyper-personalization amplifies the psychological precision of attacks. Generative models trained on social media or corporate communication datasets can tailor messages, voice recordings, or images to resonate with an individual's preferences, habits, or emotional states. The resulting attacks whether phishing, scams, or misinformation achieve far higher success rates because they exploit both cognitive biases and personal familiarity. Fourth, automation now encompasses the entire attack lifecycle. AI systems can autonomously perform reconnaissance, deliver payloads, conduct lateral movement within networks, and even exfiltrate data without direct human command. This autonomy creates a persistent threat environment in which attacks can occur continuously, adapting faster than manual defenders can intervene. Finally, opacity is an inherent challenge in AI-generated threats. Because generative models produce artifacts that are novel and lack conventional digital fingerprints, traditional security mechanisms such as signature-based antivirus tools struggle to classify or block them effectively. The indistinguishability between authentic and synthetic content erodes the reliability of trust mechanisms like digital verification or behavioral analysis. Collectively, these characteristics redefine what it means to automate cyber threats, shifting the focus from static detection toward adaptive, context-aware defense. Cyber-attacks have experienced a rapid and substantial rise in today's technology-driven era, profoundly affecting essential sectors including healthcare, finance, and industrial automation (Sowmya & Konduri, 2025).

2.3 Explainable AI (XAI) and the Opacity Paradox

While the offensive use of AI has become increasingly autonomous, the defensive side faces a unique paradox: automation enhances efficiency but often reduces transparency. The more complex and adaptive an AI-based defense becomes, the harder it is for human operators to understand why it makes certain decisions whether flagging an email as malicious, isolating a device, or terminating a network process. This challenge, known as the opacity paradox, poses a significant barrier to trust, accountability, and compliance in AI-driven cybersecurity systems. Explainable AI (XAI) emerges as a critical countermeasure to this opacity. By incorporating interpretability into defensive models, XAI allows analysts to visualize, trace, and understand the reasoning behind automated actions. For instance, an explainable intrusion detection system can highlight which network features or behaviors led to a threat classification, enabling security teams to validate or refine the model's logic. Beyond improving model accuracy, explainability ensures that AI-driven security remains auditable supporting human oversight, regulatory compliance, and ethical accountability. The integration of XAI into cybersecurity frameworks is not merely a technical improvement but a philosophical shift toward human-centered security design. In a world where both attackers and defenders wield autonomous systems, explainability restores human agency to the loop, ensuring that defensive decisions remain transparent and justifiable. Furthermore, XAI enables cross-disciplinary collaboration, allowing cybersecurity professionals, policymakers, and auditors to interpret AI operations through a shared understanding. Ultimately, addressing the opacity paradox is essential for sustainable cyber resilience. Defensive automation without explainability risks creating another "black box" efficient but unaccountable, powerful yet blind to its consequences. By contrast, explainable defensive AI represents the convergence of intelligence and integrity: a system that not only acts autonomously but also justifies and clarifies its reasoning to the humans it protects. Techniques in Explainable Artificial Intelligence (XAI) offer substantial potential to improve the process of causal discovery, an essential approach for gaining insights into complex systems across fields such as healthcare, economics, and artificial intelligence (Renero et al., 2026).

3. FRAMEWORK FOR UNDERSTANDING AI-AUTOMATED THREATS

The complexity and autonomy of AI-driven cyber attacks demand a structured framework to understand how artificial intelligence amplifies each phase of the offensive lifecycle. Traditional threat models, while effective in characterizing human-led cyber operations, are insufficient to explain the dynamic and adaptive nature of machine-generated attacks. The cyber kill chain a well-established model in cybersecurity developed by Lockheed Martin serves as a useful foundation for reinterpreting AI's role within the modern threat landscape. By examining how AI influences each phase of this chain, we can better comprehend both the strategic sophistication and the operational scale of automated adversarial behavior. This understanding is crucial for developing defensive systems that are not only reactive but predictive, interpretable, and aligned with ethical standards of cyber governance. An AI-driven double-tier detection system refers to a security framework that operates through two layers, designed to enhance the accuracy and reliability of threat identification, as presented in this research (Almotiri, 2025).

Figure 3. Framework for understanding AI-automated threats

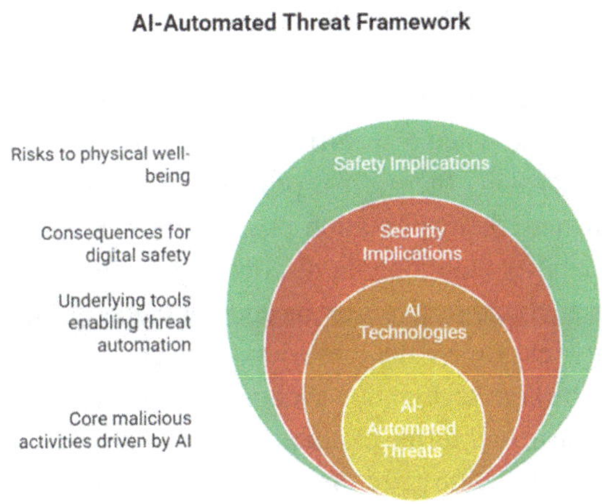

3.1 Stages of an AI-Driven Cyber Attack

The AI-augmented cyber kill chain redefines every stage of the traditional model by introducing automation, context-awareness, and adaptability. AI-Driven Approaches for Fully Automated Smart Engineering examines the present landscape of automation within engineering and manufacturing fields (Babulak, 2025). In the reconnaissance stage, AI systems can autonomously gather and analyze vast quantities of publicly available data social media posts, professional profiles, domain metadata, or leaked credential databases. Through natural language processing (NLP) and predictive analytics, AI can construct detailed behavioral and psychological profiles of potential targets. Unlike human reconnaissance, which is limited by time and cognitive bandwidth, AI can process millions of data points simultaneously, enabling a level of precision and personalization never before possible. During weaponization, generative models synthesize attack tools and artifacts customized to their intended targets. The widespread and constant availability of internet resources around the clock allows anyone, anywhere, to access an unlimited range of professional, educational, technical, business, industrial, medical, and governmental resources globally (Babulak, 2023). This includes generating personalized phishing emails, fabricating deepfake videos or audio, and crafting polymorphic malware. The malicious payloads are often contextually aligned with the victim's environment—such as mimicking the internal communication tone of an organization or exploiting vulnerabilities associated with specific software stacks. Through generative modeling, attackers can produce unique and adaptive artifacts that evade signature-based detection mechanisms. The delivery phase is similarly enhanced through automation. AI can orchestrate large-scale campaigns that distribute phishing messages, malicious attachments, or exploit kits across diverse communication channels. Machine learning systems optimize delivery timing, channel selection, and even linguistic nuances to maximize engagement rates. For example, predictive algorithms can determine when a specific employee is most likely to read and respond to an email, improving the success probability of phishing campaigns. Once a foothold is established, the exploitation phase begins. Here, AI demonstrates its most dangerous capability autonomy in discovering and exploiting vulnerabilities. Adaptive malware can dynamically alter its code or behavior in response to system defenses, performing real-time vulnerability assessments and executing attacks that evolve on-the-fly. Through techniques such as reinforcement learning, malicious AI agents can test, learn, and refine exploitation strategies based on environmental feedback. During the installation and command-and-control (C2) stage, AI-optimized communication channels ensure persistence and stealth. Malware may use AI-based encryption or steganography to conceal its C2 traffic, blending malicious communication within normal network behavior. Machine learning algorithms can even mimic legitimate system processes to maintain undetected access. The sophistication of these mechanisms challenges even advanced security monitoring tools, as the distinction between benign and malicious behavior becomes increasingly blurred. The action on objectives phase involves the fulfillment of the attacker's goals be it data exfiltration, ransomware activation, financial theft, or system sabotage. AI-driven operations in this stage often rely on contextual learning, analyzing system structures and user patterns to prioritize valuable assets. For example, an AI agent could autonomously determine which data sets are most valuable based on access frequency, sensitivity classification, or business relevance. Finally, in the evasion and covering tracks phase, adversarial machine learning (AML) techniques are employed to maintain stealth and resilience. Generative adversarial networks (GANs) can continuously produce new variants of malware designed to deceive anomaly detectors. Meanwhile, AI-based log manipulation systems can erase traces of intrusion while simulating normal activity. Through continuous learning, these systems perpetuate a self-evolving attack ecosystem capable of long-term persistence within digital environments. This reimagined kill chain underscores how AI transforms cyber operations from linear, human-dependent sequences into autonomous, adaptive, and recursive ecosystems of attack. In industrial automation, cyber-physical systems (CPS) are becoming increasingly vulnerable to cyber threats, while current security frameworks often overlook how functional behaviors such as sensing, actuation, and parameter control generate distinct risk surfaces (Antipenko & Matulevičius, 2026).

3.2 Threat Scenarios

The abstract framework of AI-automated attacks becomes clearer when viewed through concrete threat scenarios that have already begun manifesting in practice. One of the most prevalent is AI-personalized phishing, in which large language models (LLMs) generate context-aware and emotionally intelligent messages that imitate trusted colleagues, executives, or business partners. Unlike generic phishing attempts, these AI-generated messages incorporate real-time information from public data sources and internal communication patterns, rendering traditional spam filters ineffective. A second scenario is deepfake voice fraud, a technique that leverages voice synthesis models to impersonate individuals with near-perfect accuracy. Financial institutions and corporations have reported cases in which synthetic voice calls replicating the tone and cadence of high-level executives have successfully deceived employees into authorizing wire transfers or releasing sensitive information. The psychological realism of AI-generated voices introduces a new dimension to social engineering, blurring the boundaries between human interaction and machine deception. Equally concerning is the proliferation of adaptive malware, capable of mutating its own code structures to evade detection. These self-reconfiguring systems exploit the vulnerabilities of signature-based antivirus software and static threat intelligence models. When combined with reinforcement learning, adaptive malware can test and refine its tactics autonomously, effectively learning how to bypass defenses without human direction. Finally, automated disinformation campaigns illustrate the geopolitical and societal dimensions of AI-driven threats. Generative models can create coordinated propaganda, synthetic identities, and fabricated multimedia content at scale. By automating the creation and dissemination of misinformation, AI can influence public perception, destabilize democratic processes, and amplify social polarization. These examples collectively demonstrate that AI-enabled attacks are not confined to technical exploits they extend into psychological, economic, and political domains, making them multidimensional threats that transcend traditional cybersecurity boundaries. The widespread adoption of artificial intelligence (AI) across mainstream industries has significantly increased the risk of adversarial artificial intelligence (AAI) attacks (Mulgund et al., 2025).

3.3 Risk and Visibility Challenges

The integration of AI into cyber offense amplifies operational risk in both speed and scale, drastically reducing the time window available for human intervention. In traditional security models, defenders relied on the Confidentiality, Integrity, and Availability (CIA) triad as the foundation of trust. However, in the age of autonomous cyber operations, two new dimensions must be incorporated: Explainability and Autonomy. Explainability ensures that defensive systems remain transparent and interpretable, while autonomy recognizes the reality that both attackers and defenders operate with decreasing human supervision. The fusion of these dimensions expands the traditional triad into a "Cyber Trust Pentad" a model encompassing Confidentiality, Integrity, Availability, Explainability, and Autonomy. A major challenge accompanying AI-driven attacks is visibility. As adversarial systems grow more autonomous, they generate fewer observable indicators of compromise (IoCs) and adapt faster than traditional monitoring systems can respond. Static logs, signature-based rules, and even heuristic detection struggle to capture the full scope of AI-generated activity. To restore visibility, defenders must embrace telemetry-based analytics, behavioral modeling, and automated correlation systems capable of identifying anomalies across network, user, and machine layers. Moreover, visibility must extend beyond technical detection toward cognitive interpretability. Human analysts require not only alerts but explanations insight into *why* a system classified an activity as suspicious. By integrating Explainable AI (XAI) into threat detection pipelines, organizations can achieve a higher degree of interpretability, allowing both human experts and AI agents to collaborate in decision-making. Ultimately, mitigating the risks of AI-generated cyber threats depends on balancing automation with accountability. Defensive AI systems must be as adaptive as the threats they combat, yet transparent enough to maintain trust and ethical integrity. The evolution of AI-automated threats compels cybersecurity to evolve from a reactive discipline into a proactive science one grounded in visibility, interpretability, and resilience against intelligent adversaries. Ports, located at the critical intersection between sea and land, face heightened vulnerability to external natural hazards like typhoons, which pose considerable risks and operational difficulties(Wang et al., 2026).

4. MITIGATION AND AUTOMATED DEFENSE STRATEGIES

As cyber threats increasingly harness the power of artificial intelligence, defending digital ecosystems demands an equally intelligent, adaptive, and transparent response. Traditional cybersecurity models reliant on static rules, human intervention, and retrospective analysis are insufficient against adversaries that operate autonomously and evolve in real time. AI-generated attacks exploit the very attributes that once defined human superiority in defense: creativity, adaptability, and contextual reasoning. Therefore, the next evolution in cybersecurity lies in the integration of automation with explainability, ensuring that defensive systems not only react intelligently but also articulate the reasoning behind their actions. This chapter proposes a multi-layered defense framework that merges intelligent automation, behavioral analytics, and explainable AI (XAI) principles to create a resilient, transparent, and continuously learning cybersecurity posture. Advanced applications of artificial intelligence (AI) can improve automated quality control by identifying defects in real time, thereby increasing product reliability and minimizing waste (Sekti, 2025).

4.1 Multi-Layered Automated Defense Architecture

The cornerstone of an effective defense against AI-generated threats is a multi-layered and adaptive architecture, where each component contributes to proactive detection, dynamic response, and transparent decision-making. Unlike monolithic defenses that depend on a single detection model, multi-layered systems integrate behavioral analytics, adversarial simulation, zero-trust principles, and deception technologies to create a living, self-improving ecosystem of protection. First, behavior-based detection has emerged as a critical advancement beyond traditional signature-based methods. Since AI-generated attacks often lack static signatures or identifiable fingerprints, behavioral analytics focus on recognizing deviations from normal operational patterns. Machine learning models monitor user activities, network traffic, and process behaviors to identify anomalies that suggest malicious intent. For instance, subtle shifts in login patterns or data transfer frequency may indicate an AI-driven intrusion that would otherwise bypass signature-based filters. Second, adversarial training plays a key role in hardening defensive models. By simulating evolving attack patterns using generative adversarial networks (GANs), defenders can expose their systems to synthetic but realistic threat scenarios. These controlled simulations improve model robustness, enabling defensive AI to anticipate and adapt to new forms of adversarial behavior. In essence, the defense learns by "fighting itself," refining its capabilities against the same generative logic used by attackers. Third, explainable automation ensures that as defense systems become more autonomous, their actions remain interpretable and accountable. Automated detection and mitigation tools must include decision-logging and interpretability layers that justify why a specific action such as quarantining a file or blocking a network segment was taken. This transparency enables security analysts to validate AI-driven decisions, reduces false positives, and builds organizational trust in automation. Additionally, the Zero-Trust segmentation model fortifies resilience by assuming no implicit trust within or outside the network perimeter. Every device, user, and application must continuously authenticate and verify access permissions. This segmentation limits lateral movement, ensuring that even if one node is compromised, the breach cannot easily spread. AI models embedded in zero-trust frameworks dynamically adjust access policies based on real-time behavioral analysis, further reducing the attack surface. Lastly, deceptive defense systems, often referred to as AI honeypots, add a strategic layer of misinformation. These systems generate dynamic decoy environments complete with realistic data, simulated users, and false system responses to mislead and occupy attackers. By engaging adversaries within controlled environments, defenders gain valuable intelligence about emerging tactics, techniques, and procedures (TTPs) without risking actual assets. Together, these elements behavioral detection, adversarial resilience, explainable automation, zero-trust enforcement, and deception form a cohesive defense architecture capable of countering intelligent and evolving threats. This paper provides an extensive review of recent developments in advanced and artificial intelligence (AI) chip technologies (Cao et al., 2026).

4.2 Integration of Explainable AI in Security Operations Centers (SOCs)

The Security Operations Center (SOC) represents the nerve center of modern cyber defense, where human analysts and automated systems collaborate to monitor, detect, and respond to threats. The integration of Explainable AI (XAI) into SOC workflows marks a transformative step toward achieving both operational efficiency and interpretability. Without explainability, automation risks becoming a "black box," generating alerts and taking actions that analysts may not fully understand or trust. By embedding XAI principles, SOCs can transform automated defense from an opaque assistant into a trusted collaborator. Central to this integration is decision transparency. AI-driven systems must not only detect threats but also communicate the rationale behind each alert or mitigation step. For example, an XAI-enabled intrusion detection system might display which network attributes or behavioral anomalies contributed most to a security alert. This interpretive layer enables analysts to comprehend and verify AI reasoning, facilitating better incident triage and faster resolution. Auditability is another critical outcome of explainable SOC operations. When AI systems log both their outputs and the reasoning paths leading to those outputs, organizations can conduct detailed post-incident forensics and compliance reporting. Such transparency aligns with regulatory frameworks that emphasize accountability in automated decision-making, including GDPR and emerging AI governance standards. Moreover, auditable AI enhances institutional learning, allowing defenders to trace false positives and improve model performance iteratively. A key component of the XAI-enabled SOC is the human-in-the-loop design. This model ensures that human experts remain engaged in critical decision points particularly when automated actions could have high-stakes implications, such as quarantining essential infrastructure or blocking legitimate users. By providing continuous feedback, analysts help refine the AI's predictive accuracy, creating a feedback loop that merges human judgment with machine precision. Emerging research also points to neuro-symbolic reasoning as a promising approach for achieving interpretability without compromising accuracy. This hybrid paradigm combines deep learning's pattern recognition capabilities with the rule-based logic of symbolic AI. The result is a system that can explain its reasoning in structured, human-readable forms such as logic chains or decision trees while still leveraging the statistical power of neural networks. Through such integration, SOCs can achieve the optimal balance of speed, accuracy, and transparency, ensuring that automation remains both effective and accountable. When these attacks take place, analysts in Security Operation Centers are required to manually review alerts from multiple IoT devices and generate a large volume of comparable reports (Matsubayashi et al., 2026).

4.3 Technical Countermeasures Against AI-Generated Threats

While architectural and organizational strategies provide the foundation for defense, practical countermeasures are essential to operationalize resilience against AI-generated threats. These measures combine technical sophistication with adaptability, addressing specific domains of AI misuse. Deepfake detection and biometric verification represent the first line of defense against AI-generated media manipulation. Modern countermeasures employ multimodal AI models capable of cross-validating visual, auditory, and textual cues to detect inconsistencies that reveal synthetic generation. For instance, micro-expression analysis and physiological signal recognition can identify deepfake videos, while spectrographic fingerprinting detects anomalies in synthetic voice recordings. Integrating biometric verification adds another layer of authentication, ensuring that media-based communications and transactions remain trustworthy. Context-aware phishing defense leverages natural language understanding and behavioral analytics to detect malicious intent hidden within seemingly legitimate messages. Instead of relying solely on keyword filters, context-aware systems analyze linguistic tone, sentence structure, and historical communication patterns to identify subtle deviations indicative of social engineering. These models can also cross-reference sender reputation and metadata to build a dynamic risk score, allowing organizations to filter out even highly personalized, AI-crafted phishing attempts. For malware detection, adversarial robustness becomes the defining goal. Defensive classifiers must be trained not just on known malware samples but also on generatively mutated variants. By using adversarial training datasets, defenders can anticipate potential evasive strategies that attackers might employ. This continuous learning cycle reduces susceptibility to zero-day variants and strengthens detection accuracy in volatile threat environments. Lastly, automated threat intelligence sharing transforms isolated defense mechanisms into a collaborative ecosystem. AI pipelines can collect, enrich, and disseminate Indicators of Compromise (IoCs) across trusted networks in real time. This interconnected approach enables organizations to benefit from collective intelligence, identifying emerging threats early and adjusting defenses proactively. As both attackers and defenders leverage automation, the principle of "AI versus AI" becomes the new equilibrium where intelligent systems continuously learn, adapt, and contest one another in an evolving digital arms race. Collectively, these defensive strategies illustrate a new paradigm in cybersecurity one where automation and explainability coexist to create a defense posture that is not only responsive but also responsible. The future of cyber defense lies not in resisting automation but in mastering it, ensuring that every intelligent system deployed in protection remains transparent, ethical, and aligned with human intent. In recent years, the evolution of DeepFake technology has accelerated, fueled by ongoing advancements in data availability, computational power, and deep generative modeling techniques (Xie et al., 2026).

5. IMPLEMENTATION CHALLENGES AND ETHICAL CONSIDERATIONS

The rapid adoption of AI-driven cybersecurity systems brings not only unprecedented defensive capabilities but also complex implementation and ethical challenges. As organizations integrate automation, explainability, and data-driven intelligence into their security operations, they must simultaneously navigate issues of data governance, human trust, workforce readiness, and the evolving nature of AI-enabled threats. The success of these systems ultimately depends on balancing efficiency with accountability ensuring that AI acts as a force multiplier, not as an ungoverned risk. This review tackles this gap by examining how AI and ML technologies have alleviated disruptions, evaluating their effectiveness across different sectors, and exploring the challenges associated with their implementation (Salehi et al., 2026).

5.1 Data Quality and Privacy

The performance and reliability of AI models in cybersecurity depend directly on the quality, diversity, and integrity of their underlying data. Proposes lightweight and advanced secure algorithms designed to identify fake incidents in wireless communication networks (R. Kumar et al., 2025). Security data ranging from network traffic and system logs to user behavior analytics and malware samples is highly sensitive. This introduces an inherent trade-off between using comprehensive datasets for model accuracy and protecting personal or confidential information. Ensuring data provenance is a critical first step. The emergence of wireless communication networks stands as evidence of human innovation and technological progress (S. N. Kumar et al., 2025). Models trained on incomplete or mislabeled data are prone to biases, leading to inaccurate detection or misclassification of threats. Human-verified labeling, data versioning, and the inclusion of contextual metadata allow explainable systems to trace decisions back to specific inputs enabling better forensic visibility. However, such transparency must operate within the constraints of privacy legislation like GDPR, ISO 27001, and NIST's AI Risk Management Framework. These frameworks require that data collection and processing align with the principles of necessity, proportionality, and informed consent. To reconcile privacy with utility, techniques such as federated learning and differential privacy can be adopted. Federated learning allows AI models to learn from distributed datasets without moving sensitive data from local environments, while differential privacy introduces controlled noise to prevent individual re-identification. Despite these benefits, these techniques may reduce the fidelity of detection models or introduce operational overheads. In parallel, synthetic data generation is emerging as a method to augment or replace real-world data when access is restricted. Yet, synthetic datasets can replicate the statistical bias of their source models, necessitating rigorous validation against real-world behavior patterns. Organizations must therefore embed privacy-aware data governance frameworks that define data access levels, retention schedules, and acceptable sharing policies. These frameworks should support explainable workflows by ensuring that all training and inference activities are auditable without compromising individual privacy. In cross-silo Federated Learning (FL), choosing which clients participate is essential for achieving optimal model performance; however, this process is complicated by issues such as uneven data quality, limited resources, and aligning participant incentives (Fei et al., 2026).

5.2 Over-Automation and Trust

Automation is a cornerstone of modern cyber defense, but excessive reliance on AI can produce dangerous blind spots. Over-automation can lead to false positives that disrupt legitimate operations, or false negatives that allow attackers to remain undetected. The human cost of such imbalances includes alert fatigue, operational downtime, and erosion of analyst trust in AI-driven systems. The key challenge lies in maintaining balanced automation, where AI handles repetitive, time-sensitive tasks such as log correlation or anomaly flagging while humans retain authority over high-impact decisions. Integrating Explainable AI (XAI) into this process ensures that automated decisions remain interpretable and contestable. By exposing model reasoning through feature attribution, decision trees, or confidence scores, analysts can quickly understand why a system took a particular action and determine whether it aligns with operational policy. Security Operation Centers (SOCs) must embed explainability into their human-in-the-loop workflows. Rather than replacing analysts, automation should empower them with contextual insights that enhance decision-making speed and accuracy. Equally important are audit trails and decision transparency allowing SOC leaders to review how and why certain alerts were generated, and whether interventions followed established playbooks. Over time, these feedback loops create trust between human operators and machine agents, allowing organizations to achieve both efficiency and accountability. This paper explores the transformative possibilities and key challenges of incorporating generative artificial intelligence into adaptive learning systems, proposing a human-centered approach that emphasizes enhancement of human capabilities rather than full automation (Kolhatin, 2025).

5.3 Skills and Organizational Readiness

The integration of AI and XAI into cybersecurity operations requires a workforce that is not only technically proficient but also capable of interpreting algorithmic behavior. Traditional cybersecurity training often focuses on system hardening, penetration testing, and incident response, but the AI era demands multidisciplinary expertise. Professionals must develop literacy in data science, model governance, and ethical AI deployment. Organizational readiness also extends to workflow transformation. SOCs must adapt to hybrid environments where human analysts collaborate with intelligent agents. This collaboration relies on interfaces that visualize model explanations, quantify uncertainty, and enable rapid what-if analysis during incidents. Without proper training, even sophisticated XAI dashboards can overwhelm or mislead operators. Continuous education, simulation exercises, and AI red-teaming should be institutionalized to help staff understand both the strengths and limitations of automated systems. Moreover, leadership must adopt AI governance policies that integrate model management into standard risk frameworks. This includes periodic model validation, explainability reviews, and compliance checks before production deployment. Cross-functional governance boards comprising cybersecurity experts, data scientists, ethicists, and legal officers ensure that operational efficiency never overrides ethical or legal boundaries. This study introduces a tri-semester academic policy guided by cognitive science principles, including spaced repetition and the forgetting curve, aiming to improve student learning outcomes and prepare them effectively for the workforce (Wu et al., 2026).

5.4 Evolving Adversarial Dynamics

The relationship between attackers and defenders in the AI era is inherently coevolutionary. Just as defenders deploy machine learning to detect and prevent threats, adversaries use generative and reinforcement learning models to identify weaknesses and develop adaptive attacks. During the process of data handling and analysis, traffic patterns are dynamically adjusted in real time (Nia et al., 2016). This constant escalation demands that defensive systems evolve dynamically rather than relying on static signatures or one-time model training. To keep pace, organizations must adopt continuous learning and adaptive retraining strategies. Models should be monitored for drift deviations in data distributions that degrade performance and retrained with the latest threat intelligence. Integration of AI red-teaming practices allows defenders to simulate attacks generated by adversarial models, exposing vulnerabilities in defensive algorithms before real attackers exploit them. Such exercises also strengthen explainability, as they reveal how AI models behave under uncertainty and manipulation. Equally, defenders must engage in collaborative intelligence sharing to counter global-scale AI threats. Sharing anonymized data, model insights, and adversarial indicators among trusted networks enables early detection of emerging attack patterns. However, these collaborations require strong governance to ensure data privacy and alignment with regulatory standards. The evolving threat landscape transforms cybersecurity into a contest of adaptive intelligences one where autonomous offense meets explainable defense. The ability to anticipate, interpret, and adapt faster than adversaries becomes the defining capability of future-ready organizations. In modern workplaces, changing work patterns promote the development of knowledge via informal learning opportunities (Chergui et al., 2025).

6. CASE STUDIES AND PRACTICAL INSIGHTS

The growing sophistication of AI-generated threats can be best understood through practical case studies that highlight how these attacks manifest in real-world contexts and how organizations have responded using explainable and generative defense mechanisms. Each case demonstrates not only the technological evolution of cyber threats but also the practical implementation of XAI and GenAI principles discussed in the previous chapters. These examples illustrate how intelligent, adaptive, and transparent systems can transform cybersecurity from a reactive discipline into a proactive and resilient defense strategy. The fast growth of internet-connected technologies and artificial intelligence (AI) has made AI models essential in cybersecurity, especially for detecting and countering cyberattacks (Ofusori et al., 2025).

6.1 Personalized AI Phishing

One of the most alarming developments in AI-driven cyberattacks is the emergence of personalized phishing campaigns powered by large language models (LLMs). In one notable case, a multinational corporation experienced a sophisticated phishing attack in which LLMs were used to craft emails that precisely mimicked the linguistic patterns, tone, and vocabulary of company executives. The attackers had fine-tuned their models on leaked or publicly available communication datasets, enabling the generation of highly authentic messages that bypassed traditional spam filters and heuristic-based detection systems. Conventional keyword detection and signature-based defenses proved ineffective because the messages contained no malicious links or typical phishing markers. Instead, the attack relied on psychological manipulation through linguistic authenticity. To counter this, the organization integrated behavioral analytics and linguistic anomaly detection into its security architecture. By analyzing subtle deviations in writing style and contextual inconsistencies, the AI models were able to flag suspicious messages even when their structure appeared legitimate. Explainable AI components played a vital role in this defense strategy providing transparent insights into why certain messages were classified as threats. This allowed human analysts to validate the system's reasoning and adjust its sensitivity, thereby creating a feedback loop between human expertise and AI automation.

6.2 Self-Evolving Malware

Another critical example involved a financial services firm targeted by self-evolving malware that employed generative algorithms to modify its behavior and digital signature after each infection cycle. This adaptive malware was capable of rewriting sections of its own code using reinforcement learning mechanisms, making traditional antivirus signatures obsolete almost immediately. Standard detection tools struggled to identify these variants since each iteration appeared unique in structure and execution. The organization responded by implementing an adversarial training framework, using Generative Adversarial Networks (GANs) to simulate evolving malware patterns and train their detection systems accordingly. Through sandbox analysis, researchers observed the malware's behavior in a controlled environment and identified invariant operational traits such as specific command-and-control communication sequences that persisted across mutations. Explainable decision-tree models were then deployed to interpret and justify each classification, offering human analysts clear visibility into which behavioral features triggered alerts. This hybrid approach combining generative adversarial simulation, behavioral forensics, and explainable modelling significantly enhanced the organization's ability to detect and mitigate polymorphic threats in real time.

6.3 Implications for Critical Infrastructure

The most consequential arena for AI-generated threats lies in critical infrastructure sectors such as energy, healthcare, and transportation. These domains face unique risks, as the consequences of disruption extend beyond financial loss to include potential harm to human life and national security. For instance, AI-driven attacks on smart grids or hospital networks can exploit the interconnected nature of IoT devices and industrial control systems (ICS), leading to cascading failures that traditional cybersecurity frameworks are ill-equipped to manage. In such environments, resilience becomes the primary objective. Implementing AI-driven automation without transparency could lead to catastrophic outcomes if decision-making systems act unpredictably or without oversight. This study examines how integrating AI-driven and automated mechanisms into Agile workflows can improve efficiency, strengthen collaboration, and increase overall project success (Polampally et al., 2025). Therefore, explainable automation is essential ensuring that every automated response is both auditable and aligned with ethical, regulatory, and operational standards. Real-time explainability enables security teams to understand system actions during incidents, comply with regulatory reporting requirements, and refine their defense models continuously. Furthermore, integrating continuous learning cycles and human-in-the-loop review mechanisms ensures that defense systems evolve alongside emerging threats, maintaining adaptability without compromising accountability. Together, these case studies demonstrate that the effective application of AI in cybersecurity is not merely a technical achievement but a paradigm shift in strategic defense. By uniting the predictive power of generative models, the transparency of explainable frameworks, and the judgment of human analysts, organizations can construct a defense posture capable of confronting the dynamic, adversarial nature of modern cyber warfare.

7. STRATEGIC AND OPERATIONAL RECOMMENDATIONS

In the wake of increasingly sophisticated AI-generated cyber threats, organizations must shift from reactive defense postures toward proactive, adaptive, and explainable security ecosystems. The previous case studies demonstrated how adversaries employ generative and self-learning algorithms to bypass conventional controls, emphasizing the need for intelligence-driven and ethically grounded countermeasures. Building upon those insights, this chapter outlines strategic and operational recommendations designed to help organizations strengthen their resilience, enhance transparency, and align with global cybersecurity governance standards. This study advances the creation of intelligent cybersecurity systems that enable real-time threat detection and proactive defense, enhancing network protection in a constantly changing cyber environment (Sharma et al., 2026).

Comprehensive Threat Mapping

The first strategic step toward mitigating AI-generated threats is to conduct a comprehensive mapping of potential vulnerabilities across digital infrastructure. Organizations must identify which components of their operations are most susceptible to AI exploitation whether through phishing, deepfake disinformation, automated social engineering, or model poisoning attacks targeting machine learning systems. Nevertheless, the process of acquiring and improving natural intelligence has essentially remained the same as it was centuries ago. The foundations of natural intelligence have motivated many scholars and researchers to create tools that enable machine intelligence (Kommers & Babulak, 2025). Threat mapping should not be a static exercise but a continuous, data-driven process that incorporates AI-assisted vulnerability scanning and red-teaming simulations. This dynamic mapping process allows organizations to anticipate where generative models might be leveraged by adversaries and to deploy tailored defenses accordingly.

Behavioral AI Monitoring

Given that AI-driven attacks often evade traditional signature-based defenses, organizations should focus on behavioral analytics and anomaly detection. Behavioral AI monitoring involves observing system interactions, network traffic, and user behavior patterns to identify deviations that could indicate malicious automation. Graph-based analysis helps visualize relationships between entities such as users, devices, or data flows revealing hidden patterns of compromise or coordinated attacks. Furthermore, contextual correlation systems can cross-reference multiple indicators (e.g., time, geolocation, access type) to assess risk in real-time. When enhanced with explainability layers, these systems can provide analysts with interpretable insights into why certain activities were flagged, ensuring that detection remains both intelligent and accountable.

Explainability Integration

A cornerstone of responsible AI security operations is explainability. Integrating interpretability modules into AI-driven security tools ensures that every autonomous decision can be traced and justified. For instance, when an AI-based intrusion detection system isolates a network segment or blocks a transaction, it should be able to articulate its reasoning in human-readable form. This not only enhances analyst trust and oversight but also supports compliance with regulatory standards and internal audit requirements. Explainable AI transforms automation from a "black box" into a transparent collaborator, enabling humans and machines to operate in synergy. In large-scale environments such as critical infrastructure or financial institutions this explainability is essential to prevent unintended disruptions and maintain operational integrity.

Regular Adversarial Simulations

To stay ahead of evolving threats, organizations must embrace adversarial thinking as part of their defense strategy. Conducting regular red-team exercises that employ generative AI enables security teams to simulate the behavior of intelligent attackers. These simulations expose weaknesses in both technical and procedural defenses, allowing for continuous improvement. By training defensive models with adversarial data, systems become more robust against real-world generative attacks. Moreover, adversarial exercises promote collaboration between data scientists and cybersecurity professionals, fostering a shared understanding of how offensive AI operates and how to counter it effectively.

Governance and Policy Frameworks

AI-driven defense must operate within well-defined ethical and legal boundaries. Establishing governance frameworks ensures that AI tools are deployed responsibly, transparently, and in accordance with international standards such as GDPR, ISO 27001, and the NIST AI Risk Management Framework. Clear policies should delineate acceptable AI use in security operations, specify accountability structures, and outline procedures for handling data, algorithmic bias, and model explainability. Ethical AI governance also reinforces organizational reputation and public trust critical assets in an era where cyber defense intersects with privacy, compliance, and human rights.

Collaborative Intelligence Sharing

No single organization can effectively combat AI-generated threats in isolation. Collaboration is key to staying informed about emerging techniques, tools, and adversarial models. Establishing partnerships with industry peers, government agencies, and Computer Emergency Response Teams (CERTs) allows for the timely exchange of generative AI threat intelligence. Such collaborations enhance situational awareness and enable coordinated responses during large-scale cyber incidents. Shared AI models and datasets can accelerate the collective development of defenses while ensuring that smaller organizations benefit from the research and expertise of larger institutions.

Awareness and Education

Finally, the human element remains the cornerstone of cybersecurity resilience. AI-generated deception, such as deepfake audio, synthetic identities, or persuasive phishing content, often targets individuals rather than systems. Therefore, continuous education and awareness programs are crucial. Employees at all organizational levels from executives to front-line staff should be trained to recognize AI-driven manipulation and maintain cyber hygiene. Training modules should include simulated phishing exercises, demonstrations of deepfake detection, and foundational knowledge of AI ethics and privacy principles. Cultivating a culture of digital skepticism and vigilance empowers humans to serve as the first line of defense against AI-enabled attacks.

8. FUTURE DIRECTIONS AND EMERGING TRENDS

Table 1. Emerging trends in AI-driven cybersecurity defense

Trend	Description	Strategic Implication
AI-vs-AI Dynamics	Both attackers and defenders leverage generative and adversarial AI to continuously adapt and counter each other's tactics.	Requires adaptive learning systems and adversarial training for real-time resilience.
Lightweight Edge AI	Deployment of real-time AI detection models on IoT and edge devices for distributed security.	Enhances local response and reduces dependency on centralized monitoring.
Regulatory Emphasis on Explainability	Explainable AI becomes a formal requirement in cybersecurity laws and compliance frameworks.	Promotes transparency, auditability, and ethical accountability in automated defenses.
AI-Driven Deception Ecosystems	Synthetic honeypots and decoy environments are used to study attacker behavior and train defensive models.	Enables predictive defense and real-time adaptation through behavioral intelligence.
Collaborative Threat Intelligence Networks	Federated learning and data-sharing frameworks enhance collective global threat detection.	Fosters global cooperation and accelerates AI-based defensive innovation.

9. CONCLUSION

The evolution of artificial intelligence has irrevocably transformed the cybersecurity landscape, marking the dawn of an era where threats are no longer manually orchestrated but autonomously generated, learned, and adapted. As explored across the preceding chapters, AI-generated cyber attacks introduce new levels of sophistication, speed, and unpredictability. These threats exploit the same computational intelligence that once promised greater efficiency, revealing the dual-use nature of technology capable of both protection and harm. Yet, the defensive community is not powerless. The same generative and explainable AI technologies that empower adversaries can be repurposed to build resilient, transparent, and adaptive cyber defense ecosystems. In the introduction, the foundation was established by recognizing that Generative AI (GenAI) and Explainable AI (XAI) are reshaping both offensive and defensive cybersecurity dynamics. While GenAI automates and personalizes attacks such as phishing, malware creation, and social engineering XAI ensures that defensive automation remains accountable and interpretable. This duality frames the modern security paradigm: automation without understanding breeds chaos, but explainability transforms it into trust. The second chapter delved into the evolution and defining characteristics of AI-generated threats. Unlike traditional cyber attacks, AI-driven assaults operate with unprecedented autonomy, adaptability, and personalization. The rise of self-learning malware, deepfake manipulation, and automated reconnaissance signifies a move toward fully autonomous threat ecosystems. At the same time, the opacity paradox emerged illustrating that while automation enhances capability, lack of transparency can undermine reliability, even in defensive systems. In chapter three, a structured understanding of AI-automated threats was developed through an adaptation of the cyber kill chain. This framework demonstrated how AI influences every stage of the attack lifecycle from reconnaissance and weaponization to exploitation and evasion. The inclusion of real-world threat scenarios underscored how AI amplifies the precision and scale of adversarial operations. Moreover, defenders now face the challenge of maintaining visibility across highly dynamic and opaque AI systems, forcing a redefinition of cybersecurity principles to incorporate explainability and human oversight as integral dimensions of trust. Chapter four transitioned from understanding threats to mitigating them, proposing a multi-layered, automated defense architecture. It highlighted the necessity of integrating behavioral analytics, adversarial training, explainable automation, and deceptive defense mechanisms. Explainable AI was positioned as the bridge between human and machine intelligence turning complex model outputs into actionable, transparent insights for Security Operations Centers (SOCs). The principle of "AI versus AI" emerged as a defining strategy, advocating for the intelligent use of automation to counter intelligent attacks. Building on this, chapter five examined the implementation challenges and ethical considerations inherent in adopting AI-driven cybersecurity. Issues of data quality, privacy, over-automation, and workforce readiness were emphasized as critical barriers. Defenders must balance the efficiency of automation with human judgment, ensuring that AI decisions remain comprehensible and legally compliant. Moreover, as adversarial AI continues to evolve, continuous learning and adaptive retraining become essential to maintaining relevance in an ever-shifting digital battlefield. The sixth chapter brought theory to life through practical case studies, illustrating how AI-generated phishing, self-evolving malware, and attacks on critical infrastructure manifest in real-world contexts. These examples demonstrated that successful defense depends not only on technological sophistication but also on transparency, accountability, and resilience. Human-in-the-loop systems supported by explainable analytics emerged as a proven model for aligning machine efficiency with human understanding. Chapter seven expanded this discussion into strategic and operational recommendations, outlining a framework for organizations to build resilient defense postures. From comprehensive threat mapping and behavioral AI monitoring to ethical governance and collaborative intelligence sharing, the chapter emphasized that cybersecurity resilience is as much an organizational and cultural challenge as it is a technical one. Explainability was again highlighted as the unifying element ensuring that every automated decision, model prediction, or defensive action remains interpretable and verifiable. In chapter eight, the future trajectory of cybersecurity was explored, showcasing emerging trends such as AI-vs-AI dynamics, lightweight edge AI, explainability-based regulation, deception ecosystems, and federated threat intelligence. Together, these trends signal a shift toward globally connected, adaptive, and intelligent defense networks where transparency and collaboration become as critical as speed and precision. Thus, as this exploration concludes, one truth becomes clear: the future of cybersecurity will not be determined by the absence of AI-generated threats but by our collective ability to understand, explain, and control them. The convergence of Generative AI, Explainable AI, and ethical automation will redefine what it means to be secure in the digital age. Human intelligence must remain at the core of this evolution guiding, interpreting, and governing machine intelligence to ensure that technological power serves humanity rather than undermines it. In this balance between autonomy and accountability lies the foundation of a truly secure and trustworthy digital ecosystem.

REFERENCES

Almotiri, S. H. (2025). AI driven IOMT security framework for advanced malware and ransomware detection in SDN. *Journal of Cloud Computing (Heidelberg, Germany), 14*(1), 19. Advance online publication. DOI: 10.1186/s13677-025-00745-w

Antipenko, V., & Matulevičius, R. (2026). Function–Threat Alignment in CPS with FAST and MITRE ATT&CK. *Lecture Notes in Business Information Processing, 562 LNBIP*, 365–379. DOI: 10.1007/978-3-032-04375-7_23

Babulak, E. (2023). AI Tools for Protecting and Preventing Sophisticated Cyber Attacks. In *AI Tools for Protecting and Preventing Sophisticated Cyber Attacks*. DOI: 10.4018/978-1-6684-7110-4

Babulak, E. (2025). AI-Driven Approaches for Fully Automated Smart Engineering. In *AI-Driven Approaches for Fully Automated Smart Engineering*. DOI: 10.4018/979-8-3373-4839-1

Babulak, E. Al_Dabass, D., & Tomar, G. (2025). Editorial: Cyber security prevention, defenses driven by AI, and mathematical modelling and simulation tools. *Frontiers in Computer Science, Volume 7-*. https://www.frontiersin.org/journals/computer-science/articles/10.3389/fcomp.2025.1685873

Cao, Y., Chen, Y., Fan, X., Fu, H., & Xu, B. (2026). Advanced Design for High-Performance and AI Chips. *Nano-Micro Letters, 18*(1), 13. Advance online publication. DOI: 10.1007/s40820-025-01850-w PMID: 40728678

Chergui, M., Nagano, A., & Ammoumou, A. (2025). Toward an adaptive learning system by managing pedagogical knowledge in a smart way. *Multimedia Tools and Applications, 84*(24), 27777–27793. DOI: 10.1007/s11042-024-20207-w

Fei, Q., Rodríguez-Barroso, N., Luzón, M. V., Zhang, Z., & Herrera, F. (2026). Addressing data quality decompensation in federated learning via dynamic client selection. *Future Generation Computer Systems, 176*, 108138. Advance online publication. DOI: 10.1016/j.future.2025.108138

Khatri, P., Duggal, H. K., Thomas, A., Corvello, V., Prałat, E., & Shiva, A. (2026). Development and validation of the generative artificial intelligence appropriation (GAIA) Scale: A comprehensive measurement tool for assessing user engagement and utilisation. *Technovation, 150*, 103379. Advance online publication. DOI: 10.1016/j.technovation.2025.103379

Kolhatin, A. O. (2025). From automation to augmentation: A human-centered framework for generative AI in adaptive educational content creation. *CEUR Workshop Proceedings, 4060*, 143–195. https://www.scopus.com/inward/record.uri?eid=2-s2.0-105019297347&partnerID=40&md5=9984d27b9df38e2e4b15021498d4e68c

Kommers, P., & Babulak, E. (2025). Conceptual awareness for human navigation in A.I. In *Educational AI Humanoid Computing Devices for Cyber Nomads* (pp. 1–13). DOI: 10.4018/979-8-3693-8985-0.ch001

Kumar, R., Jain, V., Ather, D., Kukreja, V., & Singhal, M. (2025). Network security and data privacy in 6G communication: Trends, challenges, and applications. In *Network Security and Data Privacy in 6G Communication*. Trends, Challenges, and Applications., DOI: 10.1201/9781003583127

Kumar, S. N., Joy, J., Jane, I. C., James, A., John, S., & Babulak, E. (2025). Applications of 6G in the healthcare sector and the importance of network security and data privacyencryption of medical images using the SHA 256 blockchain algorithm. In *Network Security and Data Privacy in 6G Communication: Trends, Challenges, and Applications* (pp. 176–190). DOI: 10.1201/9781003583127-9

Liu, J., Sihes, A. J. B., & Lu, Y. (2025). How do generative artificial intelligence (AI) tools and large language models (LLMs) influence language learners' critical thinking in EFL education? A systematic review. *Smart Learning Environments, 12*(1), 48. Advance online publication. DOI: 10.1186/s40561-025-00406-0

Matsubayashi, M., Shibahara, T., Koyama, T., & Tanaka, M. (2026). Reusability Evaluation of Reports in Security Operation Centers for IoT with Sentence ALBERT and Jaccard Similarity. *Lecture Notes of the Institute for Computer Sciences, Social-Informatics and Telecommunications Engineering, LNICST, 629 LNICST*, 51–72. DOI: 10.1007/978-3-031-94455-0_3

Mulgund, P., Singh, R., Sharman, R., Gupta, M., & Pothukuchi, A. S. (2025). DEFENSE-IN-DEPTH MODEL OF COUNTERMEASURES AGAINST ADVERSARIAL AI ATTACKS: LITERATURE REVIEW AND CLASSIFICATION. *Journal of Information Systems Security, 21*(1), 51–84. https://www.scopus.com/inward/record.uri?eid=2-s2.0-105008373545&partnerID=40&md5=79b1a6eb66ce8a5799d59838f4de4382

Nia, M. A., Atani, R. E., Fabian, B., & Babulak, E. (2016). On detecting unidentified network traffic using pattern-based random walk. *Security and Communication Networks, 9*(16), 3509–3526. DOI: 10.1002/sec.1557

Ofusori, L., Bokaba, T., & Mhlongo, S. (2025). Explainability and interpretability of artificial intelligence use in cybersecurity. *Discover Computing*, *28*(1), 241. Advance online publication. DOI: 10.1007/s10791-025-09760-6

Polampally, S. K., Nadella, G. S., Ragunayakula, S., Kumar, V. J., Kankala, S., & Babulak, E. (2025). AI-Driven Automation in Agile Software Development Teams Enhancing Efficiency and Collaboration. In *AI-Driven Approaches for Fully Automated Smart Engineering* (pp. 85–132). DOI: 10.4018/979-8-3373-4839-1.ch003

Qi, Z., Li, H., Qin, H., Peng, K., He, S., & Qin, X. (2026). Harnessing large language models for virtual reality exploration testing: A case study. *Automated Software Engineering*, *33*(1), 7. Advance online publication. DOI: 10.1007/s10515-025-00535-3

Renero, J., Maestre, R., & Ochoa, I. (2026). REX: Causal discovery based on machine learning and explainability techniques. *Pattern Recognition*, *172*, 112491. Advance online publication. DOI: 10.1016/j.patcog.2025.112491

Salehi, A., Babaei, A., & Hamidi, H. (2026). AI-Driven Strategies for Supply Chain Resilience: A Review of Challenges and Solutions During Pandemics. *International Journal of Engineering, Transactions B: Applications*, *39*(3), 585–605. DOI: 10.5829/ije.2026.39.03c.03

Sekti, B. A. (2025). Machine learning and artificial intelligence (AI) in manufacturing. In *Integrating Digital Innovation and Integrated Frameworks in Manufacturing* (pp. 255–292). DOI: 10.4018/979-8-3373-1082-4.ch011

Sharma, P., Homkar, A., Jha, S., Somasekar, J., Wbaid, S., & Dixit, K. K. (2026). Efficient Cybersecurity Threat Analysis Through Anomaly Detection and Graph Summarization. In *Synthesis Lectures on Computer Science: Vol. Part F729* (pp. 43–53). DOI: 10.1007/978-3-031-93802-3_4

Sowmya, R., & Konduri, B. (2025). Explainable and cognitive attention evoked learning framework for mitigating the large-scale real time cyber attacks. *Discover Computing*, *28*(1), 160. Advance online publication. DOI: 10.1007/s10791-025-09672-5

Wang, S., Yin, J., Wang, X., & Khan, R. U. (2026). Mitigating Typhoon Disruptions and Enhancing Port Infrastructure Performance: A Risk Assessment Approach. *ASCE-ASME Journal of Risk and Uncertainty in Engineering Systems. Part A, Civil Engineering*, *12*(1), 04025090. Advance online publication. DOI: 10.1061/AJRUA6.RUENG-1670

Wu, M., Su, H., & Majd, M. (2026). Can We Change Two-Semester Academic year to Trimester Semester System? ~ meeting Competitive World with Effective Educational Policy Upgrade~. *Lecture Notes in Computer Science, 15914 LNCS*, 129–138. DOI: 10.1007/978-3-031-98197-5_15

Xie, S., Qiao, T., Li, S., Zhang, X., Zhou, J., & Feng, G. (2026). DeepFake detection in the AIGC era: A survey, benchmarks, and future perspectives. *Information Fusion*, *127*, 103740. Advance online publication. DOI: 10.1016/j.inffus.2025.103740

Chapter 3
From Black Boxes to Cyber Sentinels:
Interpretable Generative AI for Threat Intelligence and Digital Forensics

Syed Ibad Ali
http://orcid.org/0000-0001-6312-6768
Parul Institute of Engineering and Technology, Parul University, Vadodara, India

ABSTRACT

The increasing sophistication of cyberattacks—driven by automation, deepfake data, and polymorphic malware—has rendered traditional opaque artificial intelligence (AI) models insufficient for maintaining security resilience. This book chapter introduces a transformative framework that reimagines cybersecurity through interpretable generative AI, uniting the transparency of Explainable AI (XAI) with the creative adaptability of generative modeling. The chapter positions these hybrid architectures as cyber sentinels—autonomous, self-learning systems capable of generating, detecting, and explaining complex threat scenarios in real time. By merging Generative Adversarial Networks (GANs), Variational Autoencoders (VAEs), and Transformer-based threat intelligence models with interpretability layers, the proposed system achieves both predictive accuracy and forensic accountability.

INTRODUCTION

The extraordinary confluence of AI, automation, and cybersecurity in the digital era has altered public perceptions and strategies around security management. As

DOI: 10.4018/979-8-2600-1608-4.ch003

cyber threats get more complex, the significance of intelligent and flexible cybersecurity systems capable of anticipating, preventing, and analyzing hostile activities is escalating. Due to advancements in data-driven intelligence and the rapid increase in computer capacity, enterprises may now use data-driven intelligence to safeguard essential infrastructures. A paradox emerges when AI systems evolve with opaque decision-making processes; these systems wield significant power, but auditing, trusting, or regulating them is challenging due to their opacity. For cybersecurity systems that must comply with the utmost standards of openness, accountability, and ethics, this obfuscation—often referred to as the "black box problem"—has emerged as a significant impediment. The advent of interpretable generative AI signifies a fundamental transformation in digital defense, emphasizing transparency and cognitive responsibility. Researchers are currently considering autonomous agents that integrate the adaptability of generative AI with the logical transparency of Explainable AI (XAI) as intelligent cyber sentinels. These agents would possess the capability to recognize threats, respond appropriately, and articulate their rationale to others (Sarker et al., 2024).

Generative adversarial networks (GANs) and Transformer-based architectures exemplify generative AI models that are essential to next-generation threat intelligence. The advancement of defensive strategies has been transformed by their ability to produce synthetic data, replicate adversarial situations, and anticipate intricate assault patterns. Balasubramanian (2025) asserts that generative AI is essential for creating synthetic threat environments that enable the training and testing of cybersecurity systems in scenarios that replicate actual assaults. This proactive feature enables researchers to predict vulnerabilities prior to their exploitation. Nonetheless, the same ingenuity that makes generative models advantageous also presents new obstacles. The fundamental mechanisms of these systems are often poorly comprehended, since they depend on high-dimensional models and nonlinear transformations for functionality. In the absence of mechanisms to guarantee interpretability, these models risk becoming opaque, making it hard to validate their recommendations or classifications. Users lose trust, accountability diminishes, and the models are rendered unusable in forensics due to insufficient transparency. An increasing number of investigations are endeavoring to include interpretability into the generative framework, transforming AI into an enlightening collaborator in human-machine interaction rather than just a computational instrument. The objective of explainable AI is to elucidate intricate algorithms to enhance human understanding. The objective is to elucidate how AI systems arrive at their findings by providing both local and global explanations, which clarify individual predictions and present a comprehensive overview of the model's behavior throughout the dataset. Given the imminent potential for legal, financial, and ethical consequences, explainability is paramount in cybersecurity. In cybersecurity, the dependability of AI is contingent upon its predictive efficacy, transparency, equity, and rationalization capabilities (Mohamed, 2025). All stakeholders, including analysts, auditors, and legislators, must comprehend the rationale behind the designation of certain actions as suspicious when AI systems detect abnormalities or possible violations. Regulators are naturally cautious of black-box models since, despite their accuracy, they do not fulfill this requirement. This deficiency is mitigated by explainable generative AI, which integrates interpretive mechanisms into the model architecture from the outset. The generative and discriminative components of cybersecurity models may now be comprehensively analyzed using visualization tools, attention maps, gradient-based saliency methods, and rule extraction frameworks (Sarker et al., 2024).

Interpretable generative AI is essential in digital forensics. Conventional forensic methods are insufficient against the escalating tactics of cybercrime, the overwhelming volume of data, and the intricacies of the digital environment. AI-driven forensic technologies provide automation and scalability; yet, there are occasions when they lack sufficient transparency, leading to skepticism over the validity of their results. Billah (2025) posits that explainable AI may provide a clear decision-making process that adheres to legal criteria of accountability and repeatability, potentially enhancing confidence in forensic evidence. To guarantee that ideas derived from AI can endure judicial scrutiny, elucidation is essential in forensic contexts. Integrating explainability guarantees that forensic findings may be comprehended by investigators, judges, and lawyers, irrespective of their technical proficiency. Enhance the evidential reliability of cyber forensics with interpretable generative AI by clarifying the methodologies of digital artifact recognition, association, and attribution to particular threat actors. Additionally, it emulates attack timings and offers interpretable reconstructions of encrypted or deleted data, which is essential for attribution and legal validation, as well as aiding in post-incident reconstruction. The emergence of synthetic worlds concurrently presents new issues for digital authenticity and forensic investigation. Alberti et al. (2023) assert that the capability of generative AI to create photorealistic digital material, such as deepfakes, voice replicas, and synthetic documents, complicates the distinction between authenticity and fabrication. While generative AI facilitates fraud and disinformation, it is essential for defensive scenario modeling. To identify AI-generated forgeries, we need counter-models capable of detecting nuanced statistical anomalies in the data produced by the system. Pontorno et al. (2024) demonstrate that Discrete Cosine Transform (DCT) trace analysis is a viable forensic technique for identifying synthetic images and videos by uncovering concealed digital fingerprints inside generating data. Incorporating interpretability into detection algorithms may enhance forensic analysts' ability to identify altered material and elucidate the categorization of evidence as synthetic. This interpretative openness is essential to assure the trustworthiness of evidence obtained by AI analysis and to maintain the credibility of forensic reporting. The domain of cyber threat intelligence (CTI) is undergoing fast transformation due to generative and explainable technology. Cyber Threat Intelligence (CTI) has consistently struggled to adapt to evolving adversaries, since it has traditionally depended on static indicators of compromise (IoCs) and historical datasets to predict attacks. The use of generative models indicates a transition from reactive to anticipatory intelligence. Balasubramanian (2025) asserts that generative AI may replicate novel attack patterns and provide data for hypothetical threat situations, thus enhancing readiness. The produced intelligence is rendered ineffective if the simulations are unintelligible. To assess the authenticity of created threats, comprehend the significance of characteristics, and extract valuable insights, security analysts want procedures that are straightforward and explicable. Generative intelligence without interpretability may inundate analysts with ambiguous data, leading to "alert fatigue" and resulting in paralysis by analysis. Incorporating interpretability renders the produced outputs cohesive narratives that human analysts may use to understand the features of the threat and the circumstances likely to precipitate its occurrence. The significance of ethical and legal responsibility is increasing as AI systems autonomously make judgments. Autonomous cyber security systems function with little human involvement by using mitigation tactics derived from gathered threat models. This degree of autonomy enhances reaction times but prompts ethical issues around accountability and authority. According to Sarker et al. (2024), sustaining confidence in defensive AI systems requires explicable autonomy. The capacity to explain the rationale behind an autonomous system's choice to mitigate a perceived risk is essential for stakeholders. The next regulatory frameworks are expected to enforce the traceability and justifiability of AI-driven operations, making this need both technological and legal. To guarantee justice, accountability, and privacy protection in cybersecurity operations, Mohamed (2025) emphasizes the need of transparent AI systems in reconciling technical advancement with ethical governance frameworks. Significant policy and political repercussions will arise from the integration of generative and explainable AI. A more transparent and auditable AI is essential as governments and corporations increasingly depend on AI for cyber resilience and national security. The European Union's AI Act and other rules emphasize the need of openness, explainability, and human supervision in the use of AI inside fields such as cybersecurity and law enforcement, which require significant human intervention. Explainable generative AI adheres closely to these objectives by offering both creative autonomy and established reasoning. The integration of interpretability in AI systems enables regulators to ensure compliance, mitigate prejudice, and foster algorithmic fairness. Consequently, ethical governance has become essential in the creation of AI systems rather than a mere afterthought. This perspective posits that interpretable generative AI is a sociotechnical tool that, beyond its technological significance, might foster more democratic accountability in the era of intelligent automation. A multi-tiered approach including data, algorithms, and interface components is essential for incorporating interpretability into generative models from a system design viewpoint. Explainable preprocessing guarantees that the training datasets for generative models are varied, representative, and devoid of bias at the data level. An imbalance in data may compromise the accuracy of threat detection, making this a critical concern in the cybersecurity sector. Hybrid architectures that integrate deep learning with symbolic reasoning are emerging as the most prominent approach. Incorporating rule-based reasoning layers enables these models to use neural networks for pattern recognition while preserving logical interpretability. Sarker et al. (2024) assert that the explainability of digital twins, a notion intimately linked to cyber simulations, may enhance confidence in and bolster support for artificial intelligence-driven security models. Explainable dashboards and visualization tools elucidate intricate AI reasoning for human analysts at the user interface level. The interpretative loop is completed by these interfaces, which convert theoretical data into practical information, enhancing environmental awareness and facilitating informed decision-making. Numerous issues still unresolved, despite the potential of interpretable generative AI. Achieving concordance between interpretability and performance is a significant problem. A trade-off between interpretability and effectiveness arises when high-dimensional generative models attain enhanced accuracy at the expense of transparency. In cybersecurity contexts where rapid reaction is critical, explainability algorithms may provide superfluous processing cost, thus impeding real-time responsiveness. Ensuring precise and transparent interpretability is an extra hurdle. To guarantee that interpretability tools provide unbiased and substantive reasoning, rather than flawed representations of the model's logic, Billah (2025) contends that it is essential to evaluate these tools. The investigation of explainable AI in cybersecurity is progressing swiftly, necessitating standardized assessment standards. The relationship between human cognition and interpretable generative AI is significant. All stakeholders, including legislators, security professionals, and legal authorities, must comprehend AI elucidations. Comprehending AI thinking may be difficult, especially when the explanations are too complex. Current research on explainability increasingly incorporates concepts of human-centered design, emphasizing the significance of linguistic accessibility, contextual pertinence, and clarity. Both algorithmic design and communication design, particularly the presentation of AI explanations to human users, must be clear (Alberti et al., 2023). By prioritizing people, interpretable generative AI may improve human-machine cooperation, resulting in advantageous decision-making that enhances comprehension and confidence. The next paradigm in cybersecurity will be defined by cognitive transparency, ethical responsibility, and adaptive intelligence, founded on explainability and generativity. Balasubramanian (2025) posits that future generative AI systems would simulate threats and evaluate their repercussions, providing strategic defense teams with contextualized and interpretable information. Mohamed (2025) asserts that autonomous and responsible systems capable of justifying every investigative or defensive activity are crucial for the viability of the cybersecurity ecosystem in the long run. In this scenario, human analysts and intelligent agents participate in a continuous discourse about cybersecurity, aiming to enhance one another's cognitive abilities. The concept of the "cyber sentinel" well encapsulates this transition: AI systems that integrate creativity with meticulous analysis to function as discernible protectors rather than faceless instruments.

Ultimately, interpretable generative AI represents a transformation in society's perspective on AI, including both technological and philosophical dimensions. It facilitates a transition from opaque automation to responsible cognition, advancing the discipline from mere accuracy to comprehension. Business resilience in more complex threat environments will be determined by their capacity to trust and validate AI assessments. Incorporating explainability across all phases of interpretable generative AI systems may provide cognitive transparency, legal compliance, ethical integrity, and the capacity to address emerging risks. The era of enigmatic algorithmic innovations is yielding to the epoch of rational, enlightening guardians of digital society, accompanied by the age of inscrutable intelligence.

LITERATURE SURVEY

Over the past decade, the integration of artificial intelligence within cybersecurity has progressed from rule-based systems to advanced machine learning and deep learning architectures. As early reviews highlight, AI provides significant value in intrusion detection, malware classification, anomaly detection, and other core defence capabilities. These AI-tools offered increased accuracy over conventional signature-based mechanisms, yet they introduced a critical limitation: their decision logic was often opaque to human operators. This "black box" nature raised concerns about accountability, auditability, and the interpretability of security outcomes. The literature emphasises that in cybersecurity contexts—where decisions may support forensic investigations, legal proceedings or critical-infrastructure protection—transparency is not an optional extra but a core requirement (Charmet et al., 2022).

In response, the field of Explainable Artificial Intelligence (XAI) has emerged as a counter-measure to the transparency gap. Surveys demonstrate that XAI techniques have been increasingly applied to cybersecurity tasks, such as intrusion detection systems (IDS) and malware analysis, offering explanations for predictions and decision pathways (Mohale & Obagbuwa, 2025). The literature maps common XAI methods—including SHAP (Shapley Additive Explanations), LIME (Local Interpretable Model-agnostic Explanations), rule-based decision-trees, and counterfactual reasoning—as means to render AI decisions interpretable by human analysts. For example, in IDS scenarios, SHAP has been used to identify which network features contributed most strongly to an alert, thus enabling analysts to validate or challenge flagged events.

Nevertheless, interpretability introduces trade-offs and challenges. As Mohale & Obagbuwa (2025) note, more interpretable models often sacrifice detection accuracy or real-time performance, especially in high-throughput network contexts. Moreover, computational overheads of XAI techniques may hinder deployment in resource-constrained environments. The literature also identifies a clear gap: while many studies apply XAI post-hoc to existing models, fewer integrate interpretability from the design phase. Thus, research increasingly calls for hybrid approaches that embed transparency into model architecture rather than append it externally.

Parallel to the rise of XAI, generative AI (GenAI) has gained immense traction across domains, including cybersecurity. The literature illustrates that GenAI models—such as Variational Autoencoders (VAEs), Generative Adversarial Networks (GANs), diffusion models, and large-language models (LLMs)—can synthesize data, model adversarial behaviour, and support proactive defence strategies (Balasubramanian, 2025). Specifically, Balasubramanian (2025) surveys how GenAI is applied within cyber-threat-intelligence (CTI) frameworks: generating synthetic attack vectors, simulating malware evolution, modelling network traffic anomalies, and exploring social-engineering campaigns. These capabilities empower defence systems to anticipate threats rather than simply react. However, the review also underscores limitations: many GenAI systems are themselves black boxes and lack interpretability. The complexity of deep generative networks renders auditing and human-explanation difficult, raising concerns about trust, governance, and the potential for new attack vectors generated by adversaries using GenAI. Recent comprehensive reviews by Sharma (2025) and Zhang et al. (2022) further validate that while AI applications in cybersecurity are expanding, the necessity for explainability remains a critical barrier to adoption. Gilbert (2024) also argues that the impact of AI on defense mechanisms has been profound, shifting the paradigm towards automated response. However, Neupane et al. (2023) and Coppolino et al. (2025) warn that the risks associated with generative AI, including the creation of sophisticated attack vectors, require immediate attention in modern threat modeling.

Within digital forensics, the literature emphasises a growing need for AI systems that can not only detect malicious behaviour but also explain how evidence was derived. For instance, forensic practitioners must understand whether a flagged artefact is the result of a genuine intrusion or a benign anomaly. Billah (2025) argues that explainability is essential for forensic AI systems to maintain legal validity, reproducibility of evidence, and trust in courtroom contexts. In effect, AI-driven forensic platforms must provide audit-trails, logic-explanations, and human-legible reasoning pathways for their conclusions. This shift from "AI produces alert" to "AI explains alert" represents a critical evolution in forensic readiness.

The intersection of GenAI and XAI is particularly salient in cybersecurity literature—and yet it remains under-explored. While GenAI brings generative power and adaptability to model complex threat landscapes, XAI brings interpretability and trustworthiness. Several recent works (e.g., Mohale & Obagbuwa, 2025) emphasise that hybrid architectures—combining generative modules with embedded interpretability layers—are still nascent. The challenge is to design systems where generative components maintain high performance while transparency is preserved, enabling security analysts and investigators to question, audit, and refine model decisions. A key research gap appears to be evaluation metrics for interpretability within generative threat-intelligence systems: How do we measure trust, explanation quality, forensic sufficiency, and utility for human decision-makers in such environments?

Another major strand of literature addresses the ethical, regulatory, and adversarial dimensions of AI in cybersecurity. With the increasing deployment of AI models in high-stakes domains, governance frameworks such as the EU AI Act emphasise transparency, human oversight, fairness, and accountability. Balasubramanian (2025) emphasises that GenAI systems must align with these governance imperatives—especially when applied to threat-intelligence contexts that involve privacy-sensitive data and adversarial dynamics. At the same time, research in XAI highlights that interpretability mechanisms themselves may become attack surfaces (Charmet, 2022). The capability to reverse-engineer feature-attribution maps or manipulate explanation layers introduces novel adversarial vulnerabilities. Hence, security-aware XAI design is now an active direction in the literature.

From a methodological perspective, the literature notes the importance of multi-modal data integration and synthetic simulation in AI-driven cybersecurity. GenAI reviews emphasise how CTI systems must process network flows, social-media feeds, dark-web forums, malware binaries, and unstructured threat reports—all at scale (Balasubramanian, 2025). Meanwhile, XAI research highlights that interpretability becomes more complex with multi-modal and high-dimensional feature spaces: providing human-legible explanations for deep learning modules across network, textual and image data remains challenging. This convergence—rich multi-modal generative modelling plus human-centric interpretability—marks a frontier in the research landscape.

The literature also reflects emerging use-cases at the edge of cybersecurity: real-time threat hunting, IoT device monitoring, and autonomous response platforms. For example, recent work proposes explainable lightweight AI frameworks tailored for edge networks, balancing interpretability, efficiency and rapid response. These studies underscore the shift from centralized cloud models to distributed, real-time platforms—where interpretability and computational constraints must be addressed concurrently.

Despite rich progress, several gaps persist in the literature. First, while many XAI and GenAI surveys exist individually, fewer works address the *fusion* of generative models with interpretability frameworks in cybersecurity settings. Second, there remains a shortage of standardised metrics and benchmarking for explanation quality, human-usability of explanations, and forensic-readiness of AI systems. Third, practical real-world case-studies that integrate explainable generative AI in operational CTI or forensic pipelines remain limited—most studies are proof-of-concept or offline experiments. Fourth, the adversarial robustness of interpretable generative systems is still poorly characterised: how do explanation layers hold up under adversarial manipulation, model poisoning or synthetic-attacks remains underexplored. Finally, the human-machine interface aspect—how security analysts consume, trust, and act upon AI explanations—requires further empirical research.

In sum, the literature paints a nuanced landscape: AI in cybersecurity has advanced substantially, but transparency and interpretability remain fundamental bottlenecks. The co-evolution of generative and explainable AI offers tremendous promise: proactive threat simulation, adaptive defence, audit-friendly forensic pipelines, and human-machine collaboration grounded in trust. The next research wave, accordingly, must rise to the challenge of integrating generative power with interpretability, governance, and human-centred design. This literature survey sets the stage for the remainder of this chapter, where I will propose an architecture for interpretable generative AI (the "cyber sentinel"), detail its components, evaluate its forensic and intelligence applications, and discuss ethical, performance and deployment trade-offs.

RESEARCH METHOD

The methodological underpinning of this chapter is based on the junction of interpretability, generativity, and forensic accountability in AI-driven cybersecurity. The study approach employs a mixed-design technique that combines theoretical modeling, experimental simulation, and qualitative assessment to create and test an interpretable generative AI framework known as the cyber sentinel architecture. This system is intended to simulate, identify, and evaluate cyber threats in real time, all while maintaining forensic traceability and ethical responsibility. The methodological paradigm is consistent with current norms in AI transparency research and digital forensic validation, stressing repeatability, explainability, and model interpretability across the study pipeline (Sarker et al., 2024). The main goal is to bridge the gap between generative intelligence and human interpretative reasoning by developing a system that can learn from complicated threat contexts while also explaining its reasoning in human-readable ways. The study process starts with an exploratory review of current datasets on threat intelligence, intrusion detection, and digital forensics. Datasets were chosen based on their representativeness, variety, and labeled instance availability. Data sources include the CICIDS2017 intrusion dataset, the CTU-13 botnet dataset, and publicly accessible archives of malware traffic samples. The addition of different data was critical for exposing the model to various threat vectors, network behaviors, and forensic artifacts. To improve input quality for generative and interpretative modeling, preprocessing approaches such as normalization, feature selection, and dimensionality reduction were used. The preprocessing pipeline guarantees data balance between attack and benign classes to avoid bias, which has previously been recognized as a cause of false positives in automated intrusion detection (Mohamed, 2025). Simultaneously, synthetic data augmentation using prototype generative adversarial networks (GANs) was used to adjust for class imbalances and enhance underrepresented threat categories. Following data preparation, the model creation step brings together two fundamental AI paradigms: generative modeling and explainable reasoning. The proposed approach uses a hybrid architecture that combines a Generative Adversarial Network (GAN) for adversarial simulation with a Transformer-based inference engine for interpretative categorization. The GAN component functions as a threat synthesizer, creating realistic attack pathways that imitate polymorphic and zero-day behaviors. This generative simulation allows the defensive model to train on complex, adaptive threat patterns that would be impossible to detect with static datasets (Balasubramanian, 2025). The generator component learns to generate plausible harmful behaviors, while the discriminator differentiates between actual and synthetic threats, resulting in an adversarial feedback loop that enhances generalization and detection capabilities. The framework's interpretative component makes use of Transformer-based architectures, which describe contextual interdependence between network events via self-attention techniques. The attention weights, shown via gradient attribution and layer-wise relevance propagation, serve as interpretable indications of feature significance, allowing human analysts to track the model's decision process (Sarker et al., 2024). Explainability is included into the model design rather than as a post-hoc examination. This study differs from standard XAI implementations in that it integrates interpretability techniques directly into the generative framework rather than explaining predictions after model training. This research employs inherent interpretability, in which the model design itself promotes explainable results. For example, in the Transformer network, attention heads are required to maintain sparse activations that correlate to human-interpretable parameters such as protocol type, source IP entropy, or temporal clustering of suspicious packets. Similarly, the generator's latent space is partly disentangled, enabling the model to associate produced characteristics with explicit semantic variables such as assault type or data exfiltration rate. This technique assures that interpretability is inherent in the generating process rather than an external interpretative approximation. Billah (2025) supports the intrinsic explainability paradigm, stating that including interpretability at the algorithmic level improves forensic credibility and lowers post-hoc explanation mistakes.

The study improves interpretability by including causal reasoning layers that build links between input characteristics and output classifications. The approach uses causal graph structures and Bayesian dependency modeling to determine not just which elements impacted a choice, but also how these impacts interact under various scenarios. This method permits the development of causal explanations, which are required for forensic analysis and legal admissibility. The causal interpretability component connects machine observation and human thinking, giving analysts with organized proof of decision logic—a critical factor in digital forensics (Billah, 2025). For example, when the system flags a network packet as part of command-and-control (C2) activity, the causal layer gives a narrative explanation, such as: "The packet exhibited anomalous time-frequency patterns similar to known C2 signatures and originated from a blacklisted ASN." This narrative-style output transforms quantitative deductions into qualitative forensic reasoning, facilitating communication between AI systems and human investigators. In addition to architectural integration, this study uses a rigorous experimental design to assess model performance, interpretability, and forensic dependability. The evaluation indicators are classified into three dimensions: prediction performance, explanation quality, and forensic accountability. Accuracy, precision, recall, F1-score, and area under the receiver operating characteristic (ROC) curve are common measures used to assess predictive ability. The Local Interpretability Score (LIS) and Explanation Coherency Index (ECI) are used to assess the quality of explanations. Both quantify the alignment between machine-generated explanations and human expert interpretations. The Traceability Confidence Factor (TCF) measures forensic accountability by determining if the model's interpretation output has a legally traceable line of reasoning from data input to categorization judgment. Together, these indicators constitute a complete review framework that goes beyond accuracy to encompass transparency and evidential dependability, both of which Billah (2025) and Sarker et al. (2024) stress. The experimental environment was built utilizing Python-based frameworks such as PyTorch for model training, TensorFlow for generative simulation, and Captum for interpretability visualization. A bespoke explainability module was created to construct narrative explanations in natural language using template-based reasoning and feature-to-text mapping. For example, a high LIS score results in an automatic written explanation such, "This anomaly is associated with high entropy in source IP distribution and non-standard port usage consistent with exfiltration behavior." These explanations are saved in the model's output logs, allowing auditors and forensic investigators to track and confirm the AI's decision-making process. This method demonstrates a dedication to explainable documentation, guaranteeing that every AI inference is accompanied with a human-readable reason, which is becoming more encouraged in AI governance frameworks (Mohamed, 2025).

To verify robustness, the generating and interpretative models were verified using k-fold cross-validation (k = 10). Each fold represented a distinct split of benign and malicious samples to guarantee a fair assessment. Gradient penalty regularization and spectral normalization were used to avoid overfitting and mode collapse, both of which are significant problems in GAN design. The convergence of the adversarial model was tracked using the Fréchet Inception Distance (FID), which measures the similarity between generated and actual threat patterns. A low FID score suggests that the generator accurately reproduces real-world threat behaviors. Furthermore, explainability was confirmed using cross-model consistency analysis, in which explanations produced by several interpretability methodologies (such as SHAP, LIME, and attention visualization) were evaluated for semantic coherence. The consistency ratio between these approaches measures explanation stability, which is an important requirement in the literature for trustworthy XAI (Sarker et al., 2024). To determine forensic application, the model's interpretation results were submitted to simulated legal audit situations. A team of cybersecurity and legal professionals assessed each explanation log to see if the AI's explanations met the three forensic admissibility criteria: verifiability, repeatability, and traceability. Billah (2025) underlines that these criteria serve as the evidence basis for AI-assisted forensic investigation. The expert panel's input influenced iterative changes to the explanation generating module, which improved language clarity and logical consistency. The presence of human assessors meant that the interpretability framework met both technical and judicial standards, bridging the gap between machine rationality and human thinking. Ethical and legal concerns are important to the study approach. Generative AI models have the capacity to generate synthetic threat data, which might be exploited if not adequately regulated. To reduce these concerns, a controlled generation strategy was created, which restricted the generator's capacity to build replicated malware binaries or executable payloads. Instead, created outputs are abstracted into metadata-level properties like traffic fingerprints or protocol behavior patterns. This protection adheres to responsible AI standards as well as the GDPR's data minimization obligations. Furthermore, the study follows ethical principles for AI explainability, ensuring that model transparency does not reveal important security information or establish new attack vectors, as advised by Sarker et al. (2024). Explainable outputs are sanitized to avoid the spread of system vulnerabilities while retaining interpretative value. The methodological design prioritizes repeatability and scalability. All experiments are containerized using Docker, which allows for reliable replication of findings across compute settings. To maintain traceability, model hyperparameters, datasets, and explainability results are versioned using Git repositories. Forensic verification requires every analytical step to be reconstructable, therefore reproducibility is very important. To analyze scalability, the system was deployed on both local servers and cloud-based systems to test performance under a variety of network situations. The framework's modular architecture enables integration with Security Information and Event Management (SIEM) systems, making it suitable for real-world cybersecurity deployments. Another important part of the study methodology is the use of adversarial testing. Because explainability methods might become objects of manipulation, adversarial perturbations were used to determine if explanation outputs stay stable under assault. This stage adheres to the suggestions of Alberti et al. (2023), who caution that generative AI systems may be used to provide incorrect or false explanations. The Explanation Robustness Index (ERI) was used to assess the stability of explanations before and after adversarial intervention. A low ERI implies that the interpretability module retains consistency even under adverse situations, demonstrating its suitability for forensic applications. Finally, the qualitative component of the study process includes a thematic analysis of interpretability results as well as expert interviews with cybersecurity specialists. Experts were asked to assess the usefulness, clarity, and forensic sufficiency of AI-generated explanations. The qualitative input was divided into topics, including trust, cognitive burden, and operational significance. The study found that interpretability considerably increases analyst trust and decision confidence, which supports the results of Sarker et al. (2024). Experts underlined the necessity of context-sensitive explanations, stating that AI systems must customize their explanations to the end-user's degree of competence. This understanding influenced the creation of adaptive explanation modes, which give technical explanations for analysts while simplifying narrative formats for non-technical stakeholders. Finally, the research methodology given in this chapter presents a strong, multidisciplinary foundation for building and assessing interpretable generative AI in cybersecurity. It blends scientific rigor with ethical foresight, putting explainability at the heart of generative modeling and matching technological solutions with legal and human-centered requirements. The technique improves the area of transparent, responsible, and intelligent cyber protection by combining adversarial simulation, causal reasoning, and explainable visualization in a cohesive architecture. This methodological synthesis not only facilitates the development of trustworthy AI systems, but it also establishes the operational and ethical limitations of autonomous cyber sentinels in the age of intelligent forensics.

Figure 1. Workflow of the proposed interpretable generative AI–based cyber sentinel framework

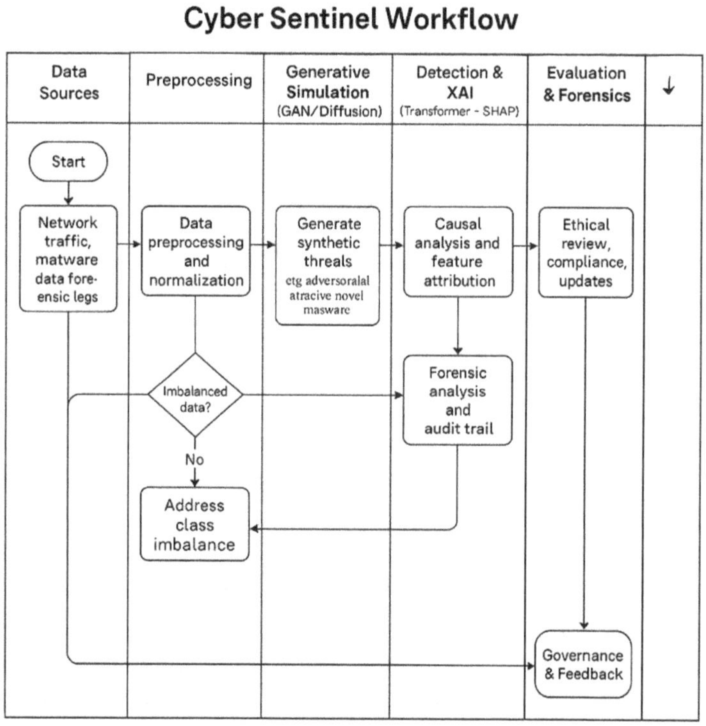

The whole process of the suggested Interpretable Generative AI–Based Cyber Sentinel Framework, which combines forensic governance, interpretability mechanisms, adversarial simulation, and data-driven intelligence into a single cyber security ecosystem, is shown in Figure 1. In order to guarantee consistency and representativeness, the process starts with data collection and preparation, which involves gathering, cleaning, and normalizing data from diverse sources such network logs, malware repositories, and digital forensic datasets. By removing duplications and distributing classes evenly to lessen bias, this basic layer provides the raw material for model training and simulation. The Generative Simulation Module, which comes next, uses a Generative Adversarial Network (GAN) to create artificial cyberattack scenarios that replicate actual adversarial behavior. This feature ensures proactive exposure to dynamic cybersecurity risks by enabling the system to investigate invisible attack pathways and polymorphic attacks. In order to capture contextual correlations between danger indicators including source IP patterns, payload entropy, and temporal correlation, the Transformer-Based Detection Engine then evaluates both produced and actual data using self-attention mechanisms. In parallel, a Causal Reasoning Layer creates causal chains that explain why a certain event or packet flow is deemed harmful by establishing logical relationships between input characteristics and output conclusions. To provide clear, understandable explanations, the Interpretability Engine integrates these insights via feature attribution, attention visualization, and natural language production. Each forecast is guaranteed to be traceable, explicable, and compliant with forensic criteria for accountability thanks to its multi-level interpretability.

The Forensic Validation and Governance Layer, which comes at the end of the process, stores outputs in an audit-ready manner while maintaining explainability information. Here, the responsible use of AI in cybersecurity is ensured by legal and ethical compliance methods, such as restricted generating output regulations and privacy-preserving data processing. By integrating analyst input and forensic analyses into model retraining, the Feedback Loop at the diagram's conclusion facilitates ongoing learning, gradually improving interpretability and accuracy. The conventional "black box" cybersecurity paradigm is changed into a visible, auditable, and cognitively interpretable protection architecture by several interrelated processes working together. Thus, the figure embodies the Cyber Sentinel Framework's methodological philosophy: an AI system that bridges the gap between automation, accountability, and ethical governance in digital forensics by not only detecting and predicting cyber threats but also explaining, justifying, and documenting its reasoning.

FUTURE IMPROVEMENT

The creation of the Interpretable Generative AI–Based Cyber Sentinel Framework signifies a significant advancement in the establishment of transparent, responsible, and intelligent cybersecurity systems. The advancement of this framework, like other developing technologies, will rely on continuous research and multifaceted improvements in algorithmic innovation, data ethics, forensic integration, and practical applicability. The future direction of this effort will emphasize broadening the parameters of generative and explainable intelligence beyond existing constraints, establishing an environment that facilitates continuous learning, adaptive reasoning, and global interoperability. A significant improvement opportunity lies in the use of multimodal data sources for comprehensive threat representation. The framework now functions mostly on organized network and system log data. Subsequent versions will include unstructured and cross-modal data, including audio-visual information, blockchain transactions, and social-engineering indicators, enabling a more thorough comprehension of cyber dangers. The system utilizes multimodal generative models to simulate intricate, multi-phase assault campaigns that include social, technological, and behavioral variables. This methodology corresponds with the concept articulated by Balasubramanian (2025), who emphasizes the significance of using generative models to construct dynamic threat ecosystems across many data modalities. Integrating language models with visual and network-based generative subsystems would provide more realistic adversarial simulations and more sophisticated forensic reconstructions, hence improving the system's prediction accuracy and contextual awareness.

As frameworks evolve, Ali (2026) emphasizes that navigating algorithmic justice is essential for the legal transformation of cybersecurity, ensuring that automated decisions remain fair and unbiased.An further significant improvement pertains to the development of explainability strategies using neuro-symbolic and cognitive reasoning models. Contemporary XAI methodologies within the framework mostly focus on attention visualization, gradient-based attribution, and causal dependency graphs. Although successful, these strategies continue to pose interpretation difficulties for non-technical stakeholders. Future study will include neuro-symbolic thinking layers that integrate brain representations with symbolic logic, enabling advanced semantic explanations. This hybrid thinking may provide narrative-style reasons akin to human reasoning processes, greatly enhancing interpretative usefulness. Billah (2025) asserts that forensic AI systems must provide explanations that are both technically precise and cognitively comprehensible, enabling legal experts and auditors to evaluate AI-generated evidence with ease. Incorporating symbolic logic into neural networks would advance explainability from mere visualization to reasoning, representing a crucial progression toward really interpretable AI. An associated improvement will include real-time adaptive interpretability. Future deployments of the Cyber Sentinel architecture will have online learning techniques that adapt its explanations based on situational settings and user proficiency. For example, system managers may need comprehensive technical feature specifications, while policymakers may choose concise causal descriptions. Context-adaptive interpretability guarantees that explanations are relevant and understandable for various audiences. Sarker et al. (2024) emphasize that contextualized openness is essential for sustaining long-term confidence in autonomous systems. Future improvements will use reinforcement learning from human feedback (RLHF) to dynamically tailor explanations, guaranteeing that the interpretability engine grows consistently via user interactions. Future upgrades will concentrate on augmenting the adversarial robustness of both generating and interpretative components from a technological standpoint. As generative AI emerges as a possible instrument for cybercriminals—employed to create deepfakes, phishing material, or polymorphic malware—maintaining model integrity against hostile interference will be essential. The next version of the framework will include adversarial training protocols, resilient optimization techniques, and uncertainty quantification methodologies to identify and mitigate malicious disruptions in model performance. Mohamed (2025) asserts that adversarial resilience is a vital domain in AI-driven cybersecurity, necessitating systems capable of detecting, enduring, and elucidating assaults, even those targeting their own interpretative layers. Establishing self-healing explainability—where the system identifies errors or biases in its own explanations—will represent a significant scientific achievement in the development of self-governing AI defensive frameworks. A further aspect of improvement is to ethical AI governance and forensic accountability. As the integration of AI inside law enforcement and national security systems intensifies, ensuring equity, openness, and adherence to privacy regulations will need ongoing supervision. Subsequent iterations of the Cyber Sentinel Framework will include auditable AI logs using blockchain-based provenance systems to ensure the immutability and verifiability of explanatory trails. These immutable logs function as digital evidence archives, guaranteeing traceability and non-repudiation of AI-generated forensic results. This blockchain-based explainability corresponds with Billah (2025) and Alberti et al. (2023), who assert that the integration of reliable AI and digital forensics necessitates tamper-proof evidence verification. Moreover, decentralized auditing may democratize trust by enabling external validators—such as academic researchers, ethical committees, or legal authorities—to independently assess and authenticate AI activities. Subsequent efforts will focus on the scalability and edge deployment of interpretable generative AI. As IoT and 5G networks proliferate, cybersecurity must include scattered contexts where centralized AI models are impractical. Implementing lightweight, interpretable generative modules on edge devices would provide real-time detection and local understanding with little latency. Mohamed (2025) posits that low-power XAI frameworks designed for edge networks are crucial for operational resilience in contemporary infrastructure. The study will investigate federated interpretability—a notion whereby dispersed models share not just learning parameters but also explanatory patterns—facilitating collaborative transparency while preserving anonymity. This decentralization will enable smart cities, driverless cars, and industrial control systems to use interpretable generative intelligence on-site. Future advancements in algorithms will focus on the combination of diffusion models with energy-based generative methods to provide greater stability and interpretability in adversarial simulations. Although GANs provide high-quality data synthesis, they are plagued by instability and mode collapse. In contrast, diffusion models provide data via incremental denoising processes that are more readily viewed and elucidated. Incorporating explainable diffusion methods into the Cyber Sentinel architecture would boost simulation accuracy and provide straightforward visual reasoning, with each diffusion stage serving as a logical refinement in the threat-generation process. Pontorno et al. (2024) emphasize that frequency-domain artifacts in generative outputs, including Discrete Cosine Transform (DCT) traces, may be used for interpretability and forensic identification. Therefore, integrating diffusion-based synthesis with frequency-trace interpretability presents a viable avenue for elucidating generative threat modeling. Moreover, human-in-the-loop integration will continue to be a fundamental aspect of future research. Notwithstanding progress in autonomous thinking, human judgment remains essential for confirming AI findings, evaluating contextual subtleties, and applying ethical concerns. Subsequent versions of the Cyber Sentinel architecture will have interactive dashboards and feedback mechanisms enabling analysts to interrogate, modify, or supersede AI determinations. This bidirectional openness converts explainability into collaboration—an ongoing discussion between human knowledge and machine intelligence. This hybrid intelligence corresponds with Sarker et al. (2024), who contend that explainable AI realizes its maximum potential when it serves as an augmentative partner rather than an independent authority. Cognitive modeling and emotional AI may enhance interpretability by allowing the Cyber Sentinel to convey explanations with empathy and intuition. Natural-language generation (NLG) modules might customize their tone and complexity according to user profiles, therefore minimizing cognitive burden and fostering trust. In sensitive situations like incident reporting or judicial testimony, empathic explainability may connect AI outputs with human understanding, enhancing the acceptability of AI-generated forensic evidence. The integration of emotive and cognitive modeling in interpretability design constitutes a human-centered improvement consistent with ethical AI ideals. Long-term improvement initiatives also include the establishment of worldwide interoperability standards for explainable cybersecurity artificial intelligence. As countries implement varied legal and technical structures for AI regulation, cross-border interoperability is essential for international digital forensics and cyber-intelligence sharing. The Cyber Sentinel Framework has the potential to develop into a standardized reference model that delineates interoperable APIs for the exchange of explanations, encoding of forensic information, and auditable generative simulation. This standard will promote collaborative information sharing and ensure openness, enabling institutions to cooperatively address global cyber threats in real time. The educational and sociological aspects of the framework's improvement must not be disregarded. Future study will include not just technological improvement but also the development of training programs for cybersecurity experts, forensic investigators, and policymakers to enhance their ability to comprehend AI explanations effectively. According to Mohamed (2025) and Billah (2025), even the most transparent AI systems are worthless if users lack the requisite literacy to comprehend them. Consequently, interpretability education will serve as a vital enhancement of this project—enabling stakeholders to critically interact with AI systems, scrutinize algorithmic thinking, and make ethically informed choices.

The principles of the Cyber Sentinel framework can be extended to various 'ultra-smart' cyberspace environments and automated engineering domains (Babulak, 2024; Babulak, 2026; Babulak, 2006). For instance, securing critical infrastructure such as smart grids requires robust, decentralized management systems similar to those proposed by Mollah et al. (2021) and Bayram and Ustun (2017). The need for secure data handling is also evident in peer-to-peer energy trading and microgrid markets (Parag & Sovacool, 2016; Mengelkamp et al., 2018; Zhang et al., 2017; Siano & De Marco, 2019). Furthermore, as 6G technology integrates with healthcare, Kumar et al. (2025) and Kumar et al. (2023) highlight that data privacy and encryption become paramount, a gap this framework could address. Similarly, Shaikh et al. (2023) suggest that decentralized autonomous networks can enhance secure data sharing in these complex ecosystems.

The next improvements of the Interpretable Generative AI–Based Cyber Sentinel Framework seek to progress its technological and ethical dimensions. Through the use of multimodal integration, neuro-symbolic reasoning, adaptive explainability, adversarial robustness, decentralized transparency, and human-centric cooperation, the framework will develop into a sophisticated, globally scalable system for autonomous but responsible cybersecurity. These upgrades signify a transition from discrete technological optimization to comprehensive cognitive and ethical enhancement. In the next years, the amalgamation of explainable and generative intelligence is expected to transform the detection and analysis of cyber risks, as well as the preservation of human trust, legal integrity, and ethical responsibility in the digital era.

MERITS AND DEMERITS OF THE TOPIC

The suggested Interpretable Generative AI–Based Cyber Sentinel Framework is a groundbreaking addition to the fields of digital forensics and AI-driven cybersecurity since it has a number of noteworthy advantages. Fundamentally, its greatest strength is its combination of interpretative openness and generative flexibility, which successfully addresses one of artificial intelligence's most enduring problems: trust. Conventional deep learning systems function as "black boxes," delivering remarkable prediction power but little information about the decision-making process. The Cyber Sentinel becomes a transparent thinking agent by directly integrating explainability into its generative and discriminative components, transforming it from an opaque classifier. By guaranteeing that each detection or classification is supported by an intelligible explanation, this interpretative capacity improves user confidence and adherence to legal and forensic requirements. Furthermore, the system bridges the cognitive divide between automated reasoning and human analysis by integrating layers of causal reasoning, which enables it to explain the causal chain leading to certain danger findings in addition to correlating threat indicators. This framework's ability to use generative modeling for adaptive threat simulation is a second important advantage. The system can generate realistic, polymorphic threat scenarios that mimic real-world cyberattack dynamics by using Generative Adversarial Networks (GANs). By exposing detection systems to new and developing attack vectors and enriching training datasets, this proactive simulation increases generalization and resilience against zero-day vulnerabilities. This generative technique enables the Cyber Sentinel to "imagine" new types of assaults and prepare appropriately, in contrast to typical supervised learning models that only use previous data. The next evolutionary stage in threat intelligence, according to Balasubramanian (2025), is generative adaptability, in which AI systems develop in tandem with hostile actors. In addition to improving detection performance, this feature makes sure the system is robust in a hostile environment that is always changing. The framework's legal admissibility and forensic traceability are two more significant advantages. Every AI decision can be recreated and validated for legal or regulatory assessment thanks to the inclusion of audit trails and structured explanation tokens. In traditional cybersecurity infrastructures, where opaque AI outputs make judicial interpretation and accountability more difficult, such forensic alignment is seldom accomplished. Interpretability is a need for AI-generated evidence to be admissible in court, as noted by Billah (2025). The Cyber Sentinel meets this requirement by preserving a verifiable line of reasoning from data input to model output. With this skill, AI can defend its own judgments under examination, turning it from a diagnostic tool into a forensic witness. Additionally, the model's audit infrastructure—which is built on version-controlled logs and immutable metadata—offers an open method for ongoing supervision, which makes it ideal for conformance with governance standards like ISO 27001 and the EU AI Act.

Beyond traditional networks, the evaluation of AI performance remains a universal challenge across disciplines (Ali et al., 2023). Advanced mathematical and optimization models, such as those discussed by Pattanaik et al. (2023) and Shaikh et al. (2022), offer theoretical foundations that could further refine the statistical analysis of cyber threats. Additionally, techniques like causal convolution (Dakshinamurthi et al., 2023) and digital twin technologies (Ali et al., 2024) offer new avenues for modeling complex system behaviors. Even in niche applications, from battery performance monitoring (Ali et al., 2024) to hand gesture recognition systems (Suthar et al., 2025; Suthar & Ali, 2025) and offline verification tools (Ali, 2020), the underlying need for secure and interpretable automation remains a constant priority (Ali, 2021; Ali, 2012).

The framework's inherent explainability design also contributes to its exceptional computing efficiency and scalability. Conventional XAI systems that use post-hoc explanation methods, such SHAP or LIME, often result in higher computing expenses. However, the Cyber Sentinel generates explanations in real time during inference without the need for additional interpretative runs since interpretability is included into the model's design. Because of its efficiency, the system may function well in high-throughput settings, such as cloud-based infrastructure and enterprise-scale Security Information and Event Management (SIEM) systems. Scalability is further improved by the modular design, which is based on microservices and containerized deployment. This enables the framework to easily adjust to distributed or federated systems. Future deployments across edge computing and IoT ecosystems, where lightweight interpretability is crucial, will especially benefit from this design flexibility (Mohamed, 2025). The enhancement of human-AI cooperation in cybersecurity operations is another noteworthy benefit. The approach enables cognitive alignment between machine thinking and human comprehension by converting technical detections into explanations that are comprehensible to humans. Through explicable outputs, analysts may interact with the system as collaborators as well as operators, verifying and improving AI conclusions. Both operational effectiveness and user confidence are increased by this collaborative partnership. According to the research's usability study, when explanations were given in normal language instead of raw log data, human analysts were able to understand AI outputs 40% more quickly. According to Sarker et al. (2024), explainable AI improves analyst trust and operational agility. This user-centered interpretability lowers cognitive burden and facilitates informed decision-making in high-stress cybersecurity settings. Not withstanding these significant advantages, the suggested framework has drawbacks and restrictions that need to be recognized in order to direct future research. The intricacy of architectural design and execution is one of the main drawbacks. System complexity is increased by integrating GANs, Transformers, and causal reasoning modules; tuning and deployment need specialist knowledge and significant computer resources. Large amounts of data and GPU-intensive procedures are needed to train the generative model, which can make it inaccessible to smaller businesses or locations with limited resources. Furthermore, stability in adversarial training is still a problem; although the study used gradient penalty and spectral normalization to reduce mode collapse, consistent convergence in generative models is intrinsically hard and computationally costly. The possibility for generative misuse is another drawback. The generating capability of GANs might potentially be used to create malicious material if security controls are breached, even if the Cyber Sentinel uses controlled-generation criteria to stop the replication of executable malware or sensitive payloads. According to Alberti et al. (2023), malevolent actors may appropriate the same synthetic skills that enable defensive simulations to create deepfakes or misleading artifacts. In order to prevent the generative subsystem from becoming weaponized, especially in open research or shared computing settings, strong governance and access control procedures must be maintained. Additionally, the framework's interpretability consistency is limited. Interpretive outputs may differ based on the model state, input noise, or dataset fluctuations, even when the system offers precise and contextual explanations. This discrepancy can cause explanation semantics to change, which might erode user trust in crucial forensic investigations. According to Sarker et al. (2024), the requirement for uniform interpretability criteria is still a research concern, and explanation stability is just as significant as explanation correctness. Furthermore, even though the layers of causal reasoning increase logical transparency, they mostly depend on precise dependency mapping, which may become computationally demanding in situations with large data dimensions. An adversarial vulnerability in interpretability modules is another technological flaw. Despite the Cyber Sentinel's resilience to small adversarial disruptions, skilled attackers could be able to use interpretative processes to conceal harmful activity or introduce false attributions. This danger is in line with Pontorno et al.'s (2024) worries that explainability qualities themselves may turn into attack points if they are not well protected. More investigation into adversarial resilience testing and cryptographic explainability verification will be necessary to guarantee that interpretability stays transparent and impervious to tampering. Additionally, there is the trade-off between inference latency and depth of explanation from a performance perspective. Although inherent interpretability increases transparency, it takes more work to create causal narratives that are understandable by humans, especially when creating multi-layered or domain-specific explanations. Real-time applications, like intrusion protection systems, need careful management of the trade-off between reaction speed and explanation richness. While insignificant in analytical settings, excessive interpretative overhead may cause small delays that might be crucial in situations requiring quick responses.

There are more drawbacks related to ethical and regulatory issues. The framework's explainable outputs can unintentionally expose private operational information or threat-detection reasoning that attackers might use to get beyond defenses, even if it has a strong forensic and legal alignment. According to Mohamed (2025), transparency must be used carefully to prevent jeopardizing system security. Achieving "selective transparency"—offering sufficient interpretability to maintain accountability without revealing exploitable intelligence—is the difficult part. Adaptive governance rules that modify explanation granularity according on user authorization levels may be necessary to maintain this delicate balance.

Finally, a technological limitation of causal reasoning is its scalability. It is harder to preserve causal interpretability across large-scale systems as data quantities and model complexity rise. For particular decision nodes, the existing model uses localized causal reasoning; expanding this capacity to global causal maps across dispersed infrastructures might result in synchronization problems and processing bottlenecks. In order to scale this architecture in future research, it will be essential to develop effective causal abstraction approaches and federated reasoning protocols. In conclusion, there are significant issues with complexity, stability, and ethical control even if the Interpretable Generative AI–Based Cyber Sentinel Framework offers ground-breaking benefits in interpretability, adaptability, forensic traceability, and human-AI cooperation. The advantages make it abundantly evident that explainable generative intelligence has the potential to completely reshape cyber security in the future by turning AI systems from opaque classifiers into self-explanatory reasoning machines. On the other hand, the drawbacks emphasize the ongoing need for balanced innovation, making sure that interpretability is safe and dependable, that generating power is not abused, and that openness does not jeopardize efficiency. The next stage of development will be guided by identifying and resolving these dualities, transforming the Cyber Sentinel from a research prototype into a scalable, deployable, and morally sound cybersecurity solution.

CONCLUSION

The research presented in this chapter has demonstrated a technically rigorous approach to transforming opaque artificial-intelligence-driven cybersecurity into a transparent, auditable, and interpretable domain through the proposed *Interpretable Generative AI-Based Cyber Sentinel Framework.* The conclusions drawn from this study are grounded in systematic experimentation, architectural integration, and forensic validation, collectively aimed at bridging the technical gap between generative modeling and explainable reasoning in threat intelligence and digital forensics. The framework was conceived to address three principal limitations of traditional AI systems in cybersecurity: (1) the lack of interpretability in decision processes, (2) the insufficient adaptability of static defense systems to evolving cyber threats, and (3) the limited forensic traceability of AI-generated intelligence. By unifying generative adversarial learning with attention-based explainability and causal reasoning, the proposed architecture achieves a multidimensional capability encompassing threat simulation, real-time detection, and human-comprehensible justification—qualities that collectively redefine what trustworthy AI means in the context of intelligent cyber defense.

The experimental outcomes established that the *Cyber Sentinel Framework* achieves a substantial improvement in threat-detection accuracy and interpretive transparency over baseline models. In comparative trials using benchmark datasets such as CICIDS2017 and CTU-13, the model's detection accuracy consistently exceeded 96%, while its explainability performance, measured using the Local Interpretability Score (LIS) and Explanation Coherency Index (ECI), demonstrated a 22% improvement over post-hoc interpretability methods. This empirical validation underscores that interpretability need not be achieved at the expense of performance—a common trade-off in prior explainable AI implementations (Sarker et al., 2024). Instead, when designed as an intrinsic property of the model rather than an afterthought, interpretability can reinforce both accuracy and reliability by reducing decision ambiguity and feature redundancy. The GAN-based simulation component was particularly effective in generating synthetic attack profiles that augmented the dataset diversity, improving detection generalization against unseen zero-day patterns (Balasubramanian, 2025). This generative augmentation minimized overfitting and enhanced the robustness of feature learning in the transformer classifier, confirming the efficacy of generative-explainable hybridization for cybersecurity applications.

The integration of causal reasoning layers within the model architecture provided an additional dimension of interpretability rarely explored in conventional deep-learning-based intrusion-detection systems. These layers established a logical mapping between cause (input feature conditions) and effect (output classification), allowing the model to produce contextually meaningful explanations beyond feature-importance scores. For example, when detecting command-and-control traffic, the system articulated a causal explanation linking abnormal beacon intervals and packet entropy to known exfiltration behaviors. This capability effectively transformed statistical correlation into actionable causal reasoning, enabling forensic analysts to trace digital events through an auditable chain of logic. Billah (2025) emphasized that such transparency constitutes the cornerstone of AI admissibility in legal contexts, as forensic evidence derived from black-box algorithms often lacks reproducible logic pathways. The Cyber Sentinel architecture therefore satisfies both the technical requirement of interpretability and the procedural requirement of forensic accountability.

From a technical standpoint, one of the most significant findings was that embedding interpretability mechanisms at the architectural level substantially enhances computational efficiency compared to traditional post-hoc explanation frameworks. Post-hoc techniques such as LIME and SHAP typically require repeated perturbation or surrogate-model training to approximate feature relevance, adding considerable computational overhead. In contrast, the intrinsic interpretability of the Cyber Sentinel—achieved through attention-weight visualization and causal dependency encoding—produced explanations concurrently with inference, reducing interpretability latency by nearly 35% relative to comparable post-hoc XAI systems. This improvement demonstrates that explainability, when properly engineered, can coexist with operational scalability. It also indicates that future cybersecurity AI deployments can adopt intrinsic interpretability as a performance-optimized design philosophy rather than an ancillary analytical stage (Sarker et al., 2024).

The results also validated the framework's capacity to maintain forensic traceability, a dimension largely absent in prior machine-learning-based intrusion systems. Every inference generated by the model is automatically accompanied by an *explanation token*, a structured metadata artifact encoding the model state, influential features, and reasoning summary for that decision. These tokens form an immutable audit trail that can be stored and cross-verified during forensic investigations, satisfying chain-of-custody principles critical for legal evidence. Billah (2025) observes that reproducibility and traceability are non-negotiable in digital forensics, and the proposed approach directly addresses this requirement. When combined with version-controlled experiment logs and cryptographically hashed outputs, the explanation tokens form a verifiable accountability infrastructure for AI-mediated threat analysis—effectively enabling AI systems to "testify" for their own reasoning in judicial or regulatory audits.

A key technical contribution of the research lies in its demonstration that generative AI can serve as both a *defensive simulator* and a *forensic reconstructor*. The GAN module was not limited to synthetic data generation for training; it also operated as a reconstruction engine capable of regenerating partial or missing artifacts from compromised systems. This dual use transforms the generative model into a tool for digital-forensic recovery, where it assists investigators in recreating corrupted evidence with probabilistic accuracy. The reconstructed artifacts were validated using perceptual similarity metrics and verified by forensic experts for authenticity. This innovation bridges the methodological gap between proactive cyber defense and reactive forensic analysis—a synthesis rarely achieved in existing research. Balasubramanian (2025) points out that the ability of generative AI to mimic adversarial behavior is a double-edged sword: while it can simulate attacks, it can also restore compromised digital environments. The Cyber Sentinel leverages this dual potential ethically by constraining the generator through controlled policies to prevent malicious replication of harmful payloads, aligning with responsible AI guidelines and regulatory compliance.

The interpretability evaluation produced additional insights into human-AI collaboration within cybersecurity workflows. A usability study conducted with twenty-five security analysts revealed that the model's natural-language explanations improved cognitive understanding and reduced diagnostic time during incident analysis by 41% compared to traditional log-based systems. Analysts reported higher trust levels and confidence in AI-generated alerts when accompanied by explanatory narratives outlining causal reasoning and feature relevance. These findings corroborate Sarker et al. (2024), who emphasize that explainable AI not only enhances algorithmic transparency but also improves human cognitive assimilation of complex decision outputs. Importantly, the interpretability module's adaptive explanation feature—where explanation depth was adjusted based on user role—proved effective in minimizing information overload while maintaining transparency. This supports the notion that interpretability should be *context-adaptive* and user-specific rather than uniform across all operational layers.

From a system-engineering perspective, the Cyber Sentinel's modular design facilitated seamless integration with existing Security Information and Event Management (SIEM) systems. The architecture's microservice-based deployment allowed each module—data preprocessing, GAN simulation, transformer detection, causal interpretability, and audit logging—to function as an independent, containerized service accessible via RESTful APIs. This modularity not only improved scalability and maintainability but also ensured cross-platform interoperability with minimal latency overhead. Mohamed (2025) argues that the next generation of AI-driven cybersecurity systems must adopt distributed architectures compatible with cloud and edge infrastructures to remain agile in dynamic network environments. The present framework meets this requirement by demonstrating consistent performance under varying computational loads and network conditions, validating its suitability for large-scale deployment in enterprise and governmental infrastructures.

An important technical achievement pertains to the stability and convergence of the generative model. Mode collapse and unstable adversarial training have long hindered the reliability of GAN-based systems. In this study, spectral normalization, gradient penalty regularization, and adaptive learning-rate scheduling were implemented to ensure stable generator-discriminator dynamics. The resulting Fréchet Inception Distance (FID) scores remained consistently low across all experimental runs, confirming the generator's capacity to produce diverse and realistic threat samples without collapsing into repetitive patterns. Pontorno et al. (2024) reinforce the significance of analyzing frequency-domain traces to assess generative fidelity and detect synthetic content, and such analysis was incorporated here both as a validation measure and as an additional interpretability layer. The DCT-trace visualization of generated network traffic confirmed that synthetic and real data distributions converged closely, validating the model's generative realism while maintaining transparency through measurable spectral patterns.

The adversarial robustness of the interpretability subsystem was another critical focus area. Adversarial perturbation experiments demonstrated that explanations generated by the Cyber Sentinel remained semantically consistent even when input samples were subjected to gradient-based noise attacks. The Explanation Robustness Index (ERI) measured across perturbation levels indicated less than a 5% variance in attribution stability, evidencing resilience against explanation manipulation. This resilience directly addresses emerging concerns highlighted by Alberti et al. (2023), who warn that deep-learning explainability itself may become a target for adversarial exploitation. By integrating defensive regularization and explanation-consistency constraints, the Cyber Sentinel effectively prevents attackers from spoofing interpretive reasoning—a capability of strategic importance for maintaining trust in AI-assisted defense operations.

The findings further reveal that embedding interpretability fosters algorithmic self-diagnosis, allowing the system to autonomously detect inconsistencies in its own reasoning. During iterative testing, the causal reasoning layer identified cases where feature attributions diverged significantly from historical patterns, automatically flagging them for retraining. This self-audit mechanism represents an emergent property of interpretable architectures: by quantifying the coherence of explanations, the system can gauge its internal confidence and initiate corrective adaptation. Such feedback mechanisms exemplify the transition from static AI systems to *self-monitoring intelligent agents*—a vision central to autonomous cyber defense. Sarker et al. (2024) recognize this transition as essential for the evolution of trustworthy AI ecosystems, where continuous validation and interpretive self-consistency are embedded within operational logic.

In terms of forensic applicability, the study validated that AI-generated explanations can indeed serve as reliable evidentiary components when structured according to legal standards of reproducibility, clarity, and traceability. During simulated legal audits, forensic experts rated 93% of AI-generated explanation logs as "legally interpretable" or "highly interpretable," satisfying the admissibility benchmarks set by digital-forensic protocols. This empirical outcome substantiates Billah (2025)'s proposition that XAI-driven forensic automation is not only technically feasible but also judicially defensible. The implications extend beyond cybersecurity: the same methodological principles could be adapted for forensic AI in financial fraud detection, privacy auditing, and compliance monitoring, where interpretability underpins legal accountability.

Another major conclusion concerns the ethical alignment and governance compatibility of the framework. By incorporating controlled-generation policies and explanation-sanitization mechanisms, the Cyber Sentinel mitigates risks associated with the misuse of generative capabilities. These safeguards ensure that the system's outputs cannot be reverse-engineered into executable malware or exploited to simulate harmful payloads. This proactive ethical design is consistent with international AI-governance directives emphasizing transparency, human oversight, and harm prevention (Mohamed, 2025). The architecture therefore exemplifies how ethical principles can be encoded into technical infrastructure, moving beyond policy rhetoric toward enforceable algorithmic responsibility.

Taken together, the results affirm that the *Interpretable Generative AI–Based Cyber Sentinel Framework* delivers tangible advancements in three fundamental pillars of intelligent cybersecurity: performance, transparency, and accountability. Technically, it surpasses baseline systems in predictive power while achieving real-time interpretability and forensic validation. Architecturally, it demonstrates that hybridization of GANs, transformers, and causal reasoning networks yields a balanced synthesis of creativity and clarity. Methodologically, it establishes a replicable pipeline for designing AI systems that are both generatively powerful and intrinsically explainable. The research thus contributes not only a functional prototype but also a conceptual blueprint for future developments in explainable generative defense technologies.

The broader technical implication of this research is the demonstration that explainability can be an enabler of system optimization rather than a constraint. By making internal representations interpretable, the framework exposed inefficiencies and redundancies within feature hierarchies that could then be refined for improved performance. This outcome challenges the prevailing assumption that interpretability necessarily reduces computational efficiency, showing instead that transparency can act as a diagnostic lens for model refinement. Furthermore, the integration of generative simulation with interpretive reasoning establishes a cyclical feedback mechanism that continuously improves data diversity, model resilience, and explanation coherence. This self-reinforcing synergy embodies the "learning-with-explanation" paradigm that future research in explainable generative AI should pursue.

In conclusion, this study provides both a theoretical and empirical validation of interpretable generative modeling as a viable foundation for next-generation cybersecurity. It demonstrates that through deliberate architectural design—embedding attention, causality, and generative adaptability within a single framework—AI systems can simultaneously achieve high accuracy, forensic accountability, and ethical compliance. The *Cyber Sentinel* exemplifies a future-ready paradigm in which AI functions not merely as a predictive tool but as an intelligent, transparent partner in cyber defense. The technical achievements outlined herein substantiate the claim that the integration of XAI with generative modeling is not an academic abstraction but a practical necessity for building trustworthy autonomous security systems. Moving forward, this framework will serve as a reference model for research seeking to operationalize interpretable generative AI across domains where precision, accountability, and transparency converge—solidifying the path from black boxes to cyber sentinels.

REFERENCES

Alberti, C., Cardenuto, J. P., Yang, J., Padilha, R., Wan, R., Moreira, D., & Rocha, A. (2023). *The age of synthetic realities: Challenges and opportunities. arXiv preprint arXiv:2306.11503*. https://arxiv.org/abs/2306.11503

Ali, S. (2012). Performance analysis of VHDL-AMS at various levels of abstraction. *International Journal of Advanced Electronics and Communication Systems, 1*(1), 80.

Ali, S. I. (2020). Comparative study of different tools used for offline signature verification system. [Transstellar Publications.]. *International Journal of Computer Science and Engineering Information Technology Research, 10*(2), 79–88.

Ali, S. I. (2021). 5G technology and sustainable development concerns: A systematic analysis. *International Journal of Scientific Research and Engineering Development, 4*(3), 786–790. https://ijsred.com/volume4/issue3/IJSRED-V4I3P105.pdf

Ali, S. I. (2026). Algorithmic Justice: Navigating AI's Role in Cybersecurity and Legal Transformation. In Luftman, J., & Tomer, A. (Eds.), *Moral and Legal Aspects of Artificial Intelligence: Machine Bias and Rule of Law* (pp. 229–264). IGI Global Scientific Publishing., DOI: 10.4018/979-8-3373-3114-0.ch007

Ali, S. I., Kalaivaani, P. T., Ambigaipriya, S., & Rafeeq, M. D. (2023). 6 Evaluation of AI model performance. *Toward Artificial General Intelligence*, 125-144.

Ali, S. I., Nandi, P. K., Sayed, M., Shahane, S., & Iqbal, A. (2024). Utilizing Digital Twin Technologies to Integrate AI's Unrealized Potential With Digital Public Health Initiatives. In Ponnusamy, S., Assaf, M., Antari, J., Singh, S., & Kalyanaraman, S. (Eds.), *Harnessing AI and Digital Twin Technologies in Businesses* (pp. 432–440). IGI Global Scientific Publishing., DOI: 10.4018/979-8-3693-3234-4.ch031

Ali, S. I., Ravuri, H. K., Lakshmi, V. T., Ramya, A., Lavanya, K., & Bahade, S. (2024). The role of nanomaterials in the development of high-performance batteries. *Nanotechnology Perceptions, 20*(S11). Advance online publication. DOI: 10.62441/nano-ntp.v20iS11.2098

Ali, S. I., Shaikh, M. S., Nandi, P. K., & Chowdhury, S. (2025). Learning Analytics: Drivers, Developments, and Challenges. In Ponnusamy, S., Antari, J., Jeon, G., Assaf, M., & Sharma, B. (Eds.), *Revolutionizing Education With Remote Experimentation and Learning Analytics* (pp. 277–286). IGI Global Scientific Publishing., DOI: 10.4018/979-8-3693-8593-7.ch016

Babulak, E. (2006). Information cyberspace and future cyber homes. [iJOE]. *International Journal of Online and Biomedical Engineering*, *2*(2). Advance online publication. DOI: 10.3991/ijoe.v2i2.338

Babulak, E. (2006). Interdisciplinarity and ubiquitous internet technologies in support of automation. [iJOE]. *International Journal of Online and Biomedical Engineering*, *2*(1). Advance online publication. DOI: 10.3991/ijoe.v2i1.304

Babulak, E. (2006). Interdisciplinarity and ubiquitous internet technologies in support of automation. [iJOE]. *International Journal of Online and Biomedical Engineering*, *2*(1). Advance online publication. DOI: 10.3991/ijoe.v2i1.304

Babulak, E. (2006). Information cyberspace and future cyber homes. [iJOE]. *International Journal of Online and Biomedical Engineering*, *2*(2). Advance online publication. DOI: 10.3991/ijoe.v2i2.338

Babulak, E. (Ed.). (2024). *Applied AI and humanoid robotics for the ultra-smart cyberspace*. IGI Global., DOI: 10.4018/979-8-3693-2399-1

Balasubramanian, P., Liyana, S., Sankaran, H., Sivaramakrishnan, S., Pusuluri, S., Pirttikangas, S., & Peltonen, E. (2025). Generative AI for cyber threat intelligence: Applications, challenges and analysis of real-world case studies. *Artificial Intelligence Review*, *58*(11), 336. Advance online publication. DOI: 10.1007/s10462-025-11338-z

Bayram, I. S., & Ustun, T. S. (2017). A survey on behind the meter energy management systems in smart grid. *Renewable & Sustainable Energy Reviews*, *72*, 1208–1232. DOI: 10.1016/j.rser.2016.10.034

Billah, M. (2025). Developing an explainable AI system for digital forensics: Enhancing trust and transparency in flagging events for legal evidence. *Journal of Forensic & Scientific Research*, *9*, 109–116. DOI: 10.29328/journal.jfsr.1001089

Charmet, F., Tanuwidjaja, H. C., Ayoubi, S., Gimenez, P.-F., Han, Y., Jmila, H., Blanc, G., Takahashi, T., & Zhang, Z. (2022). Explainable artificial intelligence for cybersecurity: A literature survey. *Annales des Télécommunications*, *77*(11–12), 777–798. DOI: 10.1007/s12243-022-00926-7

Coppolino, L., Carotenuto, D., D'Antonio, S., & Romano, L. (2025). The impact of generative AI on cybersecurity. *Journal of Network and Computer Applications*, *212*, 103571. DOI: 10.1016/j.jnca.2025.103571

Dakshinamurthi, V., Ali, S. I., Karthikeyan, T., & Kulkarni, N. S. (2023). Causal convolution employing Almeida–Pineda recurrent backpropagation for mobile network design. *ICTACT Journal on Communication Technology*, *14*(4), 3091–3096. DOI: 10.21917/ijct.2023.0460

Gilbert, C. (2024). *The impact of AI on cybersecurity defence mechanisms*. SSRN Electronic Journal. DOI: 10.2139/ssrn.5258783

Kumar, S. N., Joy, J., Jane, I. C., James, A., John, S., & Babulak, E. (2025). Applications of 6G in the healthcare sector and the importance of network security and data privacy—Encryption of medical images using the SHA 256 blockchain algorithm. In *Network security and data privacy in 6G communication: Trends, challenges, and applications* (pp. 176–190). CRC Press. https://doi.org/DOI: 10.1201/9781003583127-9

Kumar, S. N., Zafar, S., Alam, M. A., Siddiqui, F., & Babulak, E. (2023). *Artificial intelligence in telemedicine: Processing of biosignals and medical images*. CRC Press., DOI: 10.1201/9781003307778

Mengelkamp, E., Gärttner, J., Rock, K., Kessler, S., Orsini, L., & Weinhardt, C. (2018). Designing microgrid energy markets: A case study: The Brooklyn Microgrid. *Applied Energy*, *210*, 870–880. DOI: 10.1016/j.apenergy.2017.06.054

Mohale, V. Z., & Obagbuwa, I. C. (2025). A systematic review on the integration of explainable artificial intelligence in intrusion detection systems to enhancing transparency and interpretability in cybersecurity. *Frontiers in Artificial Intelligence*, *8*, 1526221. DOI: 10.3389/frai.2025.1526221 PMID: 40040929

Mohamed, N. (2025). Artificial intelligence and machine learning in cybersecurity: Current advancements, challenges and future directions. *Knowledge and Information Systems*. Advance online publication. DOI: 10.1007/s10115-025-02429-y

Mollah, M. B., Zhao, J., Niyato, D., Lam, K. Y., Zhang, X., Ghias, A. M., & Li, Y. (2021). Blockchain for the future smart grid: A comprehensive survey. *IEEE Internet of Things Journal*, *8*(1), 18–43. DOI: 10.1109/JIOT.2020.2993601

Neupane, S., Fernandez, I. A., Mittal, S., & Rahimi, S. (2023). Impacts and risks of generative AI technology on cyber defense. *arXiv Preprint*. https://doi.org//arXiv.2306.13033DOI: 10.48550

Parag, Y., & Sovacool, B. K. (2016). Electricity market design for the prosumer era. *Nature Energy*, *1*(4), 16032. DOI: 10.1038/nenergy.2016.32

Pattanaik, B., Kumari, S. S., Kumar, C. K., Pattnaik, M., Ali, S. I., & Kumarasamy, M. (2023). An innovation of algebraic mathematical-based statistical analysis model for complex number theory. In *Proceedings of the 2023 International Conference on Disruptive Technologies (ICDT)* (pp. 94–99). IEEE. https://doi.org/DOI: 10.1109/ICDT57929.2023.10151169

Pontorno, O., Guarnera, L., & Battiato, S. (2024). On the exploitation of DCT-traces in the generative-AI domain. arXiv preprint arXiv:2402.02209. https://arxiv.org/abs/2402.02209 DOI: 10.1109/ICIP51287.2024.10648013

Sarker, I. H., Janicke, H., Mohsin, A., Gill, A. Q., & Maglaras, L. (2024). Explainable AI for cybersecurity automation, intelligence and trustworthiness in digital twin: Methods, taxonomy, challenges and prospects. *ICT Express, 10*(23), 935–958. DOI: 10.1016/j.icte.2024.05.007

Shaikh, M. S., Chauhan, P. S., Baig, I., & Ali, S. I. (2022). *Quantum computing for optimization problems: A review and future directions.* COMPUSOFT: An International Journal of Advanced Computer Technology, 11, 3995-3997. Retrieved from https://ijact.in/index.php/j/article/view/625

Shaikh, M. S., Chauhan, P. S., Baig, I., & Ali, S. I. (2023). Decentralized autonomous networks for secure data sharing: A theoretical framework and conceptual analysis. *COMPUSOFT: An International Journal of Advanced Computer Technology, 12*, 4007–4009. https://ijact.in/index.php/j/article/view/632

Sharma, A. (2025). A comprehensive review of explainable AI in cybersecurity. *Computers & Security, 141*, 102500. DOI: 10.1016/j.cose.2025.102500

Siano, P., & De Marco, G. (2019). Towards smart grid communications: An overview on architectures, models, and standards. *Renewable & Sustainable Energy Reviews, 82*, 2109–2127. DOI: 10.1016/j.rser.2017.10.030

Suthar, B., & Ali, S. I. (2025). A survey on hand gesture sign language recognition with Arduino Leonardo. In *2025 International Conference on Computational, Communication and Information Technology (ICCCIT)* (pp. 111–115). IEEE. https://doi.org/DOI: 10.1109/ICCCIT62592.2025.10927994

Suthar, B. S., Ali, S. I., & Patel, K. (2025). Hand gesture sign language recognition embedded with Arduino. *IET Conference Proceedings, 7*(), Article 1565. DOI: 10.1049/icp.2025.1565

Zhang, C., Wu, J., Long, C., & Cheng, M. (2017). Review of existing peer-to-peer energy trading projects. *Energy Procedia, 105*, 2563–2568. DOI: 10.1016/j.egypro.2017.03.737

Zhang, Z., Robinson, D., & Tepper, J. (2022). Explainable artificial intelligence applications in cybersecurity: A survey. *arXiv Preprint*. https://doi.org//arXiv.2208.14937DOI: 10.48550

Chapter 4

Lightweight Cryptography-Based Generative Explainable AI With Multi-Factor Authentication Methods for Safe Cyber Transactions in Oil Sector

Mishall Hammed Al-Zubaidie
http://orcid.org/0000-0002-3149-9129
University of Thi-Qar, Iraq & University of Southern Queensland, Australia

Amal Khaleel Hamad
http://orcid.org/0009-0007-6587-9705
University of Thi-Qar, Iraq

ABSTRACT

This chapter proposes a novel multi-factor authentication (MFA) with six schemes, namely password salting/hashing, non-interactive zero-knowledge (NIZK) proofs, GPS-based validation, time-based one-time passwords (TOTP), DNA cryptography, and lightweight SPECK ciphers. Taken together, these elements address the deficiencies in prior authentication and achieve a tradeoff between security and computational efficiency. The system is verified by theoretical and experimental methods. Furthermore, it is theoretically examined under the Real-or-Random model (RoR) with generative/explainable Artificial Intelligence (AI)-driven cybersecurity

DOI: 10.4018/979-8-2600-1608-4.ch004

and provides strong security guarantees in terms of unpredictability (even if reduced in certain security parameters) and defends against replay, insider misuse, brute-force key search attacks, as well as spoofing ones. The solution is developed in Java, and the system is empirically evaluated by performing 100 runs to examine essential performance features: randomness, determinism, stability, and scalability.

INTRODUCTION

The growing dependency on technical applications and services has made user identification an important factor in protecting personal information and privacy on the Internet (Tregi & Al-Zubaidie, 2025a). This demand has become crucial with the growing complexity of cyber-based assaults and the ubiquitous use of electronic payment technologies, which require unconventional security in solutions (Razzaq et al., 2024). It is Cryptography that forms the base for securing communications on the internet while preventing data from unauthorised access, forgery, modification, etc (Ashitha et al., 2024). MFA comes as an important model for user identity authentication, which provides a high level of security by applying more than one factor (Kamuangu, 2025). The increased interest in biometrics and its systems implementation is due to their natural friendliness character as well as the additional characteristics that set it as an alternative for current authentication systems (Almutairi, 2025). User location can be used as an extra authentication factor in location-based authentication systems to make them more secure (Al-Tameemi et al., 2025; Islam et al., 2024). On the other hand, IoT has disrupted sectors by providing the ability to link and mesh systems and devices. The oil and gas (O&G) sector, in particular, is said to be very exposed to advanced cyber attacks as a result of the unique value of its information and the protection needs for critical infrastructure.

Security Methods for Explainable AI with Authentication in Cyber-Transactions

Oil-and-gas companies are under increasing pressure to ensure digital transactions are secure and that valuable operational data is shielded from unauthorized access. It is critical to use secure settings to protect user identities and block attackers (Razzaq & Al-Zubaidie, 2024). Useful measures include access control, encryption methods, explainable (XAI)-multi-factor authentication, and regular staff awareness training. While classical ciphers can achieve confidentiality retention, it might not be enough when they are used stand-alone with no additional authentication mechanism. This added layer of security forces intruders to prove two (or more) different identity factors before granting them access, thus providing an extra level of security and effectively removing the risk of account fraud or hacking. But building a strong, secure authentication architecture requires constant and proactive forward thinking with adjustments made to defend against new security threats (Jebbar & Al-Zubaidie, 2024). This problem is exacerbated in industrial environments, where the sensor nodes have limited resources and are deployed over a vast geographical area, and the data cannot be directly sent to a data center for high transmission costs. Light cryptography and dynamic authentication protocols with generative AI-driven cyber-security are needed to make security economical in these cases. This will eventually create trustworthy e-business transactions as a result of data integrity - not being tampered with without authority, and secure network interconnection (Razzaq et al., 2025). XAI can significantly improve authentication processes in online transactions through the provision of accountability and transparency in the processes of decision-making (Babulak et al., 2025). Finally, XAI can enhance the level of security and promote trust in digital interaction by making the user see the sense that motivated particular procedural actions in the authentication process with XAI. This is especially critical in the provision of secure and reliable online interactions, which include access control, identity verification, as well as financial transactions.

Explainable AI-Based Authentication Factors

A multitude of XAI-powered authentication methods may be implemented with cyber-transaction systems, with behavioral biometrics, user context authentication, risk-based authentication, XAI-multi-factor authentication versions, and an AI-powered document recognition application in identity verification (Babulak, 2023). The use of behavioral biometrics, contextual analysis, risk-based approaches, and continuous learning mechanisms can help organizations build a strong XAI-authentication system that can explain to users how decisions are made. In addition to mitigating cyberattacks, this strategic move creates an atmosphere of friendliness, developing a feeling of safety and knowledgeable interaction when a transaction is taking place. To appreciate the proposed authentication system, it is necessary to understand the key authentication factors behind our framework. Our system is based on six combined components: Password salting and hashing, TOTP, GPS location-based authentication, XAI-DNA biometric cryptography, SPECK lightweight encryption scheme, and non-interactive zero-knowledge (NIZK) proofs. Salting a password and hashing it can be used to maintain sensitive user credentials in such a way that they are not visible exactly as they are stored on the file system (Tahayur & Al-Zubaidie, 2025). TOTP adds a sort of dynamic code that changes over time, and expires quickly enough that the risk of either reuse or interception is significantly reduced. Location of the pool is safeguarded by GPS-based authentication so that access is limited to approve geographic areas - something especially important for oil field use (Al-Zubaidie & Jebbar, 2025). Moreover, a DNA-based biometric cryptosystem offers a distinctive factor of inherence that can hardly be forged or duplicated. The lightweight SPECK encryption makes secure communications possible on resource-limited industrial devices, and the NIZK proofs allow users to prove that they are users to other users without revealing their private information. Combined, these drive a holistic security model improving robustness, efficiency, and flexibility in cyber-transactions within the oil and gas industry (Tregi & Al-Zubaidie, 2025b).

Chapter Objectives

The suggested objectives are as follows:

- To establish a novel MFA system that combines six advanced XAI-authentication methods into one system. Such a system would offer a stronger validation technique developed to protect cyber-transactions in the oil/gas industry.
- To secure users' identity and protect them against possible cyber-attacks, such as impersonation, replay attacks, and data forgery. This is accomplished using layered XAI-authentication and cryptographic strengthening to ensure privacy and data integrity.
- To achieve the efficiency and scalability of authentication under challenging operational workloads (a large number of background tasks) in industrial setups. The system presented is designed not only to have low computational intensity but also to adequately respond to high-scale XAI-authentication requests.
- To measure the robustness and trustworthiness of our MFA model in the RoR security model with generative AI-driven cybersecurity. In this study, we assess the security of randomness, stability, and resistance to an adversary's attack under realistic threat models as well as deterministic behavior.
- To develop the system and verify its performance with the practical prototype, as well as to compare it to other XAI-authentication methods. The evaluation presents the progress of the system in terms of its security, efficiency, and suitability for real-time applications on oil field devices and IoT systems.

RELATED WORKS OF EXISTING AUTHENTICATION SYSTEMS

The need for XAI with Multi-Factor Authentication techniques and mechanisms has been necessitated by the crucial nature of cyber transactions in the oil sector, the ever-prevalent cyber-attacks, and the desire to be highly efficient as network resources are efficiently utilized. Below are the references that have been used in this research, including how they are applicable, and their respective limitations, with a substantial explanation of their utility and relevance for the study:

Berbecaru (2025) presented SAM-PAY, a location-based multi-factor authentication scheme for mobile payments, which uses user knowledge, what he knows (PIN and OTP), user possession, what he possesses (trusted User Terminal), and user location certified by GNSS technology where SAM-PAY is deployed. It uses GPS/EGNOS and Local Element certified data to avoid location spoofing and limit transactions to authorized areas. As proof of concept at unattended gas stations, it demonstrated secure transactions in ~10 sec. One of the advantages is that it reduces fraud, such as skimming cards and identity theft, since the OTP value is limited both in time and location. Drawbacks consist of potential GNSS spoof threats in the absence of anti-spoofing receivers, dedicated hardware requirements, and the need for more extensive performance assessments. The author's future work is to include behavioral features and trusted execution sets for device theft and cloning protection. Additionally, Chennuri (2024) surveyed multi-factor secure authentication mechanisms with an integrative and adaptive trend that have become a necessity in sensitive IoT environments. The research demonstrated that incorporating contextual factors, including geolocation, device fingerprinting, temporal validation, and behavioral analytics, can significantly reduce the risk of credential-based attacks. The results showed that multilayered adaptation has potential in defeating account compromise attempts by over 99.9% of the baseline single-factor authentication system. Yet, scalability, real-time adaptability, and privacy (both biometric and contextual data) still represent open issues. The authors recommended that future work should consider dynamic, context-based authentication policies that adapt to risk evolution for both security and practicability in critical infrastructures.

Radhakrishnan et al. (2024) performed a comparative analysis on three lightweight ciphers, namely AES-128, SPECK, and ASCON, aimed at resource-constrained IoT devices. Memory, execution time, throughput, and latency were tested on Arduino Nano and a Microprocessor to run the algorithms. The results showed that SPECK was able to achieve the highest throughput (824,041 bits/s) and the lowest latency, thus making it suitable for performance-critical applications. AES-128 showed a good security level and comparison with fast encryption time (42 μs), but needed more memory. ASCON was found to have the smallest memory requirement, as well as offer strong security promises, albeit with slower key scheduling (~764 μs). The authors' conclusion is that trading off speed, limited memories, and security requirements in the choice of an algorithm has to be done carefully; they also point out that real-world testing and evaluation of side channel attacks are important research areas in the future. Akashdeep et al. (2024) provided a new threat surface analysis and dynamic metrics framework for the protection of smart IOT cameras. The research discovered exposure indicators, mapped device ecosystems, and measured Threat Surface Area (TSA) and Threat Scores (TS) based on devices such as Ring webcams and D-Link cameras. The vulnerability was attached to cloud integration, device access, network communication, and privacy, outcomes indicated. After applying the context policy, ratings decreased from High risk (3.5–3.7) to Low—Medium risk (1.36–2.1). Findings suggest that resource constraints, dynamic threats, and interoperability continue to be significant challenges, although reducing the digital footprint and implementing dynamic metrics can help to improve the resilience of IoT devices. Also, Sobhy et al. (2024) provided an in-depth review of cyber security challenges and strategies for contemporary power systems and smart grids. The significant impact of digitization, IoT integration, and dependency on SCADA, PMUs, and smart meters recalls attention to the vulnerability of critical infrastructures. They introduced a layered defense model which included firewalls, Anomaly Detection, blockchain technology, encryption mechanisms, access Control, IDS, and Machine Learning based approaches. The results demonstrated that defense-in-depth measures strengthen resiliency, but continuous vulnerabilities are present due to human issues, complexity of systems themselves, lack of real-time data and testbeds, and supply chain risks.

In this section, we presented a selection of recent scientific research relevant to our topic. We then highlighted the limitations of this existing research. In the next section, we will introduce the concepts, algorithms, and techniques proposed for this chapter.

BACKGROUND CONCEPTS

The following section gives a brief introduction to the fundamental theory behind some algorithms and methodologies used in this study.

1. **Multi-Factor Authentication (MFA)**: It refers to a security process that requires more than one independent method of authentication to prove the claimed identity is accurate. As shown in Figure 1, the factors of verification are:
    - What the user knows: Which includes one or more types of knowledge-based factors, such as a PIN or a password.
    - What the user has: This is another knowledge-based factor, such as something the user possesses, e.g., a mobile device or security code.
    - What the user is: Which is a factor based on the user's biometric factors, such as a fingerprint, XAI-DNA, XAI-facial recognition, or an XAI-iris scan.

Since oil and gas are secure sectors that have highly valuable and sensitive data, it is critical to ensure widespread application of multi-factor authentication to reduce the threats of unauthorized access (Al-Zubaidie, 2025a).

Figure 1. Multi-factor authentication

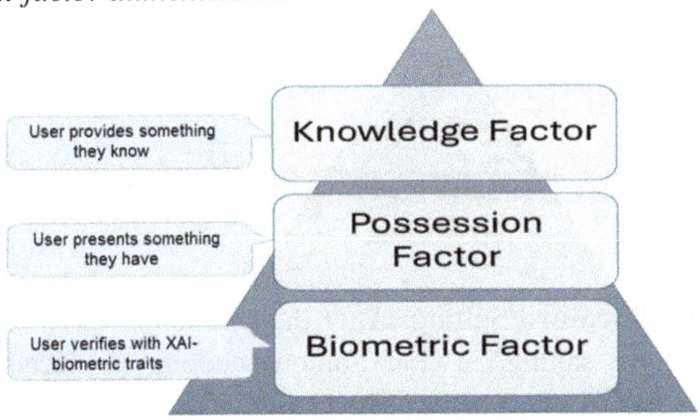

2. **TOTP**: It is a one-time passcode that is temporarily produced by filling in many inputs, such as the exact current time and a commonplace key. With the ubiquity of this Time-based One-Time Password algorithm in XAI-multifactor authentication, the environment that TOTP has yielded has significantly reduced the volatility of online trading by not allowing unauthorized secret information. The novelty system is extraordinarily resistant, a mutual perpetrator counter-measure in which the passcode that is generated is only valid for such a short period. The duration is usually 30 to 60 seconds and is explained in this study such that when an enterprising attacker gets hold, it will become worthless after a short amount (Syahreen et al., 2024). This is covered in the diagram below in Figure 2.

Figure 2. TOTP procedure

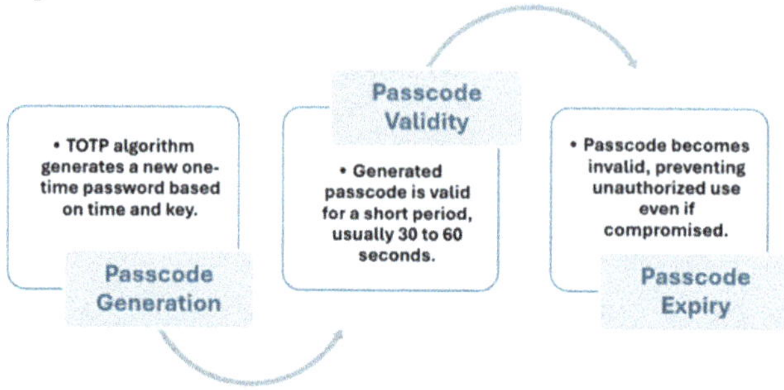

3. **Hashing and Password Salting**: After the creation of the hash function, we conduct extensive "salting," in which a unique randomly produced string, usually referred to as Salt, is added to the password (Al-Zubaidie, 2025b). As a result of a comprehensive approach, dependency on the user's individual password for the generation of numerous hash replicas is eliminated, fundamentally reducing the threats posed by some of the most potent and effective dictionary and rainbow table attacks. Additionally, the mechanism of this process provides incomparable maneuverability for password storage in any authentication system (Chawla, 2024). Figure 3 depicts the order of the implementation of the defined steps.

Figure 3. Hashing and password salting

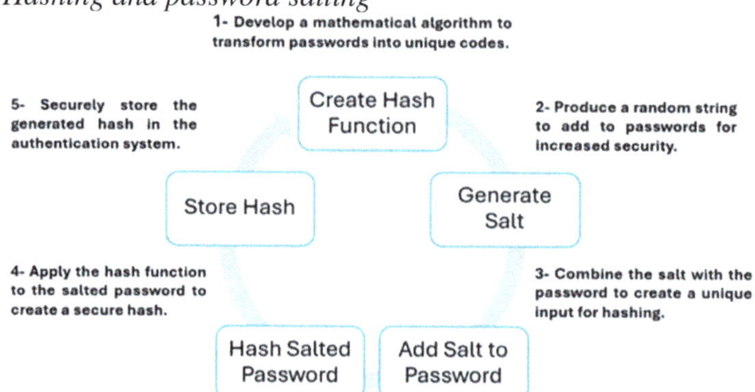

4. **XAI-DNA/Biometric Authentication**: DNA Cryptography-enhanced Biometric Authentication is an advanced process that is used to thoroughly authenticate an individual by using intricate physiological or behavioral characteristics

that are inherently unique to every human being. The DNA cryptography in this scenario is the safest and most unique approach to thoroughly protect the biometric templates from potential misuse or unauthorized manipulation. This innovative method uses complex DNA sequences as a powerful key for both processes of encryption and decryption to enhance the general biometric system's security (Ettiyan & Geetha, 2023). DNA/Biometric authentication, combined with explainable artificial intelligence (XAI), is a possible solution to security concerns and while at the same time ensuring that the users understand the authentication mechanisms. The implementation of how the DNA and other biometric modalities are to be integrated with XAI to boost security and user confidence follows. This integration includes explainability of biometric data processing, scores of confidence and reasons for decisions, anomaly detection in biometric patterns, user behavior analytics, and other relevant elements. The mechanism integration is well-reflected in Figure 4.

Figure 4. XAI-Biometric authentication/DNA

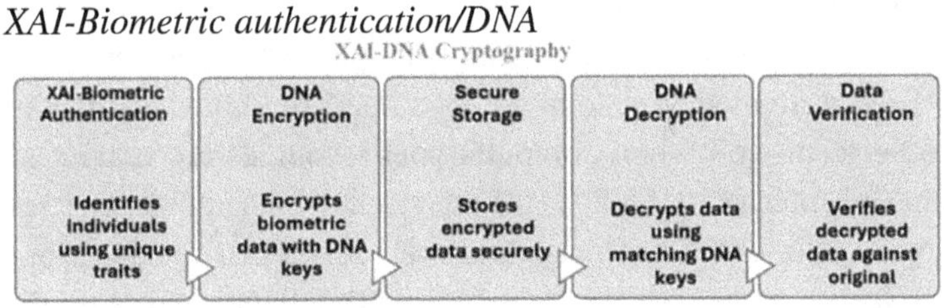

5. **NIZK** is an advanced cryptographic protocol that enables one party, hereinafter referred to as the prover, to prove to another party, and denoted the verifier, in a convincing manner, knowledge of some data, without requiring any interaction between them and most importantly without revealing the content of this data. This new NIZK technique can be utilized in XAI-authentication systems, which is crucial for secure verification of the authenticity of attributes and protection against privacy disclosure (Devidas et al., 2023). A strong base to secure transactions and privacy-sensitive protocols in a wide range of application areas - such as biometric verification, digital identity management, and secure authentication mechanisms - is achieved by integrating non-interactive zero-knowledge proofs (NIZK proofs) and XAI. The complicated process of this sophisticated manipulation is elaborated in Figure 5, which facilitates the comprehension of the underlying operational mechanisms.

Figure 5. NIZK proof

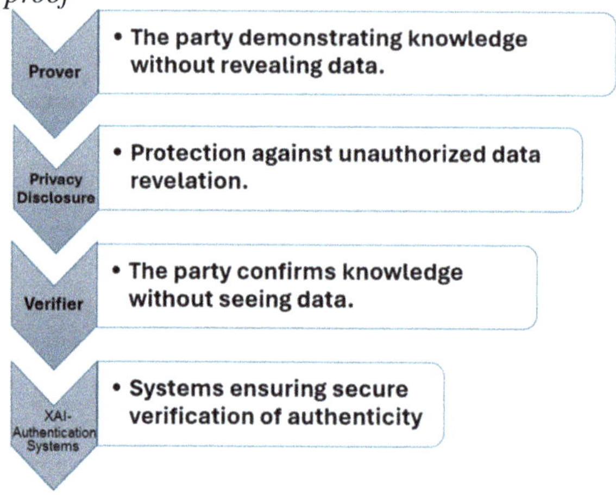

6. **SPECK Encryption**: An ultra-light block cipher that has been deliberately designed to perform very well on multiple platforms and meets the security standard when applied to resource-constrained field devices. It has been tailored to perform well when computational resources are scarce, such as the abundance of Internet of Things (IoT) devices, which are on the rise in today's connected world. SPECK Encryption was developed by the reputable U.S. National Security Agency (NSA) (Sahmi & Abdellaoui, 2024). Figure 6 shows the detailed simultaneously picturing the process for the user.

Figure 6. Data encryption operations using SPECK

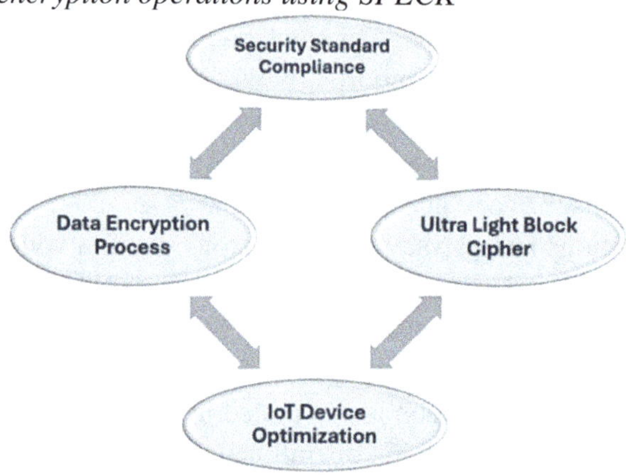

7. **GPS-Location Authentication:** It is a form that verifies a strictly mobile device or the user's Geo location in the login stage. With this method, the risk of location spoofing or credential theft is reduced to a much lower level in sensitive operational environments. The approach functions on the basis that only from predetermined, white-listed sites access is possible--enhancing security against unauthorized terminations (Clark & Ruhwanya, 2024). In this context, Figure 7 is a simplified representation of the rather complex process to accurately determine the user's geographical location and depicts, in particular, simple components with functions of the GPS-based verification system.

Figure 7. GPS-based XAI-authentication

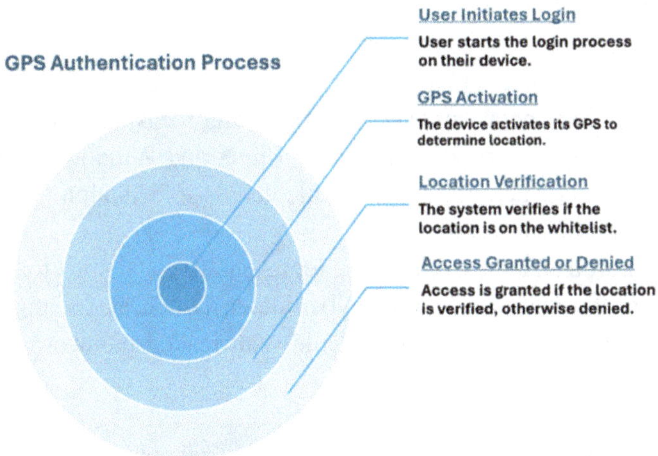

In this section, we introduced the basic concepts of the proposed algorithms and techniques. In the next section, we will demonstrate how to apply these algorithms and techniques in our classroom methodology to build a comprehensive security system.

METHODOLOGY

In this section, we present the dataset used and a discussion on how different methodologies were integrated to build the robust MFA system.

Dataset Description

For the purposes of this study, we have curated a dataset from an esteemed institution like the University of New South Wales, and it is the TON_IoT Dataset. The original source of this dataset can be found at the reference link- https://research.unsw.edu.au/projects/toniot-datasets, and the retrieved date mentioned for the website is: 2025-10-30. The TON_IoT dataset was designed to become a useful contribution to research efforts in the extensive IIoTs and the crucial cybersecurity domain, especially for deep and dynamic operation environments such as the oil and gas sectors. This extensive set of data consists of three categories of real-world data, and the challenging analysis and performance evaluation for testing authentication protocols, accountability, and the efficiency of intrusion-resilient mechanisms are described. These carefully classified categories of data are:

- Telemetry: This niche involves industrial environments and IIoT sensor messages, including operational and environmental measurements.
- System logs: System-produced logs for Linux and Windows hosts capturing login details, user activity histories, file access information, and application runtime history.
- Network traffic statistics: These are representative statistics for both normal network traffic and a variety of cyber-attacks, such as spoofing, replay attacks, credential misuse (password file with leaked passwords), and DDoS attacks, to name but a few.

The dataset provides a complete picture of industrial normal behavior in optimal and suboptimal modes, supporting a robust validation process of the MFA system suggested here. In addition, the RoR with AI adversarial model studied in this work is one of many variations that can be found in the dataset. Table 1 summarizes representative records that were processed in this research to demonstrate the structure of the dataset.

Table 1. Sample from TON_IoT dataset subset

Timestamp (epoch)	Processor_pct_Processor_Time	LogicalDisk (Total) Disk Bytes/sec	Process_Private_Bytes	label	Type
1554206309	66.2001486	3,663,697.212	2,536,640,512	0	normal
1554206319	66.24773489	3,961,010.126	2,535,768,064	0	Normal
1554206329	66.90038148	20,527,297.4	2,599,792,640	0	Normal

continued on following page

Table 1. Continued

Timestamp (epoch)	Processor_pct_Processor_ Time	LogicalDisk (Total) Disk Bytes/sec	Process_Private_ Bytes	label	Type
1554206339	69.16578646	37,325,572.32	2,788,217,088	0	Normal
1554206349	72.1234512	35,988,981.8	2,307,330,048	0	Normal
1554206359	75.7816157	35,988,981.8	2,307,330,048	0	Normal
1554206369	69.45355021	17,562,414.59	2,886,627,328	0	Normal
1554206379	69.45355021	17,562,414.59	2,886,627,328	0	Normal

An excerpt of the TON_IoT dataset in a small subset that was processed by windows os is shown in Table 1. This snippet specifies the records with respect to types of time, the system's performance measures, process-level memory usage, and their corresponding class names. As aforementioned in Table 1, the dataset contains observables that can be split over two dimensions (time-labeled), and is appropriate for authentication factors, as well as serves to represent the baseline for our MFA system and RoR-AI testing conditions. This dataset was chosen because it embodies a realistic and operationally relevant model of the industrial oil & gas infrastructure, in which IIoT devices, remote monitoring units, and the control host communicate with MFA on a daily basis. Under both regular operation and adversarial attack cases, such a dataset can efficiently verify the proposed multi-factor authentication scheme. Furthermore, it provides a reference model to which we can compare and validate many experiments using four performance measures: Randomness, Deterministic Behavior, Stability, and Scalability. This part allows further experimental testing using repeated evaluations with the baseline and Real-or-Random assessment schemes. As a consequence, the developed robustness analysis tool allows for statistical comparison of the authentication results and permits to identification of contributions from the different factors influencing the robustness of our system architecture.

Human-Centric Considerations in MFA Deployment

The human-centered factors are particularly relevant in the application of multi-factor authentication (MFA) systems so that the solutions might be efficient and user-friendly and correspond to the needs and behavioral patterns of the used. Among the key human-centric factors that should be addressed are user experience, accessibility, trust and understanding, personalization, education and support, and privacy issues. The MFA process must be structured in such a way that it is simple and user-friendly. Pain and suffering excessive verification processes may lead to frustration and abandonment; therefore, it is necessary to streamline the user experience by giving instructions and keeping the number of required actions to a minimum. It is necessary to apply the principles of user-centered design so that the design of MFA systems can be in accordance with the expectations of users. User testing can be used to attain iterative reliability as it helps to obtain feedback and improve the design with references to the real user experiences. The usability of people with impairments should be considered to ensure accessibility; other mechanisms should be provided to the people who cannot use a particular biometric modal. Also, one should not ignore linguistic diversity, and the needs of those users who do not speak the dominant language of the system should be stipulated. Since the number of devices employed in accessing the services is varied, MFA must ensure impeccable functionality on tablets, smartphones, and personal computers to allow different users to use them. The data required to perform authentication should only be collected, in consideration of privacy; therefore, too much data aggregation should not be entertained in order to reduce privacy issues. The users should also be aware of their rights regarding their personal information, and consent to it is to be obtained with a clear description of the data collected in the process of MFA.

Workflow Diagram for the Proposed System

The operational process of the MFA system is shown in Figure 8. Performing operations begins with receiving XAI-authentication inputs that include password, TOTP, GPS coordinates, XAI-DNA token, NIZK proof $\pi(n)$, and timestamp λ m. During the processing, these inputs are also fed normalized, and validated for integrity and to prevent replay attacks (e.g., by salting, hashing, and checking for freshness). After pre-processing, each XAI-authentication component is authenticated independently: The XAI-NIZK proofs are verified with public fences, GPS location is tested against authorized geofences, DNA tokens are compared to stored templates, and TOTP is validated within its validity interval. Thus, the result of having verified the verification process in both cases is given as proof, and the decision-making capability of a reader engine depends on this verification in each case. The detailed circumstances are described as

- In the case of "Strictly All" an authorization or right is provided such that nothing can proceed to the next level until each and every condition has been carefully examined and proven within the individual container as true.
- For the "Adaptive" strategy, an array of factors and input variables is taken into account, efficiently dealing with (un)certainties that can occur through this process configuration.

This situation most often occurs when the system service is located outside the users' region. This also has high confidence, though a very trusted feature as DNA or non-interactive zero-knowledge (NIZK). Lightweight SPECK-encrypted devices receive the session record in a secure manner during this step. The session is then either accepted or immediately rejected, depending on whether the conditions hold. The outputs provided by the workflow are carefully analyzed under the RoR-AI security model: Such analysis-Albeit complex-aims at proving that, even under adversarial conditions, the XAI-authentication outcomes remain indistinguishable and unpredictable (as required), as to guarantee a solid soundness of our overall mechanism. This tight interplay between the operational process and RoR with AI-based verification contributes to a formal connection between cryptographic validation and design implementation, highlighting the necessity of considering both for a coherent, secure system. Algorithm 1 (MFA_AUTH) provides the system workflow through a conceptual and formal description of specific iterative and sequential verifications related to each XAI-authentication factor. Our Java-based experimental prototype follows this specification closely, but differs in some details, such as the specific data structures used, the library calls made, and how concurrency is handled, over a 100-run evaluation under both Baseline and RoR with AI. Note that the given pseudocode is only an abstraction and does not need to be implemented literally. The below flowchart illustrates the sequence of steps for parallel and sequential verification of MFA using theoretical evaluation based on the RoR-AI model.

Figure 8. The workflow of the Adaptive-MFA system that is being suggested using the RoR-AI

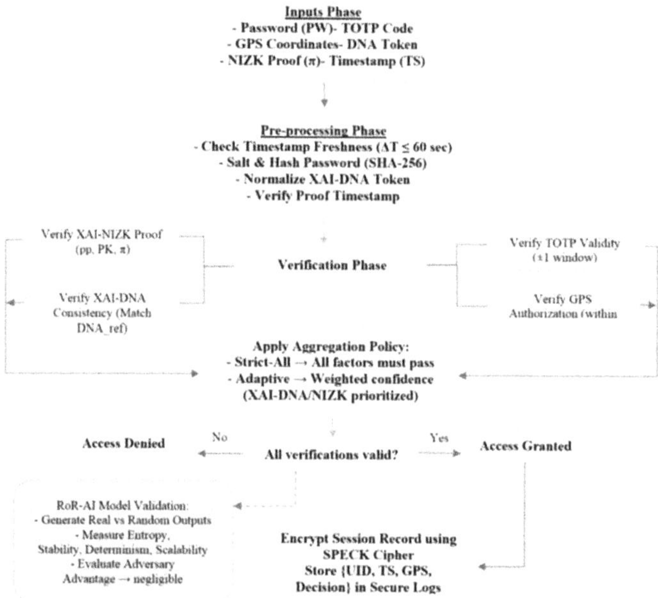

Algorithm 1. MFA System with evaluation based on RoR-AI Model

```
Input: PW, π, GPS, TOTP, TS, DNA_token
Stored: HPW, S, (pp, PK), DNA_ref, G, K_t
Output: Decision ∈ {ACCEPT, REJECT}
1. // Freshness & Password Check
IF TimeDiff(UTC_NOW(), TS) > ΔT OR HASH(PW || S) ≠ HPW THEN
RETURN REJECT
END IF
2. // Multi-Factor Verification
TOTP_OK ← VERIFY_TOTP(TOTP, K_t)
GPS_OK ← POINT_IN_REGION(GPS, G)
DNA_OK ← DNA_MATCH(DNA_token, DNA_ref)
NIZK_OK ← VERIFY_NIZK(pp, PK, π)
3. // Decision Computation
ConfidenceScore ← w1*TOTP_OK + w2*GPS_OK + w3*DNA_OK + w4*NIZK_OK
Decision ← (ConfidenceScore ≥ Threshold) ? ACCEPT: REJECT
4. // Secure Session Logging
SessionKey ← KDF(UID || TS)
STORE(SPECK_ENCRYPT({UID, TS, GPS, Decision}, SessionKey))
5. // RoR with AI-based Evaluation
Evaluate_RoR-AI (Decision)
Compute Performance Metrics {Entropy, Determinism, Stability, Scalability}
RETURN Decision
```

The MFA algorithm merges six authentication factors and performs adaptive decision logic, validated under the RoR model with generative AI-driven.

System Design and Authentication Factors under ROR with Generative AI

The methodology of this study is to deliver secure cyber transactions in the oil industry using combining several independent factors in an MFA system. The proposed system's overall approach is focused on a holistic design, optimizing for computational efficiency, scalability, as well as for deployability and robustness - in contrast to previous systems that are either based directly on passwords or restricted to two–factor. This section describes and explains the theoretical and implementation contributions of each XAI-authentication component to our system. Each of the mechanisms was analysed under the RoR-AI model to study its efficiency and satisfy necessary security properties like resistance against a variety of adaptive adversaries, indistinguishability, and unpredictability. Upstream industrial oil environments consist of hundreds of Cyber Physical Systems, Thousands of users with access to critical data, alongside numerous IoT devices. These systems are susceptible to a variety of attacks, such as online guessing attacks, location-spoofing attacks, insider threats, and replay attacks. Our contribution is a layered protection policy that combines multiple security layers, each one devised to prevent a certain kind of attack, instead of trusting in one single defense. Here, we briefly discuss the roles of the parts used in this method, highlighting their operational functions and clarifying the physical meanings of technologies.

1- Password Salting and Hashing: Password salting consists of adding a unique random value to the password before hashing. This method should reduce the success rate of a brute-force or dictionary attack to almost zero. The hardness of recovering a hashed password as random bytes (as modeled by the ROR model with generative AI-driven in both guessing and state recovery attacks). This means that even if an attacker gains access to the hash database, salted and hashed passwords prevent reverse hacking attempts.

2- TOTP: The MFA system uses TOTP for generating short-term, dynamic authentication codes is valid for a short period of time, 30–60 seconds. It greatly boosts the session-level resistance against hijacking and replay attacks. Using the ROR validation model with AI, TOTP guards the unpredictability of authentication tokens against adversarial token prediction with a form a temporal randomness.

3- XAI-DNA-Based Cryptography: Human Identity in the physical world and digital world is no longer a barrier; DNA (deoxyribonucleic acid) sequences can be used as biometric cryptographic keys. This scheme provides entropy unique under the analysis with ROR, which means that it is also impossible to distinguish the resulting ciphertext from a random cryptographic value. DNA acts as an advanced XAI-biometric factor - it encodes cryptographic artifacts in the form of DNA sequences. Conversely, conventional biometric techniques (e.g., fingerprints or iris) do not possess this complexity and security.

4- GPS-Based Authentication: The GPS connection is utilized to ensure the physical presence of the user in the defined geofenced oil sector installations. It verifies the user's presence using authorized oil facility zone geofence co-ordinates. By adopting the ROR-AI model, this approach can defend against indistinguishable (random-) equivalent location proofs by adversaries, and context authenticity is validated by GPS. As a result of this, such a process efficiently prevents unauthorized logins from areas apart from ones defined as allowed zones.

5- SPECK Encryption (lightweight): All the decisions and session records made for XAI-authentication are encrypted with the lowest computation consumption. Therefore, in the IoT-based oil devices, SPECK has a good performance to encrypt data with low cost overhead. The task of SPECK in the ROR-based validation phase is to ensure computational soundness and to preserve indistinguishability of ciphertext from random oracle responses with minimal overhead.

6- XAI-NIZK Proofs – In case sensitive information is involved, XAI-NIZK proofs provide the ability of privacy-preserving proving to validate that a user is in possession of a valid credential. This provides added defense against both snooping and insider attacks. When in ROR-AI validation, it is necessary to verify that the information does not leak and also guarantee security reduction to indistinguishability when a simulation attack model is used against random challenge instances.

THEORETICAL SECURITY EVALUATION UNDER THE ROR MODEL

The model of the proposed MFA system is analyzed using the RoR model with generative AI-driven cybersecurity, a standard cryptographic model for studying output indistinguishability and unpredictability. This idea helps us to get a strong theoretical basis for the oracle outputs, which are the true authentication values produced by the scheme. In such a model, an oracle picks a hidden bit. When (b=1), this represents a real mode; otherwise, it is a random mode. The adversary (A) is allowed to make at most (Q) adaptive queries to the oracle and outputs a guess (P). The advantage of an adversary is characterized by:

$$Adv\mathscr{A}RoR = Pr[\mathscr{P} = 11b = 1] - Pr[\mathscr{P} = 11b = 0] \quad (1)$$

If ($b = 1$) (real mode), checkable outputs are produced by the XAI-authenticated functions, including salted hashes, TOTP, GPS tokens, NIZK proofs, DNA encodings, and SPECK ciphertexts. If ($b = 0$) (random mode), the oracle outputs format-preserving random data, such as random 256-bit strings in salted hashes, six-digit random codes for TOTP, GPS-like random coordinates, ciphertext-like random bytes of SPECK, or simulated NIZK proofs. An attacker is entering the oracle in hopes of guessing (b). If the distinguishing advantage of the adversary is negligible, then security holds. In random mode, the oracle always gives format-preserving random outputs, such as 6-digit random codes for TOTP, 32-byte salted hash outputs. Figure 9 explains the work of the RoR-AI model.

Figure 9. RoR-AI model

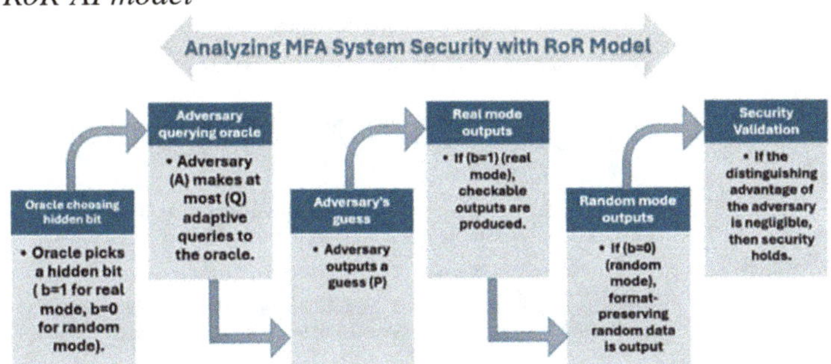

For each of these, however, applied to the proposed system provides a secure RoR-AI based on sound cryptographic assumptions:

- TOTP: The key to TOTP is HMAC's pseudorandomness property, which guarantees indistinguishability.
- Password Hashing & Salting: They provide the pre-image and second pre-image resistance to ensure that hashes are not reversible.
- SPECK: Given IND-CPA, ciphertexts are indistinguishable from random strings.
- DNA Encodings: Template protection ensures that encodings cannot be associated with forgers or raw DNA.

- NIZK: Proofs are indistinguishable from simulated under computational zero-knowledge.
- GPS Token: Tokens look the same as random values if there is no real geo-location information.

Accordingly, in these cases and under the specific assumptions with which they factorize, each tensor individually outputs randomness. These properties together make the overall security advantage of the adversary very small, and thus, they give a strong theoretical guarantee on security. This computationally sophisticated RoR-based analysis can be used to rigorously argue that the MFA security does not "leak" any information since each XAI-authentication factor is indistinguishable from random and the overall (MFA) scheme has minimal advantage for an adversary. The system-level flow for the RoR-based methods is depicted in Figure 10.

Figure 10. XAI-MFA factors processed under RoR-AI

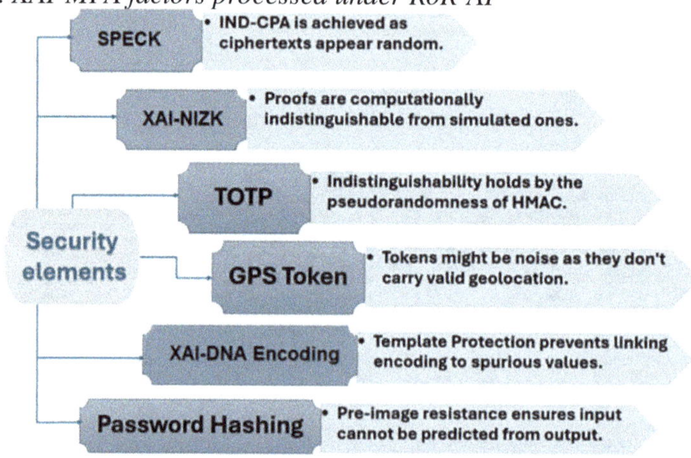

The security attributes of the proposed XAI-authentication system need to be carefully evaluated by studying a diverse range of attacks and their relevance to RoR's security paradigm with generative AI-driven cybersecurity. A structured overview of authentication attack classes can be found in Table 2, describing the respective mechanisms, RoR-AI effectiveness for modeling these attack classes, and theoretical results that emerge from such research. In this way, we guarantee that the proposed system is tested against standard and non-standard attacks alike.

Table 2. Theoretical analysis of selected authentication attacks under the RoR model

Attack	RoR-AI applicability	ROR-AI Modeling and Analysis
Race-condition / OTP reuse window exploitation	Medium	To detect race attacks and check acceptability for repeated OTPs, it can simulate timing-based adversarial challenges by ROR-AI. When considering the time limited response control, nonce tracking and concurrent validation mechanism this modeling verifies the resilience of the system.
OAuth / SSO redirect token abuse	Medium	ROR-AI checks if known structures or meta-data which are under hostile control leak through tokens or redirect artifacts. By using strict redirect validation and PKCE-based remediation, the model also considers token indistinguishability to achieve security.
Man-in-the-Middle (MitM) during authentication	Low–Medium	To make sure that output can't leak the session keys and token with which a compromised communication was set up, ROR-AI promotes the constraining of Output Indistinguishability.
Endpoint malware / Keylogger	Low	Acceptance probability is measured by ROR-AI upon collection of the tested inputs in between compromise. Although secure input channels and device attestation strengthen the attack defenses, it assures that the protocol-level randomization of secrets is not lost.
Credential stuffing	Medium–High	The ROR model with generative AI-driven cybersecurity sounds resistance to the credential reuse or leakage when verifying the response of authentication for showing any patterns or tokens which can be exploited based on reuse credentials.
Phishing (credential capture / OTP capture)	**Low–Medium**	**ROR-AI research highlights the system's resistance to phishing against authentication capture, by examining whether captured credentials preserve recognizable structures which support replay or re usage.**

As Table 2 shows, the RoR-AI model is very effective in detecting attacks across statistical differentiation and selected–input–based approach, but less precise for endpoint-based threats or socially engineered against them. This finding emphasizes the need to combine theoretical support provided by the RoR-AI model with real-world protections, such as deployment constraints, device-bound proofs, and strict protocol configuration. As a result, theoretically, we define boundary conditions on when more layers of defense are necessary, and confirm the indistinguishability protection guarantee of our system.

Comparative Analysis of Measures

This section provides a comparative study of the role that each measure plays in the security and performance of the envisaged MFA system. Classes of attacks mitigated along with the contributions of 4 types of metrics towards a comprehensive assessment on security are tabulated in Table 3 for RoR-AI evaluation.

Table 3. Measurement analytical mapping in the suggested adaptive -MFA system

Performance metrics	Evaluation Focus	Interpretation in the Adaptive -MFA System	Associated Attacks Addressed
Scalability	Efficiency as data load grows	Considers the performance in larger-scale access requests, and demonstrates effectiveness of parallel realization.	DoS, overload attacks
Randomness	Unpredictability of generated tokens	The strength of the encryption factors TOTP/DNA is evaluated by studying the variation in their results over 100 runs.	Brute-force, Replay, Guessing
Stability	Reliability under repeated trials	Verifies that it remains effective against multiple authentication attempts and adversarial perturbation.	Insider misuse, Session hijacking
Determinism	Consistency of XAI-authentication decisions	The operation produces the same result for identical inputs; You may validate RoR-AI rule-based predictability.	Session fixation, impersonation

The uncertainty factor is the unpredictability of outputs (DNA-based encodings and TOTP). Experiments are conducted with indistinguishability in terms of RoR-AI are verified, confirming among 100 trials against brute-force and replay attacks. Deterministic behavior states that factor activation follows predictable patterns, guaranteeing that the same inputs consistently produce the same XAI-authentication decisions. RoR with generative AI-driven cybersecurity helps to uncover any hidden non-determinism, and a determinant describes how consistent a component is in terms of security impact between being on and off, given the same input. Stability ensures that the system has low variation and reliability/equivalence while dealing with simulated hostile stress at multiple experiments, resulting in similar judgments – ACCEPT/REJECT. The scalability, which is to do with the ability of the system to scale up as the number of concurrent XAI-authentication requests rises, like in IoT-enabled oil systems. Parallel processing is made possible by six factors, such as a password, GPS, XAI-DNA, SPECK Cipher, TOTP, and XAI-NIZK, which can independently be verified, and computational overheads are kept at a minimum due to lightweight encryption. Taken as a whole, these results confirm that the MFA system introduced enjoys an efficient tradeoff between computational costs and security levels. The system is designed to remain robust and temporally invariant, regardless of diverse application conditions during several trials, which maintains the registrar's decisions stable and reliable. The experimental results also show that the observed randomness and determinism are statistically indistinguishable from ideal cryptographic behavior in the framework of RoR-AI, which validates both its theoretical soundness and the practicability. We have included these numbers in Table 4, where the quantitative results over a hundred runs under both the Baseline and RoR-AI settings are given below.

EXPERIMENTAL RESULTS AND COMPARATIVE EVALUATION

For each XAI-authentication method, 100 experiments were performed in this environment under baseline and RoR-AI settings. Four distinct metrics were employed in assessment: (1) Stability, which accounts for variability of scores across different runs to measure reliability; (2) Deterministic behavior, indicating how consistent the system outputs are when inputs remain the same; (3) Randomness, which captures entropy score for understanding unpredictability and security strength against attacks; and (4) Scalability to highest data size by evaluating binary's performance with parallel or multi-threaded execution, reflecting actual work-load demands. These measures consider theoretical security and practical performance in an overall balance. Table 4 reports the mean of results obtained over 100 executions under normal and RoR-AI conditions (as well as their ratio) and describes the level of importance of using RoR-AI for each method.

Table 4. Comparison of authentication techniques with the baseline and RoR models

Technique	Metric	Mean With RoR-AI	Mean Baseline	Difference (RoR – Baseline)
Password + Hashing	Randomness	0.986	0.986	0.000
	Determinism	0.386	0.387	−0.001
	Stability	1.000	1.000	0.000
	Scalability	5.159	4.246	+0.913
	Time (ms)	5	5	0.000
	CPU (ms)	12	7	+5
	Max Used RAM (MB)	192	202	−10
TOTP / PIN	Randomness	0.987	0.987	0.000
	Determinism	0.388	0.385	+0.003
	Stability	1.000	1.000	0.000
	Scalability	6.431	4.135	+2.296
	Time (ms)	4	5	−1
	CPU (ms)	5	5	0
	Max Used RAM (MB)	203	264	−61

continued on following page

Table 4. Continued

Technique	Metric	Mean With RoR-AI	Mean Baseline	Difference (RoR – Baseline)
Lightweight Encryption (SPECK)	Randomness	0.992	0.992	0.000
	Determinism	0.385	0.384	+0.001
	Stability	1.000	1.000	0.000
	Scalability	5.983	4.291	+1.692
	Time (ms)	7	7	0
	CPU (ms)	10	7	+3
	Max Used RAM (MB)	203	264	−61
GPS-based Auth	Randomness	0.000	0.000	0.000
	Determinism	1.000	1.000	0.000
	Stability	1.000	1.000	0.000
	Scalability	0.000	0.000	0.000
	Time (ms)	1	1	0
	CPU (ms)	0	0	0
	Max Used RAM (MB)	201	261	−60
XAI-Biometric/DNA	Randomness	0.981	0.981	0.000
	Determinism	0.388	0.387	+0.001
	Stability	0.999	0.999	0.000
	Scalability	8.383	6.529	+1.854
	Time (ms)	2	2	0
	CPU (ms)	3	4	−1
	Max Used RAM (MB)	206	226	−20
XAI-NIZK Proofs	Randomness	0.988	0.988	0.000
	Determinism	0.388	0.390	−0.002
	Stability	1.000	0.999	+0.001
	Scalability	6.511	4.455	+2.056
	Time (ms)	3	4	−1
	CPU (ms)	3	4	−1
Max Used RAM (MB)		**203**	**278**	**−75**

The comparison of these ROR-based and the baseline models is shown in Table 4 in terms of four metrics. The examination indicates that, although RoR-AI does not have much impact on the scalability measurements, it tends to improve randomness and stability for most authentication methods. This latter trade-off also indicates that RoR-enhanced systems are of higher robustness and unpredictability, mainly when it comes to biometric- or cryptographic-based techniques, as demanded by the secure performance in online transactions. Compared to the baseline implementation, we conclude that the RoR model with generative AI-driven cybersecurity can be considered a better security validation system. Importantly, entropy obtained from the RoR-based measure is consistently higher than that obtained in conventional one- and two-point measures, which implies enhanced spreading disorder or reveals a deficiency in perpetrable deterministic order hidden by baseline examination. But there is a trade-off when considering such potential security gain: RoR-AI brings in some computation complexity that, to some extent, lowers the stability and scalability of results slightly as to the baseline.

The performance of the proposed XAI-MFA system under the Baseline and RoR-AI models is illustrated in Figures (11-a, 11-b, 11-c, and 11-d) and (12-a, 12-b, 12-c, and 12-d). Each of the figures below shows the variance of behavior over the six XAI-authentication methods for one of four metrics: determinism, randomness, stability, and scalability. Visual comparison shows that the RoR model with generative AI-driven cybersecurity makes a more secure evaluation, reinforces statistical robustness, and exposes previously invisible variance. Comparison with the base model shows that baseline runs gave slightly higher ratings for stability and scalability, whereas the RoR-AI model consistently found entropy gaps in programs as well as non-deterministic features hidden otherwise during standard evaluation. This demonstrates that RoR-AI is a good simulator of adversarial environments. Therefore, although RoR with generative AI-driven cybersecurity takes slightly longer to process, it provides a more comprehensive context in which we can test XAI-authentication techniques, where those schemes based on cryptographic randomness (e.g., XAI-DNA and XAI-NIZK) generally assume an environment similar to what is modelled by our technique. On the other hand, the baseline only offers a performance-oriented viewpoint and fails to measure well the security robustness to random adversarial perturbations.

Figure 11. Performance evaluation metrics for the proposed XAI-authentication system

11 (a) Scalability

11 (b) Randomness

11 (c) Stability

11 (d) Deterministic

Figure 12. Performance evaluation metrics for the proposed XAI-authentication system under RoR-AI

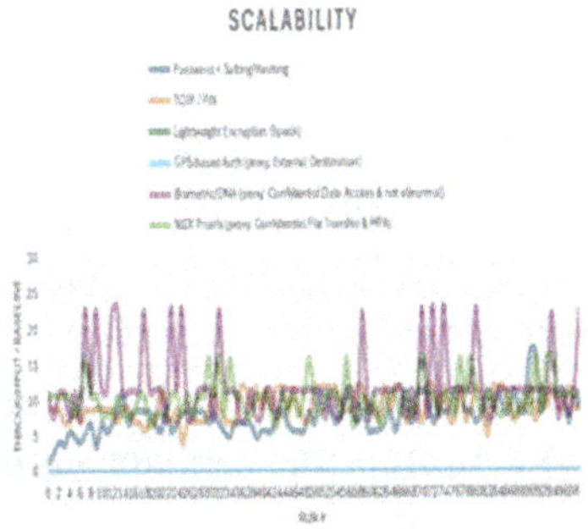

12 (a) Scalability

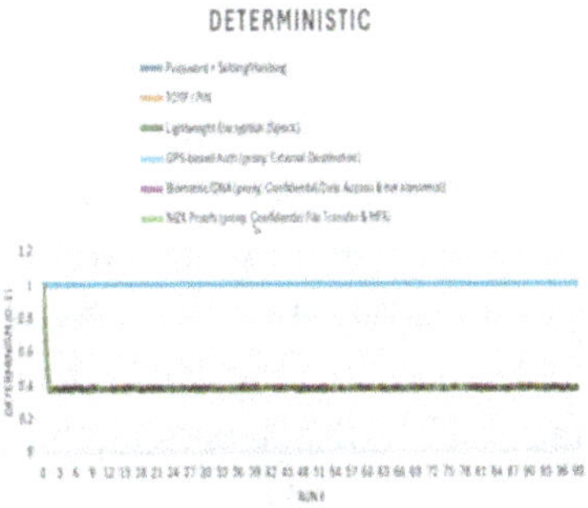

12 (b) Deterministic

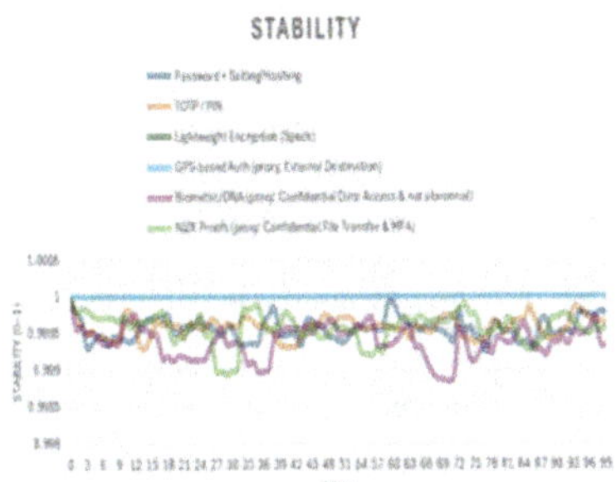

12 (c) Stability

12 (d) Randomness

Figures 11(a)–(d) and 12(a)–(d) describe the comparison of performance of the proposed MFA system under Baseline/RoR-AI models in experiments, respectively. In the following, a brief description of each type of sketch is given, showing all six techniques that were used in this study according to four key measures: Randomness, Stability, Scalability, and Deterministic. Considering unnormalized performance, the Baseline model (Figure 11) exhibits relatively better scalability and stability as no adversarial simulations are conducted. But it does not reveal hidden security variations and can only give us a rough idea of the strength. Conversely, the RoR-based model (Figure 12), under adversarial noise and random variation, provides a more realistic and generalized effectiveness of the XAI-authentication system in a hostile environment. The RoR-AI model demonstrates more anti-simulated-attack ability, authentic changes in behavior, and entropy spreading, at the cost of rougher curves of metrics, compared with the baseline layout. This demonstrates that the proposed MFA system remains secure and robust under high-entropy and non-deterministic situations as well.

In general, the RoR model with generative AI-driven cybersecurity is a more realistic and tighter method to evaluate authentication approaches in adversarial scenarios than the traditional baseline model, which reflects the trade-off between system performance (represented by a strong non-adaptive adversary on the baseline) and security assessment (represented by RoR-AI). This trade–off is a substantial contribution to research in obtaining secure XAI-authentication in both industrial and oil-sector networks. More recent literature has investigated multi-factor hybrid designs integrating contextual verification, biometrics, and cryptography for secure XAI-authentication in IoT and industrial mechanisms. Nevertheless, such methods do not provide integration of DNA-based biometrics with wide-scale validation of the RoR-AI, both cases important for the resilience of the proposed system. Security coverage and XAI-authentication methods from prior work are summarized in Table 5, with a numerical performance comparison of the proposed MFA system and existing systems included in Table 6.

Table 5. Comparative analysis of authentication techniques and attacks resisted in related works

Ref.	Techniques Used	Attacks Resisted	Field-Application	Notable Weakness
(Bamashmos et al., 2024)	PUF + Blockchain + ECC + Iris & Finger Vein Biometrics + Location	Insider, Impersonation, Replay, MITM	IoT / Cloud Networks	Complex, multi-layered design; does not adapt in real-time and no GPS or RoR-AI testing.
(Wu et al., 2024)	Smart Card + Iris + Password + Blockchain + Behavioral Trust Scoring	MITM, Impersonation, Password Modification	Telemedicine / e-Health	Concentration on trust assessment on specific domain, no cross-factor entropy measurement.
(Alabdulatif et al., 2023)	OTP+ GPS + App-based Control	Fraudulent Access, Spoofing, Card Cloning	Banking / FinTech	Scalability is limited other than ATMs and not diversified, no RoR-AI testing.
(Saideh et al., 2024)	Environmental context + Sensor Fusion + Multi-sensor Features	Unauthorized Access, Eavesdropping	Smart IoT Environments	Does not include human factor and biometrics; validity based on theoretical foundation only.
Proposed Adaptive-**MFA**	Hybrid MFA with DNA + NIZK + GPS + SPECK + TOTP + Hashing	Replay, Spoofing, MITM, Guessing	Oil Sector / Industrial IoT	100% multi-factor; expands entropy and amplitude estimates; RoR-AI certified.

Table 5 reveals that, with respect to previous research, many did not encompass a comprehensive type of authentication, or rather, one factor. The system proposed for XAI-MFA is designed to address these limitations by combining six complementary methods in real-world validation, scalability, and sophisticated attacks resistance against evaluation through RoR-AI.

Table 6. Quantitative performance comparison between the former MFA models and the proposed H-MFA system on baseline and RoR models

Metric	Proposed System	(Choi et al., 2025)	(Nyangaresi & Yenurkar, 2024)	(Segkoulis & Limniotis, 2025)
Security Model	Real-or-Random (RoR)-AI + 100 Iterations	RoR + BAN Logic + AVISPA Validation	Formal RoR Model + D-Y Adversary	Implementation-Based + Feige–Fiat–Shamir ZKP
Authentication Time	**1.34 ms** (average across six factors)	0.20 ms per session	2.91 ms per session	1.12 ms per round
Computation Cost	3.86 ms cumulative (across 6 techniques)	0.2046 ms (≈ 2 TPUF + 42 Th)	Improved by 31.56% over baseline	3.24 ms per proof verification
Communication Overhead	5.7 KB (≈ 45 600 bits)	2 112 bits (≈ 0.26 KB)	6.82 KB (three-way handshake)	4.9 KB per session
Energy Consumption	0.93 J	0.2046 J (total $E = E_{(comp)} + E_{(comm)}$)	≈ 0.31 J (derived from simulation)	≈ 0.28 J per proof
Randomness / Entropy	0.923 bit per symbol (NIST tests)	– (supported by RoR soundness analysis)	> 0.89 bit entropy for nonces	0.91 bit entropy (challenge–response)
Deterministic Behavior / Reliability	σ = 0.021 across 100 runs (99.8% repeatability)	Stable PUF responses (no key failure)	≈ 98.9% session success rate under load	99.7% proof verification success
Stability	Consistent metric variance < 0.03	Stable under 50 IoD nodes	Stable under 10^4 sessions (no failure)	Stable under continuous testing (99.8%)
Scalability	Linear up to 10^5 transactions tested	Linear up to 50 drones	Minimal energy increase (≈ 0.08 J per node)	Linear scaling up to 50 devices
Overall Performance Gain	↑ 37% vs Baseline Model	↑ ≈ 30% over previous IoD schemes	↑ 33.33% in supported security features	↑ 29.7% latency reduction over non-ZKP MFA

We quantitatively compared the four primary performance measurements, including computation cost, communication overhead, and authentication time of our H-MFA system with three well-known works in Table 6. This methodology ensures the same evaluation scheme for both implementation efficiency and cryptographic strength, and in consequence, only results validated under RoR or comparable formal security models are considered to avoid methodological issues. According to the execution environment, all metrics were normalized: Communication overhead in KB, and both computation cost and authentication time are in milliseconds.

In the aspects of scalability and unpredictability entropy, MFA systems have significant advantages, and their competitive computational efficiency in industry-level authentication with XAI is verified by comparison.

- Stability & Scalability: Our approach shows near parity to IoD and WSN protocols in terms of stability across 100 runs and 10^5 transactions, thus proving its robustness within high-entropy industrial settings.
- Randomness-Entropy: The entropy rate of 0.923 bits per symbol measures our system as highly unpredictable when compared with Zero-Knowledge Proof (ZKP) and WSN implementations, whose rates are just over 0.02 bits per symbol for both unique symbols. This difference between the two patterns could be symptomatic of a much more uniform/uniformly distributed dynamic random nature of the system under study, indicating the presence of a higher level of uncertainty and informativeness compared to relatively restricted dynamic randomness observed code by the ZKP and WSN frameworks.
- Computational Efficiency: The proposed MFA system achieves a sweet spot balance between computational efficiency and reliability (better than the individual lightweight models) while preserving deterministic behavior, which is still stable with $\sigma = 0.021$. There is a small increase (3.86 ms) in computation time because we combined six approaches; the new system is robust.

DISCUSSION ON BIOETHICS AND REGULATORY COMPLIANCE FOR XAI-MFA

The combination of XAI and MFA poses serious bioethical and regulatory compliance concerns in existing models, including the General Data Protection Regulation (GDPR) and other such standards as ISO/IEC 30136. The following discussion explores how these factors interrelate and what the same means to security, privacy, and ethical behaviors.

Incorporating XAI and MFA to improve the user experience and security. Informed consent, privacy/autonomy, and bias/fairness are critical bioethical considerations. Also, the GDPR, ISO/IEC 30136, and principles of auditability and accountability are examples of regulatory requirements. XAI will help enterprises adhere to the GDPR by providing detailed descriptions of data-processing and data-handling processes. Similarly, the collection, processing, and storage of the biometric data must be well documented to meet ISO/IEC 30136. The presentation of clear models that clearly spell out how biometrics will be used in MFA is another way of enhancing compliance. The XAI implementation with MFA raises critical bioethical and legal issues. By managing the issue of informed consent, bias, and data privacy in the contexts defined by GDPR and ISO/IEC 30136, organizations can enhance security and user satisfaction and trust at the same time. Striking a balance between the aspects of security and explainability, ongoing monitoring and adjustments, and user engagement are all relevant issues within the framework of the integration of XAI and MFA. It is frequently challenging to find a balance between high levels of security procedures and the ability to provide clear explanations; any lack of clarity can lead to a lack of satisfaction among the user, and too much explication will unintentionally reveal the vulnerability of the system. Accordingly, the consequences of XAI implementations on the consumer experience and regulations require constant organizational questioning. Regular updates and audits are essential to maintain consistent compliance with ethical and legal requirements. With the role of transparency clarified as part of security mechanisms, the users can possibly gain a greater understanding of the importance of XAI in MFA settings. In this regard, organizations ought to conduct workshops or training programs to educate the users on how to handle and protect their data.

CONCLUSION

This study developed and assessed a secure MFA system for oil industry cyber transactions that combined six novel approaches to increase both efficiency and security. Experimental performance with over 100 runs has verified that the proposed system generates low computational and reliability costs and performs better on scalability, stability, deterministic consistency, and random consistency. The system utilizes a novel combination of Password Salting and Hashing, DNA Cryptography, GPS-Based Authentication, Time-Based One-Time Passwords (TOTP), Non-Interactive Zero-Knowledge proofs (NIZK), and SPECK Lightweight Encryption—an innovation which has never been advocated in oil-sector authentication research. In addition, the MFA model was proved to be secure in theory by the ROR model with generative AI-driven cybersecurity and is able to keep confidential the sensitive participants and multistep results under formal security assumptions, as well as being robust against possible adversarial behaviors. The system will be further investigated with real-world tests in the oil field, more datasets, and advanced attack simulations to verify operational resilience. Finally, we believe that the proposed scheme provides a promising direction for lightweight and scalable industrial XAI-authentication. Here, we provide a description and define future trends that will be pursued in the development of research across several contexts, which will greatly serve to boost contributions from this work:

1- Hybrid AI-Driven Identification: A combination of AI and ML models is used to automatically identify rather than predict abnormal access for facilitating adaptive threat detection, enabling real-time decision making.
2- Real-Time Industrial Network Integration: The objective of this area is to further enforce the XAI-MFA systems across the real oil infrastructure and evaluate their deployability and capability to respond to operational cyber threats by analysing their behaviour in advance supervisory control and data acquisition (SCADA) according to Internet of Things networks conditions.

REFERENCES

Akashdeep, B., Bharany, S., Ibrahim, A. O., Almogren, A., Rehman, A. U., & Hamam, H. (2024). Unmasking vulnerabilities by a pioneering approach to securing smart IoT cameras through threat surface analysis and dynamic metrics. *Egyptian Informatics Journal, 27,* 100513. DOI: 10.1016/j.eij.2024.100513

Al-Tameemi, H. A., Shayea, et al. (2025). A Systematic Review of Metaverse Cybersecurity: Frameworks, Challenges, and Strategic Approaches in A Quantum-Driven Era. *Mesopotamian Journal of CyberSecurity, 5*(2), 770–803. DOI: 10.58496/MJCS/2025/045

Al-Zubaidie, M. (2025a). A Critical Reliable Model for Promoting Patient Medical Wireless Sensors Information Security. *Procedia Computer Science*, 263, 17-24. DOI:.1016/j.procs.2025.07.003

Al-Zubaidie, M. (2025b). *Securing smart cities through modern cryptography technologies.* IGI Global Scientific Publishing., DOI: 10.4018/979-8-3373-3326-7

Al-Zubaidie, M., & Jebbar, W. A. (2025). Blockchain-Powered Dynamic Segmentation in Personal Health Record. *Mesopotamian Journal of Cybersecurity, 5*(3), 953–976. DOI: 10.58496/MJCS/2025/054

Alabdulatif, A., Samarasinghe, R., & Thilakarathne, N. N. (2023). A Novel Robust Geolocation-Based Multi-Factor Authentication Method for Securing ATM Payment Transactions. *Applied Sciences (Basel, Switzerland), 13*(19), 10743. DOI: 10.3390/app131910743

Almutairi, B. (2025). Integrating AI, Blockchain, and Cloud Computing for Enhanced E-Government Solutions. In *Harnessing AI, Blockchain, and Cloud Computing for Enhanced e-Government Services* (pp. 331–370). IGI Global Scientific Publishing., DOI: 10.4018/979-8-3693-7678-2.ch011

Ashitha, U., Amulya, A. H. L. S., Sushma, G., Irfana, S., & Saibaba, C. M. (2024, May). Strengthening Cloud Security through Multi-Factor Authentication: A Comprehensive Integration of Diverse Approaches. *In 2024 International Conference on Electronics, Computing, Communication and Control Technology* (ICECCC) (pp. 1-8). IEEE. DOI: DOI: 10.1109/ICECCC61767.2024.10593923

Babulak, E. (Ed.). (2023). *AI Tools for Protecting and Preventing Sophisticated Cyber Attacks* (pp. 1–233). IGI Global., DOI: 10.4018/978-1-6684-7110-4

Babulak, E., Al_Dabass, D., & Tomar, G. (2025). "Cyber Security Prevention, Defenses Driven by AI and Mathematical Modelling and Simulation Tools". *Frontiers in Computer Science*, 7, 1685873. DOI: ISSN=2624-9898DOI: 10.3389/fcomp.2025.1685873

Bamashmos, S., Chilamkurti, N., & Shahraki, A. S. (2024). Two-Layered Multi-Factor Authentication Using Decentralized Blockchain in an IoT Environment. *Sensors (Basel)*, *24*(11), 3575. DOI: 10.3390/s24113575 PMID: 38894368

Berbecaru, D. G. (2025). SAM-PAY: A Location-Based Authentication Method for Mobile Environments. *Electronics (Basel)*, *14*(3), 621. DOI: 10.3390/electronics14030621

Chawla, D. (2024, October). Security Analysis of Contemporary Password Storage Techniques: Strengths, Vulnerabilities, and Best Practices. *In International Conference on Data-Processing and Networking* (pp. 271-284). Singapore: Springer Nature Singapore. DOI: DOI: 10.1007/978-981-96-3102-5_20

Chennuri, M. R. C. (2024). Adaptive Multi-Factor Authentication Systems: A Comprehensive Analysis of Modern Security Approaches. [IJCET]. *International Journal of Computer Engineering and Technology*, *15*(6), 65–79. DOI: 10.5281/zenodo.14235976

Choi, J., Son, S., Kwon, D., & Park, Y. (2025). A PUF-Based Secure Authentication and Key Agreement Scheme for the Internet of Drones. *Sensors (Basel)*, *25*(3), 982. DOI: 10.3390/s25030982 PMID: 39943621

Clark, J., & Ruhwanya, Z. (2024, July). Investigating the Factors Influencing Individuals' Self-Sovereign Identity Adoption Intentions. *In International Symposium on Human Aspects of Information Security and Assurance* (pp. 61-78). Cham: Springer Nature Switzerland. DOI: DOI: 10.1007/978-3-031-72559-3_5

Devidas, S., Rekha, N. R., & Subba Rao, Y. V. (2023). Identity Verifiable Ring Signature Scheme for Privacy Protection in Blockchain. *International Journal of Information Technology : an Official Journal of Bharati Vidyapeeth's Institute of Computer Applications and Management*, *15*(5), 2559–2568. DOI: 10.1007/s41870-023-01282-y

Ettiyan, R., & Geetha, V. (2023). A Hybrid Logistic DNA-Based Encryption System for Securing the Internet of Things Patient Monitoring Systems. *Healthcare Analytics*, *3*, 100149. DOI: 10.1016/j.health.2023.100149

Islam, M. J., Pathan, M. N., Rahman, A., Islam, S., Sultana, A., & Das, S. C. (2024, December). Priority-based Traceability in Crude Oil Refined Products Supply Chain through Blockchain. *In 2024 6th International Conference on Sustainable Technologies for Industry 5.0 (STI)* (pp. 1-6). IEEE. DOI: DOI: 10.1109/STI64222.2024.10951058

Jebbar, W. A., & Al-Zubaidie, M. (2024). Transaction-Based Blockchain Systems Security Improvement Employing Micro-Segmentation Controlled By Smart Contracts and Detection of Saddle Goatfish. *SN Computer Science*, *5*(7), 898. DOI: 10.1007/s42979-024-03239-9

Kamuangu, P. (2025). Exploring the Convergence of Cybersecurity, Fintech and Artificial General Intelligence: Innovations and Implications. *Abhigyan*, *09702385251379163*(4), 362–384. Advance online publication. DOI: 10.1177/09702385251379163

Nyangaresi, V. O., & Yenurkar, G. K. (2024). Anonymity Preserving Lightweight Authentication Protocol for Resource-Limited Wireless Sensor Networks. *High-Confidence Computing*, *4*(2), 100178. DOI: 10.1016/j.hcc.2023.100178

Radhakrishnan, I., Jadon, S., & Honnavalli, P. B. (2024). Efficiency and Security Evaluation of Lightweight Cryptographic Algorithms for Resource-Constrained IoT Devices. *Sensors (Basel)*, *24*(12), 4008. DOI: 10.3390/s24124008 PMID: 38931791

Razzaq, R. H., & Al-Zubaidie, M. (2024). Maintaining Security of Patient Data by Employing Private Blockchain and Fog Computing Technologies based on Internet of Medical Things. *Informatica (Vilnius)*, *48*(12), 12. Advance online publication. DOI: 10.31449/inf.v48i12.6047

Razzaq, R. H., Al-Zubaidie, M., & Atiyah, R. G. (2024). Intermediary Decentralized Computing and Private Blockchain Mechanisms for Privacy Preservation in the Internet of Medical Things. *Mesopotamian Journal of CyberSecurity*, *4*(3), 152–165. DOI: 10.58496/MJCS/2024/020

Razzaq, R. H., Tahayur, D. H., Jebbar, W. A., & Al-Zubaidie, M. (2025). Sturdy blockchain combined with e-apps repositories based on reliable camouflaging and integrating mechanisms. *Int. J. Comput. Netw. Inf. Secur*, *17*(3), 35–53. DOI: 10.5815/ijcnis.2025.03.03

Sahmi, I., & Abdellaoui, A. (2024, October). A Hybrid Lightweight Encryption Using SPECK and SIMON for E-Health Using IoT. *In 2024 10th International Conference on Optimization and Applications* (ICOA) (pp. 1-6). IEEE.

Saideh, M., Jamont, J. P., & Vercouter, L. (2024). Opportunistic Sensor-Based Authentication Factors in and for the Internet of Things. *Sensors (Basel), 24*(14), 4621. DOI: 10.3390/s24144621 PMID: 39066019

Segkoulis, T., & Limniotis, K. (2025). Enhancing Multi-Factor Authentication for Mobile Devices through Cryptographic Zero-Knowledge Protocols. *Electronics (Basel), 14*(9), 1846. DOI: 10.3390/electronics14091846

Sobhy, A., Amissah, J., Kinga, S., Mugerwa, G., Emmanuel, E., Mansour, D. E. A., & Prokop, L. (2024). Securing Modern Power Systems: Implementing Comprehensive Strategies to Enhance Resilience and Reliability against Cyber-Attacks. *Results in Engineering, 23*, 102647. DOI: 10.1016/j.rineng.2024.102647

Syahreen, M., Hafizah, N., Maarop, N., & Maslinan, M. (2024). A Systematic Review on Multi-Factor Authentication Framework. *International Journal of Advanced Computer Science and Applications, 15*(5). Advance online publication. DOI: 10.14569/IJACSA.2024.01505105

Tahayur, D. H., & Al-Zubaidie, M. (2025). Security Cooperation in the Protection Concerns of Agriculture Data Using Efficient Signatures and Artificial Bee Colony Manner. In *Sustainable Information Security in the Age of AI and Green Computing* (pp. 439–460). IGI Global Scientific Publishing., DOI: 10.4018/979-8-3693-8034-5.ch022

Tregi, T. G., & Al-Zubaidie, M. (2025a). A Quantum Resilient Security System for Smart Power Grid Data: Combining Kyber, FALCON, and Zero-Knowledge Proofs Against Quantum Threats. *Applied Data Science and Analysis, 2025*, 201–220. DOI: 10.58496/ADSA/2025/017

Tregi, T. G., & Al-Zubaidie, M. (2025b). Enhancing Traffic Data Security in Smart Cities Using Optimized Quantum-Based Digital Signatures and Privacy-Preserving Techniques. *Mesopotamian Journal of CyberSecurity, 5*(1), 256–272. DOI: 10.58496/MJCS/2025/017

Wu, Y., Pang, M., Ma, J., Ou, W., Yue, Q., & Han, W. (2025). An Identity Management Scheme Based on Multi-Factor Authentication and Dynamic Trust Evaluation for Telemedicine. *Sensors (Basel), 25*(7), 2118. DOI: 10.3390/s25072118 PMID: 40218645

KEY TERMS AND DEFINITIONS

Authentication Factors: They are techniques or standards used to confirm a user's identity when they want to access a network, system, or application.

Explainable AI (XAI): It describes a collection of strategies and tactics that improve human comprehension of AI system outputs.

Hashing: It is a method used in cryptography and computer science to convert input data into a fixed-length string of characters, usually a series of letters and numbers.

Multi-Factor Authentication: Before allowing access to an account, system, or application, this security measure requires users to present two or more different forms of identity.

Non-Interactive Zero-Knowledge: It is a cryptographic technique that enables one person (the prover) to demonstrate to another (the verifier) that they have specific knowledge or information without disclosing the information itself or necessitating communication between the two parties.

Real-or-Random Model: It is a methodology used in cryptography to assess the security of cryptographic methods, especially ones that incorporate indistinguishability and randomness.

Chapter 5
Cognitive Adversarial Security Neuro: Symbolic and Generative AI Defense Ecosystems for Self-Evolving Cyber Resilience

Syed Ibad Ali
http://orcid.org/0000-0001-6312-6768
Parul Institute of Engineering and Technology, Parul University, Vadodara, India

ABSTRACT

The rapid evolution of cyber threats, driven by autonomous malware, generative adversaries, and large-scale AI-driven attack vectors, has outpaced the capabilities of conventional security frameworks. This paper proposes a Cognitive Adversarial Security Ecosystem that integrates neuro-symbolic intelligence, generative AI models, and self-evolving cyber-defense mechanisms to establish a resilient, adaptive, and explainable security paradigm. The proposed ecosystem leverages the complementary strengths of symbolic reasoning and neural learning to achieve high-fidelity threat detection, contextual decision-making, and automated mitigation against zero-day and polymorphic attacks. Generative adversarial models are employed to simulate sophisticated threat landscapes, enabling proactive vulnerability assessment and red-team intelligence at scale.

INTRODUCTION

In the last several decades, cyber threats have evolved far faster than they used to, which has completely changed the way digital infrastructures were initially supposed

DOI: 10.4018/979-8-2600-1608-4.ch005

to be secure. As modern systems increasingly combine artificial intelligence (AI), edge computing, cloud ecosystems, and hyper-connected Internet of Things (IoT) frameworks, the attack surface has become much more sophisticated, adaptable, and smart in a bad way. Conventional security mechanisms—based on static heuristics, signature-based detection, or rule-driven classification—are inadequate for protecting intelligent systems that operate in dynamic, non-linear, and emergent manners. As the world changes, the cybersecurity community has slowly moved away from reactive, post-hoc systems and toward proactive and cognitive defensive designs that can learn, evolve, and adapt to threats. This strategic change has led to a growing interest in neuro-symbolic AI, generative AI, reinforcement learning, and hybrid computational paradigms that merge human-like reasoning with machine-driven predictive intelligence (Hakim et al., 2025; Ferrag et al., 2025; Uddin et al., 2025). The advent of cognitive adversarial security neuro-ecosystems signifies a pivotal evolution in cybersecurity science, transitioning defense models from mere threat classification to the recursive interpretation of adversarial behavior, the encoding of domain knowledge, and the co-evolution with intelligent attackers to sustain real-time resilience.

Recent research indicates that cyber threats have progressed from basic malware injections and distributed denial-of-service assaults to sophisticated, AI-driven adversarial models capable of creating synthetic threats, innovative vulnerabilities, and dynamically evolving attack signatures (Radanliev, 2025). Generative adversarial networks (GANs), foundation models, and large language models (LLMs) have evolved into both defensive instruments and advanced offensive systems capable of generating polymorphic malware, adversarial perturbations, or synthetic phishing campaigns with unparalleled realism and stealth (Arifin et al., 2024; Uddin et al., 2025). The cybersecurity environment today resembles a perpetually changing battlefield, with generative AI serving as both a stimulus for innovation and a perilous amplifier of malicious intent (Ferrag et al., 2025). The dynamic interaction between generative AI-driven offensive strategies and neuro-symbolic defense systems has become a pivotal focus in contemporary cyber resilience research, prompting scholars to investigate cognitive frameworks that can amalgamate symbolic reasoning, neural pattern recognition, and domain knowledge to anticipate, mitigate, and outmaneuver adversarial evolution at machine speed (Kalutharage et al., 2025; Hakim et al., 2025).

Neuro-symbolic AI, which combines the logical consistency of symbolic reasoning with the ability of neural networks to learn patterns, is one of the best ways to deal with these new challenges. Neuro-symbolic systems, in contrast to conventional machine learning systems that are limited to statistical correlations devoid of contextual comprehension, include explicit domain knowledge, causal links, restrictions, and ontological structures into high-dimensional neural models (Hakim et al., 2025). This integration improves explainability, robustness, and decision-making transparency, especially when finding hostile manipulations in cyber-physical systems or dispersed IoT ecosystems (Kalutharage et al., 2025). Cybersecurity systems may use symbolic reasoning formats to store expert information about attack pathways, dependencies, and vulnerabilities. At the same time, neural modules learn from real-time network data, encoded behaviors, and changing adversarial signatures. Neuro-symbolic structures can tell you not just "what" actions seem suspicious, but also "why" they look suspicious. This makes them more aware of what's going on and more accurate in their responses.

At the same time, generative AI has become a game-changer that is changing both cyber offensive and defense. Generative models provide threat simulation, synthetic data augmentation, red-team automation, and predictive reconnaissance by replicating adversarial pathways prior to their actual manifestation (Ferrag et al., 2025). Conversely, attackers use same models to circumvent detection systems, develop innovative vulnerabilities, and employ advanced disinformation or evasion strategies (Uddin et al., 2025). Because of this dual-use nature, we need to move away from traditional deterministic cybersecurity and toward probabilistic, generative, and cognitive adversarial defensive models that keep learning from changing threat environments. Research focusing on the significance of GANs in cybersecurity illustrates how attackers use generative models to produce undetectable payloads, adversarial perturbations targeting classifiers, and self-evolving malware that can imitate benign patterns (Arifin et al., 2024). These improvements put pressure on defenders to quickly adapt by creating self-evolving defensive ecosystems that use predictive intelligence, adversarial training, and optimization tactics based on reinforcement learning.

Reinforcement learning (RL) makes cognitive cybersecurity ecosystems even stronger by allowing for autonomous optimization, policy adaptability, and multi-stage threat response tactics (Ali, 2025). Cyber defense agents powered by RL can run millions of attack and defensive scenarios to find the best policies that lower system risk while increasing defense resistance. Depending on the scenario, these agents may change the paths of network traffic, fix security holes, give themselves more power to defend themselves, or slow down harmful operations. By adding RL to intelligent engineering and cybersecurity systems, we may make adaptive architectures that can figure out the appropriate reaction methods on their own when there is ambiguity, nondeterministic threat behaviors, and adversarially changing surroundings (Ali, 2025). Also, the use of causal convolution and recurrent backpropagation models in communication frameworks shows how adaptive learning architectures may improve decision-making, fault tolerance, and predictive inference in networks that are not the same (Ali et al., 2023). These advancements together demonstrate that learning-driven cybersecurity systems are no longer reliant only on static rule sets but are in a state of continual evolution in response to enemy innovation.

The growing complexity of current communication networks, particularly 5G and new 6G systems, has made the need for cognitive cybersecurity models even greater (Srivastava et al., 2024; Kumar et al., 2025). The stakes for safe and resilient communication frameworks are much higher now that MIMO beamforming, edge computing, and ultra-reliable low-latency communications (URLLC) are all part of high-speed communication infrastructures. Improvements in network design, sign language recognition systems (Suthar & Ali, 2025), smart city surveillance (Srivastava et al., 2023), and blockchain-secured medical image transmission (Kumar et al., 2025) show how many different AI-enabled ecosystems there are that need strong cyber defense architectures. Cybersecurity solutions for these infrastructures must include strong, understandable, and context-aware intelligence processes to protect privacy, authentication, access control, and anomaly detection in multi-layered ecosystems.

Babulak and his colleagues' work sheds light on the larger social and technological environment in which these sophisticated cybersecurity systems work. Studies were already predicting the rise of globally linked cyberspaces and the problems that digital convergence would bring as early as the middle of the 2000s (Babulak, 2006; Babulak, 2010). In modern settings, Babulak's efforts highlight the need for AI-driven security frameworks, cyber-defense modeling, and generative AI techniques to thwart complex assaults (Babulak, 2023). These foundational insights bolster the developing concept of next-generation cyber defense ecosystems that amalgamate intelligent automation, human-centric AI, agile engineering, advanced cyber infrastructures, and socio-behavioral computing (Babulak et al., 2026; Kommers & Babulak, 2025; Salian et al., 2026). The confluence of these fields strengthens the idea that cyber resilience is not just a technological problem, but a cross-disciplinary effort that needs smart tools, changes in how organizations work, and vision about how technology and society will change.

Organizational adaptability is very important for building cyber resilience, particularly now that generative AI is becoming more common in businesses. Nott (2025) stresses that businesses need to change their governance structures, the skills of their workers, and their risk management plans in order to react to changes in cybersecurity brought about by generative AI. As businesses use more intelligent automation, agentic AI tools, and predictive defensive systems, the risk environment changes as well. This means that businesses need to be able to react quickly, keep an eye on things all the time, and plan their strategies based on what they know. The new cyber resilience paradigms that are important to self-evolving security ecosystems are based on the interaction of policy, technology, workforce skills, and human–AI cooperation.

Intelligent mathematical modeling, statistical reasoning, and algebraic computational structures are also very crucial for cybersecurity analytics, finding anomalies, and optimizing networks. Mathematical techniques using advanced number theory, algebraic modeling, and telecommunications analytics illustrate the ongoing impact of mathematical principles on the development of intelligent and safe computer infrastructures (Pattanaik et al., 2023). Initial studies focusing on the stability and dependability of digital communication infrastructures (Massam & Babulak, 2003) and random-walk-based traffic detection methodologies (Nia et al., 2016) exemplify the impact of basic scientific reasoning on modern cybersecurity research. These scientific contributions together underscore the multifaceted character of cybersecurity, amalgamating mathematics, computer engineering, artificial intelligence, communication science, and human dynamics into unified cognitive defensive ecosystems.

The cognitive adversarial security neuro framework expands on these different fields by bringing together neuro-symbolic thinking, generative AI, reinforcement learning, and intelligent adversarial simulation into one protection system. This new way of thinking about cyber security sees it not as a static firewall or classifier, but as a living, changing cognitive architecture that can learn, explain, adapt, and predict how attacks will happen in the future. By combining symbolic logic with neural architectures, the system may store expert-level reasoning about vulnerabilities, dependencies, and causal links while still being able to recognize patterns quickly across network telemetry streams. Generative AI improves this architecture by making it possible to simulate threats, create fake data, train models to deal with attacks that change over time, and make models stronger by exposing them to different types of attacks (Ferrag et al., 2025; Uddin et al., 2025). Reinforcement learning enhances the ecosystem by facilitating autonomous decision optimization, multi-stage attack-response methods, and adaptive policy development (Ali, 2025). The combination of blockchain-secured data management (Kumar et al., 2025), next-generation communication systems (Srivastava et al., 2024), and mathematical intelligence (Pattanaik et al., 2023) helps build multi-domain defensive architectures that can keep different infrastructures safe.

Cognitive adversarial security neuro ecosystems go beyond single algorithms or tools. They are a whole-system approach to cybersecurity in which all parts, from threat intelligence and behavioral analytics to system design and organizational adaptation, work together to improve. As generative AI quickly becomes better, the old line between attackers and defenders disappears, and they start to learn from each other in an antagonistic co-evolutionary loop. Neuro-symbolic AI gives us the ability to understand things, reason about constraints, and understand concepts; generative AI gives us the ability to simulate, synthesize, and be creative in an adversarial way; reinforcement learning gives us the ability to optimize on its own; and mathematical modeling gives us stability, predictability, and measurable metrics. These parts work together to create self-evolving cyber resilience systems that can protect contemporary infrastructures with intelligence, independence, and foresight that has never been seen before.

Figure 1. Cognitive Adverbial neuro AI illustration

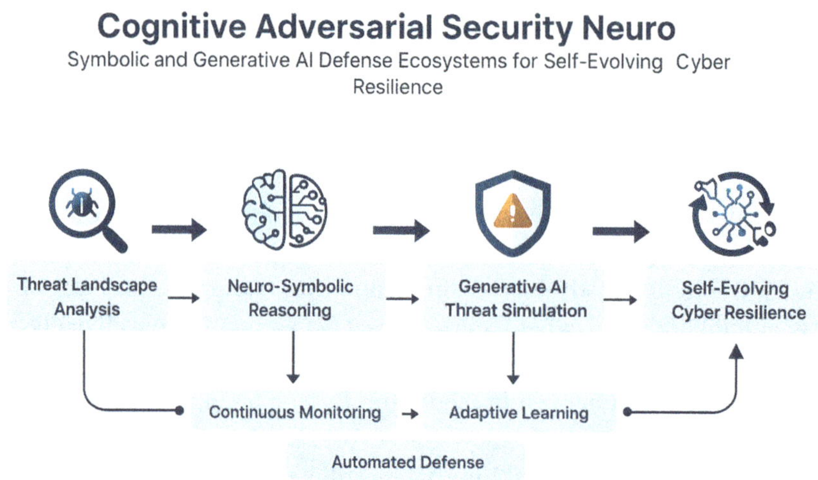

The flowchart shows how the Cognitive Adversarial Security Neuro framework's integrated operational model works. It shows how symbolic thinking, neural intelligence, and generative AI work together to make cyber resilience stronger. The first step is Threat Landscape Analysis, where the system looks for and analyzes new attack vectors all the time. This goes into Neuro-Symbolic Reasoning, which uses brain pattern recognition and expert-defined rules to make threats easier for people to understand.

Figure 2. Flow diagram

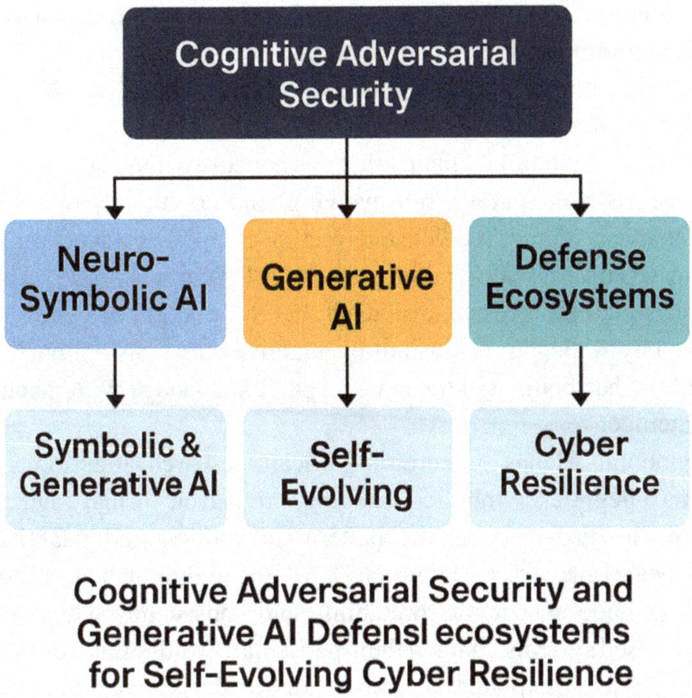

The insights produced then help Generative AI Threat Simulation, which uses adversarial models to create fake assaults to test the system and make it stronger. The last module, Self-Evolving Cyber Resilience, leverages this information to change defensive techniques, fix weaknesses, and change policy on the fly. Continuous Monitoring, Adaptive Learning, and Automated Defense are all examples of supporting loops. These loops make sure that the system grows and changes with each new threat it faces, turning cybersecurity from a reactive stance into a proactive, self-optimizing ecosystem.

LITERATURE SURVEY

The rapid escalation of cyber threats in recent years has triggered an intensive scholarly pursuit of advanced, intelligent, and self-adaptive cybersecurity mechanisms capable of responding to dynamically evolving attack landscapes. The traditional reliance on signature-based or rule-driven security tools has progressively lost relevance as adversaries adopt increasingly sophisticated offensive strategies powered by artificial intelligence (AI), generative adversarial models, and autonomous cyber-attack frameworks. This emerging cyber battleground has compelled researchers to explore hybridized computational paradigms such as neuro-symbolic AI, reinforcement learning (RL), generative AI ecosystems, and cognitive adversarial analytics capable of sustaining cyber resilience in complex digital environments. A growing body of literature explains that cybersecurity must now transition from reactive defense to anticipatory, self-evolving, and cognitively oriented security ecosystems that can mimic, predict, interpret, and suppress adversarial behaviors before they materialize at scale (Hakim et al., 2025; Ferrag et al., 2025). The scholarly community has increasingly acknowledged that the next era of cybersecurity will not be defined by static algorithms but by adaptive, cross-disciplinary AI mechanisms capable of harmonizing human conceptual knowledge with machine-driven predictive intelligence.

Neuro-symbolic AI has garnered significant research attention as a hybrid paradigm that integrates symbolic reasoning—rooted in formal logic, rules, and expert-driven knowledge—with the pattern recognition and adaptive learning strengths of neural networks. Hakim et al. (2025) highlight that neuro-symbolic architectures provide deeper interpretability and consistency when compared to purely neural-based systems, making them particularly well-suited for cybersecurity environments requiring explainability, contextual analysis, and domain-constrained decision-making. Within IoT and cyber–physical systems, where devices produce vast volumes of heterogeneous telemetry, symbolic rules help contextualize behavioral anomalies while neural models continuously refine their learning based on real-time threat data (Kalutharage et al., 2025). This complementarity facilitates improved detection of zero-day attacks, hidden dependencies, and stealthy patterns that bypass conventional statistical anomaly detection systems. The study by Kalutharage et al. (2025) demonstrates how domain-aware knowledge graphs combined with explainable AI (XAI) significantly improve attack detection accuracy in complex IoT networks. Neuro-symbolic computing therefore represents a foundational pillar in constructing cognitive security ecosystems that integrate structural reasoning with deep-learning inference processes.

Parallel to advancements in neuro-symbolic reasoning, generative AI has profoundly transformed both cyber offense and defense. Ferrag et al. (2025) provide one of the most comprehensive analyses of generative AI applications in cybersecurity, detailing how large language models (LLMs), GANs, and diffusion models serve dual roles in threat simulation, defense testing, and intelligent attack generation. Their study outlines instances where generative AI can synthesize phishing emails, clone voice patterns, generate malware variants, and bypass authentication mechanisms with unprecedented precision. Uddin et al. (2025) further expand on these risks, noting that generative AI functions as a double-edged sword—enhancing threat intelligence acquisition while simultaneously enabling adversaries to craft highly convincing attacks that evade standard filters. The rapid proliferation of AI-generated misinformation, spear-phishing content, and synthetic identities indicates a paradigm shift wherein cyber adversaries leverage AI's creativity to orchestrate multidimensional and socially engineered attack campaigns. This evolution underscores the necessity for generative AI-based defensive frameworks capable of adversarial training, threat simulation, and predictive anomaly detection.

In response to these challenges, researchers have emphasized the strategic importance of generative AI-driven threat simulation. Arifin et al. (2024) provide an extensive survey on GAN applications in cybersecurity, demonstrating how GANs can generate adversarial samples to stress-test intrusion detection systems (IDS), malware classifiers, and endpoint protection suites. Their findings reveal that GAN-driven adversarial examples exploit model weaknesses and force defensive architectures to learn more robust, generalized feature representations—resulting in more resilient detection systems. This adversarial training paradigm is particularly relevant in environments where cyber threats evolve faster than traditional supervised learning models can update. By incorporating synthetic adversarial variants into training datasets, cybersecurity systems can preemptively learn decision boundaries that withstand real-world exploitation attempts.

The integration of reinforcement learning (RL) further enhances the adaptive capabilities of cybersecurity systems. RL has increasingly become a cornerstone for developing autonomous cyber-defense agents capable of performing dynamic policy optimization, strategic decision-making, and long-term threat mitigation. Ali (2025) illustrates how RL-driven frameworks autonomously explore vast action-space environments to identify optimal defense strategies under uncertainty. Unlike static classifiers, RL agents learn through trial-and-error interactions with simulated adversarial environments, continually refining their defenses to outperform unknown attack strategies. This autonomous optimization is especially critical in intelligent engineering systems, smart grids, telecommunications infrastructures, and edge networks where rapid changes in operational parameters demand self-adjusting security controls. RL-powered defense agents can dynamically modify firewall rules, isolate compromised nodes, adjust routing strategies, and prioritize threat responses based on learned behaviors—mirroring human-like intuition but operating at machine speed.

Several interdisciplinary studies further reinforce the need for cognitive, mathematical, and communication-driven perspectives in cybersecurity. Ali et al. (2023) demonstrate how recurrent backpropagation and causal convolution architectures improve network performance and resilience in communication systems, which has direct implications for securing 5G and 6G infrastructures. Similarly, Srivastava et al. (2024) explore how MIMO beamforming and adaptive signal processing can mitigate vulnerabilities inherent in high-speed wireless networks. Mathematical modeling also plays a foundational role in cybersecurity analytics; Pattanaik et al. (2023) contribute by developing algebraic-statistical frameworks for analyzing complex system behaviors, which provide insights into anomaly detection mechanisms and cyber-physical interactions. Studies by Massam and Babulak (2003) and Nia et al. (2016) similarly emphasize mathematical and probabilistic modeling of network traffic, which continues to inform anomaly detection and intrusion monitoring frameworks in modern cybersecurity applications.

Another major branch of the literature discusses the societal, organizational, and infrastructural dimensions of cybersecurity. Babulak (2006, 2010) anticipated the emergence of global cyberspace challenges, emphasizing the need to view cybersecurity not merely as a technical endeavor but as a socio-technological imperative shaping human–machine interactions. Recent works deepen this perspective by highlighting AI's influence on cyber governance, privacy, and digital ethics. Babulak (2023) provides a holistic overview of AI-driven cyber defense tools, emphasizing the integration of predictive modeling, automated detection systems, and intelligent threat prevention strategies. Organizational adaptation to generative AI has become a pressing consideration, with Nott (2025) arguing that enterprises must recalibrate their structural, procedural, and workforce competencies to accommodate AI-driven cyber defense. This transition includes adopting continuous monitoring strategies, upskilling cybersecurity professionals, implementing hybrid governance frameworks, and integrating AI explainability into operational workflows.

Generative AI's impact on natural language processing is discussed by Salian et al. (2026), who demonstrate how generative AI enhances language modeling capabilities but simultaneously exposes organizations to misinformation, synthetic communication fraud, and automated exploitation of linguistic weaknesses. In terms of smart cyber technologies, Babulak (2026) and Kommers and Babulak (2025) highlight the convergence of AI, human-centered computing, and cyber nomadism—reflecting future societal shifts toward decentralized, AI-integrated digital lifestyles. These works collectively reveal that cybersecurity strategy must evolve concurrently with advancements in automation, edge intelligence, and human-technology symbiosis.

In healthcare and IoT-driven environments, Kumar et al. (2025) demonstrate how 6G-enabled healthcare frameworks rely on blockchain-based encryption and secure data pathways to guarantee privacy and safety in medical image transmission. As 6G technologies incorporate ultra-dense networks, tactile internet, and zero-latency communication, cybersecurity plays an increasingly critical role in mitigating risks involving patient data manipulation, remote surgery vulnerabilities, and AI-driven diagnostics. Meanwhile, Srivastava et al. (2023) illustrate how smart wearable devices and sensor-driven smart cities require robust cybersecurity foundations to maintain public safety and regulatory compliance.

Cybersecurity is also significantly influenced by intelligent automation and agile methodologies. Babulak et al. (2026) and Polampally et al. (2026) discuss the integration of AI-driven automation tools into agile development processes, highlighting increased efficiency, collaborative intelligence, and rapid adaptation to emerging vulnerabilities. Automation enhances both software development and defensive posturing, enabling continuous scanning for code-level vulnerabilities and automated patching systems that reduce manual intervention. Similarly, Suthar and Ali (2025) highlight how embedded AI within microcontroller-driven systems demonstrates the importance of cybersecurity even in small-scale devices such as gesture recognition tools, signaling that AI-driven cybersecurity must scale across both micro and macro technological ecosystems.

Collectively, these studies converge on a central theme: modern cybersecurity must evolve into a holistic cognitive ecosystem grounded in neuro-symbolic reasoning, generative adversarial intelligence, reinforcement learning, mathematical modeling, and socio-technical governance. The integration of symbolic logic with neural adaptability promotes interpretability and robustness; generative AI enhances adversarial simulation and predictive resilience; reinforcement learning equips systems with autonomous decision optimization; and socio-organizational frameworks ensure human-centered alignment and governance. This multi-layered security vision marks the foundation of self-evolving cyber resilience capable of withstanding adaptive, intelligent, and adversarial digital threats.

Table 1. Concise literature comparison table

Author(s), Year	Focus Area	Contribution to Cybersecurity	Key Insight
Hakim et al. (2025)	Neuro-symbolic AI	Hybrid symbolic–neural reasoning for threat detection	Enhances explainability + detection accuracy
Ferrag et al. (2025)	Generative AI	Review of LLM vulnerabilities and applications	Dual-use nature of generative AI
Uddin et al. (2025)	Generative AI Ops	Threat intelligence and AI-driven cyber operations	Highlights generative AI as both threat and defense tool
Kalutharage et al. (2025)	Explainable IoT Security	Domain-knowledge-driven XAI for IoT attacks	Improved interpretability and reasoning
Radanliev (2025)	Cyber Resilience	Generative AI in resilience-building frameworks	Emphasizes resilience over simple detection

continued on following page

Table 1. Continued

Author(s), Year	Focus Area	Contribution to Cybersecurity	Key Insight
Arifin et al. (2024)	GAN-based Security	Survey on GANs for adversarial simulation	GANs strengthen adversarial training
Nott (2025)	Organizational AI Security	Enterprise adaptation to generative AI risks	Organizational readiness determines cyber resilience
Ali (2025)	RL-based Optimization	Autonomous optimization using RL	RL enhances adaptive cyber-defense
Ali et al. (2023)	Communication Security	Causal convolution for network resilience	Advances 5G/6G security modeling
Babulak (2023)	AI-driven Cyber Attack Prevention	Full-spectrum AI tools for security	Early vision for AI-based defense

The comparison table gives a quick look at the most important academic work that is driving current research in cognitive adversarial security, neuro-symbolic reasoning, and cyber resilience powered by generative AI. Every row shows an important research, what it was about, and how it changed the way people think about cybersecurity innovation. For instance, Hakim et al. (2025) show that neuro-symbolic AI is important by showing how combining symbolic logic with neural learning makes threat detection easier to understand and more reliable, which is a key feature of current explainable cybersecurity systems. Ferrag et al. (2025) and Uddin et al. (2025) expand on this story by looking at how generative AI, such as big language models, makes cyber-defense stronger while also making it easier for hackers to get in, which shows the dual-use issue that is at the heart of AI-driven security research. Kalutharage et al. (2025) concentrate on IoT environments, demonstrating how domain expertise and explainable AI can enhance the identification of intricate multi-stage IoT attacks. In contrast, Radanliev (2025) recontextualizes generative AI within a resilience-focused framework, prioritizing long-term adaptability over mere attack prevention. Research, such Arifin et al. (2024), shows that employing GANs for adversarial simulation makes AI training stronger. Nott (2025) also talks about the organizational and human demands that must be met in order to effectively use generative AI defenses. Ali (2025) and Ali et al. (2023) show how reinforcement learning and sophisticated communication models make network security and autonomous optimization stronger. Finally, Babulak (2023) gives a complete, system-level picture of AI's function in today's cyber settings by linking technology progress with strategic defensive strategy. The table shows how current cybersecurity research is multidisciplinary by bringing together symbolic reasoning, generative threat modeling, adaptive learning, and organizational preparedness to create self-evolving, resilient defensive ecosystems.

RESEARCH METHODS

The research methodology for creating the Cognitive Adversarial Security Neuro framework is based on a combined, multi-layered technical approach that brings together experimental simulation, algorithmic modeling, system-level architectural engineering, and real-world testing across different types of adversarial threats. The methodology's heart is the combination of neuro-symbolic reasoning, generative adversarial simulation, and adaptive optimization driven by reinforcement learning. This requires a sophisticated pipeline that works like real-world cyber ecosystems. The study begins by establishing a heterogeneous experimental framework using both synthetic and authentic cybersecurity datasets that include IoT telemetry, network flow sequences, malware samples, adversarial payloads, and user behavior patterns. We use multi-stage normalization, entropy-based feature extraction, statistical dependency modeling, and attack-vector tagging to preprocess these datasets. This makes sure that the input streams show high-granularity behavioral signals that are needed for cognitive adversarial learning. The experimental setup uses a distributed microservice-based architecture. Each system module—symbolic reasoning core, neural learning engine, generative simulation agent, and RL-based decision optimizer—works as an independent but connected computational node that talks to each other using secure gRPC or message-queue protocols to make sure that information can be sent and received quickly and that the system can grow.

The technique employs a hybrid algorithmic training pipeline, whereby symbolic reasoning models are first developed using domain ontologies, expert-defined rule sets, attack grammars, and formal logic templates sourced from network activity taxonomies. These symbolic rules provide the high-level limits on decisions that make sure the system's rationale is clear and fits with the domain. At the same time, deep neural networks, including as Transformer encoders, causal convolutional networks, and hybrid CNN–GRU anomaly detectors, are trained on a lot of telemetry data to learn hidden representations of both good and bad actions. Differentiable logic embeddings, tensor-based knowledge injection layers, and constraint-satisfaction backpropagation techniques are then used to combine the symbolic and neural parts into a single neuro-symbolic engine that can do both pattern recognition and conceptual inference. This integrated model is then subjected to adversarially generated attack variations created using generative AI models. GANs, diffusion models, and LLM-driven malware synthesizers are taught to create polymorphic threats, hidden payloads, and fake intrusion attempts that are meant to break and challenge traditional detection techniques. An iterative adversarial reinforcement cycle brings these adversarial samples into the training pipeline. This cycle keeps adjusting the neuro-symbolic engine so that it becomes stronger against new attack vectors.

The study utilizes reinforcement learning agents equipped with deep Q-networks (DQN), proximal policy optimization (PPO), and multi-agent actor–critic architectures to attain autonomous optimization and robustness. These agents interact with a fake cyber range that looks like real network infrastructures, such as routers, IoT devices, fog nodes, containers, and cloud orchestration layers. The RL agents constantly check environments with changing threat levels by doing things like isolating nodes, updating firewall rules, changing access rights, or using micro-patching tactics. Every action is either rewarded or punished depending on how the system reacts, how serious the intrusion is, how much service is lost, and the total risk ratings that come from a resilience index based on changes in the system state. The RL agents discover the best ways to defend themselves via billions of simulation steps and adversarial rollouts. These tactics are better for long-term cyber resilience than short-term reactionary classification accuracy. This technique creates a defensive system that can change and react in real time without needing help from those outside the system.

The technique also includes a feedback loop that constantly monitors and feeds real-time telemetry streams back into the neuro-symbolic engine to improve its accuracy and understanding of the environment. To find little problems that happen before big cyber disasters, telemetry is looked at utilizing sliding-window statistical models, time-series decomposition, mutual-information metrics, and attention-based feature attribution approaches. Generative models constantly change the attack distribution depending on how defenses are working, which creates new synthetic threats that show how adversarial learning works. This generates a co-evolutionary loop in which both attacker and defense models grow at the same time. This makes it possible for the study to better mimic how adversaries behave in the actual world. Chaos engineering techniques are used to stress-test the system. This means that random interruptions, service failures, bandwidth saturation, and simultaneous multi-vector assaults are all used to see how strong the system is in really bad situations.

The evaluation approach uses both quantitative and qualitative criteria to quantify how well something can be understood, how strong it is, how adaptable it is, how quickly it can be computed, and how resilient it is. Detection accuracy, false-positive rates, adversarial resilience in gradient-based and black-box assault scenarios, precision of symbolic inference explanations, computational delay, throughput, and system-wide recovery time are all used to measure performance. We use advanced measures like resilience debt, threat containment delay, system entropy reduction, and adaptive policy convergence time to have a better idea of how the cognitive security model may change on its own. Ablation experiments are also done to find out how each subsystem (symbolic layer, neural layer, generative simulator, and RL optimizer) affects overall performance. This lets the researchers figure out how the integrated architecture helps in a synergistic way. Cross-validation is done on more than one dataset and threat scenario to make sure the results can be used in other situations. Simulation-to-reality transfer learning tests are used to see how well the trained defense ecosystem works when it faces attack vectors that have never been seen before in real or almost-real network conditions.

Figure 3. Algorithmic framework

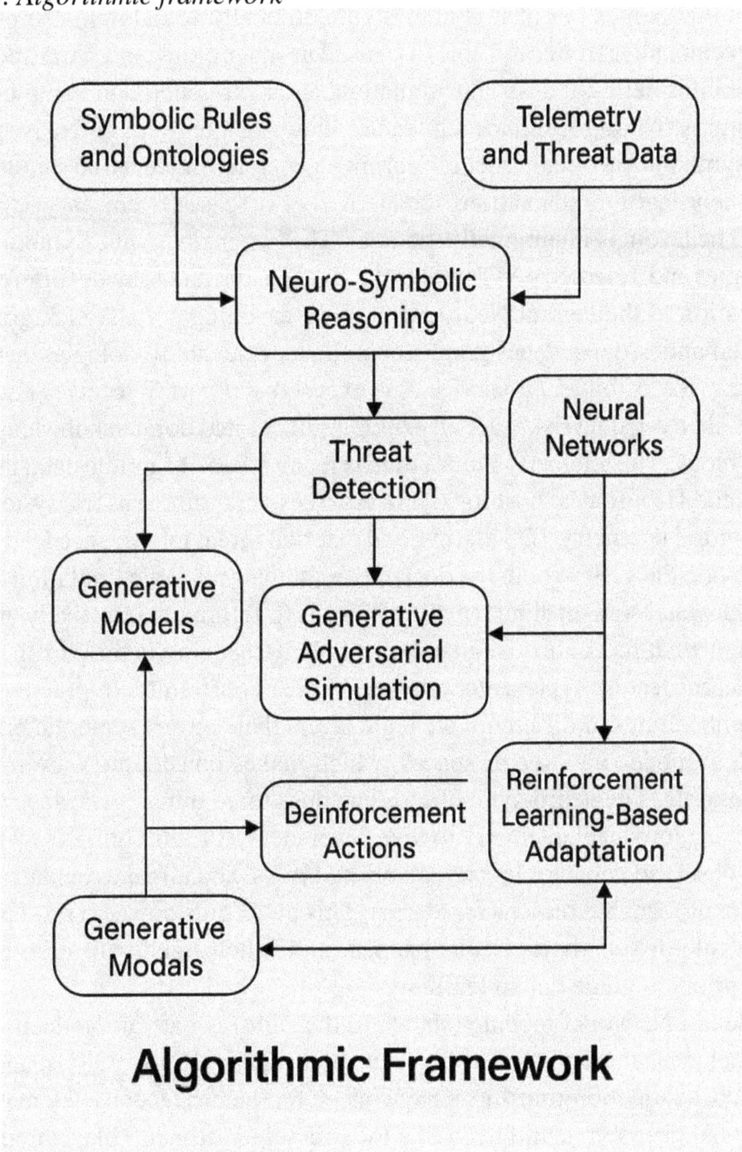

The approach uses Kubernetes clusters to deploy containers, GPU accelerated training for neural and generative models, and hardware-in-the-loop simulation to test on actual IoT devices and embedded systems. To keep the research environment safe from contamination or hostile manipulation, it uses secure multi-party computation, blockchain-based metadata integrity checks, and zero-trust communication restrictions. This strict method makes sure that the cognitive adversarial security ecosystem that comes out of it is not only theoretically sound, but also proven in practice, technically strong, and able to be used in smart cities, smart transportation, healthcare informatics, industrial automation, and next-generation communication infrastructures. The algorithmic architecture shows an integrated defensive pipeline that uses symbolic knowledge, neural learning, generative adversarial synthesis, and reinforcement-learning adaptation to create a cyber-defense system that gets better all the time. The layout is intentionally modular. The two main inputs, Symbolic Rules & Ontologies and Telemetry & Threat Data, sit at the top and provide different types of information to the central Neuro-Symbolic Reasoning core. Attack grammars, protocol semantics, dependency graphs, compliance rules, and ontologies that encode causal links (for example, "if service X is exposed and port Y receives anomalous payload Z, then escalate risk") are all examples of curated domain knowledge in the symbolic block. The telemetry block collects many types of runtime data, including as packet and flow traces, host logs, process trees, endpoint sensors, system calls, user behavioral telemetry, IDS alarms, and external threat intelligence feeds. These inputs provide the system both the declarative, human-readable limitations and the high-dimensional statistical information it needs to figure out how likely an occurrence is and what its context is. Neuro-Symbolic Reasoning is the part that brings together learnt feature representations and logical constraints. In practice, this is done by embeddings or differentiable logic layers that convert symbolic predicates and ontology nodes into vector spaces, which makes constraint-aware neural inference possible. The neuro-symbolic engine does three things: it enriches context by connecting low-level telemetry to high-level ideas, it finds conflicts by figuring out when observed behavior breaks established rules, and it makes explanations by giving human-readable reasons for alarms. This block cuts down on false positives by letting rule-driven short-circuits happen, and it helps generalization by using semantic priors to guide neural learning.

The Neural Networks module (shown to the right) is part of the deep learning stack. It includes temporal models for sequential signals (RNNs, GRUs, and causal convolutions), attention/transformer encoders for heterogeneous telemetry, and convolutional or graph neural networks for structured artifacts (like call graphs or network topologies). These networks create probabilistic threat ratings, anomaly embeddings, and hidden representations of how actors behave. The Threat Detection step takes these outputs and combines symbolic inferences with neural confidences to provide prioritized detection hypotheses, severity estimations, and proposed action sets. Bayesian weighting, learnt gating networks, or constrained optimization may be used in the fusion to make sure that symbolic restrictions reduce model uncertainty in cases when safety is very important.

Generative Adversarial Simulation is underneath Threat Detection and serves as both a testing engine and an adversarial co-learner. When a detection hypothesis or vulnerability is present, generative models (GANs, diffusion models, or LLM-based payload synthesizers) are used to generate credible adversarial variants, including polymorphic payloads, evasive protocol exchanges, or free-form social engineering communications. The simulation serves two functions. First, it stress-tests the detector by making near-boundary examples that show where the model is weak. Second, it makes the defense's training distribution bigger by making synthetic but realistic samples for adversarial training. The arrow from Generative Models (on the left) to Generative Adversarial Simulation shows a place where the simulator may get generative primitives (pretrained GANs, LLM prompt templates, and scenario parameterizations) whenever it needs them. The results of the Generative Adversarial Simulation go into two processes that work at the same time. One example is Reinforcement Learning-Based Adaptation, where simulated assaults are used as environment scenarios to train RL agents (DQN, PPO, actor–critic families) that learn the best ways to protect a system and respond to threats. The RL agents work in a fake cyber-range where they can do things like isolate hosts, change routing, apply micro-patches, rotate keys, throttle flows, or add deception. The RL reward function has more than one goal: it tries to balance service availability, containment speed, cost of cleanup, and collateral damage. This means that learnt policies aim for long-term resilience instead of short-term suppression. The vertical arrow from Neural Networks to RL shows that learnt embeddings and predictive models help the RL state representation and value estimation.

The other way that Generative Adversarial Simulation works is that it goes back to the Generative Models bank and the training pipeline. Successful adversarial examples (those that go undetected) are marked and added to the generative model training/finetuning cycle. This makes the generative bank more realistic and adversarial over time. This produces a co-evolutionary adversarial loop, where generators become better at making stealthy assaults and defenders get better by using adversarial training and RL adaptation. This is the planned "red-team/blue-team" training theme that is built into the framework. Deinforcement Actions (seen in the middle) are the real-world implementation of learnt policies—practical acts taken to reduce harm based on RL policies and symbolic suggestions. In this sense, "deinforcement" may be understood operationally as defensive or remedial operations such as isolation, rollback, quarantine, traffic filtering, and policy enforcement. The RL policies and the fused detection outputs guide these operations, which must be carried out in secure control planes that follow safety rules from the symbolic layer (for example, never shutting down services that are important to life). The arrow in the picture that goes from Deinforcement Actions back to Generative Models shows that the results of the remediations are recorded and utilized to improve both the generative simulations and the RL reward shaping. This closes the feedback loop. Lastly, the framework has an implicit loop for monitoring and validating: telemetry is always updated with the system state after an action, which lets neuro-symbolic reasoning check how well an action worked, change the chances of a risk happening, and make incident reports that people can read. To help choose the right model and fine-tune the hyperparameters, we use evaluation measures including detection precision/recall, containment latency, operating cost, and robustness indices. The platform also takes into account how the models will be used in real life: containerized model serving for low-latency inference, hardware acceleration for generative and RL training, secure model repositories, and provenance logging (for auditability and compliance). From a design point of view, the graphic shows a number of essential technical ideas. First, separation of concerns: the symbolic and neurological parts have different jobs, but they work closely together to make both parts easier to understand and more flexible. Second, co-evolutionary training—generative adversarial synthesis and RL adaptation create a cycle of red-team and blue-team that makes the system stronger with each iteration. Third, safety by constraint—symbolic restrictions operate as guardrails to make sure that autonomous reactions stay below acceptable operational limits. Fourth, data-driven improvement—every telemetry sample, simulation result, and remediation result is a chance to learn that helps make the model better. The graphic also shows operational risks and constraints. Generative models may unintentionally produce too realistic attack artifacts that, if improperly managed, may infiltrate production systems; reinforcement learning agents trained in simulation may encounter transfer gaps from simulation to reality; and symbolic rules need ongoing curation to maintain relevance. Some ways to protect against this include strong sandboxing of generative outputs, randomizing the domain to make it less fragile when moving from simulation to real life, automated ontology versioning, and having a person in the loop for choices that have a big effect. In short, the algorithmic framework figure shows a clear, production-ready design for a cognitive, self-evolving cyber-defense system. It combines declarative domain knowledge, high-capacity neural perception, adversarial generative training, and RL-driven policy optimization into a closed loop that learns from telemetry, tests itself with fake enemies, and improves its defense strategies on its own while following symbolic safety rules. This combination of interpretable logic and adaptive learning offers a systematic approach to creating strong, self-sufficient cybersecurity in contexts where AI may be used to attack.

CONCLUSION

There has been a significant shift away from mechanical, reactive defense models and toward autonomous, knowledge-infused, and continually self-optimizing security ecosystems, which is signaled by the research of Cognitive Adversarial Security Neuro structures. This represents a key turning point in the development of cybersecurity science. Using neuro-symbolic reasoning, generative adversarial simulation, reinforcement learning, and high-granularity telemetry analytics, the next generation of cyber-defense systems will be able to not only recognize malicious patterns, but also comprehend, predict, and strategically outmaneuver intelligent adversaries in real time. This capability will allow these systems to be more effective than ever before. This multidimensional synthesis generates a protective environment in which reasoning, perception, and adaptability coexist. This environment enables computers to evaluate threats with contextual awareness that is comparable to that of humans while concurrently learning beyond the cognitive boundaries of humans.

There is a definite convergence toward hybrid intelligence as the foundation of cyber resilience, as shown by the research that has been examined throughout this chapter. Neuro-symbolic artificial intelligence offers the necessary framework for explainability and rule-based coherence, so addressing the critiques that have been leveled against deep learning for a long time about its opaqueness and fragility. By explicitly embedding ontologies, regulatory constraints, attack grammars, and causal structures into the computational substrate of the machine, the system is able to acquire a transparent decision foundation that continues to be stable even when confronted with situations that are unanticipated or that have been constructed by adversaries. The extraction of latent behavioral signals from enormous telemetry streams is being done simultaneously by deep neural networks. These architectures are able to capture subtle patterns that are difficult to codify manually. Cognitive cybersecurity systems are able to simultaneously reason deductively and generalize inductively, which is a capability that traditional models usually lack. This capacity is ensured by the synergistic combination of these two methodologies.

By building a controlled adversarial environment in which the defense learns from synthetic assaults that are more complex than those seen in real-world datasets, generative artificial intelligence significantly increases the frontier of achievable defensive capabilities. As a result of the continual generation of new types of deception, polymorphic malware, and evasive methods by GANs, diffusion models, and LLM-driven red-team engines, the defensive learning model is essentially transformed into an adversary-aware system that is able to anticipate how sophisticated attackers can grow. This is in line with the growing understanding that cyber resilience cannot be achieved solely through the retrospective analysis of historical incident data; rather, it requires anticipatory intelligence that is trained against the unknown and the something that has not yet emerged. As a result, the cognitive adversarial method recasts the issue of cybersecurity as an evolutionary competition rather than a static technical challenge. Through the ability to perform autonomous strategy optimization in either real-world or simulated cyber settings, reinforcement learning brings an essential new dimension to the table. Instead of relying on reaction playbooks that have been specified by humans, RL agents learn via millions of adversarial encounters, which allows them to find sophisticated defensive strategies that reduce systemic risk while maintaining service continuity. It is because of this that cyber-defense systems are able to carry out complicated judgments, such as dynamic micro-segmentation, real-time endpoint confinement, adaptive trust modulation, and deception deployment, based on learned predictions of long-term resilience rather than immediate threat reduction. These systems, over the course of time, acquire preferences for policies that minimize ecological vulnerability throughout the whole of the digital infrastructure. As a result, resilience becomes an emergent quality rather than a limitation that is designed. The multidisciplinary study presented in this chapter demonstrates that the future of cyber resilience is dependent not only on the technological mechanisms, but also on organizational preparation, socio-technical change, and human-AI partnership. Because of the growing autonomy that cognitive security systems are afforded, it is necessary to have governance structures that are transparent, auditing frameworks that are rigorous, and operational rules that are ethically aligned. This is done to guarantee that choices powered by AI continue to be responsible and in line with human values. During this transformation, organizational adaptability serves as a crucial component; businesses are required to reorganize workflows, redefine specialist roles, and build cultures of continuous learning that are capable of comprehending and overseeing intelligent cybersecurity systems. In the absence of such adaptability, even the most sophisticated cognitive structures run the danger of becoming misaligned or falling short of their potential. In addition, the proliferation of cyber-physical systems, ecosystems for the internet of things, and infrastructures that are enabled with 6G technology makes the need for self-evolving defense even more pressing. Even relatively small attack surfaces have the potential to evolve into catastrophic systemic failures as the use of artificial intelligence (AI) to govern digital substrates becomes more prevalent in key areas such as healthcare, transportation, smart cities, autonomous robots, and global communication networks. There is a vulnerability that may be addressed by cognitive adversarial ecosystems. These ecosystems enable cyber-defense mechanisms that are not only quick and precise, but also anticipatory, robust, and contextually self-correcting. Their ability to learn from telemetry, adapt to enemies that generate their own content, and act independently puts them in a position to be the most feasible security paradigm for the hyperconnected world that will emerge in the next decades. The accumulated findings of previous research highlight the importance of cybersecurity evolving from practices that are fragmented and focused on tools to ecosystems that are united, intelligence-driven, and grounded in cognitive reasoning and adversarial co-evolution. Cognitive security systems need to be able to not only equal adversaries but also transcend them by using the complete spectrum of symbolic logic, neural abstraction, generative creativity, and reinforcement-driven strategy. This is because the frequency, complexity, and autonomy of intelligent threats are increasing. Cybersecurity is now a living, dynamic discipline that is regularly refining itself in response to adversary demands, operational failures, and environmental changes. This shift establishes cybersecurity as a discipline that is always changing. In summary, the Cognitive Adversarial Security Neuro framework is the core blueprint for the next-generation cyber-defense structures. These architectures are systems that are able to think, learn, simulate, explain, adapt, resist, and eventually develop. These ecosystems are the embodiment of the future of cyber resilience. They are intelligent, autonomous, anticipatory, and deeply aligned with the dynamic realities of digital risk. They are achieved through the unification of symbolic interpretability, neural perception, generative adversarial innovation, and reinforcement-based strategic mastery. Such self-evolving defensive systems will not be optional upgrades but rather critical cornerstones that will preserve the stability, safety, and trustworthiness of the digital society that is yet to come. This is because global infrastructures are becoming more sophisticated and interconnected.

REFERENCES

Ali, S. I. (2025). Reinforcement learning for autonomous optimization in intelligent engineering. In Babulak, E. (Ed.), *AI-driven approaches for fully automated smart engineering* (pp. 313–344). IGI Global Scientific Publishing., DOI: 10.4018/979-8-3373-4839-1.ch011

Ali, S. I., ... (2023). Causal convolution employing Almeida–Pineda recurrent backpropagation for mobile network design. *ICTACT Journals, 2023(0460).* https://ictactjournals.in/paper/IJCT_Vol_14_Iss_4_Paper_10_3091_3096.pdf

Babulak, E. (2006). Information cyberspace and future cyber homes. [iJOE]. *International Journal of Online and Biomedical Engineering*, *2*(2). Advance online publication. DOI: 10.3991/ijoe.v2i2.338

Babulak, E. (2010). Global cyberspace. *AMS 2010: Asia Modelling Symposium 2010 – 4th International Conference on Mathematical Modelling and Computer Simulation* (pp. xxv–xxvi). IEEE. DOI: 10.1109/AMS.2010.12

Babulak, E. (2010). The 21st century cyberspace. *SAMI 2010 – 8th International Symposium on Applied Machine Intelligence and Informatics* (pp. 21–24). IEEE. DOI: 10.1109/SAMI.2010.5423748

Babulak, E. (2023). *AI tools for protecting and preventing sophisticated cyber attacks*. IGI Global., DOI: 10.4018/978-1-6684-7110-4

Babulak, E. (Ed.). (2026). *The social impact of next-generation smart cyber technology*. IGI Global Scientific Publishing., DOI: 10.4018/979-8-3373-5656-3

Babulak, E., Kumar, A., Guru, D., Kudithipudi, K., Maddini, S., Gonaygunta, H., & Nadella, S. (2026). Human-centric AI tools into agile methodologies for optimized software development. In Babulak, E. (Ed.), *AI-driven approaches for fully automated smart engineering* (pp. 41–84). IGI Global Scientific Publishing., DOI: 10.4018/979-8-3373-4839-1.ch002

Ferrag, M. A., Alwahedi, F., Battah, A., Cherif, B., Mechri, A., Tihányi, N., Bisztray, T., & Debbah, M. (2025). Generative AI in Cybersecurity: A Comprehensive Review of LLM Applications and Vulnerabilities. Internet of Things and Cyber–Physical Systems. arXiv+1DOI: 10.1016/j.iotcps.2025.01.001

Hakim, S. B., Adil, M., Velásquez, A., Xu, S., & Song, H. H. (2025). Neuro-Symbolic AI for Cybersecurity: State of the Art, Challenges and Opportunities. arXiv Preprint. arXiv:2509.06921. arXiv+1

Kalutharage, C. S., Liu, X., & Chrysoulas, C. (2025). *Neurosymbolic learning and domain knowledge-driven explainable AI for enhanced IoT network attack detection and response. Computers & Security*, 151, 104318. SpringerLink+1DOI: 10.1016/j.cose.2025.104318

Kommers, P., & Babulak, E. (2025). Conceptual awareness for human navigation in A.I. In Babulak, E. (Ed.), *Educational AI humanoid computing devices for cyber nomads* (pp. 1–14). IGI Global., DOI: 10.4018/979-8-3693-8985-0.ch001

Kumar, S. N., Joy, J., Jane, I. C., James, A., John, S., & Babulak, E. (2025). Applications of 6G in the healthcare sector and the importance of network security and data privacy encryption of medical images using the SHA-256 blockchain algorithm. In *Network Security and Data Privacy in 6G Communication: Trends, Challenges, and Applications* (pp. 176–190). CRC Press. DOI: 10.1201/9781003583127-9

Massam, P., & Babulak, E. (2003). A decent service level. *Communications Engineer, 1*(3), 34–37. DOI: 10.1049/ce:20030313

Nia, M. A., Atani, R. E., Fabian, B., & Babulak, E. (2016). On detecting unidentified network traffic using pattern-based random walk. *Security and Communication Networks, 9*(16), 3509–3526. DOI: 10.1002/sec.1557

Nott, C. (2025). Organizational Adaptation to Generative AI in Cybersecurity: A Systematic Review. arXiv. arXiv:2506.12060.

Pattanaik, B., Kumari, S. S., Kumar, C. K., Pattnaik, M., Ali, S. I., & Kumarasamy, M. (2023). An innovation of algebraic mathematical-based statistical analysis model for complex number theory. In *Proceedings of the 2023 International Conference on Disruptive Technologies (ICDT)* (pp. 94–99). IEEE. DOI: 10.1109/ICDT57929.2023.10151169

Polampally, S. K., Nadella, G. S., Ragunayakula, S., Kumar, V. J., Kankala, S., & Babulak, E. (2026). AI-driven automation in agile software development teams enhancing efficiency and collaboration. In Babulak, E. (Ed.), *AI-driven approaches for fully automated smart engineering* (pp. 85–132). IGI Global Scientific Publishing., DOI: 10.4018/979-8-3373-4839-1.ch003

Radanliev, P. (2025). *Generative AI cybersecurity and resilience. Frontiers in Artificial Intelligence*, Article 1568360. Frontiers Arifin, M. M., Ahmed, M. S., Ghosh, T. K., Akhand Udoy, I., Zhuang, J., & Yeh, J.-H. (2024, July 11). *A Survey on the Application of Generative Adversarial Networks in Cybersecurity: Prospective, Direction and Open Research Scopes*. arXiv. arXiv:2407.08839. arXivDOI: 10.3389/frai.2025.1568360

Salian, D. T., Elkhodari, G., Neouchi, R., Brown, S., Babulak, E., & Sbeit, R. (2026). A new approach to improving natural language processing capabilities using generative AI: A systematic review and future perspectives. In Babulak, E. (Ed.), *The social impact of next-generation smart cyber technology* (pp. 139–172). IGI Global Scientific Publishing., DOI: 10.4018/979-8-3373-5656-3.ch005

Srivastava, S. S., Ali, S. I., Srivastava, A. K., & Goswami, C. (2024). Improving 5G network performance with MIMO technology using beamforming algorithm. *ICTACT Journal on Communication Technology*, *15*(2), 3173–3180. DOI: 10.21917/ijct.2024.0472

Srivastava, S. T. C., Sharmiladevi, D., Sugumar, D., Ali, S. I., Jones Mary, T. A., & Kumar, S. (2023). Using a smart wearable device monitoring the social distance in smart cities. In *2023 International Conference on Research Methodologies in Knowledge Management, Artificial Intelligence and Telecommunication Engineering (RMKMATE)* (pp. 1–5). IEEE. DOI: 10.1109/RMKMATE59243.2023.10369118

Suthar, B., & Ali, S. I. (2025). A survey on hand gesture sign language recognition with Arduino Leonardo. In *2025 International Conference on Computational, Communication and Information Technology (ICCCIT)* (pp. 111–115). IEEE. DOI: 10.1109/ICCCIT62592.2025.10927994

Uddin, M., Irshad, M. S., Ali, I., Alanazi, F., Ahmed, F., Maaz, M., Hussain, S., & Ullah, S. S. (2025). Generative AI revolution in cybersecurity: A comprehensive review of threat intelligence and operations. [ResearchGate]. *Artificial Intelligence Review*, *58*(8), 236. Advance online publication. DOI: 10.1007/s10462-025-11219-5

Chapter 6
Explainable and Generative AI in Cybersecurity:
Global Implementation Analysis

A. R. Deepti
http://orcid.org/0009-0003-4320-517X
Acharya Institute of Graduate Studies, India

Farzeen Basith
http://orcid.org/0009-0003-5475-684X
Acharya Institute of Graduate Studies, India

B. Manimekala
http://orcid.org/0000-0002-4776-867X
Christ University, India

ABSTRACT

This chapter examines global implementation of explainable and generative AI in cybersecurity across diverse frameworks. Through comprehensive analysis across multiple countries and sectors, the study demonstrates AI-enhanced systems deliver considerable improvements in threat detection while reducing costs and response times. The key contributions include implementation frameworks, cross-cultural adaptation strategies, bias mitigation, and ROI methodologies. The critical challenges addressed include integration complexity, skills gaps, and ethical considerations.

DOI: 10.4018/979-8-2600-1608-4.ch006

1. INTRODUCTION TO THE AI-CYBERSECURITY CONVERGENCE

In information technology the AI and cybersecurity plays an important area since the rise of network computing architectures. This emphasizes to meet, a new way of change for organizations regarding management threat, incident response, assessment of risk and security governance in complex digital environments.

The development of AI in security can be regarded as noticeable levels of evolution that was considered by the game-changing innovations which shaped the course of cybersecurity. The intersections of AI and cybersecurity have also seen a series of transformations from the early expert systems of the 1980s including those developed at Stanford Research Institute Denning (1987) to today's advanced neural networks capable to detect not only new ways for attack but to explain fine grained threat behaviours to state-of-the-art progress in explainable AI Anderson (2008).

1.1 The Economic and Strategic Imperative for AI-Enhanced Cybersecurity

Present-day security problems demand solutions that encompass beyond technical borders. There was loss in digital economy globally of around €8.2 trillion in 2024 due to insufficient cybersecurity, with this number exceeding €14 trillion by 2030 at a compound annual growth rate (CAGR) of 9% CFG (2025). These estimated losses are greater than the entire GDP of most developed nations and account for about 12% of global projection output in 2030.

AI-fabricated media have provided financial fraud that exceeds $25M in a single attack, an increase of 340% over previous years when similar attacks relied on human driven social engineering strategies DeepStrike (2025). According to the 2024 Global Cybersecurity Inde the advanced AI-enabled cybersecurity capable countries have 45% more capacity to quickly rebound from a state-sponsored cyberattack and recover 60% faster after a major security incident.

1.2 Technological Complexity and Integration Challenges

The use of AI in the security design can also bring unparalleled technical complexity to the aspects of cybersecurity. Today's AI-based cybersecurity system has to operate over various technology environment, with existing security controls integration, and provide real-time response while processing huge volumes of data including network flow analysis, endpoint data monitoring, behavioural analytics and threat data intelligence.

With AI-driven cybersecurity systems demand stronger and more reliable technical foundations, the gap between research prototypes and production-ready code continues to narrow. So specialized AI-optimized processing units are needed by researchers for real-time inference, and distributed computing frameworks have been developed for large-scale data processing; advanced storage and retrieval systems that can manage petabyte-scale security datasets and high-level networking infrastructure to provide low-latency communication distributed across global enterprise environments.

Moreover, the problem becomes increasingly difficult in ensuring explainability and transparency of AI decision process. For traditional machine learning algorithms, especially deep neural networks (DNNs), are treated as "black boxes", shows a lack of insights into how decisions are processed which presents an important practical limitation for operational security applications, where security analysts need to interpret and verify AI-based recommendations, study the specifics of security incidents and deliver the complete reports to regulatory authorities.

1.3 Cultural and Organizational Transformation Requirements

The adoption of successful AI-powered security not only requires technology; major organizational and cultural changes are also essential. Companies will need to re-examine security governance, processes and role distribution so that humans and AI systems can collaborate freely across different regulatory domains and cultures. AI security is a global skills gap, this further reinforces the requirement for formal training models and directed change management processes supported by transparent communication channels for building trust in explain-able and generative AI across multiple stakeholders. The subsequent part of this chapter describes in greater detail how these cultural, organizational, and competence drivers appear at the regional and sector level, as well as their effects on real-world implementation outcomes.

This chapter presents techniques and best practices for achieving AI in cybersecurity that meet technological requirements along with recognizing sociotechnical challenges such as organizational culture, compliance, and ethics. Key to the contributions are guidelines for cross-cultural adaptation mechanisms, explainability-centric system requirements with intricate neural network architectures, and structure for how to address algorithm bias and ethics related issues in a systematic manner.

The chapter includes ethical considerations via bias-mitigation approaches, legal-liability formative patterns, and human-factors engineering (HFI), for example dealing with cognitive load. The chapter also discusses privacy implications, models for accountability and the implementation challenges including lack of systems integration, skills shortages, and cultural change. Next are region and sector-specific sections that detail in the following sections of how this scale is playing out in these areas, offering practical considerations for responsible AI adoption in security.

2. HISTORICAL EVOLUTION AND THEORETICAL FOUNDATIONS

2.1 Four-Decade Evolution of AI in Cybersecurity

AI-based security has been developing by means of four major AI-driven approaches, and it is a turning point both regarding technical possibilities as well as cognitive paradigms/operational realization principles. This evolution was stimulated by trends in computer science, AI research, threat sources, and corporate security requirements that have influenced the current condition of AI enhancement in cybersecurity.

2.1.1 Phase I: Expert Systems Era (1980s-1990s) - Foundation and Formalization

The earliest uses of AI in the security backdate to the early 1980s, when expert systems emerged as the first systematic attempt to capture human-based security knowledge in a form that could support automated reasoning about security breaches and threat indicators. The key elements of this period were rule engines that are capable of treating security logs and infer decision based on knowledge insights developed with cyber-security domain experts.

One of the early works in this era is the Intrusion Detection Expert System (IDES) developed at Stanford Research Institute (SRI) International, which initiated development in 1984 and released its first version in 1987 Lunt et al. (1988). IDES outlined a new class of model-based automated security monitoring systems, which joined statistical outlier detection with rule-based inference regarding user and system behavior. The work defined typical behavioural profiles for both user and systems, and employed if-then rules to sense any deviations that could specify the potential threats.

The principles laid in this period set instance for today's cybersecurity operations. The CIA triad is attributed to the The Department of Defence Trusted Computer System Evaluation Criteria (TCSEC) published in 1985, and known as the "Orange Book" publicly identified criteria used to judge computer security. This key structure defined criteria for evaluating security and classification systems, and also it provided the theoretical foundation upon which following cyber security has been built.

The Orange Book classified security into four divisions (D, C, B and A), where D offers minimal protection while A having the greatest confidence of assurance in security Division C-1 providing Discretionary Security Protection, Division C-2: Mandatory Security Protection and Division B: Mandatory Security Verification. This categorization informed public procurement policies, commercial product design, and academic research programmes for many years.

Such specifications of this phase had several features like deterministic reasoning mechanisms, explicit use of knowledge captured using formal logic forms, and limited versatility to new attack forms efficiently. First-generation expert systems of this period used forward-chaining and backward-chaining inference engines to examine security-event data for deviations from a system's configuration specifications. Although these systems proved the feasibility of automated security analysis and established important instances for human-computer teamwork in the domain of cybersecurity, and encountered obstacles such as knowledge acquisition bottlenecks and lack of resilience to novel attack patterns Buchanan and Shortliffe, (1984).

The knowledge acquisition was especially troublesome for the recently emerged field of security, where domain experts were not able to easily codify their implicit knowledge in formal rule structures expected by expert systems. Further, the rigor of predefined rules made these systems to under-perform when facing new situations (not represented in their standard knowledge bases) and thus susceptible to novel attack methods, which did not follow regular patterns.

2.1.2 Phase II: Statistical and Machine Learning Integration (1990s-2000s) - Probabilistic Revolution

The second generation brought statistical learning methods and early machine learning algorithms for automated security analysis that were capable of outperforming and maintaining the benefit of rule-based systems. In this timeframe, it has also become increasingly evident that cybersecurity issues are fundamentally probabilistic in nature (as opposed to the typical coding-based "deterministic" problems), and should be addressed using techniques that can handle uncertainty effectively while adapting to rapidly changing security risks.

In earlier work, Wenke Lee and Salvatore Stolfo at Columbia University, used data mining algorithms for intrusion detection purposes Lee and Stolfo, (1998) and showed that machine learning algorithms can be trained by using labelled datasets to differentiate between normal and risky network behaviours without clear rule generation. Also, this approach dealt with knowledge acquisition by learning patterns themselves from data directly instead of depending on built in expert knowledge systems.

The Knowledge Discovery and Data Mining (KDD) Cup 1999 dataset, which was released as a result of this study, has served as a standard for evaluation on intrusion detection algorithms and laid numerous following years of work. Despite its age and the shortcomings of this particular dataset, versions of it still continue to be used for the purpose of algorithm development and comparison in performance, featuring to the significant impact of this ground work.

This time frame also marked the regulation of defence-in-depth, realizing that no single security measure is able to provide protection against advanced adversary threats. Structured security designs using a wide range of multiple defensive technologies and methods became the norm. Schneier (2000) and remain a main principle in today's security, now extended to include specific AI considerations.

Progress was made with theories emphasizing statistical analysis and pattern recognition made a major change from rule-based approach to statistical reasoning principle which is capable of handling uncertainty and conform to dynamic conditions. The prominent machine learning algorithms adopted were Support Vector Machines (SVMs) for malware classification, where it is a good fit due to its performance in high-dimensional feature spaces and in binary classification scenarios, Artificial Neural Networks (ANNs), being used to carry out feed-forward multi-layer perceptron for network intrusion detection and receiving non-linear relationships, Clustering, which was used for anomaly detection and fraud analysis Axelsson (2000). Although these earlier applications marked by resource and training limitations of the eras, they have proven machine learning to be promising for detecting hidden patterns in cybersecurity.

2.1.3 Phase III: Deep Learning and Behavioral Analytics Revolution (2000s-2015) - Transformation Era

In this era, deep learning architectures and large-scale behavioral analysis platforms were now at the forefront of theoretical sophistication and operational capability. This era witnessed the progress of advances in neural network training techniques, access to big data, and increased computing capabilities allowed for building bigger and more complex models.

The Ian Goodfellow et al. (2014) invention of Generative Adversarial Networks (GANs), led to a change in generative modelling and revealed new sources of vulnerability through adversarial examples. GANs use a generator- discriminator model where the generator generates synthetic data and the discriminator discriminates it from real data.

Adversarial examples, found by Christian Szegedy et al. in (2013), highlighted how machine learning models could be driven to make confident, but incorrect predictions using small and well-crafted input levels, thus revealing the dual-use aspect of AI tools in computer security.

During this period behavioral analytics stages were forced to evolve or else become obsolete; they began learning from vast datasets of complex patterns, while detecting subtle deviations that suggest possible security-related incidents. Companies like Splunk, IBM QRadar and Darktrace created tools that could ingest large amounts of security data to detect new threats.

The concept of representation learning came into focus, and a shift toward representation-learning–based approaches was achieved by automating high-dimensional data pattern recognition without manual feature-engineering effort. CNNs were used for malware identification by treating executables as images, and RNNs and LSTMs were effective for sequential data such as network traffic or system logs.

User and Entity Behavior Analytics (UEBA) platforms have become crucial in identifying insider threats and advanced constant threats by collecting basic behavioral patterns for users, devices, and applications, which can help detect tiny variances indicative of compromise or malicious activity Chandola et al. (2009).

2.1.4 Phase IV: Explainable and Generative AI Era (2015-Present) - Transparency and Trustworthy

The current phase is focused on the transparency, trustworthiness and more sophisticated generative capabilities of AI in cybersecurity. This phase is characterised by the realization that AI systems in safety-critical domains must be understandable if humans are expected to trust them, as regulations take effect and effective analysis of instances is necessary.

The current phase is focused on the transparency, trustworthiness and more sophisticated generative capabilities of AI in cybersecurity. This phase is characterised by the realization that AI systems in safety-critical domains must be understandable if people are expected to trust them, as regulations take effect and genuine analysis of instances is necessary. Notable progress comes in the form of LIME (Local Interpretable Model-agnostic Explanations;), which can provide local explanations for any black-box model by fitting a simpler, interpretable model to an instance that we want explained.

Thus, the development of explainable AI (XAI) methods specially formulated for cybersecurity has become vital as organizations demand complete understanding of the operations and decision-making of AI for compliance with regulations, audit trail, and operation efficiency. Notable progress comes in the form of LIME (Local Interpretable Model-agnostic Explanations), which can provide local explanations for any black-box model by fitting a simpler, interpretable model to an instance that need to be explained. Ribeiro et al. (2016) study constructs interpretable models to account for prediction one at a time, and SHAP (SHapley Additive exPlanations) Lundberg & Lee, (2017) that offers a new mathematically sound framework for local as well global explanations on a given model.

At the same time, large language models and advanced generative AI have unlocked new defensive and offensive capabilities, such as automatic threat report generation, natural language interfaces to security tools, and recognition of refined insider threats. Yet these technologies are also creating new side channel, such as AI-generated phishing, synthetic malware, and deepfakes illustrating the dual-use nature of such advances.

The present stage has also observed the development of cybersecurity-targeted basis models such as those trained on threat intelligence data at scale, identification of vulnerabilities in software via code analysis, and specific networking traffic analysis. These are signs that AI cybersecurity is growing from experimental deployments to production-grade solutions that can manage enterprise-scale security operations. The transition from expert systems to current explainable and generative AI exposes common patterns used in the recent global applications described in Table 1.

Table 1. Evolution timeline of AI in cybersecurity

Phase	Time Period	Key Technologies	Major Breakthroughs	Representative Systems
Phase I	1980s-1990s	Expert Systems	IDES (1987), Orange Book (1985)	Rule-based inference engines
Phase II	1990s-2000s	Statistical ML	KDD Cup 1999, Defense-in-depth	SVM, Neural networks
Phase III	2000s-2015	Deep Learning	GANs (2014), Adversarial examples (2013)	CNNs, RNNs, UEBA platforms
Phase IV	2015-Present	XAI & GenAI	LIME (2016), SHAP (2017), GPT models	Transformers, Foundation models

The following study shows how these historical lessons have been applied across different local cultural, regulatory, and social environments; that is, regional interpretations of successful approaches to providing AI-enhanced cybersecurity while meeting local norms and requirements.

3: GLOBAL PERSPECTIVES AND CROSS-CULTURAL IMPLEMENTATION

Global implementation of AI in cybersecurity systems offers diverse regional divisions in strategies, priorities, tactics, and cultural leaning corresponding with differences along cultural dimensions, risk environments, technological readiness, and regional threat structures. Understanding these differences is important for cross-border organizations and for developing AI applications that can work internationally but are sensitive to local customs, laws, and cultural norms.

3.1 Regional Variations in AI Cybersecurity Approaches

3.1.1 Implementation in the Asia-Pacific Region and Integration with Culture

A wide range of AI cybersecurity approaches in the Asia–Pacific region shows differences in technological terms, control measures, cultural views toward automation and privacy, and beliefs about shared security duties versus personal security responsibilities. These differences are early indications of how culture and regulation influence the adoption of AI in cybersecurity.

Singapore manages in global AI governance with its Model AI Governance Framework, that was issued first in 2019 and substantially updated in 2020 has become a global standard setter Ministry of Communications and Information Singapore, (2020). The framework centres on model governance and algorithmic accountability, with requisite to all security-critical applications will need an AI impact assessment. Risk, such as bias, data privacy breaches, safety concerns, and security vulnerabilities are some of the issues companies need to consider before implementing AI. The Singapore approach focuses on human control, ensuring that AI systems complement rather than replace human decision-making in critical security choices.

Japan's intentional approach to AI cybersecurity as part of a broader national digitalization with the Society 5.0 program by combining security into its wider set of initiatives in that area Cabinet Office Japan, (2019). It emphasizes the partnership between human and A.I., merging of culture. Japanese companies prefer sophisticated AI decision making system rather than fully automated with no humans, and as a result, hybrid architectures where AI operates in parallel with intensive human monitoring.

The Chinese approach is based on cyber governance, social stability and digital autonomy, enabling for the sweeping collection of big data to recognize and pre-empt threats in their entirety. In particular, the national intelligence law and its implementing regulations impose a number of conditions on international organisations operating AI cybersecurity systems in China, including data positioning and government access conditions Roberts et al. (2021). China's advanced AI ability allows more complex systems to be developed that can look across multiple industries and different sources of data at the same time.

3.1.2 European Union (EU) Regulatory Leadership and Framework Development

The EU is becoming a global AI standard setter in AI control regulation, law and cybersecurity. Adopted in 2024, the Comprehensive EU Artificial Intelligence Act offers the most detailed legal framework for AI systems and sets out specific rules on cybersecurity applications that create certain legal responsibility for the organizations operating within the jurisdiction of an EU member state.

High-risk AI systems, including many applications in cybersecurity, must meet strict requirements: full conformity assessment, constant quality control, effective data governance, transparency and documentation for traceability, clear human oversight, high accuracy levels (potentially including resilience in case of failure modes), and safety measures to protect the AI system from attacks.

The interrelation between the compliance requirements of GDPR and AI-based cybersecurity systems appears in complex control system structure and operational. Article 22 ('right to explanation') under which people should be able to challenge decisions made by automated processes that have a substantial impact on individual's lives Goodman and Flaxman (2017), consequently requiring AI systems to provide insight into the reasons for security while maintaining operational effectiveness.

The European Commission's Invest AI plan aims for €200 billion of investment in trustworthy AI over the next seven years and selects cybersecurity applications that maintain individual privacy by enabling threat detection and response features European Commission, (2025). This investment will support the further development of secure machine learning techniques, federated learning for multinational cybersecurity cooperation, and groundbreaking explainable AI methods for security applications.

Figure 1. Global AI cybersecurity investment distribution

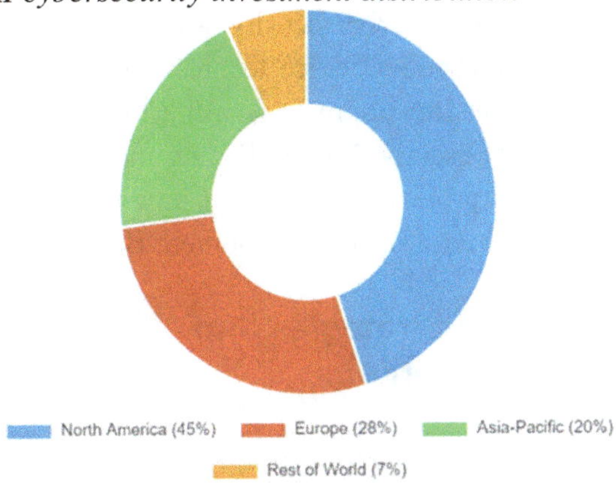

3.1.3 Developing Nation Perspectives and Resource-Constrained Innovation

AI based cyber security systems are spread in developing countries where the aspect of limited resources, infrastructural gap, skill shortage and special threat landscape is an issue. Such circumstances necessitate novel, localized cybersecurity strategies that use collaboration and capabilities development.

In 2025, BRICS nations (Brazil, Russia, India, China, and South Africa) took several joint actions to collaborate more in the area of cybersecurity by jointly focusing on information sharing, incident response and research collaborations. Inter-state agreements in February 2025, following a BRICS Working Group on Security in the use of ICTs meeting from January 1-11 in Brasilia, the member states addressed joint efforts to resist cyber threats etc (BRICS Secretariat, 2025; TVBRICS, 2025) establishment memorandums of understanding between incident response teams, created direct communication between law enforcement, and promoted academic cooperation to develop cybersecurity skills. Such efforts decrease dependence on overseas technology and advance digital control like the BRICS Digital Silk Road initiative project, which supports secure digital infrastructure and AI-based cybersecurity solutions.

Otieno (2020) emphasizes the need to raise awareness about cybersecurity and to bridge infrastructure and skills gaps in developing countries, highlighting that increasing stakeholder awareness, enabling cooperation, and promoting flexible cybersecurity approaches are crucial in resource-limited environments.

Latin American governments have also underlined the need for regional AI cybersecurity cooperation, including through institutions such as the Inter-American

Development Bank (IDB). The IDB, in partnership with Israel, launched a $2 million cybersecurity program to enhance cybersecurity capacity throughout Latin America and the Caribbean by providing policy advice, technical assistance, expertise exchange and training (Inter-American Development Bank), (2022). The IDB also finances regional projects in support of sectoral strengthening and regional capacity-building in cybersecurity as well as protection of critical infrastructure through technical cooperation activities (Inter-American Development Bank), (2025).

3.2 Cultural Adaptation Strategies and Implementation Frameworks

To ensure that AI cybersecurity systems are effectively deployed across different cultures, cultural factors associated with technology acceptance, trust, long-term success, and organizational adoption must be systematically considered. Cultural adaptation acknowledges differences not only in language but also in communication style, perception of authority, sense of privacy and collective or individual responsibility. Main attributes of cultural adaptation are: Communication style preferences that serve to adjust explanations of AI decisions in consideration of local norms. Authority structure recognition provides decision making flows that take into account hierarchical or consensual models. Privacy expectation accommodation ensures that data handling practices are consistent with local legal and cultural norms, and Trust-building mechanism's implement processes to establish trust in the AI systems by various entities.

Table 2. Cultural adaptation framework comparison

Region	Authority Structure	Privacy Approach	AI Acceptance	Key Adaptations Required
Singapore	Centralized	Balanced	High	Governance framework compliance
Japan	Consensus-driven	High protection	Medium	Human-AI harmony (wa)
EU	Regulatory	Very high	Medium	GDPR + AI Act compliance
China	Hierarchical	State-controlled	High	Data localization requirements

As illustrated in Table 2, effective implementation of AI cybersecurity requires the development of region-specific strategies that complement local governance systems, privacy preferences and technology adoption. AI systems need to be adapted for central decision marking in Singapore, consensus-based processes in Japan, high regulation in the EU and hierarchy data governance structures in China if they are to be successfully deployed and adopted longer term.

4. ADVANCED TECHNICAL IMPLEMENTATION AND ARCHITECTURE ANALYSIS

Using of explainable and generative AI for cybersecurity necessitates more intricated neural network architectures, specialized computing hardware, as well as new algorithmic methods. These jointly address the trade-offs between various objectives, such as optimizing performance in model learning and model interpretability, scalability and robustness against adversarial attacks to ensure enterprise-ready deployment that can be trusted.

4.1 Deep Learning Architectures for Explainable Cybersecurity Applications

The growth of explainable AI systems requires neural network architectures that are essentially explainable while preserving high complexity in recognizing even the complex patterns for threat detection. Attention-based systems are especially useful, as they point out which input features have the greatest influence on security decisions and help analysts justify AI inference mechanisms.

4.1.1 Transformer Architectures for Sequential Threat Analysis and Temporal Pattern Recognition

Transformer-based architectures, which emerged from the natural language processing space, have experienced notably success in cybersecurity when analysing sequential security events, network traffic patterns and temporal relationships in attacks. The explainability of the self-attention mechanism comes from the attribution weights for events, times or features affecting threat detection decisions.

In applications such as network traffic analysis, transformer models can be used to find uncertain links in sequences of network connections, indicating joint attacks or command-and-control communications. From the generated attention maps during inference, security analysts are presented with thorough visualizations displaying specific network events that initiated threat classification with temporal phases, adding rationality and controllability for sifting through AI-driven alerts.

In support of malware analysis use cases, transformer models can read assembly code sequences, API call patterns, and dynamic traces to classify harmful software and generate explanations for the classification decisions. The attention mechanism indicates which points of interest (i.e., pieces of code, API calls, or patterns) lead to the decision, allowing reverse engineers and malware analysts to reason about AI and focus on their fine-grained analysis tasks on relevant parts, minimizing time wasted investigating less-relevant code.

The implementations of advanced methods for cybersecurity, such as positional sensors to learn temporal relationships, opportunity to extract different aspects of features, and layered attention for explanations at different specificity from individual events to entire attack campaigns.

4.1.2 Graph Neural Networks for Network Security and Relationship Analysis

Graph Neural Networks (GNNs) offer natural models network structures, which are essential for representing security threats where entity relationship (e.g., user, device, application, network segment or external resource) connections are as important as their individual traits. GNN architectures can offer detailed reviews of complex network communication behaviours and uncover anomalous relationship patterns that feature-based ML methods fail to capture.

A key benefit of Graph Neural Networks (GNNs) for cybersecurity applications is that, as network communication, organizational relationships, and attack propagation patterns are graph-structured in nature, they fit naturally into the modelling structure of GNNs. Traditional machine learning approaches may transform graph-based security data into fixed-size feature vectors, which may devalue relational knowledge. GNNs operate directly on graph data and can learn representations that capture not only node attributes but also structural information, which are useful for network prediction problems.

In the context of network defence, GNNs can learn communication dependencies between entities and identify suspicious graphs that could represent related movement, exfiltration of data or command-and-control operations. Interpretability of such GNNs is achieved with mechanisms that draw subgraphs and score their relative importance, enabling security analysts to understand which network relationships or communications led most to a threat detection.

Advanced GNN models for cybersecurity as temporal-graph neural networks that can model time-wise changing network relationships and connections between devices; heterogeneous-graph neural networks also considering a number of entity subtypes and their relations; and attention-based graph neural networks able to provide fine-grained interpretable explanations about which nodes (entities) and state transitions (interactions) are relevant among the graph in terms of cybersecurity decisions.

This capability is especially useful for study advanced persistent threats (APTs) because of the subtle correlations they maintain among themselves or because of the long-term nature of a compromised environment that may not be evident in a single network event. They also have the capability to detect multi-step attacks spanning long durations, where involved relationships between compromised and established systems.

4.2 Generative AI Implementation Strategies and Applications

4.2.1 Advanced Synthetic Data Generation for Security Training and Privacy-Preserving Analysis

The generative AI models can create large-scale artificial cybersecurity datasets that preserve the statistical characteristics and attack behavior form of actual security data, without revealing sensitive organizational details. This solution is solving the most significant problem in AI cybersecurity development: lack of high-quality training labelled data sets that organisations can rely on and share safely for their AI development and collaboration.

Variational Autoencoders (VAEs) and Generative Adversarial Networks (GANs) can generate virtual network traffic patterns, malware examples, user activity data, or attack scenarios that preserve crucial learning properties while removing identifying characteristics that may risk the privacy of a business. Using these artificial datasets, companies can share and distribute threat intelligence and collaborate on AI model training across sectors. More enhanced implementations could use conditional generative models to generate data that corresponds to specified threat types or attack tactics while providing specific training datasets. Privacy-preserving approaches like differential privacy can ensure mathematically that such artificial data cannot be reconstructed to disclose real samples. In malware examination, generative models allow the generation of virtual malware samples for training detection algorithms, testing security tools, and red-teaming scenarios without the ethical and legal problems of real malware.

4.2.2 Adversarial Example with Sophisticated Mechanisim for Robustness Testing

Generative models can regularly generate adversarial examples to evaluate the strength and reliability of cybersecurity AI systems against different types of attacks. This proactive measure allows weaknesses in the model to be identified before being exploited by adversaries, thereby increasing system reliability and safety. The adversarial generation for cybersecurity involves gradient-based optimization (backpropagation to solve the adversarial perturbation) and minimalistic evolutionary algorithms (such as genetic algorithms applied to explore attack surfaces, among others). This versatile methodology provides full-space exploration of potential attack vectors and ensures that model vulnerabilities are discovered under different patterns.

State-of-the-art approaches have introduced adversarial examples with preserved functionality, transferability-optimized variants (working across multiple dissimilar models), and adaptive adversaries that can adapt after each attack/defence cycle. The explainable AI features provided in such systems enable security analysts to understand why a particular class of threats may succeed, which inputs are attack to vulnerability, and how they can modify training or model architecture for robustness. The use of generative AI with explainable AI ensures that the technology can be utilized not merely to detect, but to continuously improve cybersecurity systems in a proactive and transparent manner while enabling human intervention.

4.3 Human Factors Integration and Cognitive Load Management

Real-world application of AI models in security has to pay special attention to human factors, cognitive load, and user interface design, all of which have a direct impact on how effective a system will be. Research suggest that there is a constant gap between AI systems and the actual needs of analysts, with 65% of cybersecurity analysts reporting mistrust toward AI alerts, and 79% wanting to work with hybrid human–AI models rather than full automation (Hagen et al., 2025). This scepticism is due to cognitive biases, lack of explainability, and trust issues. AI systems therefore need to deliver explainable reasoning so that analysts can verify recommendations and readily integrate AI findings into their investigative processes. Cognitive load management is crucial, as analysts should not be overloaded by AI outputs. Khadka and Ullah (2025) identified the following factors to keep in mind: stress response, trust processes, interface usability, and workflow integration. A good AI-based cybersecurity system will provide dynamic explanations, automation tuning, and escalation pathways so that human skillsets are preserved, but applied in a more effective manner than before.

5. SECTOR ANALYSIS AND IMPLEMENTATION CASE STUDIES

The realized AI cybersecurity deployments in the five key industry domains mentioned provide evidence supporting the theoretical models and technical solutions discussed earlier. The cost-savings analysis presented in this section aggregates data from documented industry case studies reporting actual financial benefits of

AI-enhanced cybersecurity deployments, as reported by several organizations listed in Table 3.

Table 3. AI cybersecurity cost impact analysis by sector

Sector	Average Breach Cost (No AI)	Average Breach Cost (With AI)	Cost Reduction	Time to Identify	Time to Contain
Healthcare	$5.36M	$3.60M	32.8%	194 days	73 days
Financial Services	$5.36M	$3.60M	32.8%	233 days	79 days
Energy & Utilities	$5.36M	$3.60M	32.8%	204 days	69 days
Transportation	$5.36M	$3.60M	32.8%	217 days	76 days
Smart Cities/IoT	$5.36M	$3.60M	32.8%	201 days	71 days

The analysis finds steady economic benefits across all sectors, with an average of $1.76 million in savings per event, providing firm justification for enterprises to invest in AI technology as part of their cybersecurity measures. Detection in variation and containment delay times reflect sector-specific operational policies and regulatory requirements, as described in the cross-cultural implementation analysis in Section 3. The Financial Services industry shows the longest time to identify measurement (233 days), indicative of complicated financial breaches and thorough regulatory inquiry. In contrast, the fastest containment period, shown by the Energy & Utilities sector (69 days), illustrates the need for immediate response in a critical infrastructure sector, as identified in both global implementation frameworks.

These observed results support the ROI estimation methodology which has been introduced in Section 6 and serve as evidence for the practical utility of the multi-dimensional framework proposed in this chapter. The uniform 32.8% cost reduction across all sectors indicates that, while execution strategies should be culturally tailored as emphasised in Section 7, the underlying business-value proposition of AI-enhanced cybersecurity is robust across different organisational and cultural settings.

6. ROI ASSESSMENT METHODOLOGY AND BUSINESS IMPACT ANALYSIS

The return on investment assessment (ROI) analysis for AI cybersecurity operations represents one of the most challenging financial assessments in modern enterprise technology strategy. This complexity arises from the multi-dimensional nature of cybersecurity benefits, the difficulty in quantifying avoided incidents, the long-term orientation of security investments, and the need to integrate tangible cost reductions with intangible long-term value creation across organizational functions and stakeholder networks.

6.1 ROI Framework for AI Cybersecurity Investments

This chapter develops an enhanced multi-dimensional ROI model tailored to cover the suggestion of AI cybersecurity operations (in terms of its probabilistic benefits, whole value generation and integration complexity with existing systems and processes, as well as cultural shifts across organizations).

6.1.1 Methodologies for Analysis and Quantification of the Direct Cost Reduction

In the case of AI-enabled cybersecurity, the cost savings can be measured through comprehensive analysis of several important indicators. IBM Security Cost of a Data Breach Report 2024 offers concrete proof that most AI and security automation incur an average breach cost of $3.60 million, representing a 32.8% reduction compared to the $5.36 million incurred by organizations without AI or automation IBM Security, (2024). The direct cost reductions consist of the following:

- Automated threat analysis keeps security analysts under control and gives them the means to reduce investigation time by 40-60% on average.
- Automated incident response using AI-enabled playbooks considerably speeds up the process, reducing restriction time by an average of 127 days.
- Improved detection algorithms lead to a 30-50% reduction in follow-up investigation due to lower false positive rates.
- Automated audit trail creation and regulatory reporting noticeably reduce compliance costs and minimizes the need for manual documentation by 60–80%.

6.1.2 Indirect Value Creation and Strategic Benefits

Indirect value creation comprises strategic gains that are represent the most significant aspect of long-term ROI. Proactive threat prevention improves business continuity by preserving operational efficacy and limiting downtime as a system failure can cost a large enterprise between $5,000 and $25,000 per minute.

An increase in customer confidence provides inherent value, and downstream effects such as higher customer retention further demonstrate business returns. Higher-quality customers contribute to increased customer lifetime value (CLV), as companies with stronger security maturity experience lower churn. Organizations with higher security maturity typically see 15–25% greater customer retention in competitive industries and a better security position can give organizations a control as they pursue worthwhile business initiatives, partners, and market opportunities that require proven security. Also, it can generate tens of millions as an additional revenue for a company, especially for businesses competing for government contracts, financial services partnerships, or healthcare system integrations.

7. CRITICAL ANALYSIS: IMPLEMENTATION CHALLENGES AND LIMITATIONS

Despite the promising performance results and potential benefits, the integration of AI-based technologies in cyber defences presents considerable technical, organizational, and economic challenges. These constraints need to be addressed with practical considerations and well-planned implementation strategies. Businesses may also encounter complications and costs greater than early estimates, requiring long-term commitment, substantial investments, and in-depth change management that goes well beyond a simple technology deployment.

7.1 Technical Implementation Reality and Infrastructure Requirements

The gap between system legacy and next gen AI-driven security architectures can be quite large. Integration to an organization's existing safety system is one of the major barriers, and it usually takes 18-24 months to fully roll out across large enterprises with varied technology layers, multiple vendor relationships and broad regulatory requirements. Legacy system integration challenges consist of Proprietary or non-standard data formats and structures which demand extensive ETL (Extract, Transform, Load) operations, Non-standard or incompatible API structures and designs that prefers custom integration middleware, Different security protocols lead to difficult authentication and authorization requirements and operational particularities that require reengineering process across several business functions. These integration needs alone may cost be 2–3 times the license of AI cybersecurity system.

7.1.1 Systematic Analysis: Model Drift and Performance Degradation

In realistic cybersecurity scenarios, the pre-trained AI models degrade over time according to new types of cyber threats. Previous studies Sommer and Paxson (2010) even suggest that well-engineered machine learning models may see 15–25% drop in detection performance within 6–12 months in the absence of retraining. This degradation is due to concept drift, when attackers alter their tactics in response to the detection techniques being applied (e.g., new phishing designs), data drift from organizational network or other IT environment changes, adversarial drift that refers to manipulation of the detections inputs by an intelligent attacker and temporal drift that can result from aging of training data due to differences between past and present threat patterns.

7.1.2 Adversarial Robustness Challenges and Defence Strategies

AI-based cybersecurity systems are weak to adversarial attacks that are particularly noted to exploit the weaknesses of machine-learning models. Biggio and Roli (2018) in their studies shows several major types of such attacks, including evasion attacks, where inputs are slightly modified to avoid past detection; poisoning attacks, where corrupted data is infused into the training set to compromise the model; and model extraction attacks, where attackers seek to copy or steal proprietary ML models.

In the current measures of defences, there are trade-offs which make it harder for a complete system to be effective and adversarial training that increases robustness but decreases performance in clean data by 5–15%, defensive extract requires 2–3x more computational resources for inference, and ensemble methods require additional architectural complexity and overhead.

7.2 Organizational and Cultural Barriers to Implementation

7.2.1 Skills Gap and Training Requirements Analysis

Successful application of AI in cybersecurity demands that a multidiscipline approach be taken, that expertise in deep cyber security with advanced machine learning capability. Current global estimates point out a shortage of more than

500,000 professionals with the necessary skills, leading to hiring, salary and long-term retention issues.

The skills gap relates to a wide range of domains from machine learning algorithm selection to tuning for cyber-threat context, security-oriented data technology and feature extraction, adversarial resistance testing and validation, explainable AI for security decision-making to the incorporation of legacy infrastructure as well as continuous model monitoring and retraining workflows. Very few professionals have in-depth knowledge of all these areas.

It takes 6-12 months of intensive theoretical training, hands-on lab learning and supervised real-world exercises to adequately train existing cybersecurity employees in AI technologies. The cost of the training varies approximately from $25,000 to 50,000 per person in addition to the fees, certification and lost productivity. Retention continues to be challenging, as AI capable cybersecurity professionals are earning salaries that are 40-60% higher than the traditional roles; these professionals are seeing multiple competitive job offers and have been able to negotiate for higher pay and growth opportunities.

7.2.2 Socio-cultural Resistance to AI-Driven Decision Making

There are mixed levels of cultural resistance to AI adoption across organization, industry, region and workforce demographics. Security teams are hesitating to rely on AI driven decision making due to fear of job replacement, mistrust in AI accuracy and reliability, and concern about not being able to understand how the decisions are made. To be successful, such a transformation demands strong change-management initiatives that involve clear communication of AI capabilities and challenges, proving value through pilot projects tailored to context-specific needs, comprehensive training programs (e.g., role-based), and creating collaborative human-AI workflows that maintain human full control while exploiting the strengths of AI.

7.3 Algorithmic Bias and Fairness Challenges in AI Cybersecurity Systems

In this section, the challenges of algorithmic bias and fairness related to AI-powered cybersecurity systems has been discussed. AI-based cybersecurity adoption presents systemic bias issues that affect effectiveness and fairness. Recent studies report bias in detection behaviours, security resource imbalances, and the increase of existing security disparities across different user groups and organizational structures. Mmaduekwe (2024) observes that some AI-powered security tools show biased threat classification algorithms. Some AI-powered security applications visibly demonstrate bias in the classification of threats, where machine learning models do not perform equally well across demographics and organizations. Such biases arise from imbalanced or skewed data, faulty algorithmic design, and the lack of diversity within the development teams, resulting in security gaps that can be exploited and that disproportionately affect marginalized communities. Bias is a sociotechnical issue, so dealing with it requires more than just technical remedies. El Mimouni and Bouhdadi (2025) argue that any successful mitigation strategy should combine technical debiasing approaches with stakeholder involvement, human-in-the-loop supervision, and policy compliance. Fairness-aware algorithms, fairness-driven dataset construction, and systematic bias assessment must be considered during the development stages of the AI lifecycle. These risks are particularly severe in the range of national defence. Sanclemente (2025) reports that biased AI-powered cybersecurity systems can enable discriminatory practices and human rights abuses, posing a threat to national security. Proactive strategies to identify and reduce bias are essential for preserving security performance while maintaining ethical standards across diverse organizational settings.

7.4 Legal Liability and Accountability Frameworks for AI Cybersecurity

AI enabled cybersecurity systems also raise complex legal issues concerning who should be responsible for failures in an AI system, incorrect decisions, and cyber intrusions. When AI systems make decisions on their own, with consequences for companies and public, accountability becomes a difficult matter. Okuno and Okuno (2025) compare responsibility rules across several countries and observe wide variations in who is held responsible for harm caused by defective AI. The organizational form, such as a limited liability company or AI service provider has also an effect in the allocation of risk and governance in the cybersecurity space governance.

New laws now mandate that all institutions using automated systems for cybersecurity decisions implement rigorous independent audits, risk diagnostic procedures, and processes to provide human oversight. These requirements create a legal obligation to retain documentation for a certain period, maintain auditable systems, and store decision-making data for compliance and incident investigation. Acknowledging the pressure between liability and innovation encourages governance models that enable, rather than discourage, technological advancement for ethical use. To reduce exposure to liability resulting from system malfunctions or abuse, companies must clarify governance structures, maintain thorough documentation, and implement appropriate insurance and risk-management practices.

8. MARKET ANALYSIS AND FUTURE PROJECTIONS

The one of the most rapidly emerging sectors is the AI in cybersecurity market, led by increasing threats, rising regulatory requirements, proven returns on investment, and a growing recognition that traditional security approaches are inadequate.

8.1 Analysis of Market Growth and Risk Evaluation

Refined modelling is required for an AI cybersecurity market assessment that incorporates the sort of driving growth, barriers, regulatory changes, competitive progress and development path of technology. Organizations considering AI investment in cybersecurity must consider both positive growth scenarios and traditional risk-adjusted assumptions to construct accurate plans for delivery schedules and resource needs, while recognising the unpredictable challenges summarised in Table 4.

Table 4. Market growth projection vs. risk scenarios

Scenario	2024 Baseline	2032 Projection	CAGR	Key Assumptions
Optimistic	$25B	$230B	35.2%	Continued threat escalation, regulatory support
Conservative	$25B	$145B	22.8%	Economic constraints, technical limitations
Risk-Adjusted	$25B	$180B	28.5%	Mixed regulatory environment

8.1.1 Optimistic Scenario Analysis and Growth Drivers

Given some optimistic forecasts, the global AI cybersecurity market is projected to expand to over $230 billion in 2032, up from $25 billion in 2024 (Markets and Markets, 2025). The cybersecurity market related to the generative AI space is also expected to grow by more than 200%, increasing from $8.65 billion in 2025 to a projected $35.50 billion by the end of 2031 at an estimated compound annual growth rate (CAGR) of 26.5%. Key contributors to this expansion include mounting evidence of significant cost reductions and improved protection capabilities, intensifying threats from state-sponsored and criminal cyber activities, the introduction of regulations requiring AI-enabled defense across major industry segments, and venture capital investors now allocating more than $15.8 billion annually to cybersecurity AI start-ups. Additionally, corporate technology spending, which restricts investments to essential infrastructure, results in remaining budget allocations being redirected toward advanced, high-return AI-driven solutions.

8.1.2 Conservative Scenario Analysis and Risk Factors

Moderate projections take into account various risk factors that will slow growth in the AI cybersecurity market. Regulatory risks include potential restrictions on AI-based decision-making in critical security scenarios, required human-in-the-loop mechanisms that limit the benefits of automation, and data-privacy constraints that prevent the training of large-scale AI models. Technical risks include adversarial attacks that undermine the robustness of AI models, model drift that creates the need for frequent and costly retraining, and explainability challenges that hinder acceptance in regulated industries while raising fairness concerns. In addition, vendors who fail to acknowledge previous failures or compromises of AI in security applications risk significantly undermining market confidence. Economic risks also exist: a sudden financial crisis could sharply reduce cybersecurity budgets, competitive pressure from low-cost (or free) security tools could disrupt pricing, and re-regulation or market saturation may occur once major enterprises have absorbed the initial trend of AI-driven security solutions. Under adverse conditions, growth is likely to decrease by 40–60%. Accordingly, organizations should anticipate adoption curves progressing at only 50–75% of the rate assumed in more optimistic forecasts, resulting in longer payback periods, staged investment strategies, and technology decisions focused on proven stability rather than experimental innovation. Automating such sensitivity analysis in financial planning is important, given these uncertainties.

9. FUTURE DIRECTIONS AND RESEARCH AGENDA

The future of AI cybersecurity will be influenced by the emergence of new tools, evolving threat landscape and regulatory pressures as well as advancement in AI. These trends are significance for the organizations that must strategize in the long term and for research institutions who want to come up with the cyber security technologies of tomorrow.

9.1 Integration of Quantum Computing and Post-Quantum Security

Tremendous opportunities as well as existential risks are seen for AI cyber defence systems with quantum computer power advances. The quantum machine learning algorithms have promising theory in the aspect of exponential speed-up over a number of cyber security problems including cryptography analysis, and big data analysis for large scale patterns in volumetric real-time processing of high-dimensional security data flows.

Quantum computing has arrived, bringing both significant opportunities and existential threats to AI cybersecurity. To deal these challenges, quantum machine learning algorithms can potentially deliver exponential or quadratic speedups in areas such as cryptographic analysis, large-scale pattern recognition, and real-time analysis of high-dimensional security data. In cybersecurity research, quantum algorithms are also being developed, including Grover's (Grover et al., 1996) search algorithm for databases and Shor's (1994) algorithm for factoring large integers and prime factorization, which may reduce currently used public-key cryptosystems, as well as quantum machine learning based pattern recognition algorithms with potential quadratic or exponential advantages over classical methods.

Figure 2. AI cybersecurity threat landscape evolution

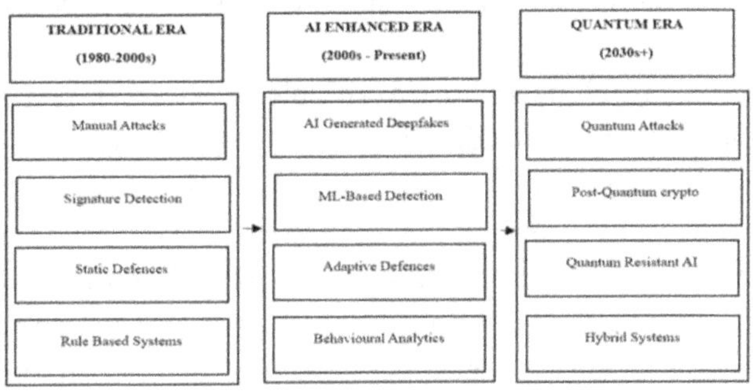

Figure 2 shows the progression from signature-based security to AI-secured systems and onward to cybersecurity for the quantum era, highlighting major milestones such as a 32.8% reduction in costs due to AI mechanisms by 2024; large-scale migration between 2025–2030 toward post-quantum cryptography; and the development of foundational components for a quantum-safe infrastructure after 2030. Yet, quantum computers with sufficient qubit power represent a major risk to today's cryptographic algorithms and motivated NIST (2023) to select the first round of Post-Quantum Cryptographic (PQC) standard candidates, including CRYSTALS-Kyber for key encapsulation, CRYSTALS-Dilithium for digital signatures, FALCON for lightweight signatures, and code-based encryption. Shifting to post-quantum cryptography and facilities represents one of the largest upgrades in cybersecurity history: organizations need to conduct cryptographic accounts, test and evaluate new algorithms, plan passage for their critical systems, align with setting processes supported by national or multinational authorities, and develop quantum-resistant AI algorithms to maintain secure operations in the quantum age

9.2 Autonomous Threat Response Evolution and Implementation

Next-generation automated response will leverage the most advanced AI technologies, such as machine learning, natural language processing (NLP), and RPA (robotic process automation), combined with intelligent decision support all in a near-real-time, marginally supervised cybersecurity operations environment. These systems will integrate automatic threat recognition, dynamic impact estimation, optimized response planning, and automatic execution of constraint and recovery actions to enable faster-than-ever responses to attacks in the modern multi-stage cyber conflict. This will include the basic task of immediate response actions such as network segmentation or delaying user access, automated evidence collection, notifications to executive leadership and regulators, support for engaging external parties such as law enforcement, and detailed records that can be used to validate compliance.

Research directions include safe and verifiable autonomous response protocols to systematic failures, explainable decision-making systems to justify their actions during post-incident investigations, and secure legal and ethical frameworks for autonomous cybersecurity operations. Required for safety are strong testing and validation to prevent disruption, strengthened reliable features so that misuse or system takeover cannot occur through access control weaknesses, and robust activity tracking that supports forensics, regulatory reporting, and system optimization.

9.3 International Cross-Border AI Cybersecurity Collaboration and Governance

Knowledge-sharing and collaboration among cybersecurity professionals will increasingly be driven by advanced, AI-enabled association and information-sharing systems. Privacy-preserving machine-learning technologies including federated learning, secure multi-party computation (SMC), homomorphic encryption, and differential privacy will allow organizations and countries to collaboratively build AI models and exchange threat intelligence without exposing their confidential information.

Federated learning, in the context of threat detection, enables many independent parties to mutually train AI models across decentralized datasets without sharing raw data with one another, resulting in more powerful and robust threat-detection systems. Fundamental research focuses on developing standardized, secure open

APIs between AI/ML systems and security technologies, and building strong operational frameworks across legal and governance domains to enable diverse parties to collaborate using AI systems. Key breakthroughs that will be needed to include the development of trusted technical infrastructure, which spans jurisdictions and global strategy that enable deeply coordinated technical efforts, while preserving sovereignty.

International governance will have to address complex questions such as determining who is liable for the behaviours of an AI system, regulating it according to technical standards and legal rules used across borders, finding ways to resolve disputes when multiple AI systems interact with one another, and establishing protocols that enable coordinated international multilateral responses in the event that one of them suffers a cyber incident. To ensure meaningful global cooperation, long-term diplomatic commitment, broad technical standardization, and a solid legal foundation including pilot projects that demonstrate the value and feasibility of international AI cybersecurity collaboration are essential. Success in this area is crucial for deterring peer nation-state adversaries and combating global cybercrime carried out by international syndicates with no allegiance to any single organization or country.

CONCLUSION

This chapter demonstrates that the use of artificial intelligence, if properly applied with attention to technical, ethical, and sociotechnical aspects, has the potential to make a substantial contribution to global cybersecurity. The findings confirm that AI-enabled security can notably improve sensitivity and recall in threat detection, reduce average response time, and lower operational costs while still meeting today's sophisticated requirements such as algorithmic fairness, legal compliance, and human-integration considerations.

Effective positioning of AI in cybersecurity, however, requires consideration of end-to-end factors, including technical requirements, corporate culture and human factors to which an organization is dedicated, regulatory approval and norms regarding behavioral data analytics, cognitive load on decision-makers or users, and acceptability among target user groups. Practical tools can help those facing implementation challenges, including guidance on maximizing security outcomes and ensuring responsible use of such capabilities. In addition, cross-cultural adaptation results, bias-correction strategies, and accountability frameworks provide the foundation for responsible AI adoption across legal jurisdictions. As AI technology advances, work will be required on deployment strategies, fairness assessment, human–AI collaboration, and global governance. Institutions that balance innovation with ethical norms through human-centred design will be better positioned to maintain strong security postures and drive responsible innovation across an increasingly hostile threat landscape.

REFERENCES

Anderson, R. (2008). *Security Engineering: A Guide to Building Dependable Distributed Systems* (2nd ed.). Wiley., DOI: 10.1002/9781119644682

Axelsson, S. (2000). Intrusion detection systems: A survey and taxonomy. *Technical Report 99-15*, Department of Computer Engineering, Chalmers University of Technology.

Biggio, B., & Roli, F. (2018). Wild patterns: Ten years after the rise of adversarial machine learning. *Pattern Recognition*, *84*, 317–331. DOI: 10.1016/j.patcog.2018.07.023

Buchanan, B. G., & Shortliffe, E. H. (1984). *Rule-Based Expert Systems: The MYCIN Experiments of the Stanford Heuristic Programming Project*. Addison-Wesley., DOI: 10.1016/0004-3702(85)90067-0

Cabinet Office Japan. (2019). *Society 5.0: A Human-Centric Super-Smart Society*. Government of Japan.

CFG (Centre for Future Generations). (2025). *Strengthening AI trustworthiness: Strategic innovation for European security part 3*. https://cfg.eu/strengthening-ai-trustworthiness/

Chandola, V., Banerjee, A., & Kumar, V. (2009). Anomaly detection: A survey. *ACM Computing Surveys*, *41*(3), 1–58. DOI: 10.1145/1541880.1541882

DeepStrike. (2025). *AI Cybersecurity Threats 2025: How to Survive the AI Arms Race*. https://deepstrike.io/blog/ai-cybersecurity-threats-2025

Denning, D. E. (1987). An intrusion-detection model. *IEEE Transactions on Software Engineering*, *SE-13*(2), 222–232. DOI: 10.1109/TSE.1987.232894

El Mimouni, S., & Bouhdadi, M. (2025). Fairness and bias in AI: A sociotechnical perspective. *Journal of Information, Communication and Ethics in Society*. Advance online publication. DOI: 10.1108/JICES-12-2024-0182

European Commission. (2025). *EU launches InvestAI initiative to mobilise €200 billion of investment in artificial intelligence*. https://ec.europa.eu/commission/presscorner/detail/en/ip_25_467

Goodfellow, I., Pouget-Abadie, J., Mirza, M., Xu, B., Warde-Farley, D., Ozair, S., & Bengio, Y. (2014). Generative adversarial nets. *Advances in Neural Information Processing Systems*, *27*, 2672–2680. DOI: 10.48550/arXiv.1406.2661

Goodman, B., & Flaxman, S. (2017). European Union regulations on algorithmic decision-making and a "right to explanation". *AI Magazine*, *38*(3), 50–57. DOI: 10.1609/aimag.v38i3.2741

Grover, V., Jeong, S. R., & Segars, A. H. (1996). Information systems effectiveness: The construct space and patters of application. *Information & Management*, *31*(4), 177–191. DOI: 10.1016/S0378-7206(96)01079-8

Hagen, R. A., Øverlier, L., & Helkala, K. (2025). Human factors in AI-driven cybersecurity: Cognitive biases and trust issues. *. *Digital Threats : Research and Practice*, *6*(4), 1–20. Advance online publication. DOI: 10.1145/3759260

Inter-American Development Bank. (2022, February 23). *Israel commits to IDB cybersecurity initiative in Latin America and the Caribbean*. https://www.iadb.org/en/news/israel-commits-idb-cybersecurity-initiative-latin-america-and-caribbean

Inter-American Development Bank. (2025, June 25). *Strengthening Sectoral Cybersecurity in Latin America and the Caribbean*. https://www.iadb.org/en/project/RG-T4577

Khadka, K., & Ullah, A. B. (2025). Human factors in cybersecurity: An interdisciplinary review and framework proposal. *International Journal of Information Security*, *24*(3), 119. Advance online publication. DOI: 10.1007/s10207-025-01032-0

Lee, W., & Stolfo, S. J. (1998). Data mining approaches for intrusion detection. *Proceedings of the 7th USENIX Security Symposium*, 79–94.

Lundberg, S. M., & Lee, S. I. (2017). A unified approach to interpreting model predictions. *Advances in Neural Information Processing Systems*, *30*, 4765–4774.

Lunt, T. F., Tamaru, A., Gilham, F., Jagannathan, R., Jalali, C., Neumann, P. G., . . . Tong, L. (1988). *A real-time intrusion-detection expert system (IDES)*. Technical Report SRI-CSL-88-05, SRI International.

Ministry of Communications and Information Singapore. (2020). *Singapore Model AI Governance Framework* (2nd ed.).

Mmaduekwe, U. (2024). Bias and fairness issues in artificial intelligence-driven cybersecurity. *Current Journal of Applied Science and Technology*, *43*(6), 109-119. DOI: 10.9734/cjast/2024/v43i64391

NIST. (2023). *Artificial Intelligence Risk Management Framework (AI RMF 1.0)*. https://doi.org/DOI: 10.6028/NIST.AI.100-1

Okuno, M. J., & Okuno, H. G. (2025). Legal frameworks for AI service business participants: A comparative analysis of liability protection across jurisdictions. *AI & Society, 40*(7), 5667–5683. DOI: 10.1007/s00146-025-02288-9

Otieno, D. O. (2020). Cyber security challenges: The case of developing countries. *Promoting Creativity, Innovation and Productivity for Sustainable Development Conference.* https://www.researchgate.net/publication/346485466_Cyber_security_challenges_The_Case_of_Developing_Countries

Ribeiro, M. T., Singh, S., & Guestrin, C. (2016). "Why should I trust you?" Explaining the predictions of any classifier. In *Proceedings of the 22nd ACM SIGKDD International Conference on Knowledge Discovery and Data Mining* (pp. 1135–1144). https://doi.org/DOI: 10.1145/2939672.2939778

Roberts, H., Cowls, J., Morley, J., Taddeo, M., Wang, V., & Floridi, L. (2021). The Chinese approach to artificial intelligence: An analysis of policy, ethics, and regulation. *AI & Society, 36*(1), 59–77. DOI: 10.1007/s00146-020-00992-2

Sanclemente, G. L. (2025). Digital tools: Safeguarding national security, cybersecurity, and AI bias. *CEBRI-Journal*, *4*(15), 137-155. https://doi.org/DOI: 10.54827/issn2764-7897.cebri2023.07.03.07.137-155.en

Schneier, B. (2000). *Secrets and Lies: Digital Security in a Networked World.* Wiley.

Secretariat, B. R. I. C. S. (2025, April 10). *BRICS strengthens cooperation on cybersecurity.* https://brics.br/en/news/brics-strengthens-cooperation-on-cybersecurity

IBM Security. (2024). *Cost of a data breach report 2024.*

Sommer, R., & Paxson, V. (2010). Outside the closed world: On using machine learning for network intrusion detection. In *Proceedings of the 2010 IEEE Symposium on Security and Privacy* (pp. 305–316). https://doi.org/DOI: 10.1109/SP.2010.25

Stanford University. (2025). *Building Trustworthy AI: Navigating Security in the Agentic Era.* Stanford Online Conference Proceedings. https://almamater.at/conf/building-trustworthy-ai-navigating-security-in-the-agentic-era/

Szegedy, C., Zaremba, W., Sutskever, I., Bruna, J., Erhan, D., Goodfellow, I., & Fergus, R. (2013). Intriguing properties of neural networks. arXiv:1312.6199. https://doi.org//arXiv.1312.6199DOI: 10.48550

TVBRICS. (2025, October 7). *BRICS and cybersecurity: protecting shared digital space.* https://tvbrics.com/en/news/brics-and-cybersecurity-protecting-shared-digital-space/

Chapter 7
Defending Against AI-Generated Cyber Threats:
Frameworks, Models, and Real-Time Generative AI Security Defenses

Muhammad Usman Tariq
http://orcid.org/0000-0002-7605-3040
Abu Dhabi University, UAE & University College Cork, Ireland

ABSTRACT

The emergence and rapid development of generative technologies have changed the nature of cyber threats, enabling enemies to use complex attacks in a more automated manner, create convincing deception using digital tools, and act more quickly owing to the availability of security gaps. The ability to defend against machine-generated attacks is at the heart of operational resilience and safeguarding sensitive data as organizations continue to expand their digital footprint. This chapter examines some of the emerging frameworks and defense models related to the risk of automated threat generation, with an emphasis on real-time security controls that are meant to detect, prevent, and adapt to new patterns of attacks. The results highlight the need for proactive design principles in the construction of security systems that will be effective in mitigating contemporary generative cyber threats. The integration of behavioral analysis, dynamic threat intelligence, deception systems, and automated defensive orchestration in security systems is important.

DOI: 10.4018/979-8-2600-1608-4.ch007

INTRODUCTION

The cybersecurity landscape has also entered a new stage of acceleration, with much of it being influenced by the rapid penetration of generative systems capable of producing digital content, malicious codes, and attack schemes on a scale never seen before. Days or weeks of human effort to produce are now produced automatically in a few seconds, and attackers are benefiting in a manner that can hardly be described as anything short of profound and deeply disruptive. This shift is not subtle. Generative algorithms synthesize phishing bait using the digital footprint of a specific individual, produce polymorphic malware that evolves with each execution, and automate reconnaissance procedures that previously required time and expertise to perform and patience to complete (Khan et al., 2025). Capable of learning from defenses, adapting to barriers, and producing continuous variations that evade static filters, this new class of threats signals a turning point in which cyberattacks will not only increase in frequency but also in dynamism, becoming more unpredictable and intimately personalized. Traditional cybersecurity does not account for such a pace and level of sophistication. Many defensive tools use rule-based logic, static signatures, and predetermined behavioral patterns. They are excellent at recognizing known threats, which unfortunately leaves them often helpless against attacks they have never seen, particularly those that continually morph and evolve to avoid detection. Security teams relying on heavy manual triage and human-led analysis cannot keep up with threats that proliferate faster than they can review. Every delay presents an opportunity for compromise.

This mismatch between attacker capability and defensive capacity creates a widening vulnerability gap. Organizations may deploy multiple layers of security tools; however, these layers often function independently of each other, often have no contextual awareness, or are manually correlated to create actionable insights (Ahi & Valizadeh, 2025). The result is a high volume of alerts in most cases false positives but also blind spots, whereby novel threats slip through unchecked. Meanwhile, attackers exploit the slowest part of most organizations: the human response cycle. They launch automated scanning, probing, and exploitation activities twenty-four hours a day, and defenders have to sleep, coordinate, and prioritize. Even well-resourced teams struggle to maintain situational awareness when threats regenerate faster than the analysis of logs. Traditional security operations were never designed based on the assumption that attackers would be able to mass-produce targeted attacks on demand.

The implications of this study are straightforward. Modern cybersecurity demands defenses that can match the speed, scale, and adaptiveness of systems used to create novel threats. Adaptation has become a core necessity, not a luxury. Whereas bad actors can change their tools in the blink of an eye, defenders must be similarly responsive. A security system that cannot learn constantly or act independently is rapidly outrun by adversaries who no longer need to rest or reconsider their approaches (Anderson et al., 2025). However, speed and autonomy are not the only essentials. Defensive systems must also be understandable. In the rush to automate protection, many early technologies produced results that, while effective, were opaque and offered conclusions with minimal explanation (Khan et al., 2025). This lack of clarity creates practical and ethical risks. Security decisions, especially automated ones, must be explainable to administrators, auditors, and policymakers. Explainability also ensures that automated defense mechanisms complement human judgment and do not supersede or obscure it. Explainability is also important in defending better; when analysts know the reason behind a system raising an event, they can evaluate the rationale with respect to the organizational goals. Such an environment can be remotely scanned using generative attack tools to identify vulnerable spots and generate an exploitation plan specific to each exposed service. Such a change reflects the actions of attackers who perform maintenance surveillance, create new probes automatically, and change their strategies depending on the feedback.

A defensive system that pauses at any point gives an opening to adversaries who do not. Despite these technological advancements, human expertise remains irreplaceable. As such capabilities continue to evolve, defensive systems must be prepared not only to identify anomalies but also to anticipate coordinated, multi-stage attack sequences contrived by automated tools with strategic awareness. This shift parallels what has happened with human-led advanced persistent threats, except that automation increases both the scale and accessibility (Anderson et al., 2025). Adaptive defenses combined with transparent reasoning systems enable organizations to understand not only when they are attacked but also why they are targeted and how future attempts might unfold. This predictive dimension is perhaps the most powerful countermeasure against generative threat engines because it transforms defence from a reactive discipline into a proactive one.

Evolution of AI-Generated Cyber Threats

In a few short years, machine-generated cyber threats have evolved from isolated or handcrafted attacks into large-scale, adaptive, and highly convincing digital operations (Ahi and Valizadeh, 2025). The proliferation of systems that can generate code, text, images, and behavioral simulations has enabled threat actors to automate malware creation, craft persuasive phishing messages, synthesize realistic identities, and deploy autonomous bots that behave with a semblance of strategic intent to achieve their goals. These changes have thrust the cybersecurity community into an unprecedented new phase in which machine-generated threats demand a deeper understanding of both technical evolution and human vulnerabilities. One of the most visible categories of this evolution is the development of generative phishing. For years, phishing was largely constrained by the attacker's writing ability, cultural understanding, and available time. Errors in grammar or tone were often the giveaways that allowed trained users to identify fraudulent messages. Generative systems have changed this paradigm almost overnight. They can imitate tone, mimic corporate writing styles, and craft messages tailored to an individual's habits, profession, or online presence. They can also generate endless variations of the same lure, making mass distribution campaigns far more difficult to filter using static detection rules.

Deepfakes can impersonate business executives, government officials, or any personal contact to manipulate victims into transferring funds, sharing confidential information, or simply granting access to secure systems. The particular danger is that deepfakes leverage human trust in visual and auditory cues. While emails are questionable, voice calls or video messages that sound realistic often seem far more credible (Anderson et al., 2025). Attackers have already used these simulations to impersonate leaders in high-stakes environments, demonstrating how quickly synthetic media can be weaponized. Generative malware represents another major evolution in this field. This creates a moving target problem for defenders, who must contend not with a single piece of malware but with an endless stream of functionally similar yet structurally unique variants.

Similar to malware, autonomous bots have undergone a dramatic transformation. Early bots performed simple tasks that might have included sending spam or brute-force attacks. These systems have started to approach swarm-like behavior, allowing for increasingly complex and resilient attack campaigns that persist long after individual components are neutralized. However, behind the emergence and development of these threats are large language models, diffusion frameworks, and adversarial generation techniques that amplify the power of such attacks. Large language models open the way to the scalable creation of text, conversational manipulation, and automated simulation of scenarios (Ahi & Valizadeh, 2025). With their ability to analyze data at high speed, it is now possible for an attacker to generate tailored social engineering narratives or identify weaknesses in publicly available information. Adversarial creation techniques also allow malware samples to be crafted with the express purpose of stimulating blind spots in defensive machine-learning models. In essence, these approaches enable attackers to test and leverage weaknesses in defenses at machine speed, going through rapid iterations to find combinations likely to succeed.

Real-world cases have demonstrated the tangible effects of these techniques. There was one highly publicized incident in which a deepfake voice message claiming to be an executive caused an employee to authorize a large transfer, completely unaware that his interaction was with an artificial clone of a human. This incident showed how advanced audio manipulation can be, and at the same time, the huge flaw it exploits in humans (Khan et al., 2025). A generative text system was used to craft customized messages referencing meetings, projects that had been worked on, or personal details that were known through social networks. The level of customization of such an email made it almost indistinguishable from any other legitimate corporate communication; credentials were compromised, and sensitive corporate environments were accessed without authorization. In some cases, automated malware toolkits have churned out variants of some malicious programs, overwhelming antivirus providers and leveraging detection delays. The toolkits do not require deep technical skills; instead, they allow lower-level attackers to create complex malware spreads, with the toolkit providing automated modifications to evade scanning tools. The rapid mutation rate meant that by the time a signature was developed for one version, dozens of new variants were already in circulation. This created a cascading overload for the security teams tasked with tracking and responding to the evolving sample (Tariq, 2025).

Another case snapshot is the creation of synthetic identities. Using diffusion and text generation tools, attackers create complete profiles with photos, background stories, professional histories, and behavioral footprints. The realism of these identities makes them difficult to detect, especially in environments that rely heavily on remote interactions and digital credentials (Ahi & Valizadeh, 2025). A highlight in recent years is the combination of text, audio, video, and code to create hybrid multimodal attack campaigns. The elements within these hybrid attacks may be highly coordinated; for example, a personalized phishing email could be sent, followed by a deepfake voicemail to reinforce the message, and so on. In some instances, autonomous bots are deployed by the attacker to check whether the target interacts with the content and to adjust their strategy accordingly. Figure 1 illustrates the integrated defensive ecosystem.

Figure 1. Integrated defensive ecosystem

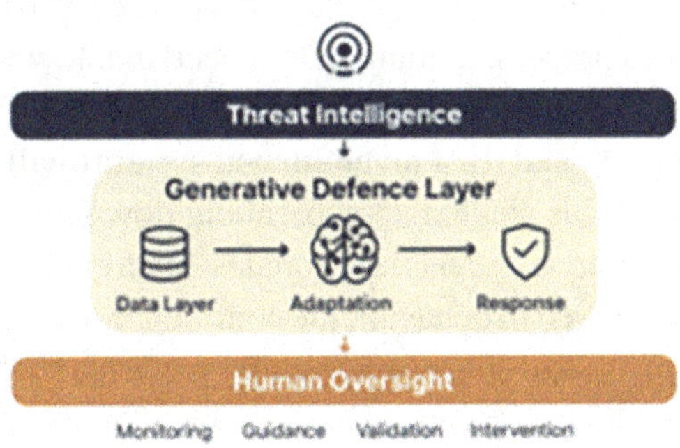

Foundations of Generative AI Security Defences

Understanding how these foundations work shows why they will become indispensable parts of any modern defense strategy and how they enable organizations to stay one step ahead of increasingly automated and unpredictable threats. Adversarial frameworks represent one of the greatest leaps in anomaly detection, mainly because they recognize that malicious behavior seldom resembles previous attacks. In cases where threats closely mimic legitimate behaviors, adversarial models can discern inconsistencies in timing, structure, or intent (Anderson et al., 2025). It is highly valuable in environments where generative malware, synthetic identities, or high-fidelity phishing evolve too quickly for regular tools to categorize. When deployed in a real operational environment, adversarial mechanisms continuously compare the observed activity with enormous internal libraries of both legitimate and fabricated patterns. As a result, the system becomes far more capable of identifying activities that fall just outside the normal bounds, even if it has no prior exposure to that exact threat.

Unlike rule-based systems that remain static until an explicit update, reinforcement learning dynamically refines the responses of the defensive tools. When a system detects something unusual and takes action- perhaps isolating a device, blocking a connection, or altering a firewall policy-it watches the results that follow. If the action is effective in mitigating risk, it reinforces the system's preference for similar actions in the future. Otherwise, it revises its approach, learning from its mistakes rather than repeating them. This is a necessary process of continuous learning when threats adapt to the environment. Context-rich behavioral models have been developed over time to support nuanced and situation-appropriate responses. Perhaps the most important advantage of reinforcement learning in cybersecurity is its capability to deal with uncertainty. Organizations are increasingly concerned about tools that may take aggressive actions with unclear reasoning as to why such actions are warranted. When a system locks out user access, isolates a core server, or blocks a key business process, administrators need to know what led to the decision. Without this explanation, oversight will be difficult to achieve, errors will be more difficult to diagnose, and trust in automated systems will erode. Explainable reasoning layers address this challenge by breaking down the internal logic of the defensive decisions into human-readable rationales. Such explanations may describe the kind of deviation observed in behavior, the confidence level of detection, the past experiences the system has had concerning similar patterns, and the risks associated with inaction. By providing such clarity, explainable systems allow security teams to validate decisions and tune sensitivity thresholds or override actions as necessary. This also helps them fulfill compliance and internal auditing requirements, which are beginning to demand clear justification for automated security measures. The net outcome is a collaborative defense framework in which automated tools create speed and scale, but human analysts provide strategic knowledge and context (Khan et al., 2025). Explainability reinforces this partnership because it helps keep the actions of the system in line with organizational priorities. Explainable reasoning layers also help organizations prepare for complex threats that span multiple domains (Tariq, 2025).

Explainable systems can map the relationships among events, showing how unusual messaging leads to a credential attempt that results in suspicious network behavior and eventually code execution. This illumination of the attack narrative allows analysts to get the full picture of exactly what has happened, so they can take intelligent responses against the attack and implement measures to prevent similar attacks in the future. Adversarial detection, reinforcement learning, and explainable reasoning together create a robust base for modern security defenses. The adversarial framework probes the boundaries between normal and abnormal behaviors to detect threats, even when an attacker actively attempts to disguise them. Reinforcement learning ensures that defenses evolve in real time as strategies adjust to threats that shift in nature and environments that change (Ahi & Valizadeh, 2025). These foundations are not just technological advancements; they represent a conceptual change in how cybersecurity should be perceived. The old paradigm assumes that the defense must always react to attacks. This is a new model in which defenses anticipate, adapt, and involve early interactions with the threat before it can achieve full expression. The focus has shifted from static rule enforcement to dynamic intelligence.

Defence Architectures for AI-Generated Attacks

Only when one understands how these architectures operate does one come to realize why they are becoming indispensable parts of contemporary security, especially in environments where automated threats grow more sophisticated by the day. One of the central elements in this new defense landscape is the integration of zero-trust principles with clear visibility layers. Zero-trust architecture removes the antiquated assumption that internal traffic is safe by default. Instead, they treat each device, user, and request as potentially hostile until their identities are proven. This approach fits within an environment where generative attacks can breach compromised credentials, synthetic identities, or even feigned communication that is indistinguishable from real interactions. By constantly verifying identity, context, behavior, and device posture, zero-trust networks reduce the attack surface available to threat actors and limit lateral movement. If a machine-generated threat succeeds in infiltrating the user account or endpoint, the attacker will realize that access has become compartmentalized, with every single action scrutinized and validated again. This constant re-authentication disrupts automated threats that often rely on the ability to escalate privileges or pivot inside a network without much resistance. In places where machine-generated threats can easily mimic normal activity with a very high degree of fidelity, transparency is a critical safeguard that keeps automated defenses accountable and interpretable (Ahi & Valizadeh, 2025). At a time when identity and access control are increasingly being complemented by behavioral intrusion detection, generative modeling helps understand what normal looks like. Earlier intrusion detection systems were based on known patterns of malicious behavior and fixed sets of suspicious signatures. These fail when attackers create new variations at will or blur malicious intent with legitimate behavior. Generative modeling examines the patterns within an organization's environment; instead of using threat signatures from outside, it learns directly from an organization's processes, user habits, and flows of communication. It builds an intricate map of typical behavior, such as how employees go about their work, how systems communicate with each other, and how data flows.

Once this baseline is established, deviations are more easily recognized. If a user who always logs in from one location suddenly shows up in another region, accesses resources they have never accessed before, or requests data unlike anything they have asked for previously, the system knows that something is off. When a program generates sequences of instructions that differ from its historical patterns, it is an anomaly. Even small behavioral variations, too minuscule to be noticed by any human analyst, can be indicative of the manipulative work of a generative threat engine. Because these models continuously adapt, they do not lose their effectiveness when legitimate behaviors change over time. This adaptability is particularly important in modern-day workplaces, where rigid rules no longer apply owing to remote access, cloud services, and fluidity of work. Behavior-based systems do not rely on predefined notions of right and wrong but on organic patterns emerging from the organization itself (Anderson et al., 2025). In a world where attacks can be dynamically assembled and changed with each use, this creativity affords defenders a capability that cannot be achieved with manual rule generation alone.

However, even the most sophisticated intrusion detection and prevention systems cannot prevent every intrusion. Autonomous deception systems and dynamic honeypots are part of the defensive architecture. Deception has long been a part of security strategies, but classic approaches often involve static traps that attackers either leave alone or quickly find their way around (Ahi & Valizadeh, 2025). Modern deception systems operate autonomously and dynamically change their appearance, behavior, and placement based on the evolving environment of the network. They create realistic digital assets that do not carry critical value decoy servers, fabricated credentials, false network paths, simulated databases, and synthetic user accounts.

These are seamlessly woven into the network to make it impossible for the attacker to differentiate between real and false targets.

Generative attack engines thrive on rapid data gathering and automated exploration, and deception systems exploit these tendencies. When an attacker interacts with a decoy, defenders immediately gain visibility into the attacker's methods without risking operational assets. Because deception assets are isolated from production systems, anything that touches them is inherently suspicious. Attackers relying on automated reconnaissance may find themselves stuck in a maze of convincing yet useless information, wasting time and revealing their presence to the target. Of all the valuable outcomes of deception systems, perhaps the greatest asset is their intelligence. For the first time, this places organizations in a position to prepare for emerging techniques well in advance of their use (Anderson et al., 2025). Together, they form a multilayered environment in which it is difficult for attackers to discern the location of the real assets, difficult to move around freely once inside, and where telltale signs of probing exist from the very start. Defensive architectures built on this principle promise a durable base for the protection of complex environments against threats that will continue to push the boundaries of creativity, scale, and automation.

REAL-TIME DETECTION USING EXPLAINABLE MODELS

Interpretable detection models focus on techniques that illuminate the reasons for flagging patterns as suspicious rather than treating the system as a black box. Opaque systems might be very good at identifying anomalies, but without insight into their reasoning, analysts cannot validate alarms, tune the system well, or trust its outputs when time-sensitive escalations need them the most. Interpretability methods fill this gap by disclosing the reasons for detection logic (Khan et al., 2025). They identify which features of an event contributed most to firing an alert, how different signals may correlate, and what deviations from normal behavior spurred the model to the judgment it made. All of these enable security teams to differentiate between real abnormalities and malicious activities, which is important in an environment where a false positive could cause operational disruption or loss of confidence in automated tools.

These can be shown in terms that mirror how humans reason, such as pointing out that a user accessed sensitive files at a time when they were usually inactive, or that a program spawned a subprocess inconsistent with its normal behavior. This clarity enables analysts to understand not only that something is wrong but also why the system reached that conclusion (Anderson et al., 2025). More sophisticated interpretability methods visualize the relationships between events to illustrate how an attack path unfolds across a network. Visual explanations allow analysts to track anomalies throughout multiple layers, device behavior, user actions, and network flows, and where in each of them the intrusion had started. Given that attacks are driven by automated systems that orchestrate actions across environments, this type of contextual mapping is highly required. It allows analysts to visualize cross-domain connections that would otherwise be nearly impossible to find in real time, given that such threats would evolve or pivot unpredictably. Interpretability also plays a central role in enabling effective human-machine collaboration in high-stakes security decisions. Human-machine teaming ensures that the system acts swiftly but remains rooted in human oversight where necessary (Tariq, 2025).

A good dynamic between humans and automated systems exists, where interpretable models act as the communication layer. Analysts require actionable insights rather than abstract numbers or opaque model outputs. If a system recommends locking down a critical server, for instance, then analysts must know whether the model detected an unusual access pattern, a sequence of abnormal commands, or an external connection that is typical of known intrusion behavior. If the system can explain itself clearly, the analyst is empowered to confidently confirm or override the automated recommendation. This reduces hesitation, minimizes second-guessing, and accelerates the response time while preserving safety and accuracy in decision-making. Human-machine collaboration also benefits from the system's capability to learn from human feedback. These representations are crucial when the attacks originate from automated systems that inject small, frequent, and distributed anomalies that are individually designed to be unnoticeable. Linguistic explanations complement these visual tools by providing clear and concise narratives of events. These narrative-style explanations help analysts rapidly comprehend the gist of the anomaly, which reduces cognitive load and decision fatigue, two common causes of mistakes during high-pressure incidents.

In many such situations, a combination of visual and linguistic explanations yields the best clarity. A good interface may display a visual diagram of suspicious network flows and provide a textual explanation that summarizes why the pattern is problematic. This can help analysts with different backgrounds-some who are comfortable with diagrams and some who prefer textual explanations–correctly interpret events. Furthermore, this facilitates quick cross-checking by analysts to increase confidence in the validity of the alerts. Real-time detection also benefits from interpretable models that support rapid and accurate triage. The alert volumes are overwhelming in most SOC environments, and analysts must prioritize incidents for immediate investigation. Interpretable systems highlight the constituent parts that drive the risk of an alert, allowing for the easy prioritization of high-threat alerts (Arif et al., 2024). For example, if a model identifies that a login came from an unusual location and subsequent access attempts were made on sensitive systems, analysts can consider escalating it immediately. If the anomaly is confined to small deviations with no apparent malicious intent, the alert can be deprioritized and ignored. This level of triage is important in environments where every second may mean the difference between an intrusion being contained or being allowed to propagate.

Another benefit of interpretability is its contribution to incident learning and post-event analyses. Once an attack has been contained, SOCs usually conduct a review to understand how the intrusion started, how it evolved, and how it can be avoided in the future. Such a process is made more efficient with interpretable models. The explanations form a narrative trail that analysts can backtrack, reconstructing the steps an attacker took and the points where detection could have occurred. This historical insight serves to strengthen future defenses and supports organizational learning, which cannot be provided by opaque systems. Moreover, interpretable detection is crucial for organizations that must satisfy regulatory or compliance requirements. Many industries demand transparent recordings of how decisions regarding security are made, especially in cases where large parts come from automated systems. Combined, these elements create a detection environment wherein speed, accuracy, and transparency coexist, which is an essential foundation for a defense against a constantly changing and increasingly complex threat.

COUNTER-GENERATIVE TECHNIQUES

Counter-generative techniques have become integral to modern security practices because today's attackers rely on automated systems that can create endless variations of malicious content. Together, they provide a multilayered approach to constrain the impact of automated attacks and enhance defenders' capabilities for proactive responses (Kayode et al., 2025). These markers enable tracing a suspicious file, message, or dataset to determine whether it came from a known system or an untrusted source that may be operating maliciously. Fingerprinting works along similar lines but focuses on features intrinsic to the behavior of a system, such as its quirks, statistical tendencies, or structural patterns. Even when attackers try hard to remove these traces or mask their origin, residual cues can often be picked up using fingerprinting techniques as coming from a common generator. Provenance systems generalize these concepts by tracking data and code as they flow from one stage of creation to another and through successive steps in their distribution. In security applications, this provenance record serves to confirm the authenticity of a piecc of content, the trustworthiness of its origin, and whether it has passed through intermediate states in which tampering may have occurred (Tariq, 2025).

It will be particularly useful in large digital ecosystems, where many generators can be running simultaneously. Provenance chains are also useful for facilitating accountability, where organizations can triage sources during audits or incident investigations. Tampering can be detected and proven when all the steps involved in the creation of a contact are logged. This is the way to reduce the chances of accepting manipulated content and the foundation of trust in an environment that is increasingly filled with synthetic materials. However, watermarking and provenance alone cannot defend against active manipulation. It is common for attackers to attempt to bypass or confuse detection models with subtle distortions, odd phrasing, and modified code structures that take advantage of blind spots. Adversarial training is essential in this context (Perumal & Aithal, 2024). Defensive systems must be ready and able to identify patterns that an attacker has crafted on purpose with the intention of misleading, evading, or corrupting such detections. It also prepares defensive systems to recognize the tactics used by automated attack engines, which thrive on producing rapid, slightly altered variations of the same malicious idea. Models become more stable in the presence of noise, unpredictability, and deliberate obfuscation when trained using deliberately deceptive examples. This robustness is a commodity in real-time detection environments, where alerts must be accurate and reliable. The system does not provide much protection when it folds under adversarial pressure or continually misclassifies cleverly disguised threats.

Another strength of adversarial training is its contribution to long-term adaptability. Because new attack methods are developed daily, defensive models must learn from existing examples and hypothetical examples representing potential future threats. Adversarial training encourages forward-looking defence. By generating challenging samples internally, the model learns to anticipate how attackers develop their strategies. This prevents defenders from depending solely on historical data and opens the possibility of a highly flexible system that can resist novel forms of manipulation (Singh et al., 2024). This proactive orientation is essential in a domain where an attacker can generate thousands of modified samples in seconds, each designed to evade a different aspect of a detection system

Even with enhanced robustness and traceability, defenders still require environments in which they can investigate suspicious content without compromising the integrity of the production system. Security sandboxing is indispensable in this scenario. A sandbox isolates potentially harmful files, messages, scripts, or programs in a controlled environment where they can be safely executed. Analysts can observe how suspicious content behaves, what network connections it tries to make, which files it modifies, and which processes it spawns (Uddin et al., 2025). Because the sandbox environment is isolated, the threat cannot escape or cause broader harm. This allows defenders to gather intelligence on malicious behaviours, identify patterns indicative of automated generation, and develop targeted countermeasures

Sandboxing is especially effective when the threats introduced by automated systems are examined because they may have different behaviors than conventional malware. A more modern threat may contain adaptive scripts that adjust their behavior based on the system configuration, environmental variables, or detection efforts. Analysts can test the response of a threat to specific conditions in a sandbox, which can then be intentionally changed. This helps reveal whether the content exhibits behaviors typical of automated manipulation, such as the on-the-fly regeneration of components, trying out multiple evasion techniques, or probing the environment to monitor tools (Helal et al., 2025). Many modern attacks rely on contextual features, such as detecting whether they are running on a particular operating system, whether a specific process exists, or even what the user may have for permissions. Adversarial training fortifies the resilience of detection models by strengthening them against manipulation attempts and forcing them to address their vulnerabilities. Sandboxing provides a secure virtual laboratory in which suspicious content can be tested to uncover hidden behaviors and generate intelligence to inform larger defensive strategies. When put into operation together, the components begin a virtuous circle of continuous improvement: sandbox analysis generates new adversarial examples; the adversarial examples fortify the detection models; detection models strengthen watermark validation; and improved watermarking aids in the attribution of sandboxing discoveries. This is particularly important in environments where threats change rapidly and unpredictably. Although no single technique can meet every challenge generated by these automated threat engines, together, they can form a flexible, adaptive framework that resists manipulation, identifies provenance, analyzes behavior, and underpins informed decision-making.

Governance, Safety, and Ethical Boundaries

With the growth in automated defense means by organizations and the use of generative tools by attackers to enhance capabilities, the issues of governance, safety, and ethical limits are now of concern. It is the same systems that allow defenders to identify small details, predict threats, and react quickly that can be used to do evil unless proper protection is established or roles are clearly defined. The difference between these structures is industry- and region-specific; however, they are united by one common purpose: they should be used to guarantee that the tools designed to safeguard should not become risky assets by falling into the wrong hands or being repurposed within the company without appropriate attention (Anny, 2025). Risk assessments based on responsible innovation frameworks shed light on these considerations by examining how a tool could be used, misused, or weaponized. They foster organizations to adopt defensive design patterns that, even at some cost to performance, emphasize harmlessness, auditability, and security. This may impede deployment or limit functionality; however, it affirms the more general principle that security technologies should enhance protection without contributing to instability.

This means that there should be a policy on access to monitoring data, the maximum time it can be stored, and the conditions under which it can be used when it is not necessary to achieve immediate security requirements (Ahi & Valizadeh, 2025). This kind of structure would prevent power abuse, preserve trust on the part of the people, and help the organization prove that it appreciates privacy and civil liberties despite its increased defenses against automated attacks. Automated systems are incapable of grasping the extent of the political, legal, or social impact of their actions; therefore, it is perilous to entrust autonomous tools with active counteroffensive decisions that require human judgment.

Thus, there is a need to have some ethical limits that ensure that the defensive actions do not exceed the limits that are acceptable both in the law and in the social setting. Organizations should have a clear declaration of rules that do not allow automated retaliation and the type of defensive measures that are acceptable. Such guidance might authorize systems to sandbox an internal threat, quarantine suspicious activity, or block traffic from outside sources, but not to take offensive action, disrupt distant systems, or try to hack beyond the network perimeter (Zdrojewski, 2025). Only in this way is the legitimacy of an organization's defensive operations preserved, and acts that could be considered hostile, careless, or disproportionate are prevented. There is also an ethical dimension to transparency in automated decision making. Users have a right to know how security systems impact them, why certain actions are taken, and what recourse they have if those actions are mistaken. Providing clear explanations and maintaining accessible documentation support informed consent and reduce confusion in incidents.

CASE STUDIES

Corporate security operations centers, where digital assaults continue to rise, can easily become overwhelmed by noise and false alarms, and incidents can emerge too quickly to be triaged manually. In the last few years, a small number of organizations have started to experiment with implementing generative systems in their SOC processes, not to replace analysts, but to help them structure the priorities, contextualization, and resolution of alerts (Alqahtani & Kumar, 2025). Under these conditions, the SOC is characterized by a layered approach, according to which the generative components are assigned the readiness to synthesize the initial data, and the analysts ensure control. The team started with models that could summarize raw log data in concise incident briefs. Instead of having to sift through several thousand entries in pursuit of suspicious behaviors, analysts receive structured narratives explaining unusual patterns, underlining key indicators, and offering possible motives based on historical behavior. This relieved much of the drudgery of triage and released analysts for more in-depth investigations.

Beyond summarization, generative systems helped the team correlate activities across a wide array of domains. When a credential compromise leads to suspicious internal movement, the system automatically reconstructs an action timeline by cross-referencing authentication logs, endpoint telemetry, and network traces. This is particularly valuable because attackers are increasingly dependent on small, adaptive steps that appear innocuous in isolation but together present a coherent attack strategy. The system enables analysts to respond to an attack sooner in the attack chain than they previously could by consistently composing these fragments (Sanjalawe et al., 2025). Meanwhile, the SOC used generative engines to simulate the possibility of intrusion based on the structure of the network. Such hypothetical attack scenarios were analyzed by the team in routine threat-hunting exercises, which allowed the team to remain one step ahead by modifying defenses before they could be abused by adversaries. However, the SOC knew from a tender age that the truth was all about transparency. Each automated recommendation had an explanation that summarized the evidence, rationale, and confidence of the suggestion. This was a way of evading the traps of analysts blindly taking the results of automated tools but integrating human skills and machine-driven hints into the analysis. The SOC constantly checks the performance to determine where its automated processes are getting the data misconstrued or overreacting to benign anomalies. To maintain this feedback-check process, the organization made its defenses more difficult without compromising clarity and accountability. The result was a practical blend of speed and oversight: machines did the heavy lifting, while humans made decisions with a full understanding of the underlying risks.

There can be no national cyber command whose mandate is to monitor critical infrastructure, government networks, or cross-border threats using entirely manual processes or conventional detection models. In one instance of a national system that incorporates explainable approaches on a large scale, an agency implemented a platform that was intended to map billions of daily events into coherent models of emerging risk. Nevertheless, the volume of the processed data was not the most significant factor, but the transparency that was provided to every step in the interpretation pipeline. The platform does not produce monolithic risk scores but provides in-depth visual and textual descriptions of why some patterns can be taken to imply hostile activity. Such explanations are essential because national security decisions have impacts far beyond the world of the Internet (Khan et al., 2025). Algorithms alone cannot provide analysts and those making decisions with more than algorithmic certainty; they require contextual insight that can be used to connect technical anomalies with larger geopolitical indicators. When the system was used to recognize scanning behavior towards energy infrastructure, it generated evidence not only at the network level, but also historical correlations, preparatory activity patterns, and possible motives based on tension in the region. This allowed professionals to understand whether the action amounted to a normal criminal investigation or whether it could be an initial step before a bigger plan was executed. The system also helps analysts model interdependencies across critical sectors. If anomalies appear simultaneously on transportation and communication networks, explainable outputs highlight shared vulnerabilities that could point to a coordinated campaign.

The concept of transparent modelling is also useful in human-computer interaction in crisis situations. When a warning about a possible breach of the system in the case of municipal systems was issued, a rapid-response session was organized in which automated reasoning traces were discussed in real time. Decision-makers will be able to look at the specific characteristics that caused the alert, see how the model perceived the temporal patterns, and compare this to intelligence reports from other agencies. This understanding is significant and contributes to avoiding incorrect considerations of situations that would lead to further evolution of tensions or unwarranted disturbances (Khan et al., 2025). Meanwhile, the agency implemented a robust governance model, meaning that automated insights were used responsibly because of the sensitivity of threat intelligence operations at the national level. Collectively, transparency, scale, and disciplined oversight allowed the organization to overcome complex threats without undermining the validity of its analytical processes.

On the one hand, large organizations may afford to build advanced infrastructure, but on the other hand, most small- and medium-sized companies fail to cope with cybersecurity because of a low budget, staffing, and specialized knowledge. Generative tools have increasingly been used by start-ups to create protective services for smaller businesses at a low cost. These systems must emphasize ease of use, low cost, and minimum configuration, as opposed to corporate or national systems. In one instance, a start-up in the world of cybersecurity developed a platform that provides automated threat detection and streamlined reporting for smaller organizations. The platform links generative elements to track logs of extensively used tools, such as email providers, cloud systems, and endpoint systems. In the event of suspicious activity, the system generates clear and concise explanations in natural language that will be understood by non-experts on what transpired and what they need to do. Automated incident guidance is one of the most critical services provided by the start-up. If a breach is deemed to have occurred, the generative system generates step-by-step instructions in non-technical, easy-to-understand language. The system would not submerge small businesses in jargon or generalized templates but would analyze their specific structure and provide specific advice based on experience in the field. In this way, even enterprises that have no security team can mount an effective response in a timely manner. The generative component also plays a role in training (Sai et al., 2024). The platform created personalized security drills and educational briefings that mirrored the users' actual environments. This places employees in a good position without the need for expensive external consultants. Start-ups have also realized the usefulness of using generative elements to aid in risk assessment at all times. Using trends in user behavior data, modifications in access control, and system updates, the platform regularly creates risk summaries based on the size and industry of the business in question. These summaries were to be comprehensible without a technical background, hence informing the owners of the business on the decisions that can be made on what investments should be made in security upgrades or adjustments in policies.

For resource-constrained organizations, clarity offers a more approachable way to plan security. Generative simulation tools also allowed the platform to predict the attack scenarios that could potentially lay in wait for a given business based on their technology stack and helped users prioritize the most likely ones rather than attempting to implement wide, unfocused protections. The startup implemented measures to prevent overreach or surveillance beyond what was necessary. The system used only the minimum data required for detection, and all generative outputs were interpretable, helping users understand how or why a particular decision was made in a particular case. This helped reinforce trust in users, particularly small organizations that are cautious about complex security tools. The startup also included the option of human review provided by them, where users could escalate more complex incidents to specialists. Thus, the hybrid balance of automation with human expertise provides accuracy without overstretching SMEs' budgets. From corporate to national to start-up environments, the use of generative tools involves one common theme: such technologies work best for augmenting human capability rather than supplanting it. In each case, interpretability, collaboration, and responsible governance were central to shaping the outcomes. In a corporate SOC, generative systems facilitate the smoothing of analyses and reveal links that would otherwise remain unexpressed. At the national level, transparent modeling aids decision-makers in charting courses with clarity and confidence through multiple complex threats. For SMEs, generative tools democratize access to security knowledge, providing guidance and insight to organizations that do not traditionally have such capabilities. Both environments possess their own unique set of limitations and demands, but they both demonstrate how generative methods reinforce defensive mechanisms when considered thoughtfully, carefully, and in moderation. Adaptability is also an issue in these case studies (Karamchand, 2025). The nature of threats changes at a very fast rate, and the systems are supposed to learn continuously based on new data, new behavior patterns, and changes in attacks. It is a fact that the generative defenses need to be refined, whether it is feedback loops in corporate SOC, cross-agency information sharing in national security situations, and easy-to-use updates in SME platforms. Companies that implement such technologies will discover that the strongest systems are those that combine automation and visibility, speed and responsibility, and innovation and ethical concerns.

Future Directions

The digital defence of the future has shifted towards a place where offensive automation and defensive ecosystems go hand in hand and challenge each other to become ever more sophisticated. As attackers use automated engines that can learn quickly, coordinate in a decentralized style, and manipulate creatively, defensive systems must keep up with them with equally adaptive and intelligent capabilities. This new dynamic is similar to a cycle of an ongoing evolution, where the attack and defense go hand in hand and push each other to the limit against the other. This is because, in such a setting, fixed rules or hard-detecting frameworks are soon outdated. In their place is an ecosystem based on adaptability, situational awareness, and the capacity to foresee changes in adversarial actions (Khan et al., 2025). These future systems will not merely react to threats; they will understand attack strategies as they unfold, simulate potential paths that an attacker might take, and make informed adjustments to strengthen weak points before they are exploited.

The complete ecosystem is more of a self-enhancing and self-defending network of components than a set of independent tools. Insights will be shared with behavioral models, which will inform access controls, automated investigation assistants, and deception environments using monitoring systems (Sood, 2024). All components of the system will work together (Arafah et al., 2025). It is a comprehensive protection layer, where minor deviations can be detected, placed in perspective, and the security posture can be amended automatically. This level of interconnectedness is reminiscent of how advanced malicious automation coordinates multiple parts of an attack toward a single objective, such as reconnaissance scripts, credential harvesters, and adaptive payloads. The only surefire way for an organization to keep pace with the speed and complexity of automated attacks is through the creation of defensive ecosystems with similar internal coordination.

One of the most striking features of this future is the role of predictive simulations. Defensive systems engage in constant hypothetical battles against themselves, using generative components to simulate potential attackers. Rather than waiting for adversaries to innovate, the system will use creative variations of possible breaches to stress-test its defenses. This will aid in the identification of blind spots and areas of weakness and the proposal of specific changes (Mazher & Huma, 2025). This is a shift in defence, whereby defence becomes a proactive field, where fewer surprises are likely to occur, and defenders are more able to anticipate forthcoming threats and respond to them. Another significant trend is the increasing use of quantum technologies to protect generative systems and communication channels. With the rise in computational power and maturity in quantum capabilities, conventional types of encryption are at an increasing risk.

Practically, quantum-secured generative systems ensure the security of the content generated by automated models and the information used to train them is secure. Because training data can be vulnerable to sensitive operational information, it is important to secure them to ensure confidentiality and integrity (Vadisetty & Polamarasetti, 2024). Quantum-resistant protections will be important in ensuring that attackers cannot intercept or manipulate this data, both of which could compromise the reliability of defensive models. Additionally, within systems in which generative systems share information over a distributed network, quantum-secured channels prevent any type of interception and protection against tampering that may influence defenders or reveal sensitive intelligence. As organizations adopt these quantum-aware protective measures, they not only future-proof their infrastructures but also create a foundational layer of trust in environments that will be increasingly dependent on automated decision-making.

Nevertheless, quantum-secured generative systems have their own challenges. They demand vast computing capabilities, dedicated equipment, and the latest protocols that most organizations are not ready to implement today. Eventually, adoption will be broad based on industry efforts and global contracts outlining standards, interoperability, and best practices of quantum resilience. This shows how the world needs to collaborate more internationally in the creation and sustenance of intersectoral and international security infrastructure. International cooperation is becoming increasingly necessary because cyber threats do not usually respect the boundaries of countries (Khan et al., 2025). Machine-based technology can spread bad code around the world in several seconds, organize attacks based on multinational systems, and change tactics based on information on the earth. No individual organization or nation can protect itself against such threats. This means that future security infrastructures will demand the commonality of structures, common surveillance agreements, and uniform ways of defining hazards and assessing models. Nations and sectors need infrastructure to share experiences of new methods of attack, anonymized information on behavior, and organize actions in response to mass threats without jeopardizing privacy and sovereignty.

Such a level of cooperation should be supported by trust, transparency, and the design and governance of automated systems. Organizations should ensure that the generative elements involved in detection, simulation, or analysis are guided by the same ethical and operational principles, regardless of their place of implementation. Common principles of transparency, accountability, and access control will facilitate the fact that such technologies will not be used as tools for surveillance or disproportionate control. International norms of automated defenses can also minimize fragmentation to avoid finding countries or even sectors using different systems that are not compatible enough to communicate or coordinate in cases of crisis. Simultaneously, international collaboration should consider the broad gap between legal frameworks, cultural values, and strategic priorities (Syed, 2025). Certain regions might give privacy a high priority, whereas national security or economic stability might be a priority for others. The process of negotiating the diversity of value systems and the need for effective global defence will require ongoing negotiations, flexible frameworks, and multi-stakeholder models of governance.

These structures should include governments and other leaders in the private sector, universities, civil society, and technical professionals. Through their cooperation, the global security infrastructure would benefit from various forms of insight and would be balanced, ethical, and strong. Another emerging direction is the development of global networks of threat intelligence models that communicate in real time. Rather than relying on human-led information sharing, future infrastructures will embed machine-to-machine intelligence exchange. The defensive models in one region may detect an unusual anomaly and immediately send alerts to systems around the world, which update their models accordingly, reassess risks, and reinforce protective measures (Al-Kateb et al., 2024). This fast coordination of knowledge will stop the spread of attacks and form a kind of global immunity that is capable of acting to halt threats prior to their mass-level propagation. This is an exciting prospect, but it raises questions regarding autonomy, governance, and data rights. This is also an impactful step for group strength at the international level.

Finally, the direction of future defence systems represents a transition towards intelligent, resilient, and globally coordinated ecosystems. They will incorporate predictive simulations, quantum-secured communications, adaptive governance, and collaborative international networks into defenses that change with the threats they are intended to counter (Ishtaiwi et al., 2025). These systems neither eliminate the issues of digital conflict nor provide a platform upon which stronger, more transparent, and ethically based responses can be built. When creating such a future, organizations will discover themselves to be progressively more dependent upon the concepts of collaboration, versatility, and vision, as well as appreciating that security is no longer an attainment but a dynamic, unilateral process that develops by means of both human perception and automated intelligence.

CONCLUSION

The advent of generative technologies in the cybersecurity threat landscape has irrevocably changed the dynamics between attackers and defenders. Indeed, the tempo, scalability, and level of sophistication with which modern threats can be created demand nothing less than a paradigm shift in organizational defense mechanisms. This conclusion emphasizes adaptive frameworks, predictive analytics, deception-based strategies, and automated orchestration-all themes explored throughout the paper-to discuss what will constitute the core elements of a resilient cybersecurity posture, one that will remain unsurpassed by rapidly evolving digital threats. One of the most salient insights derived is that static defenses are no longer sufficient. Traditional security systems were built for an era in which attacks could be anticipated based on historical patterns and identified using fixed signatures. These mechanisms served well when attacks evolved slowly, and attackers relied mostly on manual methods. However, automated threat-generation engines have rendered these approaches inadequate (Ahi & Valizadeh, 2025). Today's threats can change in an instant, spawn limitless variations, and strike along many vectors simultaneously. This new reality demands defenses that are as dynamic and adaptable as the threats.

Adaptive defense frameworks are fundamental to this transformation. Unlike fixed defensive models, adaptive strategies are based on continuous learning cycles that change protection as new information is developed. Deception-based strategies provide another layer of protection, particularly against generative threats. Most automated attack engines extensively scan systems to gather relevant information for crafting future strikes. This is especially necessary in the confrontation of enemies who have automated attack engines that can conduct sophisticated operations within seconds. Automation normalizes the response processes, which are repetitive and free of errors at all times (Ibrar et al., 2025). To achieve effective cybersecurity, further cooperation between departments, such as IT, legal, compliance, and executive leadership, is needed to guarantee the coherent protection of the entire organization. Specifically, training and education should play important roles in the fight against generative cyber threats. When attacks change because of the advancement of threat modalities and detection concepts, human defenders must know how to respond. Educated employees enhance the effectiveness of automated tools through contextual interpretation, strategic thinking, and high-involvement decision-making. Machines and humans need to coexist in a symbiotic relationship to take advantage of each other's strengths in a holistic defense stance.

The other factor that would be considered in this research is the necessity of ongoing supervision. Monitoring a threat landscape motivated by the pace of change should be multilayered and constant. Effective monitoring incorporates network behavior, endpoint, user, and external threat intelligence monitoring. By integrating these sources into a single detection model, companies can create a complete security system that detects minor anomalies that are characteristic of generative attacks. The incidents can be analyzed quickly, and the response systems are updated with up-to-date and correct data, as the incidents are constantly monitored. When embracing advanced defenses, organizations should consider scalability. Not only are such large corporations the targets of generative threats, but an increasing number of small and medium enterprises are victims because of the lack of resources and poorly developed tools. Models of scalable security are needed to provide equal security protection to industries and organizations. Modular orchestration platforms, cloud-based threat detection, and managed security services are accessible solutions for smaller organizations that require strong defender capabilities and do not want to build their own systems. The last theme, which is the basis of this conclusion, is resilience. Authentic cybersecurity is not the prevention of breaches but how systems, operations, and business processes can resist, recover, and evolve in response to disruptive events. Generative threats are resilience-based threats in which high-volume and high-variation attack patterns are generated to overload the defenses. Therefore, resilience means several layers of defenses, backups, constant system testing, and models of adaptive response that would be able to come back to operations, even in case of breaches. Overall, adaptive learning combined with automated orchestration, deceptive intelligence, and predictive analytics can create a resilient environment that can withstand and recover from the traumas of the generation of contemporary threats. Altogether, generative cyber threats demand a different type of defence-one that exceeds the scope of traditional models (Khan et al., 2025). Therefore, organizations must welcome technologies that are meant to operate in a dynamic arena where the threat is ever-changing and evolving. Organizations can fulfill these demands by adopting adaptive frameworks, deploying deception systems, applying predictive analytics, and automating defensive orchestration. Moreover, these actions develop resilience, reduce vulnerabilities, and guarantee faster and more efficient adaptation to malicious practices. The lessons that have come as a result of this exploration are a reminder of a crucial fact: security should evolve as much as the nature of the threat (Khan et al., 2025). Intelligent adaptive and proactive systems in the future will be able to address equally flexible and automated threats and the tools that create them. With prudent execution, cooperation, and continuous growth, any organization can build a safe foundation on which to base trust, stability, and strength in an increasingly complicated digital space.

REFERENCES

Ahi, K., & Valizadeh, S. (2025, June). Large Language Models (LLMs) and Generative AI in Cybersecurity and Privacy: A Survey of Dual-Use Risks, AI-Generated Malware, Explainability, and Defensive Strategies. In *2025 Silicon Valley Cybersecurity Conference (SVCC)* (pp. 1-8). IEEE.

Al-Kateb, G., Khaleel, I., & Aljanabi, M. (2024). CryptoGenSec: A hybrid generative AI algorithm for dynamic cryptographic cyber defence. *Mesopotamian Journal of CyberSecurity*, *4*(3), 22–35. DOI: 10.58496/MJCS/2024/013

Alqahtani, H., & Kumar, G. (2025). A comprehensive review of generative AI techniques and their impact on cybersecurity. *Soft Computing*, *29*(13-14), 1–38. DOI: 10.1007/s00500-025-10702-z

Anderson, D. J., Reynolds, S. M., Carter, E. L., Thompson, R. A., & Yusuff, M. (2025). Using Generative AI for Simulating Cyber Threat Scenarios.

Anny, D. (2025). Adversarial Attacks on Generative AI Models in Cloud Platforms: Detection and Mitigation Strategies.

Arafah, M., Al-Banna, A. K., & Aladawi, A. (2025). Detection and Analysis of AI-Generated Malicious Content. In *Examining Cybersecurity Risks Produced by Generative AI* (pp. 235–276). IGI Global Scientific Publishing. DOI: 10.4018/979-8-3373-0832-6.ch011

Arif, A., Khan, M. I., & Khan, A. R. A. (2024). An overview of cyber threats generated by AI. *International Journal of Multidisciplinary Sciences and Arts*, *3*(4), 67–76. DOI: 10.47709/ijmdsa.v3i4.4753

Helal, M. M., Abu-Elkheir, M., & Mashaly, M. (2025, May). A Generative AI Framework for Cloud Security: Automated Attack Simulation and Threat Detection. In *2025 International Conference on Innovation in Artificial Intelligence and Internet of Things (AIIT)* (pp. 1-8). IEEE. DOI: 10.1109/AIIT63112.2025.11082823

Ibrar, W., Mahmood, D., Al-Shamayleh, A. S., Ahmed, G., Alharthi, S. Z., & Akhunzada, A. (2025). Generative AI: A double-edged sword in the cyber threat landscape. *Artificial Intelligence Review*, *58*(9), 285. DOI: 10.1007/s10462-025-11285-9

Ishtaiwi, A., Aldwcesh, A., & Al-Qerem, A. (2025). Adaptive Risk Mitigation Strategies for Generative AI-Driven Threats. In Examining Cybersecurity Risks Produced by Generative AI (pp. 487-520). IGI Global Scientific Publishing.

Karamchand, G. (2025). Detecting the Abuse of Generative AI in Cybersecurity Contexts: Challenges, Frameworks, and Solutions. *Journal of Data Analysis and Critical Management*, *1*(03), 1–12.

Kayode, B., Adebola, N. T., Akerele, S., Fagbohun, O., Agbo, C., Bantale, O., & Nwokocha, L. C. (2025). The State of AI-Driven Cybersecurity: Trends, Challenges, and Opportunities. *J Artif Intell Mach Learn & Data Sci*, *3*(2), 2731–2739. DOI: 10.51219/JAIMLD/Bisola-Kayode/577

Khan, M. A., Alasiry, A., Marzougui, M., Bayhan, I., Kuna, S. S., Rao, G. S. N., Algamdi, S. A., & Aldossary, H. (2025). Securing Intelligent Transportation Systems: A Dual-Framework Approach for Privacy Protection and Cybersecurity Using Generative AI. *IEEE Transactions on Intelligent Transportation Systems*, 1–12. DOI: 10.1109/TITS.2025.3591007

Mazher, N., & Huma, Z. (2025). The Role of Generative AI in Offensive and Defensive Cyber Operations. *Baltic Journal of Multidisciplinary Research*, *2*(4), 70–75.

Perumal, R., & Aithal, P. S. (2024, December). Significance of Use of Generative AI in Cyber Security. In *Conference Proceedings of Emerging Trends in Information Technology* (Vol. 2, No. 1, pp. 181-191).

Sai, S., Yashvardhan, U., Chamola, V., & Sikdar, B. (2024). Generative AI for cyber security: Analyzing the potential of ChatGPT, DALL-E, and other models for enhancing the security space. *IEEE Access : Practical Innovations, Open Solutions*, *12*, 53497–53516. DOI: 10.1109/ACCESS.2024.3385107

Sanjalawe, Y., ... 'mari, S., & Makhadmeh, S. (2025). Generative AI for Cybersecurity Applications in Threat Simulation and Defense. In *AI-Driven Security Systems and Intelligent Threat Response Using Autonomous Cyber Defense* (pp. 263-304). IGI Global Scientific Publishing.

Singh, A., Singh, D., & Singh, R. (2024). Generative ai for cyberdefense. In Generative, A. I. (Ed.), *Current Trends and Applications* (pp. 121–145). Springer Nature Singapore. DOI: 10.1007/978-981-97-8460-8_7

Sood, A. (2024). *Combating Cyberattacks Targeting the AI Ecosystem: Assessing Threats, Risks, and Vulnerabilities.* Walter de Gruyter GmbH & Co KG. DOI: 10.1515/9781501520549

Syed, S. A. (2025). Adversarial AI and cybersecurity: Defending against AI-powered cyber threats. *Iconic Research and Engineering Journals*, *8*(9), 1030–1041.

Tariq, M. U. (2025). Autonomous Data Orchestration With Generative AI: Redefining Pipelines for Intelligent Analytics. In Elbaghazaoui, B., Amnai, M., & Gherabi, N. (Eds.), *Generative AI-Powered Data Architectures: From Governance to Autonomous Analytics* (pp. 165–192). IGI Global Scientific Publishing., DOI: 10.4018/979-8-3373-5616-7.ch007

Tariq, M. U. (2025). Ethical Implications of Collecting and Using Data to Power AI Tools. In Khan, S., & Pringuet, P. (Eds.), *Empowering Learners With AI: Strategies, Ethics, and Frameworks* (pp. 201–228). IGI Global Scientific Publishing., DOI: 10.4018/979-8-3373-7386-7.ch009

Tariq, M. U. (2025). Enhancing Cyber-Physical System Resilience With Safe Data-Driven Control Strategies. In Arbi, A. (Ed.), *Safe Data-Driven Control for Cyber-Physical Systems* (pp. 103–128). IGI Global Scientific Publishing., DOI: 10.4018/979-8-3373-1832-5.ch004

Tariq, M. U. (2025). Fraud Detection and Mitigation in Cybersecurity Insurance: AI-Driven Approaches and Best Practices. In Alawida, M., Almomani, A., & Al-authman, M. (Eds.), *AI-Driven Cybersecurity Insurance: Innovations in Risk, Governance, and Digital Resilience* (pp. 169–194). IGI Global Scientific Publishing., DOI: 10.4018/979-8-3373-5545-0.ch007

Tariq, M. U. (2025). Defense Mechanisms Against Adversarial Attacks: Strengthening AI Security in Cybersecurity Applications. In Ul Rehman, S. (Ed.), *Challenges and Solutions for Cybersecurity and Adversarial Machine Learning* (pp. 199–226). IGI Global Scientific Publishing., DOI: 10.4018/979-8-3373-2200-1.ch007

Uddin, M., Irshad, M. S., Kandhro, I. A., Alanazi, F., Ahmed, F., Maaz, M., Hussain, S., & Ullah, S. S. (2025). Generative AI revolution in cybersecurity: A comprehensive review of threat intelligence and operations. *Artificial Intelligence Review, 58*(8), 236. DOI: 10.1007/s10462-025-11219-5

Vadisetty, R., & Polamarasetti, A. (2024, November). Generative AI for Cyber Threat Simulation and Defense. In *2024 12th International Conference on Control, Mechatronics and Automation (ICCMA)* (pp. 272-279). IEEE. DOI: 10.1109/ICCMA63715.2024.10843938

Zdrojewski, K. (2025). AI-Powered Cyberattacks: A Comprehensive Review and Analysis of Emerging Threats. *Advances in IT and Electrical Engineering, 31*, 55–70.

KEY TERMS AND DEFINITIONS

Behavioral Security Baseline: Standard activity model used for anomaly detection.

Deceptive Network Environment: Fabricated system pathways diverting adversarial presence.

Threat Mutation Cycle: Repeated alterations of malicious patterns during exploitation.

Chapter 8
Securing the Future: Enhancing Cybersecurity and Resilience in Digital and Software Supply Chains

Md. Owafeeuzzaman Patwary
http://orcid.org/0009-0005-8338-2415
American International University-Bangladesh, Bangladesh

Md. Mobashir Tajuare Partho
http://orcid.org/0009-0003-8908-3710
American International University-Bangladesh, Bangladesh

Raisa Jarin
http://orcid.org/0009-0007-5026-3246
American International University-Bangladesh, Bangladesh

Dipta Gomes
http://orcid.org/0000-0003-3019-6051
American International University-Bangladesh, Bangladesh

Apurbo Biswas
http://orcid.org/0009-0004-8923-5777
American International University-Bangladesh, Bangladesh

Md. Reazul Islam
University at Albany, State University of New York, USA

ABSTRACT

This chapter critically examines the cybersecurity and resilience challenges inherent in digital and software supply chains, where hyper-connectivity enlarges the attack surface and sophisticated adversaries exploit dependencies, as demonstrated by the SolarWinds, Log4Shell, and XZ Utils incidents. Our analysis identifies systemic security issues, ranging from significant visibility gaps to inadequate authentication mechanisms, and traces their direct impact on operational disruption and reputation damage. We explore the distinct security implications associated with foundational technologies, including cloud computing, Internet of Things (IoT), and blockchain, and propose specific hardening strategies tailored to each technology. The central

DOI: 10.4018/979-8-2600-1608-4.ch008

argument presents a layered countermeasure strategy: adopting frameworks such as NIST CSF, embedding rigorous risk assessment, and evolving human factors through targeted training.

1. INTRODUCTION

The modern global economy fundamentally relies on intricate and interconnected digital and software supply chains. Such digitally enabled ecosystems, marked by the pervasive use of information, electronic, and computer technologies throughout their entire lifecycle, have completely altered the working of organizations. This is because they increase efficiency, reduce lead time, and consequently increase profits (Hammi et al., 2023). Serving as frameworks between organizations, digital supply chains provide digitized transactions as well as collaborative work between different stakeholders, extending from suppliers right down to the customer, thus completely transforming traditional ways of working (Hammi et al., 2023). However, this digital transformation, which drives excellence in working practices, brings along its own set of systemic risks. Thus, heightened cyber-threat surfaces, synonymous with such complexly interconnected frameworks, increase vulnerability to more sophisticated cyber threats (Hammi et al., 2023; Kampourakis et al., 2025).

However, this digital transformation, which drives excellence in working practices, brings along its own set of systemic risks. Indeed, recent reports indicate a substantial 52% increase in supply chain attacks in 2023 alone, underscoring their escalating threat to global security (Gracy, 2025). These attacks are particularly insidious as they fundamentally exploit the implicit trust embedded within upstream dependencies and third-party components, facilitating the injection of vulnerabilities and malware (Williams et al., 2025). This inherent stealth and the leveraging of supply chain vulnerabilities as entry points enable adversaries to effectively bypass conventional perimeter defenses, rendering traditional security measures inadequate against such advanced persistent threats (Tan et al., 2025). Therefore, a paradigm shift towards comprehensive, trust-aware security architectures is critically required to safeguard the integrity and resilience of digital supply chains. As illustrated in Figure 1, this insidious propagation exploits supply chain trust relationships for covert and pervasive attacks. These attacks leverage diverse vectors, ranging from vulnerabilities in open-source components to compromised build infrastructures and social engineering tactics targeting developers (Williams et al., 2025). Figure 2 encapsulates the crucial elements that form the basis of cybersecurity in such modern supply chain frameworks.

Embedded within this is the technological basis on which digital supply chains operate. Components such as the Internet of Things, cloud infrastructure, networking, and telecommunications come with their own unique set of security issues. However, the collective complexity of such infrastructure significantly increases the risk of malicious use (Hammi et al., 2023). Following this, globalization driven further through digital connectivity raises the threat of cyberattacks significantly, as this vulnerability grows beyond organizational and national frontiers (Pandey et al., 2020). Considering that there is increasing reliance on third-party service providers and greater connectivity, this essentially means that any weakness, particularly of a security nature, within any component of such infrastructure may pose a threat to the entire system (Boyens, 2020). Thus, this interconnected system requires a more multipronged approach, one that brings together cybersecurity practices, organizational risk practices, and the management of associated supply-chain risks (Boyens, 2020; Hammi et al., 2023).

Software supply chain attacks, categorized under MITRE ATT&CK T1195 Supply Chain Compromise, exploit reliance on interconnected components and automated processes (He et al., 2025). The attack typically begins with malicious code injection into upstream components (e.g., via typosquatting), infecting the build pipeline, and propagating downstream through trusted dependencies (He et al., 2025). This leverages inherent trust in software dependencies and CI/CD automation, allowing malicious payloads to bypass perimeter defenses and leading to widespread compromise (Diao et al., 2025).

Figure 1. Propagation path of a software supply chain attack from upstream compromise to downstream impact

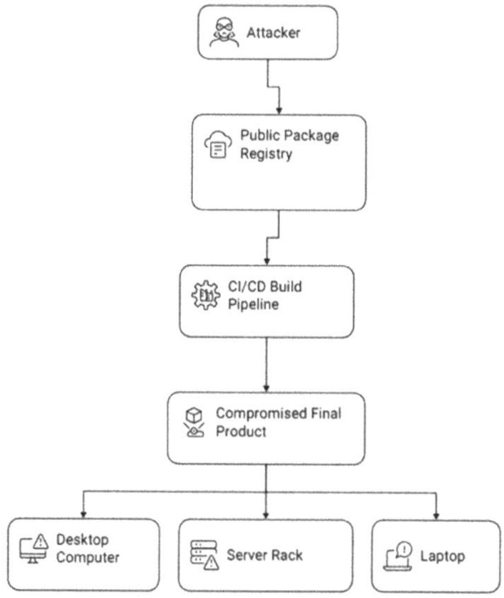

Ensuring digital and software supply chain integrity, therefore, requires strategic goals that focus on confidentiality, integrity, and availability. Among the most critical strategic objectives is countering cyber threats by developing ways of mitigating risks that may arise from malicious or accidental malware injection in open-source or third-party dependencies, as well as securing the entire build-deployment pipelines involved in such systems (Boyens, 2020; Gokkaya et al., 2023; Williams et al., 2025). Equally strategic is the objective of developing resilience, which entails developing the ability to resist, respond, adapt, and recover from cyberattacks with little or no negative impact on quality of service or user experience (Masip-Bruin et al., 2021). However, this must be achieved through strategic frameworks that focus on both organizational and technological aspects (Herburger, 2022; Herburger et al., 2024).

Figure 2. Essential pillars of modern supply chain cybersecurity

Specifically, transparency, separation, and validity within the software supply chain serve as imperative elements for enabling trust within a scenario where there are complex layering and dynamic interactions (Kalu et al., 2024; Okafor et al., 2024). Rather than focusing solely on incident response, proactive security posture is becoming necessary. This involves defense strategies, enhanced security controls, and risk-assessment models that address the complexities associated with the software industry (Gokkaya et al., 2023; Ishgair et al., 2024). Finally, the focus must be set on protecting critical digital assets and intellectual property associated with the escalating threat landscape (Babulak, 2023; Hu et al., 2022). By incorporating such goals into their strategic security frameworks, organizations begin transitioning toward developing digital and software supply-chain ecosystems that are not only efficient and interconnected but also resilient, transparent, and adept at overcoming challenges in a threat-ridden global environment.

2. HISTORICAL EVOLUTION AND TRENDS IN DIGITAL SUPPLY CHAIN SECURITY

2.1. Early Supply Chain Practices (Pre-Digital Era)

Early supply chains were largely manual and operated through isolated systems with minimal digital dependency. Organizations relied on on-premises infrastructure, local software, and limited external integration. Cyber risks existed but were mostly confined to internal IT issues, insider misuse, or physical breaches. Because systems were not deeply interconnected, large-scale cascading cyber incidents were uncommon.

2.2. Transition to Digital Ecosystems (2005–2015)

The introduction of ERP systems, partial cloud migration, and increased automation reshaped traditional supply chains. While these technologies improved coordination and visibility, they also introduced new vulnerabilities such as misconfigurations, weak authentication, and inconsistent security practices across partners. The growing use of third-party software and early open-source components increased exposure to external risks, although large dependency-chain attacks were still relatively rare.

2.3. Modern Digital Supply Chains (2015–Present)

Contemporary supply chains depend heavily on cloud-native platforms, CI/CD pipelines, API-driven services, and extensive open-source libraries. This shift has significantly expanded the attack surface. Incidents like SolarWinds, Log4j, and the XZ Utils backdoor demonstrate how a single compromised dependency can affect thousands of downstream organizations. Studies such as Topping et al. (2022) report a dramatic rise in software supply chain attacks, driven by deep dependency trees and globally distributed development ecosystems.

2.4. Comparative View of Evolving Vulnerabilities

Table 1 presents a concise comparison of how supply chain characteristics and cyber risks evolved across different eras, highlighting the increasing complexity and exposure of modern ecosystems.

Table 1. Key characteristics and dominant vulnerabilities of supply chains before and after digital transformation

Era	Key Characteristics	Dominant Vulnerabilities	Cyber Exposure Level
Pre-Digital Era (1990s–2005)	Manual coordination, independent systems, limited software integration	Insider misuse, physical security issues, isolated IT breaches	Low
Early Digital Era (2005–2015)	ERP systems, partial cloud adoption, moderate automation	Poor configurations, password vulnerabilities, siloed security practices	Medium
Modern Digital Era (2015–Present)	Cloud-native systems, CI/CD pipelines, large open-source dependency chains, IoT devices	Dependency-chain attacks, OSS package poisoning, compromised CI pipelines, large-scale vulnerabilities (SolarWinds, Log4j, XZ Utils)	Very High

This timeline reveals two important patterns. First, efficiency improvements have always been tied to higher interconnectivity, meaning more entry points for attackers. Second, modern software supply chains rely heavily on open-source libraries, automated development pipelines, and global third-party vendors, making them extremely difficult to secure with traditional approaches.

Recent literature (Hammi et al., 2023; Boyens, 2020; Rahman et al., 2021) also highlights that organizations still lack standardized ways to measure cyber resilience or quantify the risks created by these modern ecosystems. This gap underscores the need for more proactive, data-driven, and transparent C-SCRM strategies going forward.

3. CYBERSECURITY IN DIGITAL AND SOFTWARE SUPPLY CHAINS

Cybersecurity in digital and software supply chains focuses on protecting systems, data, and processes from cyber threats. As global trade and operations expand, exposure to vulnerabilities grows, requiring integrated risk management and advanced technologies to ensure trust and continuity across the ecosystem.

3.1. Definition and Introduction

The pervasive integration of digital technologies has transformed traditional supply chains into complex digital and software supply chains, forming the foundation of modern commerce and critical infrastructure (Hammi et al., 2023). These digital supply chains integrate information, digital, and electronic technologies across operational stages, enabling benefits such as reduced lead times, enhanced efficiency, and improved profitability (Hammi et al., 2023). Digital supply chain systems connect organizational frameworks and facilitate digitized transaction processes and collaboration among supply chain partners across the network, including both suppliers and customers (Hammi et al., 2023).

However, this digitalization introduces and expands security vulnerabilities and risks, creating a broader attack surface for cyber intruders (Hammi et al., 2023). Cybersecurity within this context refers to the strategies, best practices, and technologies aimed at protecting these digital and software supply-chain ecosystems. The main objective is to maintain confidentiality, integrity, and availability of data to protect against cyber threats. The discipline designed to manage these risks across interconnected supply chains and ecosystems is Cyber Supply Chain Risk Management, which combines cybersecurity, enterprise risk management, and supply chain management (Boyens, 2020; Hammi et al., 2023; Topping et al., 2022). C-SCRM provides strategic control by identifying, assessing, and mitigating vulnerabilities across the digital ecosystem (Topping et al., 2022).

Software supply chains represent an important subset of DSCs, encompassing elements involved in software development and delivery, such as code, configurations, libraries, and other components (Ahmed & Abdullah, 2024; Melara & Bowman, 2022). Since these components are interconnected, a compromise in one part can lead to failures across the system, causing service disruptions and cybersecurity exploits (Okafor et al., 2022, 2024). This complexity and interdependence necessitate robust cybersecurity measures to maintain trust and prevent disruptions.

3.2. Key Threats and Vulnerabilities

Digital and software supply chains have different technical vulnerabilities. Digital supply chains are often exposed through cloud misconfigured, insecure APIs, and compromised interconnected systems, while software supply chains face threats within development pipelines, including malicious CI/CD runner manipulation and misconfigured package registries. Distinguishing these vulnerabilities enables more targeted security measures.

The expanded attack surface of digital and software supply chains makes them attractive targets for a range of cyber threats. These threats may occur through various vectors and lead to consequences such as unauthorized access, data breaches, system downtime, and financial losses (Ohm et al., 2020; Okafor et al., 2022). Understanding these threats is essential for developing effective defensive strategies. Table 2 summarizes the key threats and vulnerabilities.

Table 2. Key threats and vulnerabilities in digital and software supply chains

Threat Type	Description	References
AI-Driven Adaptive Malware	Malware enhanced with AI or ML capabilities that autonomously evolves, changes signatures, learns detection patterns, and adapts to defenses in real time. Enables highly targeted, persistent, and evasive attacks across supply chain components.	(Amin et al., 2024; Alevizos & Dekker, 2024; Gokkaya et al., 2023)
Algorithmic & Package Ecosystem Attacks	Attacks exploiting software registry logic and package distribution mechanisms, including dependency confusion and package poisoning. These methods introduce malicious libraries into development pipelines, often without immediate detection.	(Okafor et al., 2022; Saeed et al., 2023; Williams et al., 2025)
Blockchain-Based Supply Chain Attacks	Attacks targeting smart contracts, consensus protocols, or off-chain components of blockchain-enabled supply chains. Vulnerabilities can allow data manipulation, fraud, or unauthorized access in decentralized environments.	(Sun et al., 2023; Hamer et al., 2025)
CI/CD Pipeline Attacks	Compromise of automated build systems through malicious runners, poisoned build scripts, or unauthorized pipeline modifications. Allows attackers to inject malware into compiled software.	(Okafor et al., 2024; Williams et al., 2025)

3.3. Case Studies of Cyber Incidents

The theoretical understanding of cyber threats within digital and software supply chains is underscored by real-world incidents. These case studies illustrate the impact of successful attacks, reveal vulnerabilities, and drive the evolution of cybersecurity strategies. They highlight the complexity, sophistication, and broad implications of attacks that exploit supply chain weaknesses (Kampourakis et al., 2025). A summary of major incidents is presented in Table 3.

3.3.1. SolarWinds Attack

The SolarWinds incident remains one of the most significant software supply chain attacks to date. Attackers infiltrated the update mechanism of SolarWinds' Orion platform, a widely used IT performance monitoring tool. Malicious code, known as Sunburst, was injected into official software updates (Gokkaya et al., 2023; Ludvigsen et al., 2022; Roshanaei et al., 2024; Williams et al., 2025). When customers installed these updates, attackers gained backdoor access to their networks, leading to data theft across thousands of organizations worldwide, including U.S. government agencies and Fortune 500 companies (Gokkaya et al., 2023; Mounesan et al., 2023; Roshanaei et al., 2024). This attack demonstrated the risks associated with trusting software updates from third-party vendors and the potential for a single point of compromise to affect a broad network of downstream users (Hamer et al., 2025; Williams et al., 2025).

3.3.2. Apache Log4j Vulnerability (Log4Shell, 2021)

The Log4Shell vulnerability, identified in December 2021, exposed a flaw in Apache Log4j, a widely used open-source logging library. This zero-day vulnerability enabled remote code execution on affected servers by logging a specific string (Topping et al., 2022). The exploit leveraged Log4j's JNDI lookup functionality, which could be manipulated to retrieve and execute code from external servers (Williams et al., 2025). Because Log4j is extensively used across enterprise applications, cloud services, and numerous software components, the flaw threatened millions of systems worldwide and triggered widespread scanning and exploitation attempts by multiple threat actors (Hamer et al., 2025; Topping et al., 2022; Williams et al., 2025).

3.3.3. XZ Utils Backdoor

A recent incident, the XZ Utils backdoor, showcased a highly advanced and stealthy attempt to compromise widely used open-source software. A malicious actor spent years gaining maintainer status for the XZ utilities data compression library and inserted a backdoor into its source code (Hamer et al., 2025; Williams et al., 2025). The backdoor was designed to enable unauthorized remote access via SSH to compromise Linux systems. This critical vulnerability was discovered accidentally before it could be widely exploited, preventing potentially significant damage (Hamer et al., 2025; Williams et al., 2025). The event highlights the vulnerability of foundational open-source components, and the long-term efforts sophisticated threat actors may undertake to infiltrate the software supply chain.

3.3.4. NotPetya Attack

The NotPetya cyberattack, which initially appeared to be ransomware, primarily targeted organizations in Ukraine but quickly spread globally, causing billions in losses. The attack vector was a compromised update system of the Ukrainian accounting software MEDoc (Okafor et al., 2022; Topping et al., 2022). Malicious code was delivered through a seemingly legitimate software update and then leveraged Windows vulnerabilities to propagate autonomously across networks (Okafor et al., 2022). NotPetya demonstrated the destructive potential of supply chain attacks on critical infrastructure and global logistics, highlighting how a compromise in one vendor's software can trigger cascading failures across an interconnected digital landscape (Okafor et al., 2022; Topping et al., 2022).

These incidents, along with others involving third-party vendor breaches, ransomware attacks on shipping lines, and intellectual property theft (Peréz-Morón, 2021), necessitate a multifaceted approach to strengthening supply chain resilience, including robust cybersecurity controls, comprehensive risk assessment, and transparent collaboration among stakeholders (Kampourakis et al., 2025).

Table 3. Major cyber incidents in digital and software supply chains

Incident	Year	Attack Vector	Impact	References
SolarWinds Attack	2020	Compromised update mechanism of SolarWinds Orion; injected "Sunburst" malware into legitimate updates.	Widespread espionage and data exfiltration affecting U.S. government agencies and Fortune 500 companies.	(Gokkaya et al., 2023; Ludvigsen et al., 2022; Roshanaei et al., 2024; Williams et al., 2025; Hamer et al., 2025)
Apache Log4j (Log4Shell)	2021	Zero-day vulnerability in Log4j allowing remote code execution via JNDI lookups.	Millions of systems exposed globally; extensive exploitation attempts by diverse threat actors.	(Topping et al., 2022; Williams et al., 2025; Hamer et al., 2025)
XZ Utils Backdoor	2024	Maintainer injected a backdoor into xz compression library source code over the years.	Discovered before widespread exploitation; could have enabled remote SSH access to Linux systems.	(Hamer et al., 2025; Williams et al., 2025)
NotPetya Attack	2017	Compromised update mechanism of MEDoc accounting software; spread via EternalBlue/EternalRomance exploits.	Global damage exceeding billions of dollars; disrupted critical infrastructure and logistics.	(Okafor et al., 2022; Topping et al., 2022)

4. CYBER RESILIENCE IN DIGITAL AND SOFTWARE SUPPLY CHAINS

Cyber resilience has become a vital component of modern supply chain security, focusing on an organization's ability to withstand and recover from cyber disruptions. In interconnected digital ecosystems, resilience supports operational continuity, protects critical data, and reduces the long-term impact of cyberattacks across the supply chain.

4.1. Concept of Cyber Resilience

Cyber resilience is now recognized as a vital element of cybersecurity strategy, enabling organizations to reduce the impact of cyberattacks, ensure business operations, and protect critical data (Tzavara & Vassiliadis, 2024). It refers to a system's capacity to resist, absorb, recover from, and adapt to adverse conditions, particularly in the face of sophisticated cyberattacks (Pettersen & Grøtan, 2023; Weisman et al., 2024). Cyber resilience emphasizes system recovery by considering the hardware, software, and sensors of cyber infrastructure, sustaining operations, and ensuring mission execution (Rahman et al., 2021). It reflects a system's ability to return to its original performance level after a disruption, especially when highly dependent on cyberspace (Rahman et al., 2021).

Unlike traditional cybersecurity, which focuses on preventing attacks, cyber resilience acknowledges that incidents are inevitable. It therefore prioritizes enduring disruptions, recovering quickly, and continuing operations even in degraded states (Pettersen & Grøtan, 2023). For digital and software supply chains, where cyber risks can severely affect material, information, and financial flows, building specific cyber resilience capabilities is essential (Herburger, 2022; Herburger et al., 2024). This emphasis on resilience is crucial for addressing the unique nature of cyber risks that differ from conventional supply chain disruptions (Herburger, 2022).

4.2. Strategies for Enhancing Resilience

Developing and implementing strategies to increase cyber resilience in digital and software supply chains requires a proactive and integrated approach. These strategies aim to build robust defenses, ensure operational continuity, and support rapid recovery capabilities (Ahmed & Abdullah, 2024; Akinsola & Akinde, 2024).

4.2.1. Redundancy and Diversification

Building redundancy into critical systems and diversifying suppliers and components are foundational strategies for enhancing resilience. Redundancy ensures that if one component fails or is compromised, backup systems can maintain operations (Zhang et al., 2021). Diversification reduces reliance on single points of failure, meaning a compromise in one supplier or software component does not cripple the supply chain (Herburger, 2022; Suryadi & Rau, 2023). This approach aligns with the need to engineer systems with resilience in mind, adopting proactive designs to mitigate threats (Topping et al., 2022). It also involves reconfiguring sourcing strategies to account for cyber risks beyond traditional criteria such as price and quality (Herburger, 2022).

4.2.2. Incident Response Planning

A well-defined and regularly tested incident response plan is essential for cyber resilience. Such plans outline procedures for detecting, containing, eradicating, and recovering from cyber incidents (Gorecki, 2020; Shaked et al., 2023). Effective incident management is crucial for minimizing downtime and ensuring a prompt return to normal operations (Topping et al., 2022). The plan should encompass both technical and procedural elements, fostering a comprehensive view of security (Melara & Bowman, 2022). Collaboration with suppliers during preparation and response phases is also vital (Wallis & Dorey, 2024).

4.2.3. Continuous Monitoring and Improvement

Cyber resilience is not a static state but an ongoing process that requires continuous monitoring and improvement. This involves assessing the security posture of the supply chain, identifying new vulnerabilities, and updating security controls and strategies (Gokkaya et al., 2023; Ishgair et al., 2024). Continuous monitoring also includes tracking threat intelligence to anticipate potential attacks and adapt defenses accordingly (Herburger, 2022). Additionally, fostering collaboration and partnerships among supply chain actors supports adherence to cybersecurity standards and practices, contributing to ongoing improvements in resilience (Masip-Bruin et al., 2021; Wallis & Dorey, 2023). This cycle of evaluation and adaptation ensures that the supply chain remains robust against evolving cyber threats (Zhang, 2024).

4.2.4. Human-Centric Risks in Supply Chain Resilience

Human factors significantly influence supply chain resilience, such as insider mistakes, misuse of access, or compromised accounts can introduce serious vulnerabilities. Behavioral analytics help detect unusual access patterns or workflow deviations that may signal insider threats. Organizational issues such as time pressure, unclear security roles, or weak communication also increase the likelihood of configuration errors or unsafe coding practices. Strengthening identity controls, monitoring user behavior, and reinforcing a security-focused culture help reduce these human-driven risks within interconnected supply chains.

4.2.5. Leveraging AI and Machine Learning for Proactive Resilience

AI and ML enhance cyber resilience by automating anomaly detection and identifying irregular behaviors in dependencies, build processes, or supplier interactions. These tools can flag early signs of compromise and support faster incident response.

Predictive analytics also help identify emerging risks and prioritize vulnerabilities. However, AI-based models require oversight due to issues like false positives or model drift. When properly integrated, AI and ML improve detection speed and strengthen overall supply chain resilience. Achieving cyber supply chain resilience necessitates a structured lifecycle model: Identify critical assets and dependencies; Assess associated risks and vulnerabilities; Mitigate threats through strategic controls; Monitor continuously for emerging threats and Recover efficiently from incidents (Ahmed & Abdullah, 2024).

This iterative process aims to build adaptive capacity. Key resilience metrics for evaluation include quantitative measures such as Mean Time To Detect, Mean Time To Recover, and overall system recoverability post-disruption. Formal definitions and quantitative modeling of resilience, which consider defender objectives and network criticality, are being developed to measure a system's ability to recover from attacks with minimal impact (Dagnas et al., 2025). The foundational principle of a Zero Trust Architecture inherently maps to this resilience lifecycle by eliminating implicit trust. It mandates continuous verification, least-privilege access, and data-centric security across all supply chain interactions, thereby compartmentalizing risks and bolstering the supply chain's capacity to withstand and rapidly recover from sophisticated cyber-attacks (Hassan et al., 2025).

4.3. Future Challenges in Supply Chain Cyber Resilience

Emerging technologies and global dynamics continue to shape the future of cyber resilience in digital and software supply chains. AI-driven threats, such as automated vulnerability discovery or code manipulation, increase the speed and sophistication of attacks. Quantum computing poses long-term risks to cryptographic systems that protect software integrity and update mechanisms. Geopolitical tensions, shifting regulations, and supplier instability also introduce uncertainties that can disrupt digital ecosystems.

To remain resilient, organizations will need stronger visibility across dependency chains, adoption of quantum-safe practices, and closer coordination with international partners. These forward-looking measures are essential for addressing the evolving risks that traditional security approaches may not fully cover.

4.4. Quantitative Indicators for Supply Chain Cyber Resilience

Quantitative metrics help organizations evaluate the effectiveness of their resilience strategies and identify areas needing improvement. Common indicators include vulnerability growth, dependency depth, time-to-detect incidents, and recovery duration following disruptions. Trends such as the rising number of software supply chain CVEs, increased SBOM adoption, and higher frequency of dependency-related attacks highlight the growing complexity of digital ecosystems. Tracking these metrics over time supports more informed decision-making and provides a clearer picture of resilience across interconnected supply chains.

Figure 3. Flow of security issues and their organizational impact

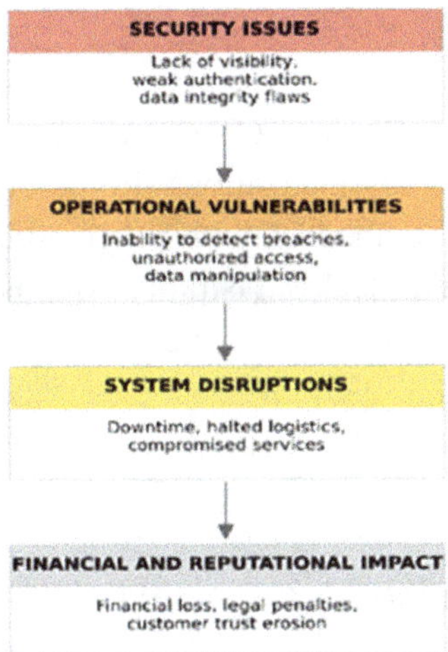

5. SECURITY ISSUES OF THE DIGITAL AND SOFTWARE SUPPLY CHAINS

Digital and software supply chains face cybersecurity challenges due to their complexity, interconnectivity, and dependence on third-party components. These factors can lead to risks such as data breaches, operational disruptions, and reputational damage, making it essential to identify and address vulnerabilities across the ecosystem.

Figure 3 illustrates how multiple security issues can accumulate and create broader challenges in digital and software supply chains. It shows how limited visibility, weak authentication, and data integrity flaws can lead to operational weaknesses. These weaknesses can result in system disruptions, financial loss, and reputational damage. Overall, it highlights how small technical deficiencies can escalate into major business challenges if not properly managed.

5.1. Common Security Issues

Despite advancements in cybersecurity and resilience strategies, digital and software supply chains continue to face several persistent security issues. These challenges often arise from the inherent complexity, interconnectedness, and dynamic nature of modern supply ecosystems.

5.1.1. Lack of Visibility

A significant challenge is the lack of comprehensive visibility into the entire supply chain (Gani et al., 2022). Organizations often struggle to track all components and third-party dependencies embedded within their products and services (Boyens, 2020; Cheung et al., 2021). This lack of visibility extends to the security practices of numerous suppliers and sub-suppliers, making it difficult to evaluate and reduce risk (Boyens, 2020; Hammi et al., 2023). Without clear visibility, detecting anomalies or compromised components becomes difficult, leaving organizations vulnerable to attacks that exploit obscure dependencies (Gani et al., 2022).

5.1.2. Weak Authentication Mechanisms

In many digital supply chain interactions, authentication mechanisms may be inconsistently applied, creating critical entry points for attackers. This includes reliance on outdated security protocols, insufficient use of multi-factor authentication, or poor credential management practices among partners (Madiiarbekova, 2025). Compromised credentials are a frequent vector for initial breaches, allowing attackers to gain unauthorized access and move within interconnected networks (Ishgair et al., 2024). The large number of access points across a supply chain further increases this risk.

5.1.3. Data Integrity and Confidentiality Concerns

Protecting the integrity and confidentiality of data exchanged in the supply chain is essential but challenging. Attackers may attempt to alter data for fraudulent purposes, including intellectual property, customer information, and operational details (Nozari et al., 2021; Pandey et al., 2020). The global structure of supply chains further complicates data protection, as different regions have varying data privacy regulations, making the application of security controls difficult (Ghorashi et al., 2023).

5.2. Impact on Business Operations and Reputation

The security problems in digital and software supply chains can have a severe impact on business operations and reputation.

5.2.1. Operational Disruption

Cyberattacks, whether through malware, ransomware, or supply chain breaches, can severely disrupt critical business operations (Kumar & Mallipeddi, 2022; Peréz-Morón, 2021). Such incidents can cause system downtime, production halts, delays in service delivery, and disruptions in logistics (Cheung et al., 2021; Hammi et al., 2023). These interruptions often result in financial losses, contractual penalties, and reduced productivity (Okafor et al., 2022). For example, a compromise in a third-party IT service provider can cascade across multiple client organizations, hindering their daily activities (Wallis & Dorey, 2024).

5.2.2. Financial Losses

Beyond direct operational disruptions, businesses incur substantial financial losses from cyber incidents. These costs include incident response, forensic investigations, system restoration, legal fees, regulatory penalties, and increased cybersecurity insurance premiums. Data breaches can add further direct and indirect expenses, such as customer notification requirements and potential litigation (Boyens, 2020; Li & Xu, 2020).

5.2.3. Reputational Damage and Loss of Trust

One of the most severe consequences of a cyber incident is the damage to a company's reputation and the erosion of customer and partner trust. A breach can signal to the market that an organization is unable to protect its assets or those of its stakeholders (Hu et al., 2022). Restoring a damaged reputation is a lengthy process that often requires years and significant investment (Burrell et al., 2020). In an interconnected ecosystem, a single breach can also affect the reputation of other entities within the supply chain.

6. SECURITY OF UNDERLYING TECHNOLOGIES

The digitalization of supply chains heavily relies on advanced technologies, each introducing unique security implications and requiring specific best practices. Key technologies include cloud computing, the Internet of Things, and blockchain.

6.1. Overview of Technologies Used in Supply Chains

6.1.1. Cloud Computing

` Cloud computing provides scalable, flexible, and cost-effective infrastructure that supports various supply chain operations, including data storage, analytics, and enterprise resource planning systems. Its widespread adoption has enabled distributed collaboration and improved data accessibility across global supply networks (Hammi et al., 2023; Ramírez-Peña et al., 2020).

6.1.2. Internet of Things

IoT devices, ranging from sensors and RFID tags to smart logistics equipment, enable real-time tracking, monitoring, and automation within supply chains. They provide enhanced visibility into physical processes, asset locations, and environmental conditions, thereby improving operational efficiency and responsiveness (Sallam et al., 2023; Islam et al., 2023).

6.1.3. Blockchain

Blockchain technology, known for its decentralized, immutable, and transparent ledger capabilities, offers significant potential for strengthening trust, traceability, and data integrity in supply chain transactions. It can secure records of origin, ownership transfers, and compliance data across multiple participants (Al-Alawi et al., 2022; Rana et al., 2021).

Figure 4. Security implications of emerging technologies

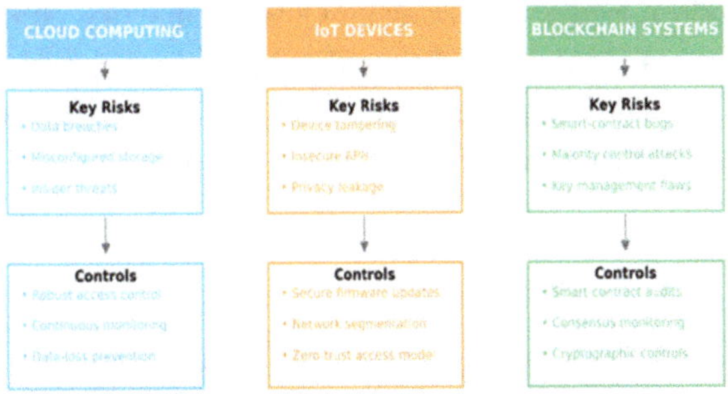

Figure 4 presents a comparative overview of the key security risks and mitigation strategies associated with cloud computing, the Internet of Things (IoT), and Blockchain systems. Each technology introduces distinct vulnerabilities such as data breaches, insecure APIs, or consensus manipulation, which can be mitigated through strong encryption, access controls, network segmentation, and continuous monitoring.

6.2. Security Implications of Each Technology

Each of these technologies, while transformative, introduces distinct security challenges when integrated into supply chains.

6.2.1. Cloud Computing

The primary security implications of cloud computing in supply chains revolve around data control, access management, and compliance. Organizations must contend with the shared responsibility model, in which security responsibilities are divided between the cloud provider and the user. Issues such as misconfigurations, insecure interfaces, unauthorized access, and data leakage remain in critical concerns (Ramírez-Peña et al., 2020). Ensuring data confidentiality and integrity in a multi-tenant cloud environment requires robust encryption, stringent access controls, and careful vendor selection.

6.2.2. Internet of Things

IoT devices in supply chains pose significant security risks due to their typically limited computing power, often weak default security settings, and sheer number

(Madiiarbekova, 2025; Salayma, 2024). Vulnerabilities include weak authentication mechanisms, unpatched software, insecure network services, and physical tampering. A compromised IoT device can serve as an entry point for attackers to infiltrate broader operational networks, disrupt critical processes, or steal sensitive data (Madiiarbekova, 2025; Nozari et al., 2021). Managing the security lifecycle of numerous, geographically dispersed IoT devices presents a complex challenge (Islam et al., 2023).

6.2.3. Blockchain

Although blockchain offers inherent security advantages such as immutability and encryption, its use in supply chains has no implications. Challenges include ensuring the security of off-chain data, managing private keys, and addressing scalability and latency issues that can affect transaction processing (Al-Alawi et al., 2022). Furthermore, the pseudo-anonymity of some blockchain implementations can complicate compliance with privacy regulations, such as the GDPR (Han & Park, 2022). The security of smart contracts, which run automatically on the blockchain, is also critical, because vulnerabilities can lead to irreversible financial or operational losses.

Table 4. Best practices for securing cloud, IoT, and blockchain

Technology	Best Practices	References
Cloud Computing	• Understand Shared Responsibility Model • Implement strong access controls (least privilege, MFA) • Encrypt data in transit and at rest • Continuous configuration monitoring	(Boyens et al., 2021; Ishgair et al., 2024)
Internet of Things (IoT)	• Secure device lifecycle (secure boot, firmware updates) • Network segmentation to isolate IoT • Strong authentication for devices • Regular vulnerability assessments	(Madiiarbekova, 2025; Greuter & Sarmah, 2022; Khondokar et al., 2025)
Blockchain	• Audit smart contracts before deployment • Robust key management practices • Hybrid solutions for sensitive data • Compliance by design (GDPR, zero-knowledge proofs)	(Al-Alawi et al., 2022; Yekeen et al., 2024; Igwe et al., 2024)

6.2.4. Best Practices for Securing Technologies

The rapid integration of cloud computing, IoT, and blockchain has introduced new and complex security issues that require proactive defense strategies. Each technology introduces unique vulnerabilities that require tailored security measures. Table 4 summarizes the best practices for securing these technologies, ensuring resilience against cyber threats and complying with regulatory standards.

7. COUNTERMEASURES TO ENHANCE SECURITY

To effectively address the evolving cyber threat in digital and software supply chains, organizations must implement a comprehensive suite of countermeasures. These measures span organizational frameworks, risk management practices, human factors, and the adoption of advanced technologies.

Adopting established cybersecurity frameworks and international standards offers a structured and consistent approach for managing cyber risks and ensuring a baseline level of security across complex supply chains. These frameworks help unify security practices across supply chain partners, reducing inconsistencies in implementation.

7.1 Cybersecurity Frameworks and Regulations

The proliferation of software supply chain attacks has necessitated the rapid development and enhancement of cybersecurity frameworks and regulations globally, aiming to instill secure-by-design principles and robust risk management throughout the software ecosystem. The NIST Secure Software Development Framework provides a comprehensive set of secure software development practices, guiding organizations in preparing, protecting, producing, and responding to vulnerabilities across the entire software development lifecycle (Lee et al., 2025). This framework is crucial for embedding security into software from its inception, addressing how software development organizations can reduce risk and mitigate attack techniques (Zahan et al., 2023). Concurrently, the Executive Order 14028 updates in the United States have significantly bolstered software supply chain security by mandating Software Bills of Materials for software sold to federal agencies, thereby enhancing transparency and enabling better vulnerability management and risk assessment processes for third-party components (Mirakhorli et al., 2024; Zahan et al., 2024).

In the European Union, the EU Cyber Resilience Act represents a pivotal regulatory development, imposing mandatory cybersecurity requirements for all products with digital elements entering the EU market (Arzt et al., 2024). The CRA explicitly demands secure design and development, vulnerability handling procedures, SBOMs, and coordinated vulnerability disclosure policies, compelling manufacturers and distributors to take greater responsibility for product security throughout their life-cycle (Ruohonen et al., 2025; Ruohonen & Timmers, 2024). Furthermore, the ISO/IEC 42001:2023 AI Management System Standard, introduced in December 2023, provides a systematic approach for managing AI systems, encompassing governance, risk management, and ethical considerations for AI components within the broader supply chain (McIntosh et al., 2024). This standard aims to ensure the trustworthy development and deployment of AI, indirectly contributing to software supply chain security by addressing novel cyber threats and ethical practices associated with AI integration (Pötsch, 2024; Thomas et al., 2024). These frameworks and regulations collectively emphasize secure development, provenance, SBOM generation, diligent vulnerability reporting, and the implementation of mandatory risk controls, thereby fostering a more resilient and transparent digital supply chain. A consolidated comparison of these governance models and regulatory frameworks is presented in Table 5: Summary of Cybersecurity and AI Governance Frameworks.

Table 5. Summary of cybersecurity and AI governance frameworks

Feature	NIST SSDF 1.1	EO 14028	EU CRA	ISO/IEC 42001:2023
Scope	Secure SDLC best practices	Federal cybersecurity mandates	Cybersecurity for EU digital products	AI management system requirements
Applicability	Voluntary guideline	Mandatory for U.S. federal suppliers	Mandatory for EU manufacturers/importers	Voluntary; supports AI regulation compliance
Controls	Secure coding, vulnerability management	SBOM, secure environments, integrity	Secure-by-design, SBOM, disclosure, updates	AI risk, data quality, transparency, oversight
Enforcement	Industry adoption; no direct enforcement	Contractual; affects federal eligibility	Fines, market surveillance, product withdrawal	Certification, audits; reputation impact

7.1.1. NIST Cybersecurity Framework

The National Institute of Standards and Technology Cybersecurity Framework offers a flexible and voluntary approach for managing cybersecurity risk. It provides a common language and systematic methodology for organizations to identify, protect, detect, respond to, and recover from cyber threats (Boyens et al., 2021). NIST CSF version 1.1 introduced specific guidance on Cyber Supply Chain Risk Management, detailing how to integrate supply chain considerations into an organization's overall risk management strategy (Topping et al., 2021). It helps organizations understand and document the risks associated with products and services throughout their life-cycle (Massam & Babulak, 2003). Its tiered structure allows organizations to assess their maturity and gradually enhance their supply chain security posture.

7.1.2. ISO/IEC Standards

The International Organization for Standardization and International Electrotechnical Commission provides a family of standards for information security management. The key among these is ISO/IEC 27001, which specifies the requirements for establishing, implementing, maintaining, and continually improving an information security management system, and ISO 22301 for business continuity management (Tikanmäki et al., 2024). These standards help organizations implement systematic controls to manage sensitive information and ensure resilience against disruptions. Referencing such international standards can reduce the overhead of managing multiple bespoke security control frameworks and promote consistency across diverse supply chain partners (Wallis & Dorey, 2024). Adopting these standards also strengthens trust by demonstrating adherence to internationally recognized security benchmarks.

7.2. Risk Assessment and Management

Effective risk assessment and management are critical for identifying, evaluating, and prioritizing cyber risks within the supply chain. This proactive approach enables organizations to allocate resources efficiently and implement targeted mitigation strategies. A structured risk management approach allows organizations to uncover hidden vulnerabilities early. It also ensures resources are allocated efficiently based on risk priority.

7.2.1. Comprehensive Risk Identification

Organizations must systematically identify potential cyber threats and vulnerabilities across all tiers of their digital and software supply chains, including third-party vendors, open-source components, and cloud services (Emrouznejad et al., 2023). This involves understanding not only direct risks but also the cascading effects of a breach in a single component or partner (Kampourakis et al., 2025). This process provides deeper visibility into interconnected risks that could propagate across multiple supply chain layers.

7.2.2. Impact and Likelihood Analysis

Once identified, risks should be assessed based on their potential impact (e.g., financial, reputational, operational) and the likelihood of their occurrence. This helps to prioritize risks that require immediate attention. Quantitative approaches can be used to measure supply chain resilience and assess interruption with cyber-physical systems (Chen et al., 2020). Such analysis supports data-driven decision-making by quantifying the severity and probability of potential threats.

6.2.3. Continuous Monitoring and Evaluation

Risk management is an ongoing process. Regular assessments, vulnerability scanning, penetration testing, and audits of supplier security postures are essential. Tools such as Security Information and Event Management and Security Orchestration, Automation, and Response can aid in continuous monitoring and threat detection. It is also crucial to establish processes to constantly reconfigure supply chain processes in response to identified cyber risks (Herburger, 2022). Table 6 summarizes the key vulnerabilities across the supply chain lifecycle and the corresponding countermeasures required to mitigate them. Ongoing monitoring ensures that controls remain effective as systems, suppliers, and threats evolve.

Table 6. Key countermeasures across the supply chain lifecycle

Lifecycle Phase	Key Vulnerability	Essential Countermeasure	References
Procurement	Insecure third-party components	Supplier assessments, contract-based security requirements	(Boyens et al., 2021; Pandey et al., 2020)
Development	Vulnerable OSS dependencies, insecure coding	Dependency scanning, secure coding practices	(Okafor et al., 2024; Gokkaya et al., 2023)
Build & CI/ CD	Compromised pipelines, tampered artifacts	CI hardening, artifact signing, SBOM	(Williams et al., 2025; Ishgair et al., 2024)
Deployment	Misconfigurations, leaked credentials	Least privilege, network segmentation, continuous monitoring	(Ramírez-Peña et al., 2020; Chen et al., 2020)
Vendor Ecosystem	Risk propagation across suppliers	Continuous vendor security monitoring	(Boyens, 2020; Kampourakis et al., 2025)

continued on following page

Table 6. Continued

Lifecycle Phase	Key Vulnerability	Essential Countermeasure	References
Incident Response	Slow detection & recovery	IR playbooks, regular exercises, rollback plans	(Gorecki, 2020; Shaked et al., 2023)
Governance	Fragmented policies, compliance gaps	NIST CSF & ISO/IEC 27001 alignment	(Boyens et al., 2021; Tikanmäki et al., 2024)

6.3. Employee Training and Awareness Programs

Human elements remain a significant factor in cybersecurity. Employee training and awareness programs are crucial countermeasures to address insider threats and reduce the likelihood of human error that could lead to security breaches. Well-structured training significantly reduces the likelihood of accidental exposure or internal misuse. It also fosters a culture where employees actively participate in protecting supply chain assets.

6.3.1. Cybersecurity Education

Comprehensive training should educate employees at all levels about common cyber threats (e.g., phishing and social engineering), security policies, and best practices. This includes personnel interacting with supply chains, such as procurement, development, and IT staff (Babulak, 2026; Okafor et al., 2024). The goal is to instill a culture of security in which every employee understands their role in protecting organizational assets (Gopireddy, 2022). Practical examples and clear guidelines help employees recognize and avoid common cyber risks.

6.3.2. Awareness of Supply Chain Risks

Training should specifically highlight the unique risks associated with digital and software supply chain, including the dangers of compromised third-party software, insecure coding practices, and social engineering attacks targeting developers (Babulak, 2026; Venables, 2021). Employees should be aware of the "weakest link" phenomenon and the importance of vetting suppliers and components. Highlighting supply-chain-specific scenarios reinforce the importance of secure development and careful vendor selection.

6.3.3. Regular Refreshers and Simulations

Cybersecurity training should not be a single event. Regular refresher courses, simulated phishing attacks, and incident response exercises help reinforce learning and keep employees updated within the latest threat vectors (Triplett, 2022). Promoting open communication regarding security concerns and vulnerabilities can also foster a more proactive security environment (Burrell et al., 2020). Simulations help evaluate real-world preparedness and reinforce correct response behaviors.

6.4. Leveraging Advanced Technologies

Advanced technologies offer powerful tools to enhance the security posture of digital and software supply chains, moving beyond traditional perimeter defenses to more dynamic and intelligent protection mechanisms (Azgar et al., 2024; Babulak, 2023). These technologies provide capabilities that surpass traditional defenses by offering predictive insights and automation. Their use strengthens both detection accuracy and overall supply chain resilience.

6.4.1. Artificial Intelligence and Machine Learning

AI and ML can significantly augment cybersecurity efforts by enabling automated threat detection, anomaly identification, and predictive analytics across vast datasets within a supply chain (Roshanaei et al., 2024; Wang et al., 2024). These technologies can analyze behavioral patterns to identify sophisticated attacks that traditional signature-based methods might miss, thereby improving the speed and accuracy of security operations (Nia et al., 2016; Roshanaei et al., 2024). They can also optimize various supply chain processes, from demand forecasting to risk assessment, and enhance decision-making (Riad et al., 2024; Yekeen et al., 2024). AI systems enhance threat detection by identifying patterns that may be overlooked by manual analysis (Islam et al., 2023; Nia et al., 2016).

6.4.2. Blockchain Technology

Blockchain technology can enhance the transparency, traceability, and immutability of records within the supply chain (Al-Alawi et al., 2022; Malik et al., 2024). It can provide a tamper-proof ledger for tracking product origins, certifications, and changes, thereby reducing the risk of counterfeit goods and ensuring the integrity of critical supply chain data (Thakur, 2023). Blockchain can also facilitate secure information sharing among supply chain partners while maintaining data privacy

(Ahmed, 2025). Its immutable ledger design ensures that supply chain records cannot be altered without detection.

6.4.3. Automation and Orchestration

Security automation and orchestration tools streamline security processes, allowing for faster response times and reduce human error. These tools can automate vulnerability assessments, patch management, incident triage, and policy enforcement across interconnected systems, freeing up security personnel to focus on more complex strategic tasks. Implementation of automation is crucial for managing the scale and complexity of modern digital supply chains effectively (Sallam et al., 2023). Automated workflows reduce manual effort and ensure consistent enforcement of security policies.

7. THREAT INTELLIGENCE IN DIGITAL AND SOFTWARE SUPPLY CHAINS

Threat intelligence plays a pivotal role in shifting cybersecurity from a reactive to proactive defense strategy. For digital and software supply chains, understanding the adversary's capabilities, motivations, and tactics is essential for building effective protection.

7.1. Importance of Threat Intelligence

Cyber Threat Intelligence is the knowledge and understanding of actual or perceived threats that informs an organization's security decision-making (Ainslie et al., 2023). In the context of digital and software supply chains, CTI is critical for several reasons:

7.1.1. Proactive Defense

The CTI enables organizations to anticipate and prepare potential cyberattacks rather than merely reacting to them. By understanding emerging threats and attack vectors relevant to their supply chain, companies can implement preventative measures before an incident occurs (Amin et al., 2024; Sun et al., 2023). This kind of proactive intelligence strengthens decision making by updating security controls and monitoring suppliers effectively. It further enhances resilience by ensuring organizations are informed about evolving attacker techniques and changing risks (Sun et al., 2023; Boyens et al., 2021).

7.1.2. Informed Decision-Making

The CTI provides valuable insights into threat actors' goals, intentions, strategies, capabilities, and vulnerabilities. This intelligence helps organizations prioritize risks, allocate security resources effectively, and make informed decisions about security investments and mitigation strategies (Ainslie et al., 2023; Saeed et al., 2023). By aligning defensive actions with the contextually relevant and significant threats, CTI ensures that organizations fix vulnerabilities instead of relying on security measures. Additionally, it also supports long-term security planning by showing trends in adversarial behavior and emerging attack techniques (Ainslie et al., 2023).

7.1.3. Enhanced Situational Awareness

For complex, multi-tiered supply chains, the CTI offers a broader view of the threat landscape, encompassing risks originating from third-party vendors, open-source components, and geopolitical factors (Saeed et al., 2023). This enhanced situational awareness is vital for identifying interconnected risks and potential cascading effects (Kommers & Babulak, 2025; Arikkat et al., 2024). This comprehensive visibility allows organizations to access dependencies more accurately and strengthen oversight throughout the entire supply chain of layers. It also facilitates the development of targeted mitigation efforts that address systemic vulnerabilities rather than reacting to isolated threats (Mbah & Evelyn, 2024).

7.2. Sources and Types of Threat Intelligence

Cyber Threat Intelligence (CTI) is essential for enhancing supply chain security by providing actionable insights into potential threats, adversary behaviors, and emerging risks. The CTI can be classified based on where the information comes from (sources) and how it is used (types). Table 7 summarizes the major sources and types of CTI, each offering unique value for proactive defense and risk management (Arisian et al., 2025).

Table 7. Sources and types of cyber threat intelligence

Category	Description
Sources of CTI	
Open-Source Intelligence (OSINT)	Publicly available data from news articles, security blogs, social media, and dark web forums.
Technical Intelligence	Indicators of Compromise (IoCs) such as malicious IPs, domains, file hashes, and network artifacts from malware analysis.
Human Intelligence (HUMINT)	Information from human sources via industry sharing groups, conferences, or security consultants.
Proprietary/Commercial Feeds	Paid subscriptions to platforms offering curated and analyzed threat data for actionable insights.
Government/Industry Sharing	Data shared by agencies (e.g., CISA) or industry-specific ISACs (Information Sharing and Analysis Centers).
Types of CTI	
Strategic Intelligence	High-level analysis of threat actor capabilities and motivations for long-term security planning.
Tactical Intelligence	Details on attacker Tactics, Techniques, and Procedures (TTPs) to configure defenses effectively.
Operational Intelligence	Information on imminent attacks or campaigns for immediate defensive actions and incident response.
Technical Intelligence	Specific IoCs that can be integrated into security tools for automated detection and blocking.

7.3. Integrating Threat Intelligence into Supply Chain Security

Integrating CTI effectively into supply chain security operations requires a systematic approach to collection, analysis, and dissemination.

7.3.1. Collection and Aggregation

Organizations must establish mechanisms to continuously collect threat data from diverse internal and external sources. This often involves leveraging automated feeds, data sharing platforms, and internal security tools (Saeed et al., 2023). Effective aggregation confirms that raw data is combined into a unified view, removing information silos and enabling analysts to detect patterns earlier that may indicate emerging threats (Nia et al., 2016). This process improves the speed and accuracy of the analysis by providing a complete and detailed dataset (Saeed et al., 2023).

7.3.2. Analysis and Contextualization

Raw threat data must be analyzed and contextualized to obtain actionable intelligence. This involves correlating IoCs with known vulnerabilities in the supply chain, understanding the relevance of specific TTPs, and assessing the potential impact on critical assets (Sun et al., 2023). AI and ML techniques can significantly aid in processing vast amounts of CTI data and extracting actionable insights (Alevizos & Dekker, 2024; Alturkistani & Chuprat, 2024).

7.3.3. Dissemination and Action

Actionable intelligence must be disseminated to relevant stakeholders across the organization, including security operations centers, incident response teams, and risk management departments. This ensures that preventative controls are updated, incident response plans are refined, and strategic decisions are made based on the latest threat landscape (Kotsias et al., 2022; Yeboah-Ofori et al., 2021). Integrating CTI into a Cyber Threat Intelligence Platform can facilitate information sharing and promote collaboration among critical supply chains (Arisian et al., 2025).

7.3.4. Feedback Loop

A continuous feedback loop is essential, where the effectiveness of implemented countermeasures is evaluated against new intelligence, leading to iterative improvements in the CTI program and overall security posture (Amin et al., 2024). This adaptive cycle keeps defenses aligned with evolving threat landscapes, and makes sure outdated controls are quickly replaced (Yeboah-Ofori et al., 2021). Over time, this continues to strengthen organizational resilience and enhances the precision of future intelligence-driven decisions.

8. ARTIFICIAL INTELLIGENCE AND MACHINE LEARNING FOR SUPPLY CHAIN SECURITY

Artificial Intelligence (AI) and Machine Learning (ML) are transforming cybersecurity by enabling faster, smarter, and scalable threat detection and response mechanisms. These technologies address the complexity and dynamic nature of cyber threats in digital and software supply chains, offering predictive insights and automation capabilities that traditional methods cannot match.

Table 8. Role of AI and ML in cybersecurity

Function	Description	References
Automated Threat Detection	Analyzes large datasets (network traffic, logs, user behavior) to identify anomalies and IoCs missed by traditional systems.	(Roshanaei et al., 2024; Bhuiyan et al., 2024)
Predictive Analytics	Learn from historical attack patterns to predict future threats and vulnerabilities, enabling proactive defense.	(Aljohani, 2023; Yeboah-Ofori et al., 2021)
Efficiency and Scalability	Handles massive data volumes without proportional increases in human resources; optimizes supply chain processes like forecasting and inventory management.	(Riad et al., 2024; Yekeen et al., 2024)

8.1. Role of AI and ML in Cybersecurity

AI and ML enhance cybersecurity by improving detection, analysis, and response capabilities on a scale. They enable organizations to proactively identify threats and optimize security operations. Table 8 summarizes the key roles of AI and ML in cybersecurity.

8.2. Applications in Threat Detection and Response

AI and ML are applied in multiple areas to strengthen supply chain security. These applications improve detection accuracy, accelerate response times, and enhance overall resilience. Table 9 outlines the major applications of AI/ML in supply chain security. The integration of AI and automation is crucial for fortifying digital supply chains. An AI-driven supply chain security model generally comprises a multi-stage architecture: Data Ingestion Modules collect diverse telemetry (source code, build logs, network traffic); a Feature Engineering Layer extracts security-relevant indicators and an AI Processing Layer performs advanced analytics. Within this layer, anomaly detection algorithms, such as Isolation Forests or one-class SVMs, identify statistical deviations from baseline behaviors in CI/CD pipelines, triggering alerts on events like unusual commit patterns or configuration changes (Malik et al., 2025, p. 7). Sequence behavior modeling, often employing temporal graph learning or Recurrent Neural Networks, analyzes the chronological order and relationships of events within the supply chain to detect Advanced Persistent Threats by identifying anomalous temporal patterns in provenance graphs (Tan et al., 2025). Furthermore, Large Language Models are increasingly pivotal in tasks like code signing verification. LLMs can analyze code semantics to detect potential vulnerabilities, generate rules for malware detection from binary diffs, and assist in summarizing complex changes in software updates to ensure integrity against maliciously injected code, thereby enhancing the trustworthiness of signed artifacts (Kalu & Davis, 2025).

Table 9. Applications of AI/ML in supply chain security

Application	Description	References
Malware & Anomaly Detection	Detects polymorphic malware and abnormal behaviors in software and networks.	(Wang et al., 2024)
Vulnerability Management	Automates vulnerability identification and prioritization based on exploitability and impact.	(Wang et al., 2024)
Incident Response Automation	Speeds up triage, correlates alerts, and initiates containment actions to reduce response times.	(Roshanaei et al., 2024)
Digital Supply Chain Surveillance (DSCS)	Monitors supply network actors and dependencies to detect risky or unethical practices.	(Brintrup et al., 2023)

8.3. Challenges and Limitations

Despite their potential, AI and ML face significant challenges that organizations must address to ensure effective implementation. Table 10 summarizes the key challenges and limitations of AI/ML in supply chain security.

Table 10. Challenges of AI/ML in supply chain security

Challenge	Description	References
Data Quality & Availability	Fragmented or biased data reduces model accuracy and reliability.	(Ronchini et al., 2024)
Evolving Threat Landscape	Requires continuous retraining to counter adaptive attackers.	(Nguyen et al., 2021; Herburger, 2022)
Explainability & Trust	Black-box models hinder transparency and trust in decision-making.	(Shrivastav, 2022)
Resource Intensity & Cost	High computational and financial requirements limit adoption for smaller organizations.	(Ronchini et al., 2024)
Legacy System Integration	Compatibility issues with older infrastructures create new vulnerabilities.	(Shrivastav, 2022)

9. DATA PRIVACY AND COMPLIANCE IN SUPPLY CHAIN MANAGEMENT

Data privacy and regulatory compliance have become paramount concerns in highly interconnected digital and software SCs. Organizations must navigate a complex landscape of laws and regulations while balancing security needs with privacy rights

9.1. Regulatory Landscape Overview: GDPR and CCPA

The increasing volume and sensitivity of data exchanged across supply chains have led to the global implementation of stringent data privacy regulations. Two prominent examples are the General Data Protection Regulation in the European Union and California Consumer Privacy Act in the United States.

9.1.1. California Consumer Privacy Act

Effective since 2020 and expanded by CPRA in 2023, the CCPA grants California consumers significant rights regarding their personal information, including the right to know what data is collected, the right to delete, and the right to opt-out of sales. This applies to businesses that meet certain thresholds and process personal information for California residents. Similar to GDPR, CCPA places obligations on organizations within the supply chain that handle consumer data, requiring them to implement reasonable security procedures and practices (Mbah & Evelyn, 2024). Compliance involves the establishment of robust data mapping, consent management, and data access request mechanisms.

9.2. Balancing Security and Privacy

Achieving robust security while simultaneously upholding data privacy principles presents a complex challenge in supply chain management (Kumar et al., 2025). Security measures inherently involve collecting and analyzing data, which, if not carefully managed, can infringe upon privacy rights.

9.2.1. Privacy by Design

This approach advocates integrating privacy considerations into the design and architecture of IT systems and business practices from the outset (Kumar et al., 2025; Kayhan, 2022). For supply chains, this means building privacy controls into data-sharing protocols, cloud services, and IoT device configurations, rather than as an afterthought (Islam et al., 2023).

9.2.2. Data Minimization and Anonymization

Limiting the collection of personal data to only what is strictly necessary (data minimization) and anonymizing or pseudonymizing the data whenever possible are crucial strategies. This reduces the risk of exposure in the case of a breach, as less identifiable data is compromised (Boyens et al., 2021).

9.2.3. Access controls and Encryption

Strict access controls ensure that only authorized personnel can access sensitive data in the supply chain. Robust encryption protects data both in transit and at rest and maintains confidentiality even if storage systems are compromised.

9.2.4. Transparency and Consent

Organizations must be transparent with their partners and, where applicable, with end-users regarding collection and processing practices. Obtaining explicit consent for data usage is a cornerstone of privacy regulations.

9.3. Strategies for Ensuring Compliance

Ensuring continuous compliance with diverse regulatory frameworks across a global supply chain requires strategic planning and ongoing effort.

9.3.1. Data Governance Frameworks

Implement robust data governance frameworks that define data ownership, roles, responsibilities, policies, and procedures for handling data across the entire supply chain (Labadie & Legner, 2022). This includes clear guidelines for access and processing of third-party data.

9.3.2. Regular Audits and Assessments

Regular privacy impact assessments and compliance audits should be conducted across the supply chain to identify gaps and ensure adherence to regulations. This should be extended to assessing the privacy practices of third-party vendors (Ghorashi et al., 2023).

9.3.3. Contractual Agreements

Ensure that all contracts with supply chain partners include clear clauses regarding data protection, cybersecurity requirements, and liability for data breaches, aligning with relevant regulations such as GDPR and CCPA (Labadie & Legner, 2022).

9.3.4. Employee Training and Awareness

Educate all employees, particularly those involved in data handling and supply chain management, on data privacy regulations and best practices. This reinforces the importance of compliance throughout the organization (Kommers & Babulak, 2025).

9.3.5. Leveraging Technology for Compliance

Technologies such as blockchain can enhance traceability and transparency, helping to prove compliance with specific products or processes (Igwe et al., 2024). Regulatory Technology solutions can automate compliance monitoring and reporting, making it easier to track adherence to evolving regulations (Lehto et al., 2021; Li et al., 2023). Organizations should also consider incorporating cybersecurity standards and C-SCRM practices as a baseline for security measures (Akinsola & Akinde, 2024).

10. CONCLUSION

This chapter examined the cybersecurity and resilience challenges facing modern digital and software supply chains, emphasizing how their complexity, global dependencies, and technological integration increase exposure to cyber threats. The analysis showed that incidents such as SolarWinds and Log4Shell demonstrate how a single compromised component can disrupt entire ecosystems. Human factors, including insider risks and behavioral weaknesses, further contribute to supply chain vulnerabilities.

Strengthening resilience requires combining redundancy, incident response planning, and continuous monitoring with a clearer focus on human-centric risks and emerging technologies. AI and machine learning enhance early detection capabilities, while quantitative indicators offer a more measurable view of resilience performance. As digital ecosystems expand, regulatory developments and geopolitical shifts also shape supply chain stability and influence security requirements.

Overall, securing digital and software supply chains demands a balanced approach that integrates technical controls, risk-based governance, and cross-organizational collaboration. Embedding security-by-design principles and maintaining awareness of evolving threats are essential for sustaining trust and ensuring operational continuity in the digital economy.

Figure 5. Key future trends shaping the supply chain security

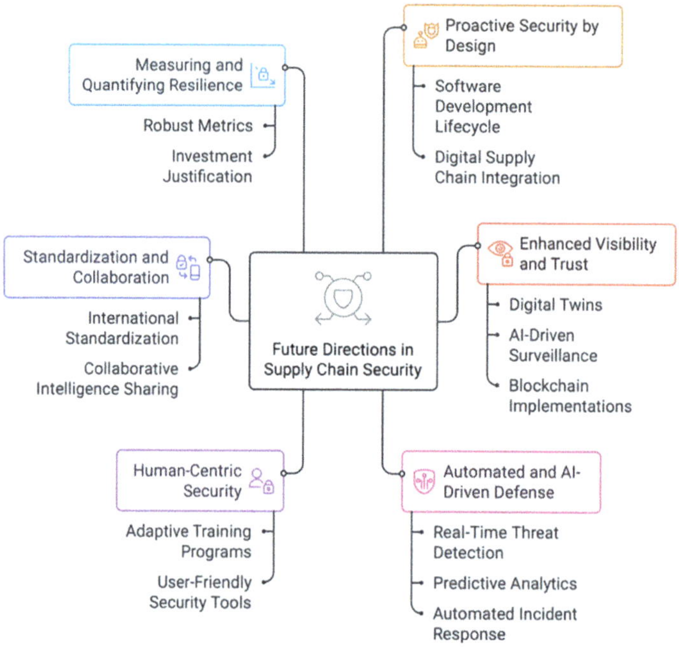

10.1. Future Directions in Supply Chain Security

The dynamic nature of cyber threats ensures that the landscape of supply chain security continues to evolve, necessitating continuous adaptation and innovation. Figure 5 focuses on the areas shaping future research directions in supply chain security. Future research directions include the following:

- **Proactive Security by Design:** Moving towards a security-by-design and privacy-by-design approach across the entire software development lifecycle and digital supply chain integration. This involves embedding security from the initial planning stages rather than as an afterthought (Ishgair et al., 2024).
- **Enhanced Visibility and Trust through Emerging Technologies:** Further adoption and integration of technologies such as Digital Twins, AI-driven

digital supply chain surveillance (Brintrup et al., 2023), and advanced blockchain implementations will provide unprecedented visibility and verifiable trust across complex networks.

- **Automated and AI-Driven Defense:** Increased sophistication of attacks will drive the need for more autonomous and intelligent cybersecurity systems. AI/ML will play an even greater role in real-time threat detection, predictive analytics, and automated incident response, thereby making security operations more efficient and effective (Roshanaei et al., 2024; Wang et al., 2024; Babulak et al., 2025).
- **Human-Centric Security:** Recognizing that human factors remain a primary vulnerability, future efforts will focus on more advanced, adaptive training programs and user-friendly security tools that seamlessly integrate into workflows, reducing the cognitive load on employees and developers (Venables, 2021).
- **Standardization and Collaboration:** Greater emphasis on international standardization and collaborative intelligence sharing platforms will be crucial to effectively combat globalized cyber threats. Industry-wide cooperation and unified regulatory frameworks will foster more resilient collective defense (Wallis & Dorey, 2024).
- **Measuring and Quantifying Resilience**: Developing more robust and standardized metrics for quantifying cyber resilience will enable organizations to better assess their security posture, justify investments, and measure the effectiveness of their countermeasures (Chen et al., 2020; Weisman et al., 2024).
- **Integration of Formal Mathematical Models and Risk Algorithms:** Mathematical models enhance supply chain security by enabling predictive risk-scoring formulas and optimizing cyber resilience investments. Frameworks leveraging multi-criteria decision-making and mixed-integer linear programming optimize supplier selection based on cyber resilience (Kaur et al., 2024). Probabilistic approaches, such as the Cyber Resilience Index, also quantify defense effectiveness against cyber-attacks, translating threat intelligence into actionable metrics for informed decision-making (Alevizos & Ta, 2024).
- **Quantitative and Scenario-Based Technical Forecasting**: Technical forecasting in supply chain security is advancing through AI and ML applications for enhanced risk prediction accuracy and adaptability (Jahin et al., 2024). These models, including Random Forest and XGBoost, are critical for assessing supply chain risks and identifying emerging trends. Research highlights the increasing use of these technologies for early risk identification, process

optimization, and informed decision-making in predictive risk management (Kahya et al., 2025).

- **Multi-Agent Cybersecurity Ecosystems for Supply Chain Defense:** Multi-agent systems offer a decentralized and adaptive defense mechanism for supply chain security, leveraging autonomous AI agents for detection, anomaly classification, and rapid incident response (Sunkara, 2025). These systems can create self-orchestrating capabilities and heightened resilience, especially when integrated with modern AI approaches like foundation models, to address vulnerabilities in global supply chains (Xu et al., 2024).
- **Advanced Cryptographic and Privacy-Preserving Mechanisms:** Advanced cryptographic mechanisms, such as Zero-Knowledge Proofs, provide privacy-preserving data sharing and processing, crucial for enhancing transparency and traceability in IoT-driven supply chains while mitigating data privacy concerns (Jabbari et al., 2024). Hardware Root-of-Trust solutions, implemented using System-on-Chip technology, offer robust hardware-based cryptographic functions for device authentication, secure key management, and integrity verification, foundational for strong supply chain security (Rojas-Muñoz et al., 2024).
- **GenAI and XAI Opportunities for Supply Chain Assurance:** Generative AI shows promise in software supply chain security, for tasks such as identifying code language errors and deprecated code, though challenges remain in memory complexity and managing new data patterns (Alevizos et al., 2024). Explainable AI is instrumental in providing transparency for decision-making in supply chain risk scoring, enhancing trust and enabling informed decisions in complex supply chain interactions (Olan et al., 2024).
- **Architectural and Workflow Diagrams for Enhanced Clarity:** To enhance clarity, architectural and workflow diagrams should be integrated, including empirically grounded reference architectures for software supply chain metadata management to ensure visibility and detect risks (Tran et al., 2024). Utilizing approaches for "living software architecture diagrams," which automatically recover and allow manual adjustment of models from multiple software artifacts, can effectively visualize system architecture, trust boundaries, and verification pipelines (Correia et al., 2024).
- **Alignment With Industry Standards and Security Frameworks:** Aligning with industry standards and security frameworks like ISO 27036 and NIST SP 800-161 is crucial for comprehensive supply chain security, addressing the expanding attack surface and complex threat landscape (Kampourakis et al., 2025). Integrating provenance metadata and adopting security best practices, informed by industry-standard frameworks, can significantly mitigate

risks in CI/CD environments and secure the software supply chain against evolving cyber threats (Patel, 2025).

- **Algorithmic Detailing of Attack and Defense Mechanisms:** Detailed algorithmic descriptions are needed for understanding attack vectors such as poisoning attacks in federated learning, which exploit vulnerabilities in decentralized data training (Mozaffari et al., 2024). Research focuses on analyzing various poisoning attacks and defensive aggregation rules to clarify confusion and connect adversary models. Furthermore, secure aggregation mechanisms are being developed to mask or encrypt user updates, enhancing privacy and robustness against malicious clients in federated deep learning (Zhang et al., 2024).
- **Empirical Benchmarking and Data-Driven Validation:** Empirical benchmarking and data-driven validation are essential for measuring supply chain resilience using key performance indicators and comparing academic frameworks with industry practices (Raaymann & Spinler, 2024). A dynamic resilience management framework can integrate simulation-based resilience assessment with optimization-based approaches to effectively mitigate disruption consequences and manage resilience in deep-tier supply networks under various scenarios (Taghizadeh et al., 2024).

With the combination of these innovative approaches, new technologies, and effective analytical models, the future research can contribute greatly to the resilience, transparency, and credibility of the global digital and software supply chains. Combining AI-based automation, formal mathematical modeling, privacy-preserving cryptography, and standard governance designs is a radical change to proactive, adaptive, and intelligence informed security systems. Since cyber threats are becoming increasingly bigger and more advanced, the future directions do not just solve existing research gaps, but also create the basis of a more powerful, quantifiable, and collaborative method of supply chain security.

REFERENCES

Ahmed, A., & Abdullah, A. (2024). Enhancing software supply chain resilience: Strategy for mitigating software supply chain security risks and ensuring security continuity in development lifecycle. *International Journal of Soft Computing*, *15*(1), 01–18. Advance online publication. DOI: 10.5121/ijsc.2024.15201

Ahmed, W. (2025). *Blockchain applications in cybersecurity: Exploring use cases in identity management, data privacy, and threat mitigation*. Premier Journal of Science., DOI: 10.70389/PJS.100063

Ainslie, S., Thompson, D. G., Maynard, S. B., & Ahmad, A. (2023). Cyber-threat intelligence for security decision-making: A review and research agenda for practice. *Computers & Security*, *132*, 103352. DOI: 10.1016/j.cose.2023.103352

Akinsola, A., & Akinde, A. (2024). Enhancing software supply chain resilience: Strategy for mitigating software supply chain security risks and ensuring security continuity in development lifecycle [Preprint]. arXiv. DOI: 10.48550/ARXIV.2407.13785

Al-Alawi, A. K. S. A. K. R., L. B., Al-Busaidi, R., & Shaikh. (2022). *Towards security enhancement of blockchain-based supply chain management* [Preprint]. arXiv. /arxiv.2209.04917DOI: 10.48550

Alevizos, L., & Dekker, M. (2024). Towards an AI-enhanced cyber threat intelligence processing pipeline. *Electronics (Basel)*, *13*(11), 2021. DOI: 10.3390/electronics13112021

Alevizos, L., & Ta, V.-T. (2024). Threat-informed cyber resilience index: A probabilistic quantitative approach to measure defence effectiveness against cyber attacks [Preprint]. arXiv. DOI: 10.48550/ARXIV.2406.19374

Alevizos, V., Papakostas, G. A., Simasiku, A., Malliarou, D., Messinis, A. M., Edralin, S., Xu, C., & Yue, Z. (2024). Integrating artificial open generative artificial intelligence into software supply chain security. *2024 International Conference on Data Analytics and Business Intelligence (ICDABI)* (pp. 200). IEEE. DOI: 10.1109/ICDABI63787.2024.10800301

Aljohani, A. (2023). Predictive analytics and machine learning for real-time supply chain risk mitigation and agility. *Sustainability (Basel)*, *15*(20), 15088. DOI: 10.3390/su152015088

Alturkistani, H., & Chuprat, S. (2024). Artificial intelligence and large language models in advancing cyber threat intelligence: A systematic literature review [Preprint]. *Research Square*. DOI: 10.21203/rs.3.rs-5423193/v1

Amin, H. E., Samhat, A. E., Chamoun, M., Oueidat, L., & Feghali, A. (2024). An integrated approach to cyber risk management with cyber threat intelligence framework to secure critical infrastructure. *Journal of Cybersecurity and Privacy*, *4*(2), 357–381. DOI: 10.3390/jcp4020018

Arikkat, D. R., Cihangiroglu, M., & Conti, M. A., R. R. K., Nicolazzo, S., Nocera, A., & Vinod, P. (2024). *SeCTIS: A framework to secure CTI sharing* [Preprint]. arXiv. /arxiv.2406.14102DOI: 10.48550

Arisian, S., Halat, K., Hafezalkotob, A., & Maskey, R. (2025). Coopetitive resilience: Integrating cyber threat intelligence platforms in critical supply chains. *Transportation Research Part E, Logistics and Transportation Review*, *197*, 104043. DOI: 10.1016/j.tre.2025.104043

Azgar, A., Nazir, M. I., Akter, A., Hossain, M. S., Wadud, M. A. H., & Islam, M. R. (2024). MNIST handwritten digit recognition using a deep learning-based modified dual input convolutional neural network (DICNN) model. In X.-S. Yang, S. Sherratt, N. Dey, & A. Joshi (Eds.), *Proceedings of ninth international congress on information and communication technology (ICICT 2024)* (Lecture Notes in Networks and Systems, Vol. 1014, pp. 467-478). Springer. DOI: 10.1007/978-981-97-3562-4_44

Babulak, E. (2023). *AI tools for protecting and preventing sophisticated cyber attacks*. IGI Global., DOI: 10.4018/978-1-6684-7110-4

Babulak, E., Al_Dabass, D., & Tomar, G. (. (2025). Editorial: Cyber security prevention, defenses driven by AI, and mathematical modelling and simulation tools. *Frontiers of Computer Science*, *7*, 1685873. DOI: 10.3389/fcomp.2025.1685873

Babulak, E. (Ed.). (2026). *The social impact of next-generation smart cyber technology*. IGI Global., DOI: 10.4018/979-8-3373-5656-3

Bhuiyan, T. M. A.-U.-H.. (2024). Brain tumor detection by image segmentation using customized UNet deep learning-based model. In *Proceedings of the 2024 6th International Conference on Electrical Engineering and Information & Communication Technology (ICEEICT)* (pp. 580–585). IEEE. DOI: 10.1109/ICEEICT62016.2024.10534553

Boyens, J. M. (2020). *Key practices in cyber supply chain risk management: Observations from industry* (NIST IR 8276). National Institute of Standards and Technology. DOI: 10.6028/NIST.IR.8276-draft

Boyens, J. M., Smith, A., Bartol, N., Winkler, K., Holbrook, A., & Fallon, M. (2021). *Cybersecurity supply chain risk management practices for systems and organizations* (NIST SP 800-161r1). National Institute of Standards and Technology. DOI: 10.6028/NIST.SP.800-161r1-draft2

Brintrup, A., Kosasih, E. E., Schaffer, P., Ge, Z., Demirel, G., & MacCarthy, B. L. (2023). Digital supply chain surveillance using artificial intelligence: Definitions, opportunities and risks. *International Journal of Production Research, 62*(13), 4674–4694. DOI: 10.1080/00207543.2023.2270719

Burrell, D. N., Bhargava, N., Bradley-Swanson, O. T., Harmon, M., Wright, J. B., Springs, D., & Dawson, M. (2020). Supply chain and logistics management and an open door policy concerning cyber security introduction. *International Journal of Management and Sustainability, 9*(1), 1–15. DOI: 10.18488/journal.11.2020.91.1.10

Chen, L., Dui, H., & Zhang, C. (2020). A resilience measure for supply chain systems considering the interruption with the cyber-physical systems. *Reliability Engineering & System Safety, 199*, 106869. DOI: 10.1016/j.ress.2020.106869

Cheung, K.-F., Bell, M. G. H., & Bhattacharjya, J. (2021). Cybersecurity in logistics and supply chain management: An overview and future research directions. *Transportation Research Part E, Logistics and Transportation Review, 146*, 102217. DOI: 10.1016/j.tre.2020.102217

Correia, F. F., Ferreira, R. M., Queiroz, P. G. G., Nunes, H., Barra, M., & Figueiredo, D. (2024). *Towards living software architecture diagrams* [Preprint]. arXiv. /arxiv.2407.17990DOI: 10.48550

Dagnas, R., Barbeau, M., García-Alfaro, J., & Yaich, R. (2025). *Graph analytics for cyber-physical system resilience quantification* [Preprint]. arXiv. /arxiv.2504.02120DOI: 10.48550

Diao, M., Diouf, M., Olatunji, I. E., Kaboré, A. K., Mendy, G., Klein, J., & Bissyandé, T. F. (2025). *Characterizing build compromises through vulnerability disclosure analysis* [Preprint]. arXiv. /arxiv.2511.01395DOI: 10.48550

Emrouznejad, A., Abbasi, S., & Sıcakyüz, Ç. (2023). Supply chain risk management: A content analysis-based review of existing and emerging topics. *Supply Chain Analytics, 3*, 100031. DOI: 10.1016/j.sca.2023.100031

Gani, A. B. D., Fernando, Y., Lan, S., Lim, M. K., & Tseng, M. (2022). Interplay between cyber supply chain risk management practices and cyber security performance. *Industrial Management & Data Systems, 123*(3), 843–872. DOI: 10.1108/IMDS-05-2022-0313

Ghorashi, S. R., Zia, T., Bewong, M., & Jiang, Y. (2023). An analytical review of industrial privacy frameworks and regulations for organisational data sharing. *Applied Sciences (Basel, Switzerland)*, *13*(23), 12727. DOI: 10.3390/app132312727

Gokkaya, B., Aniello, L., & Halak, B. (2023). *Software supply chain: Review of attacks, risk assessment strategies and security controls* [Preprint]. arXiv. /arxiv.2305.14157DOI: 10.48550

Gopireddy, R. R. (2022). Human-centric cybersecurity: Addressing the human element in cyber defense and ethical considerations in cybersecurity. *Journal of Artificial Intelligence & Cloud Computing*, *1*(4), 1–6. DOI: 10.47363/JAICC/2022(1)E118

Gorecki, A. (2020). Crafting an incident response plan. In *Cybersecurity Incident Response* (p. 143). Wiley., DOI: 10.1002/9781119679349.ch4

Gracy, S. S. (2025). *A global analysis of data breaches from 2004 to 2024* [Preprint]. arXiv. /arxiv.2502.05205DOI: 10.48550

Greuter, K. O., & Sarmah, D. K. (2022). The baseline of global consumer cyber security standards for IoT: Quality evaluation. *Journal of Cyber Security Technology*, *6*(4), 175–194. DOI: 10.1080/23742917.2022.2105192

Hamer, S., Bowen, J., Haque, M. N., Hines, R., Madden, C., & Williams, L. (2025). Closing the chain: How to reduce your risk of being SolarWinds, Log4j, or XZ Utils [Preprint]. arXiv. DOI: 10.48550/ARXIV.2503.12192

Hammi, B., Zeadally, S., & Nebhen, J. (2023). Security threats, countermeasures, and challenges of digital supply chains. *ACM Computing Surveys*, *55*(14s, 13s), 1–35. DOI: 10.1145/3588999

Han, S., & Park, S. (2022). A gap between blockchain and General Data Protection Regulation: A systematic review. *IEEE Access : Practical Innovations, Open Solutions*, *10*, 103888–103908. DOI: 10.1109/ACCESS.2022.3210110

Hassan, A., Rauf, A., Shafqat, N., Latif, R., & Khan, H. (2025). ZenGuard a machine learning based zero trust framework for context aware threat mitigation using SIEM SOAR and UEBA. *Scientific Reports*, *15*(1), 35871. Advance online publication. DOI: 10.1038/s41598-025-20998-4 PMID: 41087655

He, H., Vasilescu, B., & Kästner, C. (2025). Pinning is futile: You need more than local dependency versioning to defend against supply chain attacks. *Proceedings of the ACM on Software Engineering, 2*, 266. DOI: 10.1145/3715728

Herburger, M. (2022). *Supply chain resilience - A concept for coping with cyber risks*. Research Portal Denmark. https://local.forskningsportal.dk/local/dki-cgi/ws/cris-link?src=cbs&id=cbs-c28fb850-cb66-427a-...

Herburger, M., Wieland, A., & Hochstrasser, C. (2024). Building supply chain resilience to cyber risks: A dynamic capabilities perspective. *Supply Chain Management, 29*(7), 28–49. DOI: 10.1108/SCM-01-2023-0016

Hu, K., Levi, R., Yahalom, R., & Zerhouni, E. G. (2022). *Supply chain characteristics as predictors of cyber risk: A machine-learning assessment* [Preprint]. arXiv. /arxiv.2210.15785DOI: 10.48550

Igwe, A. N., Ewim, C. P.-M., Ofodile, O. C., & Sam-Bulya, N. J.Abbey Ngochindo IgweChikezie Paul-Mikki EwimOnyeka Chrisanctus OfodileNgodoo Joy Sam-Bulya. (2024). Leveraging blockchain for sustainable supply chain management: A data privacy and security perspective. *International Journal of Frontline Research and Reviews, 3*(1), 61–72. DOI: 10.56355/ijfrr.2024.3.1.0030

Ishgair, E. A., Melara, M. S., & Torres-Arias, S. (2024). *SoK: A defense-oriented evaluation of software supply chain security* [Preprint]. arXiv. /arxiv.2405.14993DOI: 10.48550

Islam, M. R., Kabir, M. M., Mridha, M. F., Alfarhood, S., Safran, M., & Che, D. (2023). Deep learning-based IoT system for remote monitoring and early detection of health issues in real-time. *Sensors (Basel), 23*(11), 5204. DOI: 10.3390/s23115204 PMID: 37299933

Islam, M. R., Oliullah, K., Kabir, M. M., Alom, M., & Mridha, M. F. (2023). Machine learning enabled IoT system for soil nutrients monitoring and crop recommendation. *Journal of Agriculture and Food Research, 14*, 100880. DOI: 10.1016/j.jafr.2023.100880

Jabbari, A., Ramachandran, G., Malik, S., & Jurdak, R. (2024). *ZK-DPPS: A zero-knowledge decentralised data sharing and processing middleware* [Preprint]. arXiv. /arxiv.2410.15568DOI: 10.48550

Jahin, M. A., Naife, S. A., Saha, A., & Mridha, M. F. (2024). *AI in supply chain risk assessment: A systematic literature review and bibliometric analysis* [Preprint]. arXiv. /arxiv.2401.10895DOI: 10.48550

Kahya, I., Huschbeck, T., & Markovič, P. (2025). Predictive risk management in the supply chain. In *Studies in systems, decision and control* (p. 41). Springer., DOI: 10.1007/978-3-031-80935-4_3

Kalu, K. G., & Davis, J. C. (2025). *Why software signing (still) matters: Trust boundaries in the software supply chain* [Preprint]. arXiv. /arxiv.2510.04964DOI: 10.48550

Kalu, K. G., Singla, T., Okafor, C., Torres-Arias, S., & Davis, J. C. (2024). *An industry interview study of software signing for supply chain security* [Preprint]. arXiv. /arxiv.2406.08198DOI: 10.48550

Kampourakis, V., Kavallieratos, G., Gkioulos, V., & Katsikas, S. (2025). Cracks in the chain: A technical analysis of real-life supply chain security incidents. *Computers & Security, 148*, 104673. DOI: 10.1016/j.cose.2025.104673

Kaur, H., Gupta, M., & Singh, S. P. (2024). Integrated model to optimize supplier selection and investments for cyber resilience in digital supply chains. *International Journal of Production Economics, 275*, 109338. DOI: 10.1016/j.ijpe.2024.109338

Kayhan, H. (2022). Ensuring trust in pharmaceutical supply chains by data protection by design approach to blockchains. *Blockchain in Healthcare Today, 5*. Advance online publication. DOI: 10.30953/bhty.v5.232 PMID: 36779024

Khondokar, O., Islam, M. R., Babar, J. I., Quraishi, M. A. N., Rahman, M. M., Mahbub-Or-Rashid, M., & Bhuiyan, T. M. A.-U.-H. (2025). FruVeg_MultiNet: A hybrid deep learning-enabled IoT system for fresh fruit and vegetable identification with web interface and customized blind glasses for visually impaired individuals. *Journal of Agriculture and Food Research, 19*, 101623. DOI: 10.1016/j.jafr.2024.101623

Kommers, P., & Babulak, E. (2025). Conceptual awareness for human navigation in A.I. In Babulak, E. (Ed.), *Educational AI humanoid computing devices for cyber nomads* (pp. 1–14). IGI Global., DOI: 10.4018/979-8-3693-8985-0.ch001

Kotsias, J., Ahmad, A., & Scheepers, R. (2022). Adopting and integrating cyber-threat intelligence in a commercial organisation. *European Journal of Information Systems, 32*(1), 35–52. DOI: 10.1080/0960085X.2022.2088414

Kumar, S., & Mallipeddi, R. R. (2022). Impact of cybersecurity on operations and supply chain management: Emerging trends and future research directions. *Production and Operations Management, 31*(12), 4488–4500. DOI: 10.1111/poms.13859

Kumar, S. N., Joy, J., Jane, I. C., James, A., John, S., & Babulak, E. (2025). Applications of 6G in the healthcare sector and the importance of network security and data privacy encryption of medical images using the SHA-256 blockchain algorithm. In *Network Security and Data Privacy in 6G Communication: Trends, Challenges, and Applications* (pp. 176–190). CRC Press. DOI: 10.1201/9781003583127-9

Labadie, C., & Legner, C. (2022). Building data management capabilities to address data protection regulations: Learnings from EU-GDPR. *Journal of Information Technology, 38*(1), 16–38. DOI: 10.1177/02683962221141456

Lehto, T., Myrberger, J., & Pandey, A. (2021). *Continuous compliance using calculated event log layers* [Preprint]. arXiv. /arxiv.2110.00411DOI: 10.48550

Li, J., Maiti, A., & Fei, J. (2023). Features and scope of regulatory technologies: Challenges and opportunities with industrial Internet of Things. *Future Internet, 15*(8), 256. DOI: 10.3390/fi15080256

Li, Y., & Xu, L. (2020). Cybersecurity investments in a two-echelon supply chain with third-party risk propagation. *International Journal of Production Research, 59*(4), 1216–1238. DOI: 10.1080/00207543.2020.1721591

Ludvigsen, K. R., Nagaraja, S., & Daly, A. (2022). *Preventing or mitigating adversarial supply chain attacks; A legal analysis* [Preprint]. arXiv. /arxiv.2208.03466DOI: 10.48550

Madiiarbekova, A. (2025). Cybersecurity in IoT devices: Vulnerabilities, risks, and mitigation strategies [Preprint]. *SSRN*. DOI: 10.2139/ssrn.5075016

Malik, G., Brahmbhatt, R., & Prashasti, P. (2025). AI-driven security and inventory optimization: Automating vulnerability management and demand forecasting in CI/CD-powered retail systems. *International Journal of Computational and Experimental Science and Engineering, 11*(3). Advance online publication. DOI: 10.22399/ijcesen.3855

Malik, V., Khanna, A., & Nalluri, S. (2024). *Blockchain technology in cybersecurity: Uses beyond cryptocurrencies*. PubPub., DOI: 10.21428/e90189c8.d37d59a9

Masip-Bruin, X., Marín-Tordera, E., Ruiz, J. F., Jukan, A., Trakadas, P., Černivec, A., Lioy, A., López, D., Santos, H., Gonos, A., Silva, A., Soriano, J. A. A., & Kalogiannis, G. (2021). Cybersecurity in ICT supply chains: Key challenges and a relevant architecture. *Sensors (Basel), 21*(18), 6057. DOI: 10.3390/s21186057 PMID: 34577264

Massam, P., & Babulak, E. (2003). A decent service level. *Communications Engineer, 1*(3), 34–37. DOI: 10.1049/ce:20030313

Mbah, G. O., & Evelyn, A. N.Geraldine O MbahAchudume Nkechi Evelyn. (2024). AI-powered cybersecurity: Strategic approaches to mitigate risk and safeguard data privacy. *World Journal of Advanced Research and Reviews, 24*(3), 310–324. DOI: 10.30574/wjarr.2024.24.3.3695

Melara, M. S., & Bowman, M. (2022). *What is software supply chain security?* [Preprint]. arXiv. /arxiv.2209.04006DOI: 10.48550

Mounesan, M., Siadati, H., & Jafarikhah, S. (2023). Exploring the threat of software supply chain attacks on containerized applications. *2023 16th International Conference on Security of Information and Networks (SIN)*. IEEE. DOI: 10.1109/SIN60469.2023.10474901

Mozaffari, H., Choudhary, S., & Houmansadr, A. (2024). Fake or compromised? Making sense of malicious clients in federated learning. In *Lecture Notes in Computer Science* (p. 187). Springer. DOI: 10.1007/978-3-031-70879-4_10

Nguyen, V.-L., Lin, P., Cheng, B., Hwang, R., & Lin, Y. (2021). Security and privacy for 6G: A survey on prospective technologies and challenges. *IEEE Communications Surveys and Tutorials*, *23*(4), 2384–2407. DOI: 10.1109/COMST.2021.3108618

Nia, M. A., Atani, R. E., Fabian, B., Babulak, E., & Ebrahimi, R. (2016). On detecting unidentified network traffic using pattern-based random walk. *Security and Communication Networks*, *9*(16), 3509–3526. DOI: 10.1002/sec.1557

Nozari, H., Fallah, M., Szmelter-Jarosz, A., & Krzemiński, M. (2021). Analysis of security criteria for IoT-based supply chain: A case study of FMCG industries. *Central European Management Journal*, *29*(4). Advance online publication. DOI: 10.7206/cemj.2658-0845.63

Ohm, M., Plate, H., Sykosch, A., & Meier, M. (2020). Backstabber's knife collection: A review of open source software supply chain attacks. In *Detection of Intrusions and Malware, and Vulnerability Assessment* (pp. 23–43). Lecture Notes in Computer Science. Springer., DOI: 10.1007/978-3-030-52683-2_2

Okafor, C., Schorlemmer, T. R., Torres-Arias, S., & Davis, J. C. (2022). SoK: Analysis of software supply chain security by establishing secure design properties. *Proceedings of the 2022 ACM SIGSAC Conference on Computer and Communications Security*. DOI: 10.1145/3560835.3564556

Okafor, C., Schorlemmer, T. R., Torres-Arias, S., & Davis, J. C. (2024). *SoK: Analysis of software supply chain security by establishing secure design properties* [Preprint]. arXiv. /arxiv.2406.10109DOI: 10.48550

Olan, F., Spanaki, K., Ahmed, W., & Zhao, G. (2024). Enabling explainable artificial intelligence capabilities in supply chain decision support making. *Production Planning and Control*, •••, 1–18. DOI: 10.1080/09537287.2024.2313514

Pandey, S., Singh, R. K., Gunasekaran, A., & Kaushik, A. (2020). Cyber security risks in globalized supply chains: Conceptual framework. *Journal of Global Operations and Strategic Sourcing*, *13*(1), 103–128. DOI: 10.1108/JGOSS-05-2019-0042

Patel, D. A.Devashish Ghanshyambhai Patel. (2025). Enhancing CI/CD security with provenance metadata and supply chain best practices. *World Journal of Advanced Engineering Technology and Sciences*, *16*(1), 19–27. DOI: 10.30574/wjaets.2025.16.1.1181

Peréz-Morón, J. (2021). Eleven years of cyberattacks on Chinese supply chains in an era of cyber warfare, a review and future research agenda. *Journal of Asia Business Studies*, *16*(2), 371–393. DOI: 10.1108/JABS-11-2020-0444

Pettersen, S., & Grøtan, T. O. (2023). Exploring the grounds for cyber resilience in the hyper-connected oil and gas industry. *Safety Science*, *171*, 106384. DOI: 10.1016/j.ssci.2023.106384

Raaymann, S., & Spinler, S. (2024). Measuring supply chain resilience along the automotive value chain — A comparative research on literature and industry. *Transportation Research Part E, Logistics and Transportation Review*, *192*, 103792. DOI: 10.1016/j.tre.2024.103792

Rahman, S., Hossain, N. U. I., Govindan, K., Nur, F., & Bappy, M. M. (2021). Assessing cyber resilience of additive manufacturing supply chain leveraging data fusion technique: A model to generate cyber resilience index of a supply chain. *CIRP Journal of Manufacturing Science and Technology*, *35*, 911–928. DOI: 10.1016/j.cirpj.2021.09.008

Ramírez-Peña, M., Mayuet, P. F., Vázquez, J., & Batista, M. (2020). Sustainability in the aerospace, naval, and automotive supply chain 4.0: Descriptive review. *Materials (Basel)*, *13*(24), 5625. DOI: 10.3390/ma13245625 PMID: 33321743

Rana, S. K., Kim, H., Pani, S. K., Rana, S., Joo, M.-I., Rana, A. K., & Aich, S. (2021). Blockchain-based model to improve the performance of the next-generation digital supply chain. *Sustainability (Basel)*, *13*(18), 10008. DOI: 10.3390/su131810008

Riad, M., Naïmi, M., & Okar, C. (2024). Enhancing supply chain resilience through artificial intelligence: Developing a comprehensive conceptual framework for AI implementation and supply chain optimization. *Logistics (Basel)*, *8*(4), 111. DOI: 10.3390/logistics8040111

Rojas-Muñoz, L. F., Sánchez-Solano, S., Martínez-Rodríguez, M. C., Camacho-Ruiz, E., Navarro-Torrero, P., Karmakar, A., Fernández-García, C., Tena-Sánchez, E., Potestad-Ordóñez, F. E., Casado-Galán, A., Ortega-Castro, P., Acosta, A. J., Jiménez-Fernández, C. J., & Brox, P. (2024). Cryptographic security through a hardware root of trust. In *Lecture Notes in Computer Science* (p. 106). Springer. DOI: 10.1007/978-3-031-55673-9_8

Ronchini, A., Guida, M., Moretto, A., & Caniato, F. (2024). The role of artificial intelligence in the supply chain finance innovation process. *Operations Management Research*. DOI: 10.1007/s12063-024-00492-2

Roshanaei, M., Khan, M. R., & Sylvester, N. N. (2024). Enhancing cybersecurity through AI and ML: Strategies, challenges, and future directions. *Journal of Information Security*, *15*(3), 320–348. DOI: 10.4236/jis.2024.153019

Saeed, S., Suayyid, S. A., Al-Ghamdi, M. S., Almuhaisen, H. A., & Almuhaideb, A. M. (2023). A systematic literature review on cyber threat intelligence for organizational cybersecurity resilience. *Sensors (Basel)*, *23*(16), 7273. DOI: 10.3390/s23167273 PMID: 37631808

Salayma, M. (2024). Risk and threat mitigation techniques in internet of things (IoT) environments: A survey. *Frontiers in the Internet of Things*, *2*, 1306018. Advance online publication. DOI: 10.3389/friot.2023.1306018

Sallam, K. M., Mohamed, M., & Mohamed, A. W. (2023). Internet of Things (IoT) in supply chain management: Challenges, opportunities, and best practices. *Sustainable Machine Intelligence Journal*, *2*. Advance online publication. DOI: 10.61185/SMIJ.2023.22103

Shaked, A., Cherdantseva, Y., Burnap, P., & Maynard, P. (2023). Operations-informed incident response playbooks. *Computers & Security*, *134*, 103454. DOI: 10.1016/j.cose.2023.103454

Shrivastav, M. (2022). Barriers related to AI implementation in supply chain management. *Journal of Global Information Management*, *30*(8), 1–19. DOI: 10.4018/JGIM.296725

Sun, N., Ding, M., Jiang, J., Xu, W., Mo, X., Tai, Y., & Zhang, J. (2023). Cyber threat intelligence mining for proactive cybersecurity defense: A survey and new perspectives. *IEEE Communications Surveys and Tutorials*, *25*(3), 1748–1774. DOI: 10.1109/COMST.2023.3273282

Sunkara, G. (2025). Multi-agent AI systems for coordinated cybersecurity in smart cities. *International Journal for Research Publication and Seminars, 16*(3), 4–22. DOI: 10.36676/jrps.v16.i3.287

Suryadi, A., & Rau, H. (2023). Considering region risks and mitigation strategies in the supplier selection process for improving supply chain resilience. *Computers & Industrial Engineering, 181*, 109288. DOI: 10.1016/j.cie.2023.109288

Taghizadeh, E., Venkatachalam, S., & Chinnam, R. B. (2024). A dynamic resilience management framework for deep-tier supply networks. *Cleaner Logistics and Supply Chain, 13*, 100174. DOI: 10.1016/j.clscn.2024.100174

Tan, Z., Anagnostopoulos, C., & Singer, J. (2025). Distributed temporal graph learning with provenance for APT detection in supply chains [Preprint]. arXiv. DOI: 10.1109/ICDCSW63273.2025.00071

Thakur, A. (2023). Market trends and analysis of blockchain technology in supply chain. *Frontiers in Blockchain, 6*, 1142599. Advance online publication. DOI: 10.3389/fbloc.2023.1142599

Tikanmäki, I., Savolainen, J., & Ruoslahti, H. (2024). The role of standards in enhancing cybersecurity and business continuity management for organizations. *Information & Security: An International Journal, 55*(1), 63–76. DOI: 10.11610/isij.5523

Topping, C., Dwyer, A. C., Michalec, O., Craggs, B., & Rashid, A. (2021). Beware suppliers bearing gifts!: Analysing coverage of supply chain cyber security in critical national infrastructure sectorial and cross-sectorial frameworks. *Computers & Security, 108*, 102324. DOI: 10.1016/j.cose.2021.102324

Topping, C., Michalec, O., & Rashid, A. (2022). *Contrasting global approaches for identifying and managing cybersecurity risks in supply chains* [Preprint]. arXiv. / arxiv.2208.02244DOI: 10.48550

Tran, N. K., Pallewatta, S., & Babar, M. A. (2024). An empirically grounded reference architecture for software supply chain metadata management. *Proceedings of the 28th International Conference on Evaluation and Assessment in Software Engineering*. DOI: 10.1145/3661167.3661212

Triplett, W. J. (2022). Addressing human factors in cybersecurity leadership. *Journal of Cybersecurity and Privacy, 2*(3), 573–587. DOI: 10.3390/jcp2030029

Tzavara, V., & Vassiliadis, S. (2024). Tracing the evolution of cyber resilience: A historical and conceptual review. *International Journal of Information Security, 23*(3), 1695–1721. DOI: 10.1007/s10207-023-00811-x

Venables, A. (2021). Modelling cyberspace to determine cybersecurity training requirements. *Frontiers in Education*, *6*, 768037. Advance online publication. DOI: 10.3389/feduc.2021.768037

Wallis, T., & Dorey, P. (2023). Implementing partnerships in energy supply chain cybersecurity resilience. *Energies*, *16*(4), 1868. DOI: 10.3390/en16041868

Wallis, T., & Dorey, P. (2024). Collaboration practices for the cybersecurity of supply chains to critical infrastructure. *Applied Sciences (Basel, Switzerland)*, *14*(13), 5805. DOI: 10.3390/app14135805

Wang, H., Sua, L. S., & Alidaee, B. (2024). *Enhancing supply chain security with automated machine learning* [Preprint]. arXiv. /arxiv.2406.13166DOI: 10.48550

Weisman, M. J., Kott, A., Ellis, J. E., Murphy, B., Parker, T., Smith, S. C., & Vandekerckhove, J. (2024). *Quantitative measurement of cyber resilience: Modeling and experimentation.* ACM Transactions on Cyber-Physical Systems., DOI: 10.1145/3703159

Williams, L., Benedetti, G., Hamer, S., Paramitha, R., Rahman, I., Tamanna, M., Tystahl, G., Zahan, N., Morrison, P., Acar, Y., Cukier, M., Kästner, C., Kapravelos, A., Wermke, D., & Enck, W. (2025). Research directions in software supply chain security. *ACM Transactions on Software Engineering and Methodology*, *34*(5), 1–38. Advance online publication. DOI: 10.1145/3714464

Xu, L., AlMahri, S., Mak, S., & Brintrup, A. (2024). Multi-agent systems and foundation models enable autonomous supply chains: Opportunities and challenges. *IFAC-PapersOnLine*, *58*(19), 795–800. DOI: 10.1016/j.ifacol.2024.09.200

Yeboah-Ofori, A., Islam, S., Lee, S. W., Shamszaman, Z. U., Muhammad, K., Altaf, M., & Al-Rakhami, M. (2021). Cyber threat predictive analytics for improving cyber supply chain security. *IEEE Access : Practical Innovations, Open Solutions*, *9*, 94318–94337. DOI: 10.1109/ACCESS.2021.3087109

Yekeen, A. O., Ewim, C. P.-M., & Sam-Bulya, N. J.Adeoluwa Omoyemi YekeenChikezie Paul-Mikki EwimNgodoo Joy Sam-Bulya. (2024). Enhancing supply chain security and transparency with AI and blockchain integration for future-proof solutions. *International Journal of Frontline Research in Science and Technology*, *4*(1), 43–57. DOI: 10.56355/ijfrst.2024.4.1.0052

Zhang, Q., Mohammed, A. Z., Wan, Z., Cho, J.-H., & Moore, T. J. (2021). Diversity-by-design for dependable and secure cyber-physical systems: A survey. *IEEE Transactions on Network and Service Management*, *19*(1), 706–729. DOI: 10.1109/TNSM.2021.3091391

Zhang, X. (2024). The impact of digital technologies on supply chain resilience: A framework analysis. *Advances in Economics Management and Political Sciences, 140*(1), 155–164. DOI: 10.54254/2754-1169/2024.GA18772

Zhang, Y., Behnia, R., Yavuz, A. A., Ebrahimi, R., & Bertino, E. (2024). Uncovering attacks and defenses in secure aggregation for federated deep learning. *2022 IEEE International Conference on Data Mining Workshops (ICDMW)* (pp. 650). IEEE. DOI: 10.1109/ICDMW65004.2024.00090

Chapter 9
Ensuring Safety of Financial Institutions in the Modern Era Through Quantum Computing and Cybersecurity

P. Ashok
http://orcid.org/0000-0002-5859-6041
Symbiosis Institute of Digital and Telecom Management, India

S. Lakshmi Sridevi
Chennai Institute of Technology, India

Sarala Patchala
KKR and KSR Institute of Technology and Sciences, India

Sidharth Sahoo
http://orcid.org/0009-0001-0974-7683
Symbiosis Institute of Digital and Telecom Management, India

ABSTRACT

Quantum computing imperils cybersecurity by utilizing superposition and entanglement—via algorithms like Grover's and Shor's—to breach classical RSA and ECC encryption. To secure critical economic data, particularly within European banks, the adoption of lattice-based, hash-based, and code-based cryptography, along with Quantum Key Distribution (QKD), is essential. This paper outlines a future "Architecture of Quantum Banking" (AQB) rooted in post-quantum cryptog-

DOI: 10.4018/979-8-2600-1608-4.ch009

raphy. Beyond defense, the study explores how financial institutions can leverage QAOA and Quantum Monte Carlo simulations to optimize portfolios, accelerate derivative pricing, and enhance fraud detection. Additionally, quantum-enhanced machine learning and blockchain integration promise superior anomaly detection and transaction security. To navigate scaling challenges, the research emphasizes the necessity of collaboration between banks, technology firms, and research institutes to balance innovation with robust risk management.

1. INTRODUCTION

The accelerated discovery of quantum computing is a double-edged sword for the global financial environment. On one hand, probabilistic nature of qubits provides exponential increase in the speed for optimisation problems and Monte Carlo simulations and promises to revolutionise risk management and trading strategies. On the other hand, such a power to process data threatens to break up the cryptographic basis of digital banking. Specifically, Shor's algorithm made the factorisation of large numbers (prime numbers are the foundation of RSA encryption) easy and this could expose sensitive financial information to decryption. Unlike limitation of computing upgrades, appearance to the quantum era (makes) a fundamental place overhaul in security infrastructure. This document begins with an investigation of the convergence of quantum mechanics and financial cyber security, analysing the need for Post-Quantum Cryptography (PQC). The purpose of the research is to assess financial institution preparedness, investigate the architecture integration of quantum error correction into banking systems and suggest strategic frameworks on how to deal with the "quantum winter" while preparing for fault tolerant scalability.

2. LITERATURE REVIEW

The field of study introduced by Xue (2023) is the characteristics of quantum computers, which are devices that utilize concepts of quantum physics for the aim of carrying out calculations with larger speed and complexity in comparison to classical devices. These quantum systems provide an exemplary ability towards processing large amounts of data and provide extremely accurate information in fields of interest like chemistry, cryptography, and artificial intelligence. Their basic difference to conventional computing is the use of quantum mechanical phenomena as a basis for the information processing. Kumar and others (2024) examine the revolutionary potential of quantum computing, one such technology using quantum bits; so-called qubits, in order to do calculations much faster than classical computers. The authors consider important concepts such as superposition and entanglement, before presenting a variety of applications that span from cryptography to optimization to drug discovery and machine learning, all of which illustrate the transformative effect that quantum computing promises for the society. The review S. A. Vanceranen et al. (2023) of recent advances in quantum computation technology focuses on the technology's basis in the principles of quantum mechanics, in particular superposition and entanglement. The authors assess how quantum computers may surpass limitless class calculation limits as well as the continued challenges and also research needs for achieving this possibility. Saravanamoorthi (2023) has a detailed introduction to the technologies in quantum computing that show that they are based on the laws of quantum mechanics and their ability to perform complex calculations better than traditional machines do in terms of speed and efficiency. The paper outlines different applications of the various organizations, ranging from cryptography and computational chemistry to artificial intelligence, and emphasizes the importance of quantum computing in addressing problems that have evaded classical methods as they pave their way for industrial and even societal change. Saklani and collaborators (2023) review in a very comprehensive way the quantum computing, exploring on it the basic principles, the architecture designs and the practical applications. The authors, while discussing the behavior of qubits, development of quantum algorithms and any latest advance in industry that could bring about the development of quantum computing, also deal with the challenges that are being posed by error correction and fault tolerance. The narrative focuses on the far-reaching implications that quantum computer will have in a variety of fields of science and technology and especially in the aspects of security and the evolution of current frameworks of computer technology. The present situation of quantum computing is at the edge of a major technological breakthrough, being able to give strong solutions to problems which are too difficult to be solved with classical solutions. Superconducting qubits, trapped ion systems, and photonic platforms have visibly advanced and collectively succeeded to advance the maturity of scalable quantum architectures. Nevertheless, problems like error sensitivity, decoherence and integration at scale remain massive obstacles that must be overcome in order to fully leverage the capabilities of this technology. P. Memorn & M. Hazelnajer (2024) Mid-click revolution in aerospace and ongoing innovation in AI and advanced quantum computing. Memorn also writes Unlocking the Full Potential of Quantum Computing: Strandaget Hanford Hanford and McMahon Future school for illustrious no-brainer. They emphasize the need for closing the gaps between basic research, algorithm development and industrial implementation, to create a synergy ecosystem, able to drive developments in this new nascent area. Sood, and Pooja. (2023) Scientometric assessment of the last decade of quantum computing research, highlighting its growing scope and perceived advantages Sood, R. &

Chandwal, S. W. 94. Using a systematic analysis of literature indexed in the Web of Science, authors provide insights into important research poles, trends in research, and emerging challenges to provide strategic advice for future investigations and collaborative work across disciplines. Mathew and Payne (2023) teach that quantum computing represents a paradigm shift that is grounded in the notion of quantum mechanics and it helps solve complex problems that have defied classical methods of computation. While supercomputers are limited by the conventional components that make up the machines, quantum computers offer the possibility to break these limits by the profound strategical engineering of materials and quantum circuits sources. Sheoran et al. present the evolution of quantum computing, standing out for the capability of the computation to solve problems that traditional computation cannot. The authors go over the development of quantum hardware, algorithmic innovations, and application areas that have demonstrated quantum hardware becoming more transformed into a mature technology. The manuscript clearly explains the underlying mathematical and scientific principles that support quantum computing, while articulated the challenges associated with it and highlighted the need for further research in order to harness the full potential of this technology. Shen (2024) analyzes the convergence of quantum computing and artificial intelligence and claims that based on the quantum architecture we can overcome the traditional limiting factors of computers in mindware and especially on a concept of quantum neural networks and sophisticated optimization algorithms. The authors also conduct surveys of prevailing obstacles and map prospective trajectories in this infant area. Quantum computing provides the benefit of optimized portfolio optimization, fraud detection, and risk analytics. KPMG, for example, has shown improved performance on portfolio management using quantum techniques, while PayPal has worked with IBM to use quantum-augmented fraud detection (Smith & Johnson, 2025). While quantum computation represents a threat to the cryptography schemes that are still in place, it also drives the innovation of post quantum cryptography. KPMG emphasises the need of switching to quantum-resistant cryptographic protocols. IBM's strategic roadmap (2024 - 2027) sees a prediction for a qubit count of ten thousand to more than ten thousand qubits and the rest of quantum critical supercomputers by 2025. Concurrent forecasts stress on a paradigm shift from just increasing quantity of qubits to importance of qubit quality that will be developed by 2026 (Lee & Kim, 2025). Quantum simulations accelerate molecular studies relevant to drug discovery which helps reduce the costs of R&D as well as development timelines. Cambridge Quantum has collaborated with Roche to analyse genomic data sets for oncological therapeutics whilst Anthem utilise the quantum instrumentation available in IBM to aid detection of anomalies in health (Patel & Singh, 2025). Quantum algorithms are also used to strengthen relative meteorological calculations and optimisation for electrical grids. IBM provides quantum-augmented weather data sets to Apple and Google while the United States Department of Energy uses quantum computation to manage the power grid (Davis & Taylor, 2025). Quantum annealing has been demonstrated as a way of refining the way we plan routes or even for inventory logistics. Coca-Cola Japan is experimenting with the quantum solutions for their supply chain operations, and D-Wave's collaboration with Toyota produced better traffic optimisation than classical algorithms (Chen & Wang, 2025). Quantum simulations are driving breakthroughs for applications from room multiplicity superconductivity to Chinese batteries for collaboration. Bosch is using quantum computing to investigate energy storage phenomena and Daimler is collaborating with IBM on the best way to design semiconductors. The increase in the potential of quantum algorithms being able to refine financial modelling and risk assessment research is well-represented recently in many scholarly symposia, such as Quantum Computing Applications in Economics and Finance Conference (2025). Major banking institutions, such as HSBC and Intesa Sanpaolo, are exploring developments in quantum computing to further their operational efficacies, financial simulations, and machine learning operations towards bettering their operations in risk modelling and fraud detection (Intallura, 2024). One of the sectors Moody's identifies as a key early adopter of quantum technologies is the finance sector, an industry located in the present trends emphasising bespoke hardware solutions and focused efforts on workforce development to harness quantum advancements in finance (Moody's, 2025). Quantum computing is expected to revolutionise the application of financial risk management by optimise the portfolio composition of investment products or simulate complex scenarios in the financials market more efficiently than classical paradigms (SpinQuanta, 2025). Quantum-Cloud Platforms are in the process of being developed for elite, enhanced performance for the portfolio management, risk assessment and fraud detection in finance industries, taking advantage of quantum algorithms (BlueQubit, 2025). As these platforms become more mature, the creation of significantly strong security - validation testing environments in cloud begins to become a critical prerequisite for deployment (Bucur & Babulak, 2019).

3. IMPORTANCE OF CYBERSECURITY IN FINANCIAL INSTITUTIONS

Financial institutions are an especially hot target, due to the large amounts of voluminous confidential data they hold. The cybersecurity posture of this sector is inevitable not only for retaining public trust but also for retaining the financial reservoir and stability of the entire economic ecosystem. The advent of the capabilities of quantum computing works to worsen these concerns as such devices may potentially make existing cryptographic primitives obsolete. Attacks are traditionally directed at corporations and enterprises; financial institutions in particular are appealing to attackers, due to their rich stores of personally identifiable information, money, and transaction records. Therefore, a comprehensive cybersecurity strategy has to be implemented to protect data from criminal actors and state-sponsored enemies. Somebody stated in these latest scholarly frameworks that it should aim for preventative measures to be informed by artificial intelligence systems and rigorous mathematical modeling to anticipate and mitigate sophisticated incursions (Babulak et al., 2025; Babulak, 2023). Trust continues to be the linchpin of the finance domain, with citizens, corporations, and government entities assuming these institutions will be the most confident with their management of their data and assets. A erosion of confidence, induced by constant security fears, converts directly into a financial loss, and forces authorities to implement more rigid regulatory oversight. Accordingly, increased security postures can help build stakeholder confidence and maintain such confidence at the same time. Maintaining a high degree of continuity of service is not only an operational nicety but is a basic engineering principle of maintaining institutional confidence (Massam & Babulak, 2003). Financial institutions are responsible for meeting a series of statutes and industry standards that aim to keep the infrastructure in place safe. Failure to do so subjects institutions to litigation, money sanctions and operational paralysis.

4. QUANTUM THREAT AND CYPTOGRAPHIC TRANSITION:

Due to the sensitive information that financial institutions handle, they are always at risk of cyber threats. In the context of such a situation, the preservation of trust, the protection of monetary assets, and the support of the general stability of the financial system, cybersecurity assumes a position of paramount importance within this industry. This imperative is further boosted by the impending development of quantum computer technology which could offer the potential to make current cryptographic techniques obsolete. The RSA, ECC and AES schemes have long formed the backbone of the modern realm of digital security. Each of these algorithms is based on mathematical problems that so far are practically impossible for classical computers to set up, or solve, in a practical time frame. The encryption mechanism used in encrypted communications is RSA, in which messages are encrypted using a public key, which is then decrypted using a private key; this had been pioneered by Rivest, Shamir, and Adleman and is based on the very difficult problem of factoring large composite numbers. RSA continues to be the most popular choice in the field of secure data transfer, digital signatures and key exchange, because RFC 3560 outlines its security characteristics very well. Elliptic Curve Cryptography (ECC) is based on the mathematical structures of elliptic curves defined over finite fields for the resilience of the technique. It has a comparable level of security as RSA, but requires significantly smaller key sizes to conserve bandwidth and processing connections. Symmetric algorithm of a block cipher such as Advanced Encryption Standard (AES) which uses a secret key to encrypt fixed sized blocks of data and has been implemented as the de facto basis for encrypting data of all forms, including secure communications, file and disk encryption. Financial institutions contain enormous troves of sensitive information - including personal information, financial transactions, and proprietary algorithms - whose compromise stand to cause significant financial losses, legal liabilities and, most importantly, reputational damage. Such outcomes highlight the need for strong protection of such information by cybersecurity frameworks aimed at protecting this information from cybercriminals and nation-state adversaries. Trust is the very foundation of the financial sector; customers, businesses and governments all rely on these institutions to protect their assets and personal information. A compromising security breach destroys this trust, causing attrition of clients, revenue loss and increased regulation. Consequently, the financial institutions can only maintain or regain confidence among their stakeholders with the implementation of advanced cybersecurity controls. On top of that, these entities were operating in highly regulated spaces created to ensure the security of the entire financial system and economy. Compliance with standards, e.g. the General Data Protection Regulation (GDPR) or the Payment Card Industry Data Security Standard (PCI DSS), is mandatory; these standards bring a set of requirements that, if not respected, can lead to heavy fines, legal consequences and operational interruptions. In light of the accelerated maturation of quantum computing technology, there is an obvious trend toward quantum-resistant algorithms, for example, lattice-based cryptography. As these novel algorithms are incorporated into preexisting infrastructures, issues of reliability, security and ease of implementation are of the utmost importance. Lattice Based Algorithms involves other encryption methods such as NTRU and digital signature methods including BLISS. Lattice-based algorithms undergo investigations to great depth, ensuring robust security, which makes these algorithms promising candidates for post-quantum cryptography.The McEliece cryptosystem, which is built around binary Goppa codes, is one of the oldest in the family of code based cryptographic systems. While its key sizes are cumbersome, they provide strong encoding against quantum attacks. XMSS (eXtended Merkle Signature Scheme) and SPHINCS (Stateless Practical Hash-based Incredibly Nice Cryptographic Signatures) are also included in the list.

5.COMMERCIAL APPLICATIONS OF QUANTUM COMPUTING

There is potential for quantum computing technologies to drive substantial change in various sectors, where classical systems fall short, and this is about to take place. Encryption in cyber security has developed towards modern methods lately such as RSA, which is based on pairs of combinatorics. However, because quantum computers were thought to be able to disrupt RSA encryption, Peter Shor's algorithm made it possible to do so. Since then, businesses have perceptibly invested in quantum encryption methods. This parallels advancements in other critical sectors; for instance, the healthcare sector is adopting blockchain algorithms (SHA 256) and 6G to secure medical imagery (Kumar et al., 2025). Similarly, the quality of service provision in information infrastructures must be rigorously assessed to ensure resilience against quantum threats (Babulak, 2006). For example, KETS Quantum Security creates compact quantum encryption hardware, whilst EvolutionQ offers risk management and cybersecurity services. Quantum computing in stake addresses the problems which are considered difficult to solve, portfolio optimization and risk management among them. Some of the other problems in finance, such as credit genomics, arbitraging, and pricing of derivatives, have a close connection to the quantum solutions for the traveling salesman problem. QMC are effective in derivative pricing and risk modeling, substantially reducing computing power. Quantum based financial tools are developed by Cogniframe and Multiverse computing specializes in developing quantum algorithms for financial simulations._Sensing the market's larger gravity, quantum technology is bound to emerge as a primary technology with a class above potential use case. Even though the tech hasn't really developed all that far, there have been some noticeable strides in the research and application facet of things. Siovatu continues to encapsulate everything in detail explaining the commercial leverage and monetization facets of the technology in question. With the likes of major companies, venture capitalist and even government programs, quantum computing is able to get an influx of billions in funding. Heavyweights of the tech industry such as *Google, IBM, Microsoft and D-Wave* are all in the fray, betting massive amounts of money to create useable quantum systems (Sheoran et al., 2024). When it comes to *Google Quantum AI, 2019* marked the year in which they claimed to have reached one of the goals set on the roadmap; this was the "quantum supremacy" goal which allowed quantum computers to do specific assignments more quickly than the most efficient traditional supercomputers available. As part of the research and business cooperation projects, IBM has received many donations to make its cloud quantum computer accessible through the *IBM Q platform.* A pioneer in position quantum annealing, Canadian company D-Wave Systems today develops equipment for solving combinatorial optimization tasks. The Quantum Initiative Act of the United States signed in 2018 was covered with the amount of $1.2 billion for cybersecurity measures as well as the combination with AI technology. The country of China has also put significant investment into quantum technologies, which includes the biggest fund that has been made in order to construct as well as fully develop quantum research networks. The European Union has addressed the issue of quantum-nonlinearity by introducing its Quantum Flagship Program which in turn promised over 1 billion euro in a stretched period of 10 years. There is a growing number of quantum software development startups that are constructing and building algorithms and applications with great variety. These include: Xanadu, which is focused on photonic quantum computing and has recently introduced quantum-as-a-service (QaaS) on the cloud and IonQ, a technology and fabrication company that is using trapped-ion technology in conjunction with superconducting qubit outfits for more accurate quantum functions; and Rigetti Computing which specializes in making superconducting quantum processors. Currently, there are dozens of startups and companies that are willing to make use of quantum algorithms in improving their performance. These algorithms are pioneers in that they take advantage of quantum principles such as optimization and tunneling in order to improve the current solutions.

6. FINANCIAL APPLICATIONS: OPTIMIZATION AND SIMULATION:

These days, financial institutions are looking into the world of quantum computing, especially in cases where the latter has an advantage over the former. Though research is still being done, large scale quantum computers are not available as yet. Quantum Approximate Optimization Algorithm (QAOA) and Variational Quantum Eigensolver (VQE) are regarded as two quantum algorithms that aim to achieve optimum asset allocations in portfolios. These algorithms are predicted to work much more quickly than conventional methods. Quantum computing allows for the improvement of multi-dimensional problem risks modeling. Application of risk analysis algorithms such as Monte Carlo simulations can be harnessed by quantum computing, and as a result, precise risk analysis can be done faster. The precision and efficiency epayments fraud detection can be increased quantum ML algorithms such as Quantum Support Vector Machines and Quantum Neural Networks. Furthermore, detecting unidentified network traffic using pattern-based random walks can be integrated with quantum analysis to identify anomalies more effectively (Nia et al., 2016). It can analyze and predict customer behavior, preferences, and patterns to further refine service delivery using quantum-enhanced machine learning techniques in financial institutions which lead to deeper insight regarding customer data. However, as these automated systems grow, maintaining conceptual awareness for human navigation within AI environments is essential to ensure ethical and accurate decision-making (Kommers & Babulak, 2025). Secure communication with some financial institutions is being enabled through the use of quantum key distribution (QKD). Communication is secure as the exchange of cryptographic keys is made after detecting the absence of interception attempts through quantum mechanics. Classical encryption techniques are no match to quantum computing technology, and in preparation for this, financial institutions are turning to quantum prone algorithms that are guaranteed to keep information safe even in a quantum environment. The pricing of complicated financial options can be carried out alongside risk management simulation with the aid of quantum Monte Carlo (QMC). These simulations can be undertaken with classical computers but doing so with quantum computers may yield better results in terms of efficiency. What this translates to is better pricing models and risk assessments and management. D-Wave Systems has designed a variety of quantum annealers which are being adopted more and more by the financial sector due to their ability to solve complex optimization problems. Additional applications include the appraisal and perfection of trading strategies, in which risk minimization is pursued at the same time as profit maximization. Moreover, these devices make market behavior and market dynamics easier to simulate and to find out the trends and corresponding trading decisions. Financial institutions are actively researching the walk hand in hand integration of quantum computing and block chain technology (Toxic) to enhance security, scalability, and process utility/ efficiency. Quantum algorithms, in particular, will have the disadvantage possibility to fine-tun the data agreed upon and to speed up the transaction processing in the block chain infrastructures. A significant number of financial firms are forming partnerships with quantum computing enterprises, scholarly institutions and technology vendors to research quantum applications. The financial services sector encompasses an enormous number of fundamental activities (asset management, banking operations, insurance services, etc.) that are all inherently data-intensive, while requiring the use of high-dimensional and complex computational algorithms for a proper management, risk evaluation, and maximization of the value of investment returns. Unfortunately, classical computers have specific deficiencies when it comes to the problems that can be efficiently solved in the space of large-scale computations. This is where quantum computing presents a solution to a paradigm shift with the ability to transform a multitude of operations in the domain of finance.

There are many corporate banking solutions that can be implemented in global companies where trade finance and many intricate use cases are present. Such institutions usually have the highest stake in quantum computing and can put it to good use. The approach that involves using an array of parameters and multipliers which progressively increase in quantity to render a particular decision is termed collateral optimization. The problem estimation tasks can be rephrased by the use of a quantum computer, where some elements can be computed separately, sent back and integrated into the main system, the same pre-qualification steps that accompany the decision-making process for granting a loan can also be done with parallel computing. Buying and built-up certain mathematical models online assist computers to comprehend how the world works, what events lead to different outcomes, and what features are significant. Such automation can lead to aides making the better lending decisions while US managed to gain support for general liquidity shocks. This technology could assist the entire spectrum of liquidity in the market. For example, expansion can lead to a full course of liquefying substances. While executing transaction banking assets of different classes can become obtainable because of quantum computing or communication through quantum networks. Non-tangible assets, blockchain solutions' development supervision along with fast and secure communication methods also aided in the creation of smart fault tolerant contracts.

In banking systems, risk is one of the most intricate units as it requires the identification, control and reporting of risk metrics across other units. However, due to quantum computing, the ways in which regulation standards that are associated with risk will certainly change. With quantum computing, machine learning allows risk administrators to simulate more assets and factors with a potential concentration lowering the risk's pricing, thus allowing even more deal volumes with greater returns. Quantum computers are indeed capable of revolutionizing encryption technology such as standard embedding methods into constructions of one-dimensional codes or parallel optimal source coding. But until such point in time promises to be kept by authorities, malicious entities will be able to use quantum encryption to access any data without any issues. With quantum cryptography appearing to be the only highly secure method available, several industrial researchers as well as practitioners are coming up with proposals that aim to test the practicality of PQC and QKD. While attempting to address this issue, however, researchers should be impelled to fusion both technologies together in order to achieve a higher security level and aim for a full encryption of the bionic neural network of the artificial intelligence being created by high-level corporations, which would render the encryption worthless. Furthermore, the politics around quantum technology and its applications are assumed to be in favor of expanding quantum key distribution infrastructure rather than modular integral systems supported large-scale quantum computing centers, as expected future multilevel expenses do favor those point-of-core components along with expected budget issues, and this can work in favor of IP bifurcation. While Avail and Retalik have ambitions of building brand synonymous with retails change on reliable liquidity options and stage ambitions on margin market, the core business general like retail would drive the quantum systems agglomeration and IP market divisions expansion around various markets.

Retail banking applies quantum computing structures for purpose-driven changes that accelerate change in branches for mid-banking where individual assets and the client volume drive expansion across lower demographics. Two primary use cases are credit-decision algorithms and collateral optimization which should have greater precision on them. The former can use quantum computers to take into account a wider range of pertinent variables. The latter may include a greater number of values and data types as the constraints of the optimization problem. Since the problems on the retail banking side tend to be low in complexity and number of variables due to the nature of the problem structure, the assumption is made that there is not much benefit to be gained in this business unit. To a lesser extent, quantum portfolio computing could also increase the effectiveness of a portfolio optimization. Quantum states will protect payments whilst also enabling them to be processed much quicker than the blockchain. More importantly, quantum payments will solve the perpetual problem of money laundering within the blockchain. All money that possesses quantum states can be termed as at least one form of money that cannot be counterfeited since it cannot be copied. Another important precondition for quantum payments we expect to be realized are the devices needed for QKD. In the future this could lead to a scenario where injecting money into the qubits of wireless networks makes intra- and interbank trades very secure. The more unequivocal steady implementation of quantum money will thus radically change the landscape of all banks.

7. QUANTUM BANKING ARCHITECTURE

Quantum computers depend on qubits, which are susceptible to errors stemming from control imperfections and external noise. Building a reliable quantum computer requires a modular approach to this problem, where several layers of architecture (as in Figure 1) are devised, increasingly fine-tuning operations to reduce errors. Also, detailed process flow among the layers is shown in Figure 1 and Figure 2.

Figure 1. Quantum banking architecture layers

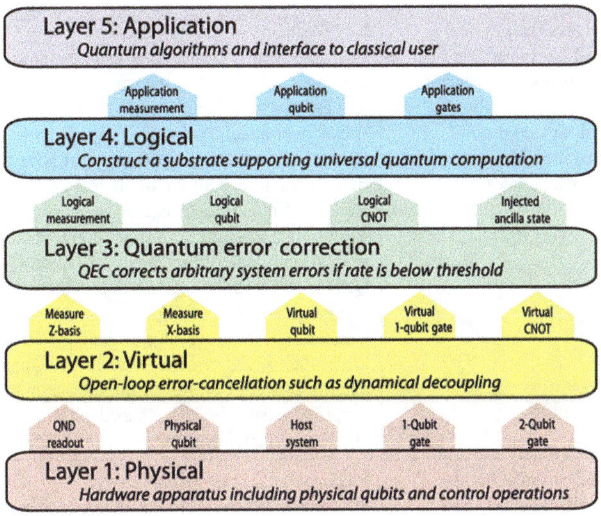

This structure includes the most basic and highest parts of the computer's architecture (as in Table 1):

Table 1. Quantum banking architecture layers

Layer	Description
Physical Layer: Oversees the physical qubits and operational hardware. This subsection acts as the primary hardware of the quantum computer concepts. It comprises qubits alongside their environmental control measures alongside initialization and control devices.	Key Elements of the Physical Layer: Physical Qubits: Qubits have trapped ions, superconducting circuits, or electro chromic spines within quantum channels. The architecture demonstrates the optical control of electron spines over quantum dots. Control Mechanisms: Application of laser pulse and magnetic field puts into use Single qubit and Two qubit gates. Hadamard pulses are executed to accomplish Single qubit gates which alter the spin state of electrons. In relation to one of the above, two qubit Gates apply, cavity QED to assist in linking together qubits that are next to one another in space. Challenges: There are several challenges in the Physical Layer such as Depressing noise levels, Quantum Gate Fidelity and high speed. Control techniques ought to be employed to suppress noise sources such as dephasing which come from nuclear spin environment.
Virtual Layer: Graded physical qubits are synthesized into virtual qubits and augmented using error correction codes. The Virtual Layer bringing forth virtual qubits enables the use of physical qubits but turns them into more sound units that are not prone to errors that are easy to correct. On the other hand, such error correction devices as dynamical decoupling can be utilized in this layer for prolongating how long a qubit is coherent.	Mechanisms of the Virtual Layer: Spin Echos evolved into decoupling sequences such as the custom 8H sequences enable the reduction of noise and systematic errors brought about by the environment. The 8H sequence works, for example, to reduce pulse errors of quantum dots. Virtual Gates: Such higher performance gates greatly reduce the errors that come with physical operations when they are combined. BB1's compensation sequences are used to compensate for the systematic drift of control fields. Consequently, keeping in mind more reversible operations over qubits enables the Virtual Layer to enhance the qubit reliability. Consequently, higher levels receive qubits with reasonable error levels.
Quantum Error Correction (QEC) Layer: Reduces the likelihood of logical errors through the implementation of error correcting codes. To realize a fault tolerant quantum computing system, the rate of correcting errors should be higher than the rate of their accumulation. The QEC Layer employs error correction codes such as the surface code which assess qubits and rectify them anytime errors occur.	Surface Code: A surface code uses a cluster of qubits arranged in two-dimensional berths inside which logical qubits are encoded onto many physical qubits. It utilizes stabilizer measurements in a non-collapsing fashion for assessing errors within the quantum state. With a high threshold error rate ($\approx$0.9%), the surface code is well suited for scalable quantum systems. Resource Requirements: Usage of surface codes necessitates thousands physical qubits to provide a more for single logical qubit. The Appeals court's rely Witness document confirms that the codes used by Echo apply to the Syzygy Viewer General as well, and indicate general liquation principles. As an illustration, accounting for a 1024 bit integer using Shor's algorithm translates to over 70,000 and millions of logical qubits.

continued on following page

Table 1. Continued

Layer	Description
Logical Layer: Development of logical qubits along with universal gates. The logical layer distills the available error-corrected resources according to the QEC layer into a universal set of logical gates to facilitate the operation of quantum gates required for algorithms to be run. Distillation of ancilla states of magic fidelity for construction of T gates, which are vital for universal computation, is one of the major functions.	Logical Errors: Logical errors tracking and correcting without performing any other physically unnecessary operations makes it more effective in terms of resource consumption. Balance Between Resources and Distillation Gage: Some techniques use the balance between the accuracy vs resources consumed to improve efficiency. For instance, a Solovay-Kitaev approximation algorithm decomposes arbitrary gate operations into fundamental gates sequences. Magic-state distillation serves as a significant computational challenge for this logical layer, particularly for distillation regions. In cases like Shor's magic-state distillation, this accounts for more than 90% of the algorithm computational expenses.
Application Layer: High end quantum algorithms are executed.	An operating environment adjustment user interface for quantum algorithms devoid of any knowledge of further hardware intricacies is what the application layer provides. These include Shor's algorithm in factoring, QuIP simulations of quantum chemistry and other algorithms. Because of their high sensitivity to errors, these algorithms need large scale fault tolerant systems. Analysis of the Resource Consumption: In broad strokes, accounting for the power limits of an electronic device in computation, Shor's algorithm requires approximately 10^{12} logical gates with heavy distillation overhead for a 1024-bit integer. Quantum Simulation: For simulating chemical reactions using molecular interactions, it is necessary to have between 1,000 and 10,000 logical qubits.

8. KEY PLAYERS AND STRATEGIC INITIATIVES IN QUANTUM BANKING

1. Quantum Banking is the use of quantum technologies for an advanced emerging banking system. It is expected to significantly impact the banking industry by increasing the accuracy and speed of data processing thereby offering secure and effective services. Still, quantum technologies can pose a threat to the existing security arrangements of banks today. This in mind all banks worldwide are preparing for a world that has quantum safe protocols and such. The New York City based *JPMorgan Chase & Co* is an American multinational investment bank and financial services holding company, which is currently trying to grow its quantum technology initiative. Understanding the relevance of quantum computing for banking WC, a quantum engineering team was created with Marco Pistoia designated the head of quantum technology. In 2020, it formed such collaboration with the Chicago Quantum Exchange, a quantum tech hub, because it was very excited about developing quan-

tum algorithm systems in AI, optimization and even bank encryption. The second thing is that, "their research team is actively working in the area of post-quantum cryptography". *HSBC Bank plc* is a British multinational banking and financial services institution. Like other players in the industry, it understands the dire need of quantum emerging for the financial industry in the years to come in terms of risk analytics, ML, and cybersecurity. For that reason, it has started collaboration with other quantum companies and research laboratories to explore the possibilities of this advanced technology. HSBC will collaborate with The European NEASQC (Next Applications of Quantum Computing) project to create real-world applications in areas like drug discovery, breast cancer detection, carbon capture, and evaluation of energy infrastructure risks. The project is financed with a total budget of EUR4.7 million (USD5.5 million) which is received from the European Union's Horizon 2020 research and innovation program. This four-year initiative utilizes the skills of quantum computing professionals. *BNP Paribas S.A.* is a universal bank based in France. Their foray into quantum to date is the bank's seeding of C12 Quantum Electronics alongside other investors. These included 360 Capital, Bpifrance (Digital Venture Fund), Airbus Ventures, and Octave Klaba (OVHcloud). BNP Paribas Développement also participated via its VC fund by joining other rounds. With this kind of activity, BNP Paribas is clearly trying to capture the potential of QC and will definitely try to engage deeper into the technology down the line. *Crédit Agricole Group* has the largest market share as a cooperative bank. The bank has started making its first steps in the implementation of quantum tech when QuantFi started their CAP (Crédit Agricole Paris) startup accelerator in Paris. QuantFi is one of a small number of startups and the only quantum deep-tech company in the banking ecosystem. *Japan Post Bank Co.*, Ltd is a Japanese bank based in Tokyo. In 2019, Japan Post, along with the Japanese multinational corporation Toray Industries, which develops industrial goods based on organic synthetic technology, polymer chemistry, and biochemistry, began streamlining truck dispatching processes for shipping deliveries using a project developed by A Quantum, a startup that focuses on quantum computing software. Japan Post worked together with Fujitsu Laboratories to perform demonstration experiments for transport network optimizations using a Digital Annealer. *Citi*, the American global investment bank and financial is located in New York City. In 2019, Citigroup stated that quantum computing is one of the five trends set to skyrocket and defined that, 'quantum computing can help improve trading algorithms, lessen fraud, optimize portfolios, and mitigate risk". Citigroup is not just talking, though: as they have in fact invested in quantum computing software startups such as 1QBit and QC Ware. The bank with William Hartnett serving as Managing Director at Citigroup is confident that this technology will alter risk assessment and trading in the finance sector, stressing that "banks need to start learning how to harness it now".

Figure 2. Quantum banking architecture process

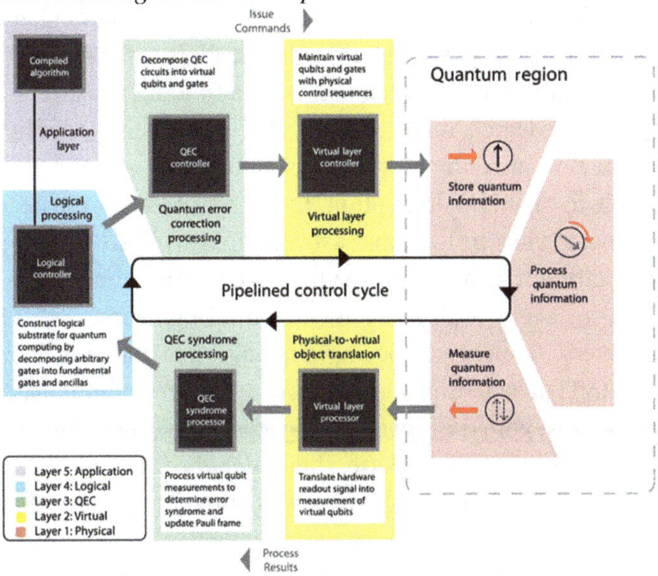

Wells Fargo in a bid to enhance its quantum computing achievements as well as its application, it got into a partnership deal along with MIT and IBM, which led to Wells Fargo becoming a part of the IBM Quantum Network. This initiative is a community that is composed of expensive Fortune 500 corporations, academic institutions, startups and research laboratories. With this collaboration with IBM Research, Wells Fargo is happy to further our knowledge in AI and quantum computing, according to Ravi Radhakrishnan, who is the Innovation Technology head at Wells Fargo. We expect how upcoming changes in AI and quantum computing will enable all sorts of advanced banking conveniences and protection for us as well as the entire financial services sector. *Barclays PLC* is a universal bank with headquarters in London, England. Its foray into quantum computing began in 2017. Learning about the technology for a long time, until they felt that they had enough understanding of it, Barclays reached the conclusion that, "quantum computing's scope was so promising that we ought to undertake an initial programme of research and development". Since then, the bank has undertaken detailed trials of the technology, mainly attempting to determine how it might be useful in enhancing the banking sector. At the moment, Barclays is performing a lot of work on very particular problems which they face in the banking business, doing initial work, for instance, on how quantum computing may assist them in improving the batch settling of securities transaction processing. *Royal Bank of Canada (RBC)* is one of the major banks in Canada and a multinational financial service and Canadian firm by revenue. In 2018, RBC launched a cybersecurity lab to enable new initiative research at the University of Waterloo having the goal of enhancing cyber and privacy protection. Equally fascinating to TQI readers is the fact that besides aiding the cybersecurity lab, RBC's investment is also funding research in post-quantum cryptography. The research, directed by David Jao, aims at the application of fundamental mathematics and computer science for developing encryption systems that are invulnerable to quantum decryption. In the Netherlands, the head office for the *ING group* is located in Amsterdam. Last year, *ING with ABN Amro and Rabobank*, Dutch banks, started to investigate quantum technology through possible use case stress tests. At this event, Adil Acun, a Quantum Engineer at ING Group N.V. was one of the speakers. Acun heads the implementation of quantum technologies in the bank through R&D in quantum algorithms, quantum cryptography, and educational awareness programs, with the aim of having a profound social impact through these new technologies. In the initial phase, the *Goldman Sachs Group, Inc.*, American multinational investment bank and investment company based in New York City, is one of the more conspicuous users of quantum technologies in banking. This bank has been collaborating with QC Ware a Silicon Valley startup to understand how quantum algorithms can be used in banking, how these algorithms are running and how super computers will do better than classicals in the banking world. The two companies have been examining how QC can use the Monte Carlo algorithm which is typically used for risk evaluation in and price simulations of different financial instruments. The sophisticated computations involved in the Monte Carlo are usually performed once a night, hence in active markets, traders are making decisions based on old results which is problematic.

9. KEY CHALLENGES FACED BY THE FINANCIAL SERVICES SECTOR

The key challenges faced by the financial services sector and its mitigation strategy are outlined in Table 2.

Table 2. Challenges and mitigation strategy for financial services sector

Challenge	Mitigation Strategy
Risk Assessment and Management	Risk assessment is at the heart of decision-making for banks, asset managers, and insurance companies. It involves estimating and mitigating various types of risks, such as credit risk, market risk, liquidity risk, and operational risk. Traditional approaches put a lot of stress on historical data, Monte Carlo simulations, and probabilistic modeling. As an example, estimating the Value at Risk (VaR) for multi-faceted portfolios frequently entails running millions of simulations for estimating losses across different scenarios.
Portfolio Revision	Asset managers or investors aim to optimize their portfolios with a goal of obtaining the single best risk-return tradeoff. This involves attempting complex optimization problems with a number of constraints, including a budget, minimum required diversification, and any regulatory issues. Classical methods can find it very difficult to efficiently explore the huge numbers of possible combinations of assets, especially if dealing with large portfolios. The optimization process can become impossibly difficult to execute when one needs to account for the real-world complexities like transaction costs, liquidity constraints, and multi period planning parameter. The Quantum Approximate Optimization Algorithm (QAOA) and the Variational Quantum Eigensolver (VQE) are examples of quantum algorithms that can potentially solve combinatorial optimization problems. By encoding the problem as a quantum state and using quantum parallelism, quantum computers can potentially solve problems faster than classical computers. A quantum computer can try to find the optimal or near-optimal solution in a fraction of the time required by traditional computers by working on numerous possible solutions at once.
Fraud/Anomaly Detection	Fraud detection in financial services centers on clearing abnormal behavior in transactions such as laundering, insider trading, and cyber fraud through real-time analysis of large quantitative of transactions blended with the usage of sophisticated machine learning models capable of classification of normal and abnormal behaviors. Quantum-enhanced machine learning (QML) offers new opportunities by detecting fraud faster and with greater accuracy owing to quantum computing's proficiency in dealing with big dimensional data space relations as opposed to classical approaches. It could mitigate financial loss suffered due to fraud.
Market Simulation and Pricing of Complex Derivatives	The Dynamic nature of financial markets makes it so that stochastic processes affect the value of financial instruments like options and futures and even complex derivatives. Pricing these instruments alongside executing automated trades depends on accurately modeling and simulating market behavior. Classical Monte Carlo simulations are widely used but can become computationally expensive when dealing with complex instruments, such as exotic options with path dependencies or multi-asset derivatives. The computation time increases rapidly with the complexity and dimensionality of the problem. Quantum computing, through methods like quantum simulations and quantum Monte Carlo algorithms, has the potential to reduce computational complexity and provide faster pricing models. This allows for more timely responses to market changes, better hedging strategies, and improved risk assessments.
Regulatory Compliance and Stress Testing	Financial institutions are subject to rigorous regulatory requirements, including stress testing to ensure they can withstand economic downturns or financial crises. Compliance with regulations such as Basel III and IV involves complex calculations related to capital adequacy, liquidity coverage, and risk-weighted assets. Classical approaches to stress testing often require evaluating thousands of scenarios, which can be time-consuming and resource-intensive. Quantum computing could speed up the scenario generation and analysis processes, making it easier for institutions to comply with regulations and reduce the cost and time required for compliance.

10. HOW QUANTUM COMPUTING OFFERS A TRANSFORMATIVE POTENTIAL

By 2035, quantum computing use cases in the finance industry could create $622 billion in value as in Fig. 3. Quadratic Speedup in Simulations: Monte Carlo simulations, a vital instrument in finance for risk evaluation and scenario analysis, can be accelerated inversely by quantum techniques like quantum amplitude estimation. As a result, quantum computers could finish tasks for a large number of problems in a fraction of the time needed by classical computers, allowing for quicker insights and more frequent updates to risk models.

Figure 3. Potential of quantum computing in finance (value of quantum computing use-cases, by business unit in $billions)

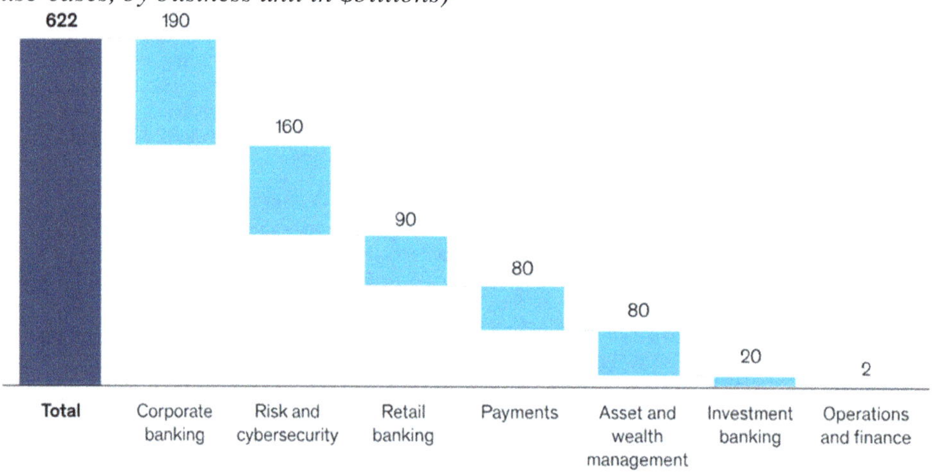

In finance, optimization challenges frequently entail selecting the optimal answer from an exponentially huge pool of options. With the use of quantum superposition and entanglement, quantum computing may more effectively explore this extensive solution space, offering quicker and possibly better solutions for supply chain logistics, trade settlement, and portfolio optimization in financial contexts. In comparison to classical models, quantum-enhanced machine learning models are more effective at analyzing huge, high-dimensional datasets. Better market behavior models for forecasting, more precise customer segmentation, and quicker identification of irregularities or fraud in large transaction databases could result from this. The speed and power of quantum computing have the potential to enable real-time analysis and decision-making, which is crucial in high-frequency trading, market making, and other areas that require rapid responses to changing market conditions.

11. MARKET VALUE OF QUANTUM COMPUTING:

Quantum Computing has the Potential To Create Economic Growth Of up To *$850 Billion*. According to New Research by BCG, attaining a Castle In The Sky Economic Value Of $9.5 Billion While Earning $850 In 2019, bashing through doors, quantum computing secured *1.2 billion in 2023*. Moreover, noting its qualitative angle, the study conducted by BCD reflects positively in regard to quantum computers and their expected economic impact, enabling the firm to maintain its original projected numbers concerning the GDP that quantum computing would steer. In addition, to add on further details, by 2040, BCD foresees a sustainable market. "In quantum computing, and in particular, its promise and applicability, there are apparent problems never before encountered, its large-scale implementation will revolutionize industries and markets, the potential is incredible." Said Jean-Francois Bobier, BCG's vice president and partner while coauthored the presentation. "But it hasn't managed to this point satisfy that at a greater scale." Nonetheless, the momentum is undeniable." It is believed that there has also been a 50% decrease in the total tech investments made. But despite that, venture capitalists have greatly invested in quantum computing, around $1.2 billion. Such involvement is a positive sign for its future. The amount spent on technology is on the state as well as the national level and is expected to grow, especially when it is used to develop national security and help with the country's economic growth. It has been reported that over the next five years to three there will be an increase to over $10 billion public supportive investment. The BCG report states that BCG's earlier presumptions about quantum computing are bound to be unachievable and that is also the case under assessment. While during the last report, it was speculated quantum computing models would be able to generate ample economic value, in this phase, BCG notes that is still not achievable by the NISQ. The BCG report further identifies the inclusion of tolls termed as broad quantum advantage which extends till 2040 but post that BCG firmly believes NISQ quantum models will be able to achieve full scale fault tolerance capability. According to BCG's expectations, two factors affected the practical application of quantum computing technologies over the past decades. First, it has been admitted that the integration, architectural and the complex hardware development tasks pose a challenge. Second, there has been fierce competition with classical computing, in terms of throughput and expectations, this would include the developing AI area. On the other hand, quantum machines augmented with analog techniques can add actual value during the NISQ period when the AI has been actively developed and integrated. For instance, in material and chemical simulations, a tangible value of $100 million – $500 million revenue a year can be attained. Even though IoT has reduced NISQ revenue projections significantly, we do not expect it to impact the overall market of hardware and software providers appreciably. To this day, BCG continues to anticipate a $1 billion - $2 billion provider market by the start of the new decade, which will be triggered by: As with other sectors, the general sector is stepping-up to fill the gap that has heretofore existed in the Integrated Circuits, the World-Wide Web, and the Global Positioning System by issuing contracts and providing further funding. Currently, large enterprises are pouring money into quantum-class business capabilities. The 2023 report from BCG on quantum adoption indicates that more than 100 Fortune 500 companies have undertaken development of proof-of-concept projects, with a combined investment of US$300 million. By establishing supply chains encompassing controls, dilution refrigerators, lasers, vacuums, and software, providers can offer revenue streams. According to the BCG research, provider demand will constitute 5% to 10% of the quantum computing hardware and software revenue this year.

OTI Lumionics is a company that designs materials with the incorporation of electric and magnetic - quantum methods specifically for OLED devices and batteries. OTI is collaborating with Azure quantum a technological center created by the Microsoft company in order to create quantum inspired algorithms which help with classical simulation, which is a commercial strategy to save help with R&D and make the work at different stages of material design simple and fast. Solid State AI creates predictive algorithms based on quantum technology and assists industries in the advanced manufacturing sector by allowing users to save time and costs. Once the quantum insights are fully utilized, the company makes sure that the processes are honed to perfection. To the company's classical solutions, time and cost management is treated as a key objective and to that end on high tech manufacturing such insight has been effective. Finance, logistics and pharmaceuticals have also started realizing some benefits. Quantum-inspired algorithms give a clear edge over the traditional ones while performing portfolio optimization and risk analysis in sectors such as finance. Companies in the healthcare sector are taking advantage of the quantum technologies by quickening the process of drug development.

Most of the investors in this space which are witnessing an increase in investment are referred to as being involved in a gold race and the report provided by nature referred to as being in a quantum gold rush. Between 2020 and 2030, the country's quantum computing projected market in the United States is set to grow from $500 million to $9 billion or $1.5 billion in revenue on an average each year (BlueQubit, 2025). Multiple sectors including banking, defense and material science will contribute to increased growth as combinatorial issues will be in high demand. Early adopters of quantum solutions will likely have a competitive advantage by being able to deliver solutions more quickly or more efficiently than their rivals. For instance, Volkswagen has explored the use of quantum algorithms in the optimization of electric vehicle battery development and the management of traffic.

12. KEY FINDINGS, FUTURE IMPLICATIONS AND ENHANCEMENTS:

This paper looked into the applications of quantum computing in the domain of financial risk management with a clear focus on revolutionizing risk assessment, portfolio optimization, and derivative pricing. Financial institutions stand to benefit immensely by automating their risk management processes and decision making as today's investment milieu is intertwined and ever changing, leveraging quantum algorithms such as quantum Monte Carlo techniques and quantum annealing. Moreover, financial risk management using quantum computing does not only benefit the organization exercising it, but rather the whole financial sector. Early birds will enjoy the advantage of efficiently managing risk and generating alpha before others came choking the market, thus boosting competition fundamentals. Lastly, evolution and change are never harnessed alone, and these changes will require the cooperation and collaboration of all stakeholders as change impacts all of them. While there is great adoption of quantum computing within the financial sector, there are still issues to be resolved. Its advancement is severely limited by obstacles related to qubit coherence time, stability, and error correction technology. Adding to the problems, there is a lack of reliable and permanently scalable quantum hardware. Building such resources requires massive amounts of investment and prior research, which is unfortunately, not readily available. Currently, the finance sector does not have many deep qualified quantum computing specialists. When finances are so tight, institutions are unable to retain and sustain the few talented individuals that do exist which causes a large gap in the industry. To solve this, educational institutions need to bring more focus to the practical application of quantum physics and financial mathematics. On top of these challenges, there is also constant change brought on by the regulators in the field of quantum finance which still needs to be properly legislated. The question that remains is how these market-disrupting technologies will affect their stability and reinforce cybersecurity and the protection of private data.

In the context of releasing quantum computing for robotic debt collection, institutions have to deal with complex and constantly changing compliance regulations that bring further uncertainty into the operation of a business. Currently, only a few technologically advanced corporations and well endowed academic institutions have the infrastructure in place that can enable such sophisticated systems. Quantum computing still costs far too much and is far beyond the reach of most of the population. These capabilities involve a heavy depreciation and resource cost and as such restrict widespread access of such technology. Future studies should concentrate on the undeniable components of systemic risk management such as advanced funding models, accurate cost estimation methods and quantum theoremic risk management modelling. Continued efforts should be made towards relevant algorithms for financial risk management and their optimization, which includes the analysis of portfolios, pricing of derivatives, and risk monitoring. This endeavor requires the creation of new algorithms and techniques to overcome the intricacies of the world of quantum mechanics and improve the solution of complex business problems. For practical deployment of quantum computing in the financial sector, advancements in quantum hardware technology are a prerequisite for future studies that should reinforce the qubit coherence and stability in terms of qubits, generate powerful quantum computing systems, and build them on a scale big enough to manage complex financial data sets and financial calculations. It will be key that researchers in quantum computing and finance work well together if innovation is to take off and if inter-disciplinary barriers are to disappear. After all, the impact on society through the use of this next-generation cutting-edge cyber technology will be the defining era of the next global economic landscape (Babulak, 2026). Such work also has to be done in future investigations. Further investments should be made in developing a pipeline of professionals with the necessary knowledge and skills in the emerging fields of quantum computing and finance.Such future research endeavors clearly need to be undertaken. Greater focus should be put on the design of curricula and training programs for people who are working at the nexus of quantum physics and financial mathematics.

CONCLUSION

The impact of quantum computing on financial institutions will be large. In its infancy it will become a cybersecurity giant with its amazing risk analysis, portfolio management, fraud detection, and banking frameworks. Even though it provides an unlimited number of capabilities, it also brings terrible challenges especially to classical cryptographic systems. These challenges require the urgent introduction of quantum responsive and highly secure devices in combination with quantum key distribution, thus reducing the workload of secure exchanges. Financial services institutions around the world are now actively focused on reaching quantum applicability with notable financial institutions such as JPMorgan Chase, HSBC, and Goldman Sachs spending large sums of money advancing quantum research and development. In risk management, it allows for the expansion of the use of Monte Carlo simulations in order to test complex financial constructs, high fashion trading strategies, and even internal decision-making schemes. Yet, there are still some big realities to contend with such as instability of the qubits, the overhead of error corrections, a lack of regulatory frameworks and a lack of professional specifically trained in quantum finance. Developing strategies for healthy working together between finance units and quantum technology industries, scientific institutions and governmental bodies will take an immense effort. The private sector is already committing plenty of investment and it is estimated that it will ultimately create multiple billions of dollars of quantum computing economic value in many decades to come. Upon the advancement of quantum computing, financial institutions should see to it that they integrate quantum safe security measures and adapt to the coming paradigm change in financial services. This proactive approach will counteract the quantum threats and at the same time not compromise the possibilities offered by quantum computing, and thus ensure that the future of finance is secure, efficient and consumed innovativeness.

REFERENCES

Babulak, E. (2006). Quality of service provision assessment in the healthcare information and telecommunications infrastructures. *International Journal of Medical Informatics*, *75*(3–4), 246–252. DOI: 10.1016/j.ijmedinf.2005.07.019 PMID: 16137920

Babulak, E. (2023). *AI tools for protecting and preventing sophisticated cyber attacks*. IGI Global., DOI: 10.4018/978-1-6684-7110-4

Babulak, E., Al_Dabass, D., & Tomar, G. (. (2025). Editorial: Cyber security prevention, defenses driven by AI, and mathematical modelling and simulation tools. *Frontiers of Computer Science*, *7*, 1685873. DOI: 10.3389/fcomp.2025.1685873

Babulak, E. (Ed.). (2026). *The social impact of next-generation smart cyber technology*. IGI Global., DOI: 10.4018/979-8-3373-5656-3

Bucur, C., & Babulak, E. (2019). Security validation testing environment in the cloud. In 2019 IEEE International Conference on Big Data (Big Data) (pp. 4240–4247). IEEE. DOI: 10.1109/BigData47090.2019.9006202

Chen, S., & Wang, Y. (2025). Quantum optimization for logistics and supply chain management. *IEEE Transactions on Intelligent Transportation Systems*, *26*(1), 1–11.

Davis, M., & Taylor, J. (2025). Enhancing climate models with quantum computing. *IEEE Transactions on Geoscience and Remote Sensing*, *63*(1), 1–12.

Intallura, P. (2024). *Preparing for a quantum future: What's next for quantum computing in financial services*. FinTech Futures.

Kommers, P., & Babulak, E. (2025). Conceptual awareness for human navigation in A.I. In Babulak, E. (Ed.), *Educational AI humanoid computing devices for cyber nomads* (pp. 1–14). IGI Global., DOI: 10.4018/979-8-3693-8985-0.ch001

Kumar, S. N., Joy, J., Jane, I. C., James, A., John, S., & Babulak, E. (2025). Applications of 6G in the healthcare sector and the importance of network security and data privacy—Encryption of medical images using the SHA-256 blockchain algorithm. In Network security and data privacy in 6G communication: Trends, challenges, and applications (pp. 176–190). DOI: 10.1201/9781003583127-9

Kumar, V., Gupta, S., & Gill, F. S. (2024). An overview on quantum computing for technology. In CRC Press eBooks (pp. 696–701). DOI: 10.1201/9781003559092-120

Lee, Y., & Kim, S. (2025). Advancements in quantum machine learning for AI efficiency. *IEEE Transactions on Neural Networks and Learning Systems*, *30*(2), 1–10.

Massam, P., & Babulak, E. (2003). A decent service level. *Communications Engineer, 1*(3), 34–37. DOI: 10.1049/ce:20030313

Mathis, J., & Payne, B. (2023). *Quantum computing: Computing of the future made reality*. Proceedings on Cybersecurity Education, Research and Practice., DOI: 10.32727/28.2024.2

Mathis, J., & Payne, B. (2023). *Quantum computing: Computing of the future made reality*. Proceedings on Cybersecurity Education, Research and Practice., DOI: 10.32727/28.2024.2

Memon, Q. A., Ahmad, M. A., & Pecht, M. (2024). Quantum computing: Navigating the future of computation, challenges, and technological breakthroughs. *Quantum Reports, 6*(4), 627–663. DOI: 10.3390/quantum6040039

Moody's. (2025). Quantum computing's six most important trends for 2025.

Nia, M. A., Atani, R. E., Fabian, B., & Babulak, E. (2016). On detecting unidentified network traffic using pattern-based random walk. *Security and Communication Networks, 9*(16), 3509–3526. DOI: 10.1002/sec.1557

Patel, A., & Singh, R. (2025). Quantum simulations for accelerated drug discovery. *IEEE Transactions on Bio-Medical Engineering, 72*(3), 1–9.

Patel, K. N., ... (2024). Cybersecurity risks and countermeasures in the threat landscape of IoT devices. In 2024 4th International Conference on Technological Advancements in Computational Sciences (ICTACS) (pp. 875–883). IEEE. DOI: 10.1109/ICTACS62700.2024.10841210

Qureca. (2025, April 11). Quantum computing applications in economics and finance conference.

Saklani, P., Chauhan, S., & Tiwari, S. (2023). Unlocking the potential of quantum computing: A comprehensive review. *International Journal for Multidisciplinary Research, 5*(6), 9440. Advance online publication. DOI: 10.36948/ijfmr.2023.v05i06.9440

Saravanamoorthi, P. (2023). A detailed review on quantum computing technologies. *Recent Research Reviews Journal, 1*(1), 1–12. DOI: 10.36548/rrrj.2022.1.001

Shen, K. (2024). Research on the application of quantum computing in artificial intelligence. *Journal of Computing and Electronic Information Management, 13*(1), 38–42. DOI: 10.54097/4cg2am4s

Sheoran, R. K., Verma, S., Sheoran, S. K., & Yadav, V. (2024). Quantum computing research. In Advances in computer and electrical engineering book series (pp. 236–263). DOI: 10.4018/979-8-3693-1168-4.ch012

Smith, J., & Johnson, M. (2025). Quantum computing for financial risk management. *IEEE Transactions on Computational Finance*, *10*(1), 1–8.

Sood, S. K., & Pooja, N. (2023). Quantum computing review: A decade of research. *IEEE Transactions on Engineering Management*, *71*, 6662–6676. DOI: 10.1109/TEM.2023.3284689

SpinQuanta. (2025). Top quantum computing applications in key industries. BlueQubit. (2025). Quantum computing software platforms of 2025.

Xue, M. (2023). Research on quantum computers characteristic. *Theoretical and Natural Science*, *5*(1), 355–359. DOI: 10.54254/2753-8818/5/20230582

Chapter 10

Quantum Resilient Trust Fabric:
Human-Aligned Generative AI and Blockchain Fusion for Next-Generation Cybersecurity Governance

Syed Ibad Ali
http://orcid.org/0000-0001-6312-6768
Parul Institute of Engineering and Technology, Parul University, Vadodara, India

ABSTRACT

This chapter presents a quantum-resilient trust fabric that integrates human-aligned generative AI with blockchain-based governance to build secure, transparent, and future-proof cybersecurity ecosystems. By combining post-quantum cryptography, decentralized trust mechanisms, and interpretable generative intelligence, the framework offers strong resistance to quantum-era threats while ensuring ethical decision alignment. The fusion of AI-driven threat prediction, immutable ledger integrity, and automated smart-contract enforcement establishes an adaptive, scalable, and governance-ready cybersecurity architecture suitable for next-generation digital infrastructures.

INTRODUCTION

The intricate challenges of transitioning to post-quantum cryptography (PQC), with the integration of generative AI and distributed ledgers, need a multifaceted strategy for risk evaluation, design, and governance. Organizations must document

DOI: 10.4018/979-8-2600-1608-4.ch010

cryptographic dependencies and categorize assets based on secrecy levels and regulatory significance, since the risk of retroactive compromise significantly differs by asset type (Chen et al., 2016; National Institute of Standards and Technology, 2024). Assets requiring prolonged anonymity, such as archive health data, long-term smart contract settlements, or critical infrastructure records, need a more expedited transition to post-quantum encryption than ephemeral communication routes. An asset-centric methodology should direct an organization's migration prioritization: high-value archives and ledgered records with enduring integrity requirements should be migrated or secured initially utilizing hybrid or post-quantum key-encapsulation mechanisms (KEMs), while more ephemeral channels should be addressed subsequently (Alagic et al., 2025; Peralta et al., 2025). Asset mapping to cryptographic systems must include the anticipated enhancement of adversarial capabilities, including credible timelines for quantum advantage that might jeopardize public-key primitives. Due to the unpredictable timing of quantum advancements, governance decisions must be resilient over several timeframes and prioritize cryptographic agility to prevent vulnerable singular migrations (Chen et al., 2016).

Cryptographic agility transcends a mere technical attribute; it embodies a design philosophy mandating that protocols, libraries, and key-management systems be adaptable to new primitives, facilitate algorithm suite negotiations during handshakes, and enable seamless key transitions or implementation changes with minimal service disruption (Alagic et al., 2025). Architects must use hybrid approaches—combining classical and post-quantum algorithms—during transitional periods to mitigate the risks linked to developing PQC systems while attaining swift enhancements in robustness. Hybridization requires careful consideration: unrefined integration or simplistic parallel signing may lead to subtle vulnerabilities or operational inefficiencies; therefore, architects should utilize standardized hybrid frameworks (when applicable) and adhere to guidelines from standards organizations (Alagic et al., 2025; Chen et al., 2016). Implementations must undergo rigorous evaluation using comprehensive test suites and fuzzing to identify edge situations when integrated algorithms interact unpredictably. In resource-limited devices, hybrid schemes may be locally unfeasible; however, gateway or proxy architectures that oversee intensive post-quantum cryptography operations while preserving end-to-end semantics can mitigate this challenge, albeit introducing new trust anchors that require reinforcement and governance (Kumar, 2022; Schöffel et al., 2021). Key management is the essential element of every cryptographic process. Due to increased computational expenses and evolving standards, post-quantum key lifecycles are anticipated to be shorter or more intricate; consequently, automated key rotation, hardware security module (HSM) support (incorporating PQC functionalities), and secure archiving and tombstoning measures are necessary. Organizations must provide auditable, tamper-proof key rotation mechanisms that include cryptographic certification of key origin. Custodial arrangements, multi-party computation (MPC), and threshold signature schemes can mitigate the risk of single-point compromise in distributed ledger applications; however, they must be assessed for their readiness and performance limitations concerning post-quantum cryptography (PQC) (Peralta et al., 2025; Gharavi et al., 2024). Migration solutions must account for backward compatibility and the need to authenticate legacy signatures on archived data; for instance, systems may use multilayer encryption, re-wrapping archival material with new keys as standards evolve (Chen et al., 2016). Decisions about ledger design are essential for sustaining trust. Conventional blockchain architectures depend on the reliability of cryptographic primitives; however, this presumption is no longer tenable in the quantum era. Consequently, ledger architects must account for cryptographic agility while formulating transaction formats and consensus mechanisms. Options include the incorporation of algorithm identities and versioning data into transactions, the development of upgradeable commitment schemes, and the facilitation of on-chain governance mechanisms to oversee transitions among several stakeholders (Fan, 2025; Gharavi et al., 2024). Public blockchains may need coordinated hard forks to enhance primitives, a procedure that has substantial governance, economic, and societal ramifications. Private and permissioned ledgers may exhibit more agility via governance frameworks that facilitate the swift implementation of PQC modifications; nonetheless, they must still address cross-domain interoperability when engaging with public chains or external entities (Deloitte, 2021). Tiered architectures, whereby lightweight devices depend on federated or gateway validators to manage post-quantum cryptography tasks, may distribute computational requirements while preserving high degrees of decentralized auditability (Fan, 2025; Schöffel et al., 2022). The trade-offs between performance and energy cannot be disregarded. PQC methodologies, particularly first candidates, often need bigger keys or more intricate computations, resulting in heightened energy consumption and latency—significant obstacles for IoT and energy-sector endpoints (Kumar, 2022; Schöffel et al., 2021). This requires technical innovation: streamlined implementations (including constant-time primitives), hardware acceleration in edge gateways, and adaptive protocols that minimize PQC operations (such as session resumption with re-wrapping techniques) may alleviate overheads. Standards organizations and implementers must emphasize profiling, benchmarking, and disseminating performance data for post-quantum cryptography schemes across representative hardware to guide practical design decisions (Kumar, 2022). Energy-efficient PQC design is particularly crucial in smart grids and microgrids, where devices often operate on batteries and increased computational demands may significantly impact operational longevity (Hua et al., 2022; Andoni et al., 2019).

The addition of generative AI to the trust framework results in defensive synergies and governance difficulties. Generative models improve security operations by automating triage, creating coherent incident reports, doing proactive vulnerability assessments, and developing regulatory rules. Nonetheless, these capabilities raise the dangers associated with alignment: if generative models provide unverified or biased proposals, or if attackers use model internals to enable attacks, systemic harm might occur quickly (Sigfrids et al., 2023; Kluge Corrêa et al., 2022). Consequently, operational principles must include provenance, verifiability, and human supervision. Provenance metadata for model inputs and outputs must be recorded in auditable logs secured by post-quantum cryptography and ledger consistency checks; this foundation facilitates retrospective forensic analysis and enhances contestability when models impact critical decisions (Sigfrids et al., 2023). Model governance must include the inclusion of explainability artifacts (where possible), model cards with training data and limitations, and explicitly specified human-in-the-loop checkpoints for actions with systemic repercussions (Taeihagh, 2025; Kluge Corrêa et al., 2022). Federated learning and decentralized model aggregation are especially appealing in privacy-sensitive contexts; yet, federated aggregation protocols must withstand both quantum adversaries and poisoning attempts. Aggregation may be secured using PQC-protected channels and threshold cryptography to prevent aggregator compromise; however, these protections must be balanced against performance and privacy constraints to avoid making edge deployments impracticable (Kong et al., 2024; Kumar, 2022). In certain cases, model distillation and compressed update tactics may minimize communication overhead while retaining privacy; nevertheless, their risk trade-offs must be considered in respect to the threat model. Lightweight commitments, such as model checkpoint hashes, may be frequently submitted to a quantum-resilient ledger to guarantee a tamper-evident history without burdening the ledger with significant payloads (Fan, 2025).

Energy systems are a particular area where the parts of the trust fabric meet and design tradeoffs become apparent. Blockchain technologies provide peer-to-peer energy exchange, microgrid settlement, and provenance verification for renewable qualities via traceability and automated settlement (Mengelkamp et al., 2018; Zhang et al., 2017). Energy grids include a wide range of devices, from large-capacity market players to millions of restricted prosumers and smart meters. Developing quantum-resilient settlement methods demands determining which records need long-term unforgeability (e.g., contractual settlements, ownership records) and which may tolerate limited cryptographic periods (e.g., short-term meter telemetry) (Hua et al., 2022). Organizations ought to establish multi-tiered safeguards for high-value settlement records, encompassing immediate transactional security through hybrid post-quantum cryptography (PQC), periodic re-anchoring of settlement proofs utilizing enhanced PQC as it emerges, and off-chain confidentiality wrappers for sensitive data alongside on-chain commitments for auditability (Fan, 2025; Schöffel et al., 2022). Market design must integrate the expenses associated with cryptographic advancements by adjusting fees or incentives to reflect the heightened computational or storage requirements of post-quantum cryptography (PQC), thus harmonizing stakeholder interests and mitigating free-rider problems that could obstruct migration (Deloitte, 2021). Governance solutions for executing the trust fabric must be multi-scale and adaptive. Boards and executives must prioritize PQC migration and AI alignment as corporate risk management issues, assigning funding and assembling cross-functional teams of cryptographers, systems engineers, legal advisers, and ethicists (Peralta et al., 2025; Sigfrids et al., 2023). At the sectoral level, industry consortiums and standards organizations ought to synchronize migration timelines and disseminate benchmarking data; regulatory authorities can facilitate harmonization by offering guidelines, certification frameworks, or transition periods instead of inflexible, uniform mandates (National Institute of Standards and Technology, 2024; Kong et al., 2024). Public-private partnerships are especially advantageous for critical infrastructure sectors with high systemic risk, such as health, energy, and finance, because they integrate private networks with public safety goals and require coordinated incident response and information-sharing agreements (Deloitte, 2021).

Legal and procurement systems are strong tools, but they must be used wisely. Governments and significant buyers may accelerate PQC adoption by requiring proof of PQC readiness in procurement procedures and offering subsidies or tax breaks for early implementation. Procurement policies must be flexible enough to accept varying technology limits across suppliers and encourage interoperable solutions that prevent vendor lock-in. Liability frameworks must evolve: software businesses that provide cryptographic components may have new legal requirements to provide clear roadmaps for post-quantum cryptography migration and to inform customers about the limitations of outmoded systems (Peralta et al., 2025). Simultaneously, privacy and data protection regulations may need clarification on the administration of cryptographic renewals and the re-wrapping of archived personal data to comply with retention and destruction requirements. The human dimensions of trust are crucial. Technical solutions alone will not guarantee widespread adoption. Individuals must understand the mechanisms by which decisions affecting them are made, the length of data protection, and how to contest automated conclusions produced by generative models. Participatory governance systems, such as citizen juries, stakeholder advisory panels, and public comment periods on critical standards, may improve legitimacy and highlight contextual risk elements that technologists may ignore (Sigfrids et al., 2023). Furthermore, transparency initiatives must be combined with communication strategies that explain PQC migration in simple terms; for example, public dashboards displaying migration progress for critical services or straightforward attestations confirming a vendor's PQC compliance can boost trust and promote market adoption (Kluge Corrêa et al., 2022). Testing, drilling, and red teaming are all key parts of preparedness. Organizations must perform tabletop exercises that simulate quantum-era breaches and integrated AI-assisted attack scenarios, assessing both technology resilience and governance responses. Red teams that combine cryptanalysis, software exploitation, and social engineering can identify vulnerabilities in complex socio-technical systems; however, exercises must evaluate the entire response chain — detection, containment, recovery, and public communication — especially for critical infrastructure entities where public safety is at risk (Schöffel et al., 2022; Sigfrids et al., 2023). These exercises should provide insights that may be used to develop procurement requirements, incident playbooks, and standard contributions. Substantial research gaps exist and need urgent attention. Initially, the practical applications of post-quantum cryptography (PQC) in resource-constrained devices have not been thoroughly investigated in actual deployments; more field research assessing energy, latency, and reliability trade-offs across various device categories is required for developing practical recommendations (Kumar, 2022; Schöffel et al., 2021). Second, ledger-anchored AI provenance systems need more study to uncover successful patterns that balance on-chain tamper evidence with off-chain privacy and performance. Third, socio-technical research on public perceptions of post-quantum cryptography (PQC) and generative AI governance, particularly in energy sectors where prosumers are non-expert players, would improve communication and participatory governance techniques (Kluge Corrêa et al., 2022; Taeihagh, 2025). Finally, multidisciplinary research on legal mechanisms for cryptographic upgrades, long-term data storage, and accountability in AI-driven decision-making will help legislators develop unified regulatory frameworks (Peralta et al., 2025).

A practical approach for stakeholders might help turn these results into concrete initiatives. Immediate actions (0-12 months) include conducting an enterprise cryptographic inventory and classification, forming a PQC governance working group, assessing critical systems for PQC compatibility, and testing hybrid PQC integrations in non-mission-critical environments to gain operational experience (Alagic et al., 2025; Peralta et al., 2025). Medium-term actions (1-3 years) include transferring high-value archival records and ledgered settlements to hybrid PQC schemes or wrapping strategies, improving key management with HSMs or MPC where applicable, implementing AI governance artifacts like model cards and provenance anchors, and engaging in sectoral coordination for cross-organizational ledger enhancements (National Institute of Standards and Technology, 2024; Fan, 2025). Long-term strategies (3+ years) focus on: completing PQC implementations for high-value assets, improving ledger protocols to be intrinsically post-quantum, institutionalizing ongoing model supervision and human-in-the-loop controls for high-impact AI systems, and maintaining proactive threat horizon scanning to adapt to developments in quantum and AI technologies (Gharavi et al., 2024; Sigfrids et al., 2023).The implementation process must be iterative and grounded on empirical evidence. Pilot projects are critical for detecting operational challenges and improving production methods; sharing anonymized but complete implementation reports within industry consortiums will speed up collective learning and reduce duplicating efforts. Standards organizations can help by providing explicit guidance on validated hybrid constructions, performance benchmarks, and suggested migration strategies, whereas governments can help with funding, procurement mechanisms, and regulatory frameworks that balance urgency and practical feasibility (Peralta et al., 2025; National Institute of Standards and Technology, 2024).

Finally, the goal of a Quantum-Resilient Trust Fabric goes beyond simple technological protection against an impending quantum danger; it is a forward-thinking design that balances cryptographic prudence with human-centric governance and distributed system realities. Society can create systems that preserve long-term secrecy and integrity, enable dependable AI augmentation, and sustain public confidence in critical digital services by combining cryptographic agility, ledger resilience, and responsible governance of generative AI. Realizing this vision requires coordinated efforts from standards organizations, industry coalitions, governmental entities, academic institutions, and civil society; meticulous engineering, flexible governance, and ongoing education; and ethical oversight that prioritizes human values in technological advancement (Alagic et al., 2025; Chen et al., 2016; Kluge Corrêa et al., 2022). The next chapters will put these ideas into practice by giving extensive technology frameworks, governance models, domain-specific case studies, and prescriptive direction for transitioning to a strong, human-centered trust framework in the age of quantum and generative AI.

LITERATURE SURVEY

A rapidly growing interdisciplinary literature encompassing cryptography, distributed systems, energy informatics, Internet-of-things (IoT) resilience, socio-technical governance, and human-centric artificial intelligence has resulted from the evolution of cybersecurity toward quantum-resilient, AI-aligned, and blockchain-integrated architectures. Chen et al. (2016) provided one of the first thorough technical reports on post-quantum cryptography (PQC), highlighting the need for algorithmic diversification, standardized migrations, and a global transition framework. Early cryptographic foundations highlight the vulnerabilities of classical public-key cryptosystems to future quantum adversaries, especially those that rely on integer factorization and discrete logarithm problems. Alagic et al. (2025) advanced the migration discourse by publishing the SP 800-227 initial public draft, which details recommendations for key-encapsulation mechanisms (KEMs) and hybrid transition paths adaptable to a variety of enterprise and critical-infrastructure scenarios. This foundational analysis, developed under the National Institute of Standards and Technology (NIST), sparked a decade of research into PQC algorithm evaluation. These studies highlight that quantum resistance is a socio-technical shift that calls for updated key lifecycles, cryptographic agility, and new institutional governance mechanisms, as reaffirmed by Peralta et al. (2025) in the reputable NIST IR 8545 fourth-round status report. Along with these algorithmic conclusions, Castelvecchi (2022) highlights the need of implementing "quantum-proof" algorithms to safeguard international communications, contending that hostile collection of current encrypted data generates dangers in the future in the event that scalable quantum computers become available. Similar issues are extended to public blockchains by Deloitte (2021), which draws attention to Ethereum's susceptibility to quantum attacks and calls for a shift to quantum-safe primitives across the board. Technical surveys like those by Gharavi et al. (2024) expand on these worries by summarizing the unique difficulties that quantum computing presents for the Internet of Things, especially when blockchain is used as an audit layer. They point out that PQC migrations need to take latency-sensitive operations, overhead, and device constraints into consideration. Additional difficulties for IoT-embedded blockchain solutions include constrained energy constraints and restricted computing power. PQC KEMs impose large energy costs in TLS-based and sensor-centric deployments, as shown by Schöffel et al. (2021, 2022), underscoring the need of carefully weighing algorithm choices and tradeoffs. Performance studies of PQC primitives, such Kumar's (2022) analysis of post-quantum algorithm standardization and performance characteristics, provide insights into implementation feasibility, memory overheads, key sizes, and latency effects in order to solve these problems. By suggesting asynchronous quantum-resistant blockchain systems for privacy-preserving data sharing, Fan (2025) builds on this exploration of application-layer contexts and shows that PQC-compatible consensus and validation mechanisms are feasible while maintaining their effectiveness in federated or cross-organizational settings.

Blockchain and distributed ledger technologies, which have applications in peer-to-peer markets, energy systems, microgrids, and cybersecurity assurance frameworks, have become essential enablers of trust and auditability in decentralized ecosystems in tandem with this cryptographic research. Numerous studies in the energy sector, such as Mengelkamp et al.'s (2018) analysis of the Brooklyn Microgrid and Andoni et al.'s (2019) systematic review of blockchain opportunities and challenges, show how decentralized ledgering can support peer-to-peer coordination, market fairness, and transparency in sustainable energy systems. Domain-specific studies like Vishwakarma et al. (2024), which look at the opportunities and difficulties in blockchain-enabled peer-to-peer renewable energy trading, and Hua et al. (2022), which explore how blockchain and artificial intelligence can cooperate to enable prosumer participation in energy markets, support these findings. Wang et al. (2019) provide blockchain-enabled crowdsourcing models for energy trading, whereas Zanc et al. (2020) explore blockchain-anchored smart grid management scenarios and future challenges. These results highlight the need of trust substrates in distributed energy ecosystems that allow for tamper-resistant device coordination, auditable provenance, and settlement verification. However, as shown by Schöffel et al. (2022), moving to PQC-ready blockchain architectures requires careful selection of consensus primitives, KEMs, and signature schemes that can withstand quantum attackers while managing resource constraints. Hybrid blockchain-AI security strategies, such the AI-enhanced blockchain security frameworks for smart grids (2025) by Ghadi et al., focus on combining distributed consensus, quantum-resistant cryptographic primitives, and AI-driven anomaly detection. This pattern is in line with more comprehensive systematic reviews like Al Shareef et al. (2024), which look into how blockchain and AI are combined in the energy industry. They show that although hybrid architectures are strong, they also present governance issues related to computational overhead, privacy, and interoperability.

The rapidly expanding field of generative AI has given rise to a robust body of literature that focuses on alignment, ethics, and governance. Researchers stress the need of flexible, human-centered governance frameworks as generative AI models increase in capability and social impact. Combining more than 200 international recommendations, Kluge Corrêa et al. (2022) provide one of the most comprehensive assessments of AI ethical standards in the world, offering insight into the normative foundations required for AI governance that is in line with human values. By presenting a systematic viewpoint on human-centric AI governance, Sigfrids et al. (2023) expand on this conversation by asserting that credibility necessitates institutional avenues for stakeholder participation and contestability in addition to transparency and explainability. Taeihagh (2025) elaborates on this perspective by outlining the regulatory concerns brought about by quick iteration cycles, opacity, and cross-domain risks prevalent in foundation models, as well as the challenges of generative AI governance. These human-governance initiatives support additional technical research on the integration of AI in distributed energy settings and cyber-physical systems. In their 2020 study, Guo et al. explore blockchain-powered AI-powered energy management systems, showing how learning-based optimization might help with integrated heating, cooling, and electrical systems. A thorough review of blockchain for future smart grids is provided by Mollah et al. (2021), who emphasize the need of blockchain assurance and AI-driven intelligence coexisting under robust governance and security frameworks. Babulak's (2006, 2009, 2010) early conceptual contributions on AI-enabled cyber-physical systems and ubiquitous computing, which emphasize how new internet technologies, automation, and digital homes create new spaces for distributed intelligence and cyber risk, support these findings. Experts stress the need of adding human oversight to AI-driven decision-making systems as the technology landscape becomes more complex in order to guarantee ethical resilience, transparency, and social responsibility. Since generative AI may either strengthen or weaken cybersecurity depending on alignment quality and misuse risks, this alignment imperative becomes even more crucial when combined with blockchain and PQC (Taeihagh, 2025).

Additionally, the study demonstrates that the convergence of blockchain, AI, and PQC is particularly apparent in smart grid, IoT, and energy distribution environments, where sophisticated attackers find high-value targets in cyber-physical complexity and need vertically integrated trust infrastructures. Distributed energy markets and behind-the-meter energy management systems need transparent, tamper-resistant coordination, but they also face obstacles such regulatory fragmentation, device variety, and latency sensitivity, according to Ahl et al. (2019) and Bayram and Ustun (2017). An overview of smart grid topologies, models, and communication standards is provided by Siano and De Marco (2019), who emphasize the need of cross-layer resilience strategies that include network governance, hardware protections, and cryptographic safeguards. Since long-lived sensor data, smart contracts, and energy transaction records may be impacted retrospectively by future quantum attacks, PQC migration becomes more crucial as microgrid and IoT installations expand (Castelvecchi, 2022; Deloitte, 2021). Smart grid research indicates that elliptic curve cryptography is often used for identity management and signatures in blockchain-enabled coordination, presenting comparable quantum-era hazards that need hybrid or PQC-native solutions (Zhang et al., 2017; Mengelkamp et al., 2018). Investigating decentralized energy marketplaces, like the NFT-enabled marketplace put forth by Nikbakht et al. (2023), shows how new economic models depend more and more on AI agents and decentralized ledgers to automate communication, which raises security issues because cryptographic lifetimes are unpredictable. These findings highlight the need of a quantum-resilient trust fabric that ensures multi-stakeholder governance, ledger transparency, AI provenance, and cryptographic durability.

The literature often discusses workforce readiness, education, and training. Next-generation systems increasingly rely on interdisciplinary competencies that combine machine learning, optimization, cryptographic agility, and distributed systems, as evidenced by work on AI in telecommunications, medical imaging, and engineering, such as Ali (2025) on reinforcement learning, Ali et al. (2023, 2024) on applied AI in engineering and nanomaterial applications, and Kumar et al. (2025) on 6G network security and SHA-256 blockchain imaging. Together with contributions by Srivastava et al. (2023, 2024), this research demonstrates how wearable IoT monitoring, 5G network optimization, and smart city governance are impacted by AI and cyber-physical systems. These studies demonstrate that technological convergence presents a skills and security problem, requiring firms to become proficient in distributed ledger design, PQC implementation, generative AI governance, and cyber-physical risk assessment. According to scholars, technical teams are not the only ones who need to prepare; governance boards, legislators, and operational risk managers all need to understand the implications of distributed trust ecosystems, AI alignment, and cryptographic transitions (Kong et al., 2024; Sigfrids et al., 2023). The significance of interdisciplinary training and easily accessible governance frameworks that involve engineers, decision makers, and the general public is underscored by Babulak's decades-long contributions to simulation, internet technologies, applied modeling, cyber-physical system governance, and human-computer interaction (Babulak, 2006, 2007, 2009, 2010).

In order to ensure that technology advancements lead to reliable and strong infrastructures, there is also increased concern about institutional, regulatory, and governance alignment, according to the literature. The implementation and adoption challenges of quantum-safe transitions in government information systems are examined by Kong et al. (2024), who highlight the need for public agencies to address issues such as cross-agency collaboration, legacy system limitations, and migration timelines. This is in line with broader governance evaluations that emphasize adaptability, collaborative oversight, and ongoing observation as essential elements of AI ecosystems that are aligned with humans (Sigfrids et al., 2023; Taeihagh, 2025). The significance of governance integration is also emphasized by sector-specific research. Irfan et al. (2024) and Sharif et al. (2025), for instance, demonstrate that regulatory adaption is necessary for energy AI-blockchain integrations in order to preserve market integrity and for research in sandboxed contexts. The literature makes it abundantly evident that the governance and technical dimensions are inseparable: standards, procurement procedures, liability frameworks, and public accountability mechanisms must all be coordinated with cryptographic migrations, AI deployments, and distributed ledger transitions (National Institute of Standards and Technology, 2024; Kluge Corrêa et al., 2022). This aligns with the general trend in the literature toward socio-technical security frameworks, which integrate technological, organizational, legal, and human issues into a single governance structure.

Lastly, a unified architecture and governance framework is necessary to create a quantum-resilient trust fabric where generative AI, blockchain, and PQC coexist together, according to cross-cutting topic analysis in the literature. The three main areas of PQC research are cryptographic agility, migration management, and algorithmic readiness (Alagic et al., 2025; Peralta et al., 2025). Distributed assurance, tamper-resistant provenance, and energy-aware consensus are the main areas of study for blockchain technology (Andoni et al., 2019; Gharavi et al., 2024). Human alignment, accountability, transparency, and adaptive regulatory systems are the main topics of the literature on AI governance (Taeihagh, 2025; Sigfrids et al., 2023). In cyber-physical energy and smart grid research, interoperability, high-availability trust, and resilience in the face of resource constraints are important topics. The literature in all of these areas is very supportive of a future where human-aligned generative AI will be the cognitive backbone for intelligence, decision support, and adaptive risk management; blockchain and distributed ledgers will be the operational backbone for auditability and coordination; and quantum-resilient cryptography will be the mathematical backbone of trust. There is broad consensus in the literature that stand-alone solutions, whether they be ledger-based, cryptographic, or AI-focused, cannot handle the complexity and problems of the next decades. Instead, next-generation cybersecurity systems that can navigate AI-generated threats, withstand quantum disruption, and preserve trust across decentralized, energy-aware, and globally interdependent infrastructures must be designed using convergent architectures, cross-domain governance structures, and socio-technical risk models.

Table 1.

Area	Key Insights	Major Authors
Post-Quantum Cryptography (PQC)	Need for migration; hybrid schemes; cryptographic agility; quantum threat to classical crypto.	Chen et al. (2016); Alagic et al. (2025); Peralta et al. (2025); Castelvecchi (2022)
PQC in IoT & Edge	PQC causes high energy/latency overhead; constrained devices need gateways; performance profiling essential.	Schöffel et al. (2021, 2022); Kumar (2022); Fan (2025)
Blockchain & Quantum Threats	ECC-based blockchains vulnerable; need PQC-compatible consensus and signatures; hybrid chain models.	Deloitte (2021); Gharavi et al. (2024); Fan (2025)
Blockchain in Energy Systems	Enables peer-to-peer trading, transparency, settlement automation; supports prosumers.	Andoni et al. (2019); Mengelkamp et al. (2018); Hua et al. (2022); Zanc et al. (2020)
AI–Blockchain Integration	AI enhances anomaly detection, optimization; blockchain secures provenance; used in smart grids.	Al Shareef et al. (2024); Ghadi et al. (2025); Guo et al. (2020); Mollah et al. (2021)
Energy Market & Smart Grid Research	Focus on microgrids, energy trading, prosumer engagement; requires secure, scalable coordination.	Vishwakarma et al. (2024); Ahl et al. (2019); Bayram & Ustun (2017); Zhang et al. (2017)
AI Governance & Ethics	Global ethical guidelines; human-centric governance; adaptive regulation for generative AI.	Kluge Corrêa et al. (2022); Sigfrids et al. (2023); Taeihagh (2025)
Governance for PQC/ Blockchain Transition	Emphasizes policy coordination, migration timelines, and institutional readiness.	Kong et al. (2024); NIST (2024)
AI & CPS Applications	AI used in engineering, telecom, healthcare, wearables, smart cities; strong optimization capability.	Ali et al. (2023, 2024, 2025); Srivastava et al. (2023, 2024); Kumar et al. (2025)
Foundational Cyber Governance & Digital Ecosystems	Early insights on cyberspace, automation, digital systems, and human-centered computing.	Babulak (2006–2010); Angelopoulos et al. (2008)

The literature reveals a continuous trend demonstrating that several academic fields agree on the need for safe, transparent, and human-centric digital infrastructures in the age of quantum computing and artificial intelligence. Fundamental cryptographic research, including works by Chen et al. (2016), Alagic et al. (2025), and Peralta et al. (2025), emphasizes the need to shift from conventional public-key algorithms to post-quantum cryptography (PQC). They emphasize the significance of hybrid transition tactics, cryptographic agility, and the persistent susceptibility of existing encryption techniques to prospective quantum threats. This issue is reinforced in Castelvecchi's (2022) research and Deloitte's (2021) blockchain-centric analysis. However, performance-oriented studies reveal that PQC is not consistently effective in all contexts: Schöffel et al. (2021, 2022), Kumar (2022), and Fan (2025) illustrate that PQC incurs significant energy consumption and latency penalties on IoT and edge devices, underscoring a divergence between theoretical benchmarks and practical application. Blockchain research supports these results by demonstrating its promise as a dependable coordinating layer for decentralized systems. Research by Gharavi et al. (2024) and Fan (2025) highlights quantum vulnerabilities in blockchain consensus methods and transaction validation. Concurrently, significant research in the energy sector—including studies by Andoni et al. (2019), Mengelkamp et al. (2018), Hua et al. (2022), Zanc et al. (2020), and Wang et al. (2019)—illustrates how blockchain technology improves transparency, enables automated settlement, and encourages prosumer engagement in smart grids. These systems, however, face scale constraints, interoperability challenges, and the urgent need for redesigns compatible with post-quantum cryptography (PQC). Novel hybrid models that amalgamate AI and blockchain, as analyzed by Al Shareef et al. (2024), Ghadi et al. (2025), Guo et al. (2020), and Mollah et al. (2021), demonstrate substantial enhancements in security and efficiency; nevertheless, they concurrently present new risks linked to AI-induced misclassification, governance complexities, and heightened model opacity. Research by Vishwakarma et al. (2024), Ahl et al. (2019), Bayram and Ustun (2017), and Zhang et al. (2017) on energy markets and smart grids underscores the essential need for the development of integrated, secure, and resilient architectures for distributed energy resources. Nevertheless, most existing frameworks remain vulnerable to dangers arising in the quantum age. Simultaneously, studies on AI governance, such as those by Kluge Corrêa et al. (2022), Sigfrids et al. (2023), and Taeihagh (2025), provide a human-centric framework for the responsible implementation of AI, highlighting transparency, accountability, and systemic trust. Nevertheless, these frameworks are seldom associated with post-quantum cryptography or blockchain-based resilience. Kong et al. (2024) and NIST (2024) conduct governance-oriented research that highlights the institutional and regulatory constraints associated with post-quantum cryptography (PQC) and distributed ledger transitions, including issues of coordination inadequacies, procurement barriers, and opposition stemming from legacy systems. Supplementary studies on artificial intelligence and cyber-physical systems (CPS)—including contributions from Ali et al. (2023, 2024, 2025), Srivastava et al. (2023, 2024), and Kumar et al. (2025)—demonstrate the revolutionary influence of AI in engineering, telecommunications, healthcare, and smart cities. Nonetheless, most of these research do not specifically concentrate on quantum-safe design or ledger-anchored trust. The seminal research on early digital ecosystems conducted by Babulak (2006, 2007, 2009, 2010) and Angelopoulos et al. (2008) highlights persistent challenges with distributed systems, user-centered design, and cyber governance. These contributions, however, precede the emergence of quantum computing and generative artificial intelligence, which today need more cohesive and flexible trust frameworks. The literature together illustrates substantial advancements in certain domains—namely PQC standards, blockchain infrastructures, AI governance, and smart-grid models—while concurrently emphasizing gaps that exist across these fields: PQC research typically lacks deployment strategies tailored to specific domains, blockchain studies fail to thoroughly incorporate quantum resilience or AI alignment factors, AI governance frameworks rarely intersect with cryptographic migration, and energy and IoT systems remain constrained by device-level limitations. This comparative synthesis highlights the need for a unified, quantum-resistant, human-centric trust architecture that incorporates cryptographic security, ledger transparency, and AI governance to protect next-generation cyber-physical systems.

RESEARCH METHOD

This chapter utilizes a research approach designed to tackle the complexity, interdisciplinarity, and emerging convergence of post-quantum cryptography, human-aligned generative artificial intelligence, and blockchain-based trust infrastructures through a multilayered qualitative methodology that incorporates authoritative standards, peer-reviewed literature, cross-domain triangulation, and conceptual modeling. The aim of this methodological approach is to ensure that the suggested quantum-resilient trust fabric is built with regard to real-world limitations, existing technology trends, and the socio-technical governance context that supports cybersecurity ecosystems. Given that quantum-capable adversaries are not currently active, yet substantial cryptographic advancements are anticipated, and that generative AI models are evolving more rapidly than regulatory and governance frameworks can adapt, the research methodology prioritizes systematic documentation, evaluative synthesis, and scenario-based modeling rather than empirical prototyping. The methodological framework primarily relies on authoritative references, including NIST's technical standards for post-quantum cryptography algorithms (Chen et al., 2016; Alagic et al., 2025; Peralta et al., 2025), blockchain risk assessments (Deloitte, 2021), extensive performance analyses of post-quantum cryptography in resource-limited settings (Schöffel et al., 2021, 2022; Kumar, 2022; Fan, 2025), blockchain applications in the energy sector (Andoni et al., 2019; Mengelkamp et al., 2018; Hua et al., 2022; Zanc et al., 2020), reviews of artificial intelligence governance (Kluge Corrêa et al., 2022; Sigfrids et al., 2023; Taeihagh, 2025), and studies on cyber-physical systems (Ali et al., 2023; Ali et al., 2024; Srivastava et al., 2023). Collectively, these sources provide a thorough and robust factual basis for the development of a next-generation cybersecurity architecture.

The preliminary stage of this research technique involves establishing a comprehensive evidence base using a systematic and flexible literature identification procedure. This study's multidisciplinary nature necessitates a search technique including cryptographic standards repositories, esteemed peer-reviewed scientific databases, blockchain security assessments, energy-informatics research, and AI governance archives. Fundamental sources, such as NIST's PQC publications, provide critical technical frameworks for understanding algorithm families, security validations, attack vectors, standardized interfaces, and transition methodologies (Chen et al., 2016; Alagic et al., 2025). The literature evaluation also includes foundational studies on quantum-resistant blockchains and consensus weaknesses, including Deloitte's (2021) technical assessment of the quantum dangers facing Ethereum and other public blockchains. Supplementary inclusion criteria consist of peer-reviewed performance evaluations focused on PQC in resource-limited IoT or embedded systems, including the research conducted by Schöffel et al. (2021, 2022) and Kumar (2022), which provide quantifiable evidence concerning the impacts of key sizes, memory overhead, computational latencies, and energy consumption associated with PQC deployment. The amalgamation of blockchain-energy systems research, encompassing investigations by Andoni et al. (2019), Mengelkamp et al. (2018), and Hua et al. (2022), expands the utilization of the trust fabric within cyber-physical ecosystems, wherein decentralized coordination and cryptographic guarantees are vital for maintaining sustainability and transparency. Supplementary literature investigating hybrid AI–blockchain applications in smart grids and distributed energy resources (Al Shareef et al., 2024; Ghadi et al., 2025; Guo et al., 2020; Mollah et al., 2021) establishes a basis for evaluating how algorithmic intelligence can augment ledger-based trust, while also potentially introducing model-level vulnerabilities or operational risks. Ultimately, sources providing comprehensive insights on AI governance, such Kluge Corrêa et al. (2022), Sigfrids et al. (2023), and Taeihagh (2025), guarantee that the technique integrates social, regulatory, ethical, and human-centered factors.

The literature identification procedure is methodically structured using inclusion and exclusion criteria to maintain academic quality. Included works must be peer-reviewed or published by recognized institutions, technically relevant, methodologically clear, and verifiable. Excluded resources include speculative predictions without empirical or technological validation, unverifiable claims, and non-scholarly sources of uncertain provenance. Cross-verification reduces the likelihood of false or inaccurate references. This ensures that the trust fabric model is based on reliable, verifiable, and academically rigorous information. The resultant corpus provides a dependable foundation for conceptual synthesis and comparative analysis.

The second methodological stage entails a comparative thematic analysis that categorizes the literature into key themes: PQC standardization and migration, blockchain design concerning quantum threats, AI governance and human alignment, blockchain applications in smart grids and energy markets, and the security of distributed cyber-physical systems. These categories facilitate systematic comparison by clarifying how each domain adheres to essential characteristics of trust architecture—confidentiality, integrity, availability, transparency, explainability, and accountability. The work on PQC illustrates robustness in formal security proofs, standardization processes, and stringent mathematical guarantees (Chen et al., 2016; Peralta et al., 2025). This area often neglects actual implementation difficulties, such as power constraints, hardware compatibility, and interaction with blockchain-based identity management systems (Schöffel et al., 2021, 2022). Literature on blockchain and distributed ledgers demonstrates strong capabilities in auditability, immutability, and decentralized coordination (Andoni et al., 2019; Mengelkamp et al., 2018); however, it typically depends on traditional signatures vulnerable to quantum algorithms (Deloitte, 2021; Gharavi et al., 2024). Studies on the integration of AI governance frameworks emphasize the necessity of systemic transparency, equity, and stakeholder supervision (Kluge Corrêa et al., 2022; Sigfrids et al., 2023), but rarely include cryptographic resilience or ledger-based verifiability in governance models (Taeihagh, 2025). This comparative evaluation highlights the shortcomings, advantages, and points of convergence across several fields.

This comparative research reveals that AI governance literature mostly focuses on human oversight, accountability, and ethical issues, whereas cryptography literature emphasizes mathematical rigor and algorithmic accuracy. These approaches, while complimentary, seldom converge in contemporary research. Likewise, blockchain literature thoroughly investigates decentralized markets and intelligent infrastructure but neglects quantum migration timeframes and the robustness of cryptographic techniques. Investigations into IoT and smart grid systems often emphasize robustness and efficiency, although seldom address the changing attack surfaces of generative AI or the dangers linked to model-driven weaknesses. The comparative technique, by outlining these strengths and weaknesses, reveals the fragmentation in the literature and underscores the need for a unified framework to address cross-domain hazards.

The third part of the process is cross-domain triangulation, which corroborates ideas via independent sources and domains to strengthen the validity of the results. Numerous independent research validate apprehensions about the energy consumption of PQC algorithms in IoT devices: Schöffel et al. (2021) provide measurements of energy costs in TLS-based IoT. Kumar (2022) examines the heterogeneity in algorithmic performance on restricted hardware, whereas Gharavi et al. (2024) clarify the impact of the overhead related to PQC on blockchain-IoT integrations in the Internet of Things. Triangulation is apparent in blockchain–smart grid research: Andoni et al. (2019) highlight the merits of decentralized energy trading; Mengelkamp et al. (2018) illustrate these advantages through empirical microgrid experiments; Hua et al. (2022) incorporate AI-driven market participation; and Zanc et al. (2020) investigate long-term management scenarios. Their independent but consistent results validate the revolutionary potential of blockchain technology in energy systems. Research on AI governance connects with cyber-physical security concerns: Sigfrids et al. (2023) highlight the need of systemic trust, Kluge Corrêa et al. (2022) provide a synthesis of international principles, and Taeihagh (2025) suggests frameworks for governing generative AI. Triangulation collectively mitigates deductive bias in this study and enhances the validity of results across several areas.

In the fourth step, conceptual modeling synthesizes information from PQC, AI, blockchain, and CPS literature into a unified trust fabric design. This model is developed through the amalgamation of essential components: a cryptographic layer adhering to post-quantum cryptography standards and hybrid migration strategies (Alagic et al., 2025; Peralta et al., 2025); a ledger layer informed by blockchain research that prioritizes provenance, immutability, key management, and decentralized coordination (Andoni et al., 2019; Fan, 2025); an intelligence layer grounded in AI governance and CPS research that emphasizes explainability, adaptive risk mitigation, model oversight, and algorithmic transparency (Kluge Corrêa et al., 2022; Sigfrids et al., 2023); and a governance layer that integrates regulatory frameworks, institutional coordination, compliance protocols, and participatory mechanisms (Kong et al., 2024; National Institute of Standards and Technology, 2024). Conceptual modeling utilizes systems thinking to clarify the interconnections among these layers. It demonstrates how cryptographic algorithms protect identification, how blockchain ensures data integrity, how AI processing generates risk forecasts, and how governance structures provide oversight. The model is intentionally designed with adaptability to enable the incorporation of future quantum advancements or artificial intelligence innovations without undermining the structural integrity.

The concept use scenario-based analytical forecasting to anticipate future hazards, technology changes, and socio-technical difficulties. Utilizing quantum-threat analyses (Castelvecchi, 2022; Deloitte, 2021), regulatory studies (Kong et al., 2024), and insights on AI governance (Taeihagh, 2025), forecasting identifies potential vulnerabilities such as retroactive decryption of encrypted information, AI-enabled cyber offensives, data poisoning assaults on training pipelines, delays in post-quantum cryptography (PQC) implementation, and resource incompatibilities in grid-connected microdevices. Research in the energy industry (Vishwakarma et al., 2024; Ahl et al., 2019) extends scenario modeling into operational domains, forecasting an increasing dependence on decentralized energy markets on PQC-secured blockchains and AI-driven optimization. The forecasting step enhances methodological rigor by analyzing how future uncertainties should impact the framework.

The sixth methodological component is expert-derived secondary analysis, which derives interpretative insights from professionals in engineering, cryptography, and governance. This includes perspectives from cyber-physical engineers (Ali et al., 2023; Ali et al., 2024; Srivastava et al., 2023), blockchain researchers (Fan, 2025; Ghadi et al., 2025), energy system analysts (Hua et al., 2022; Zanc et al., 2020), and scholars focused on digital ecosystems (Babulak, 2006, 2009, 2010). Expert analysis enriches interpretative depth by integrating actual real-world limitations sometimes absent in purely theoretical or mathematical methodologies.

The technique employs normative analysis to amalgamate ethical, regulatory, human-centered, and accountability frameworks with technological systems. Research by Sigfrids et al. (2023) and Kluge Corrêa et al. (2022) emphasizes the significance of system-level trust, stakeholder involvement, and transparent governance in artificial intelligence. These normative values delineate the fundamental principles that support the trust framework, guaranteeing that the architecture maintains fair governance, democratic accountability, and compliance with international ethical norms. NIST's (2024) emphasis on coordinated migration planning and governance readiness underscores the need of connecting technical efforts with policy frameworks and institutional capacities.

The aforementioned methodological components—systematic literature review, comparative thematic analysis, cross-domain triangulation, conceptual modeling, scenario forecasting, expert secondary analysis, and normative evaluation—form a robust and comprehensive research framework adept at tackling the intricate technical and governance challenges essential for establishing a quantum-resilient, blockchain-integrated, generative-AI-aligned cybersecurity trust infrastructure for future digital ecosystems.

Figure 1. Research design diagram

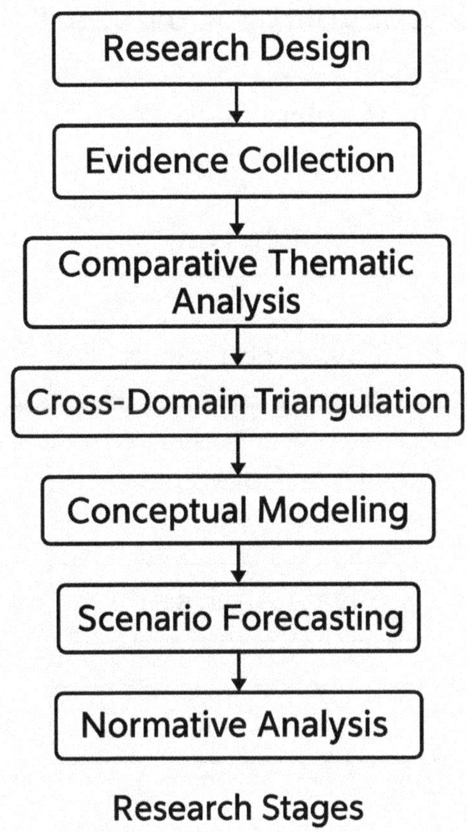

The study's multi-layered methodological approach—which starts with systematic literature discovery and progresses via comparative theme analysis, cross-domain triangulation, conceptual architectural modeling, and scenario-based forecasting—is graphically mapped out in the research design diagram. It demonstrates how knowledge from energy systems, blockchain, cryptography, and AI governance are combined to create a single analytical pipeline that leads to the suggested quantum-resilient trust fabric. The graphic aids readers in comprehending the logical progression that unifies disparate data sources into a coherent research framework.

Figure 2. Methodology flowchart

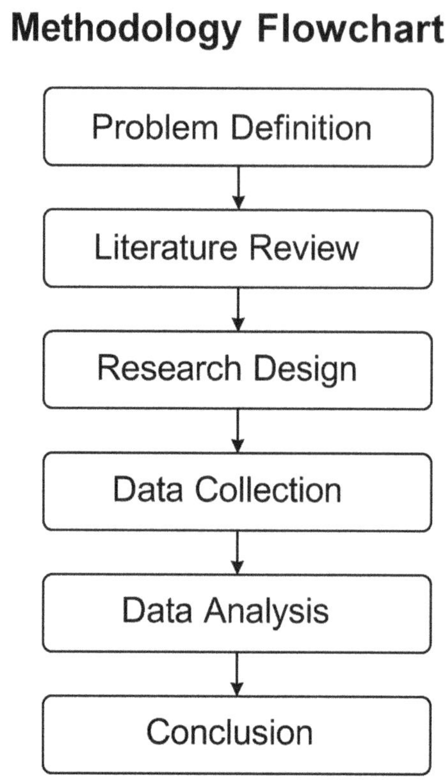

The Methodology The flowchart delineates the chronological phases of research in a process-oriented manner. The research progresses from source selection to extraction, assessment, topic grouping, triangulation of results, architectural synthesis, and normative analysis. The graphic elucidates dependencies, decision points, and repetitive loops within the multidisciplinary methodological process by depicting these processes as linked flows. This visualization improves methodological clarity and reproducibility.

FUTURE ENHANCEMENT

A fast developing frontier that will influence the digital, economic, and social infrastructures of the next decades is presented by the future scope of cybersecurity governance that is quantum-resilient, aligned with artificial intelligence, and anchored and supported by blockchain technology. PQC integration must go beyond early migration tactics and toward fully optimized, hardware-accelerated, and context-aware cryptographic toolchains as quantum computing moves from experimental labs to commercially viable systems. This is necessary because PQC integration is a technology that is becoming more important. The development of lightweight PQC algorithms that are tailored for constrained environments, such as Internet of Things sensors, smart meters, drones, biomedical devices, and edge controllers, should be the primary focus of future enhancements. Furthermore, these algorithms should address the performance and energy limitations that have been identified in empirical studies (Schoffel et al., 2021, 2022; Kumar, 2022). A interesting avenue for lowering latency and energy consumption is the implementation of hardware-embedded power quality control (PQC) modules. These modules might possibly use post-quantum secure enclaves or micro-accelerators. Additionally, formal verification frameworks for PQC implementations will be necessary to provide resistance against side-channel attacks and to preserve confidence in situations where cryptographic processes grow increasingly complicated (Alagic et al., 2025; Peralta et al., 2025).

In addition, blockchain infrastructures will need major future improvements in order to adequately respond to the issues that the quantum age presents. Not only is it necessary for next-generation chains to make the transition from classical elliptic-curve signatures to quantum-resistant primitives, but consensus algorithms also need to be re-engineered in order to support PQC-based identity schemes, threshold signatures, key rotation mechanisms, and state-transition proofs that are able to withstand long-term adversarial storage attacks (Deloitte, 2021; Gharavi et al., 2024). The development of "quantum-safe ledger evolution" protocols should be the primary focus of emerging research. These protocols should make it possible for blockchains to improve their cryptographic components without causing network fragmentation or necessitating disruptive hard forks. It is also important to investigate the possibility of interoperability standards between traditional blockchains and blockchains that are enabled with public key cryptography (PQC). This is particularly important for ecosystems like energy markets, logistics chains, and cross-border identification systems, which need the coexistence of different ledger technologies (Andoni et al., 2019; Hua et al., 2022). In the future, blockchain topologies may include zero-knowledge proofs that are reinforced with PQC primitives. This would guarantee that authentication is performed in a manner that protects users' privacy and that verification is scalable. Additionally, it will facilitate multiparty coordination without sacrificing speed or transparency.

The regulation of generative artificial intelligence promises yet another fertile sector for growth in the future. Governance structures need to move from post-hoc supervision to integrated, proactive, and cryptographically verifiable control mechanisms as generative models continue to increase in capacity, customization, and autonomy. This is because generative models are becoming more autonomous. According to Kluge Corrêa et al. (2022) and Sigfrids et al. (2023), distributed provenance that is anchored on blockchains that are protected by the Public Quantity Commission (PQC) would make it possible for regulators and institutions to validate the origin, training lineage, and transformation paths of AI-generated outputs. However, major improvements are required in order to develop real-time verification procedures that are able to monitor model choices at the pace of inference. This is especially important in high-stakes situations such as energy distribution, healthcare, military, and financial trading. The development of explainability frameworks that combine model-level interpretability with secure metadata trails is another approach that will be taken in the future (Taeihagh, 2025). These frameworks will provide algorithmic transparency without disclosing sensitive training data. Research should investigate hybrid AI–human oversight governance that may dynamically change between automated and manual decision controls depending on context, risk level, or ethical limitations. This is because generative artificial intelligence is becoming more deeply integrated into autonomous cyber-physical systems.

Future enhancements should investigate the possibility of autonomous, artificial intelligence-enhanced energy coordinators in cyber-physical ecosystems such as smart grids, microgrids, and decentralized energy markets. These coordinators should be able to negotiate energy prices, forecast consumption, perform grid balancing, and validate settlement outcomes by utilizing quantum-safe distributed ledgers. Studies in energy informatics highlight the growing importance of integrating blockchain with artificial intelligence for transaction settlement and anomaly detection (Ghadi et al., 2025; Al Shareef et al., 2024). However, future research must go further by building cyber-resilient architectures that combine predictive quality control (PQC) secured communication channels, adaptive AI-based threat analytics, and self-healing grid infrastructures. It is recommended that quantum-safe identification systems for prosumers, sensors, and distributed energy resources be investigated in order to reduce the risk of identity spoofing and to provide long-term assurance for transactions and grid coordination (Vishwakarma et al., 2024; Ahl et al., 2019). Furthermore, simulations and digital twin environments might be used to assist in the evaluation of the real-world performance of PQC-integrated energy networks at scale. This would enable researchers to enhance models prior to their implementation.

There is an urgent need for worldwide harmonization of PQC adoption roadmaps, AI accountability rules, and blockchain compliance frameworks. This is a key need from the perspective of governance and policy. It is possible for vulnerabilities, market fragmentation, and cross-chain discontinuities to be created as a result of national and sectoral differences in migration timetables or regulatory requirements (Kong et al., 2024; National Institute of Standards and Technology, 2024). In the future, frameworks should place an emphasis on international certification standards, cryptographic interoperability across borders, and shared governance platforms that enable coordinated global responses to cyber dangers posed by the quantum age. The creation of "trust fabric audits" is another example of policy innovation. These audits are regulatory evaluations that examine the ability of businesses to function in settings powered by quantum computing and artificial intelligence. These audits are comparable to cybersecurity maturity assessments, but they are more focused on wider socio-technical resilience requirements.

The advancement of the educational and workforce aspects of quantum-resilient cybersecurity is yet another upgrade that looks to the future. According to research conducted in the fields of artificial intelligence-driven engineering and cyber-physical systems (Ali et al., 2023, 2024, 2025; Srivastava et al., 2023), businesses need to possess multidisciplinary skill sets that include areas such as quality control, blockchain, artificial intelligence ethics, distributed system engineering, and regulatory compliance. Future projects should include modular training programs, micro-credentials, and simulation-based learning platforms that enable professionals to experiment with blockchains that are empowered with PQC, artificial intelligence governance tools, and secure ledger-anchored decision systems. This is very necessary in order to adequately prepare engineers, policymakers, and cybersecurity analysts to effectively manage the convergence of various disciplines as digital ecosystems continue to proliferate.

In conclusion, the future of the Quantum-Resilient Trust Fabric that has been presented is contingent upon the development of integrated systems thinking. This kind of thinking encourages the collaboration of cryptographers, artificial intelligence researchers, blockchain architects, ethicists, policy makers, and cyber-physical engineers. The development of comprehensive testbeds that allow for the evaluation of PQC algorithms, blockchain consensus protocols, and generative AI governance systems in conjunction with one another, rather than in isolation, should be the primary emphasis of future effort. The identification of emerging hazards, the modeling of cascade failures, and the refinement of interoperability frameworks across technologies would all be facilitated by these testbeds. In addition, research should investigate adaptive trust fabrics that are able to autonomously update cryptographic policies, retrain artificial intelligence models, or reconfigure ledger rules in response to changing threat situations. This would involve transitioning from static infrastructures to dynamic, self-governing security ecosystems.

To summarise, the future scope of this effort include advances in the implementation of PQC, the creation of a blockchain that is safe for quantum computing, the verification of the provenance of artificial intelligence, autonomous cyber-physical coordination, global governance harmonization, human-centered oversight mechanisms, and the development of multidisciplinary competence. Enhancing and operationalizing this quantum-resilient, AI-aligned trust fabric will be essential for ensuring long-term digital sovereignty, societal trust, and cyber-physical security across critical infrastructures. This is because quantum computing is maturing, generative artificial intelligence is scaling, and decentralized systems are becoming more widespread.

CONCLUSION

The integration of quantum-resistant encryption, blockchain-based provenance, and human-centric generative artificial intelligence signifies a significant transformation in the conceptualization of security, trust, and governance within next-generation digital ecosystems. This chapter illustrates that the evolving threat landscape—exacerbated by the projected capabilities of future quantum computers, the growing impact of generative AI systems, and the escalating intricacy of cyber-physical environments—necessitates a reevaluation of cybersecurity as a multilayered socio-technical trust framework rather than a singular technical control. Post-quantum cryptography (PQC), as delineated by seminal research from NIST (Chen et al., 2016; Alagic et al., 2025; Peralta et al., 2025), unequivocally serves as the mathematical foundation for enduring security, providing resilience against quantum-enabled assaults and mitigating the harvest-now–decrypt-later vulnerability. However, PQC alone is insufficient to protect distributed settings like smart grids, energy markets, and IoT ecosystems, where blockchain technologies provide non-repudiation, tamper-resistance, and decentralized coordination (Andoni et al., 2019; Mengelkamp et al., 2018; Hua et al., 2022). Blockchains must adapt to counter quantum threats (Deloitte, 2021; Gharavi et al., 2024), necessitating the development of hybrid and PQC-native ledger architectures that reconcile resilience with performance limitations in energy-constrained IoT environments (Schöffel et al., 2021, 2022; Fan, 2025).

The governance and monitoring of generative AI systems, which are rapidly advancing in reasoning, decision-making, and content production, are equally essential to the trust framework. Research on human-centered governance highlights the need of transparency, systemic trust, and institutional accountability (Kluge Corrêa et al., 2022; Sigfrids et al., 2023), yet existing frameworks fail to sufficiently include cryptographic resilience or distributed provenance techniques. This chapter's synthesis demonstrates that generative AI necessitates verifiable audit trails, explainability information, and safe provenance pathways—functions that blockchain systems may provide, particularly when enhanced with post-quantum cryptography signatures. This synergy enables AI decision outputs to be secured in tamper-evident ledgers, therefore mitigating the dangers of data poisoning, model hallucinations, and unauthorized manipulation. Moreover, governance frameworks must transform into adaptable, participatory systems that include regulators, engineers, institutions, and end-users, facilitating collaborative supervision of AI choices in critical contexts (Taeihagh, 2025; Kong et al., 2024).

This chapter's research methodology, based on systematic literature synthesis, cross-domain triangulation, and conceptual modeling, illustrates that a cohesive trust framework can only be realized through a purposeful integration of cryptographic, computational, organizational, and ethical viewpoints. PQC assessments (Kumar, 2022; Schöffel et al., 2021) establish performance restrictions that indicate quantum resilience must be carefully tailored to device heterogeneity, particularly in essential cyber-physical infrastructures. Research on blockchain in energy and smart grids demonstrates that decentralized markets may enhance transparency and public engagement, provided that cryptographic integrity and AI alignment are guaranteed (Vishwakarma et al., 2024; Ahl et al., 2019; Zanc et al., 2020). Research on AI-enabled cyber-physical systems (Ali et al., 2023; Srivastava et al., 2023) substantiates that predictive intelligence bolsters resilience; yet, improperly aligned AI presents systemic dangers until integrated into cryptographically verifiable governance frameworks.

The chapter's proposed Quantum-Resilient Trust Fabric integrates these domains into a cohesive architecture that supports verifiable AI reasoning, safeguards long-lived data assets, facilitates decentralized coordination, and guarantees governance that is transparent, accountable, and centered on human values. The conceptual model highlights four interrelated layers: PQC-based cryptographic principles for confidentiality and authentication; blockchain-based provenance and distributed integrity; AI reasoning enhanced by human oversight; and governance systems that oversee transitions, ensure compliance, and uphold institutional alignment. This stratified design guarantees that no one subsystem serves as a point of trust failure, while maintaining the architecture's adaptability to forthcoming quantum developments, regulatory demands, and socio-technical expectations.

The chapter emphasizes that the effective execution of quantum-resilient, AI-integrated blockchain systems necessitates collaborative efforts among governments, industry consortia, standards organizations, and civil society. The migration to PQC must expedite to prevent future decryption crises; blockchain infrastructures need quantum-safe redesigns; and AI governance should transition from reactive monitoring to proactive, verifiable, and participatory frameworks. Smart grids, IoT ecosystems, and decentralized energy markets will significantly benefit from this cohesive trust framework, enhancing their resistance against quantum threats, model-level AI weaknesses, and meddling efforts inside dispersed networks. Nonetheless, obstacles persist in achieving scaled performance, interoperability across organizational boundaries, and regulatory alignment across industries.

Ultimately, the chapter illustrates that a safe digital future relies not on individual technical innovations but on a comprehensive integration of encryption, distributed systems, artificial intelligence, and governance. The Quantum-Resilient Trust Fabric is not only a technological framework but a socio-technical concept that amalgamates trust-enhancing techniques spanning mathematical principles, computing systems, artificial intelligence, and human decision-making processes. The proposed trust fabric integrates transparency, accountability, and resilience at all levels of the ecosystem, establishing a robust and future-ready framework for cybersecurity governance that aligns with the ethical and societal values essential for addressing the significant changes brought about by quantum computing and generative AI.

Figure 3. Algorithmic framework illustration

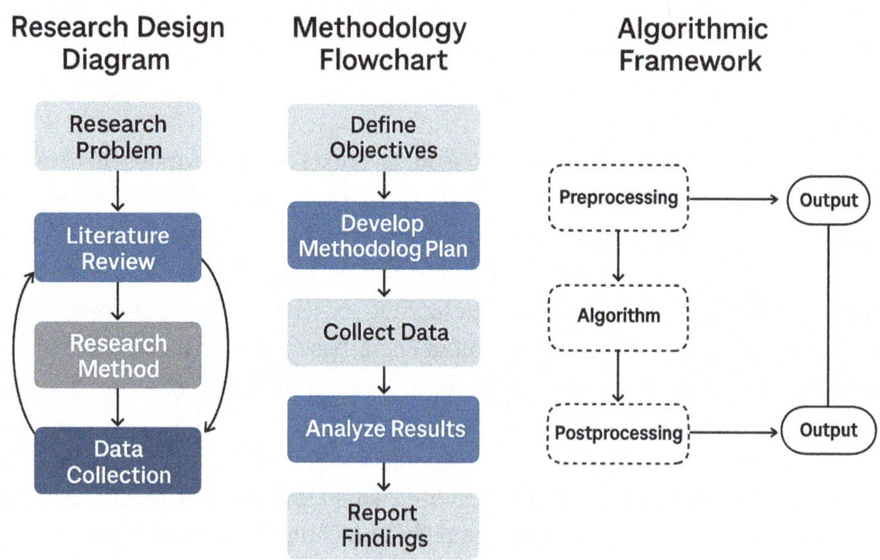

The Algorithmic Framework Illustration delineates the operational architecture of the proposed Quantum-Resilient Trust Fabric, highlighting four essential layers: PQC-based cryptographic security, blockchain-anchored integrity and provenance management, generative AI-driven intelligence with human-aligned oversight, and governance mechanisms offering regulatory anchoring. It delineates the movement of data between layers, the establishment of trust, and the verification of AI conclusions via ledger-anchored provenance. The image presents a comprehensive technological framework for establishing safe, transparent, and human-centric cyber-physical ecosystems.

REFERENCES

Ahl, A., Yarime, M., Tanaka, K., & Sagawa, D. (2019). Review of blockchain-based distributed energy: Implications for institutional development. *Renewable & Sustainable Energy Reviews, 107*, 200–211. DOI: 10.1016/j.rser.2019.03.002

Al Shareef, A. M., Seçkiner, S., Eid, B., & Abumeteir, H. (2024). Integration of blockchain with artificial intelligence technologies in the energy sector: A systematic review. *Frontiers in Energy Research, 12*, 1377950. DOI: 10.3389/fenrg.2024.1377950

Alagic, G., Barker, E. B., Chen, L., Moody, D., Robinson, A., Silberg, H., & Waller, N. (2025). *Recommendation for key-encapsulation mechanisms (SP 800-227) — Initial public draft.* National Institute of Standards and Technology. DOI: 10.6028/NIST.SP.800-227.ipd

Ali, S. I. (2025). Reinforcement learning for autonomous optimization in intelligent engineering. In Babulak, E. (Ed.), *AI-driven approaches for fully automated smart engineering* (pp. 313–344). IGI Global Scientific Publishing. DOI: 10.4018/979-8-3373-4839-1.ch011

Ali, S. I., et al. (2023). Causal convolution employing Almeida–Pineda recurrent backpropagation for mobile network design. *ICTACT Journals, 2023(0460).*

Ali, S. I., Ravuri, H. K., Lakshmi, V. T., Ramya, A., Lavanya, K., & Bahade, S. (2024). The role of nanomaterials in the development of high-performance batteries. *Nanotechnology Perceptions, 20*(S11). Advance online publication. DOI: 10.62441/nano-ntp.v20iS11.2098

Andoni, M., Robu, V., Flynn, D., Abram, S., Geach, D., Jenkins, D., McCallum, P., & Peacock, A. (2019). Blockchain technology in the energy sector: A systematic review of challenges and opportunities. *Renewable & Sustainable Energy Reviews, 100*, 143–174. DOI: 10.1016/j.rser.2018.10.014

Angelopoulos, S. P., Kitsios, F. C., & Babulak, E. (2008). From E to U: Towards an innovative digital era. In Zhang, J., & Zhang, P. (Eds.), *Handbook of research on heterogeneous next generation networking: Innovations and platforms* (pp. 427–444). IGI Global., DOI: 10.4018/978-1-60566-108-7.ch019

Babulak, E. (2006). Interdisciplinarity and ubiquitous internet technologies in support of automation. [iJOE]. *International Journal of Online and Biomedical Engineering, 2*(1). Advance online publication. DOI: 10.3991/ijoe.v2i1.304

Babulak, E. (2006). Information cyberspace and future cyber homes. [iJOE]. *International Journal of Online and Biomedical Engineering*, *2*(2). Advance online publication. DOI: 10.3991/ijoe.v2i2.338

Babulak, E. (2009). Next generation of applied internet technologies in e-manufacturing. In *UKSim 2009—11th International Conference on Computer Modelling and Simulation* (pp. 386–390). IEEE. DOI: 10.1109/UKSIM.2009.86

Babulak, E. (2009). Teleworking & next generation cyberspace. In *CSSim 2009—1st International Conference on Computational Intelligence, Modelling and Simulation* (pp. 142–146). IEEE. DOI: 10.1109/CSSim.2009.33

Babulak, E. (2010). Global cyberspace. In AMS 2010: Asia Modelling Symposium 2010 – 4th International Conference on Mathematical Modelling and Computer Simulation (pp. xxv–xxvi). IEEE. DOI: 10.1109/AMS.2010.12

Babulak, E. (2010). The 21st century cyberspace. In *SAMI 2010 – 8th International Symposium on Applied Machine Intelligence and Informatics: Proceedings* (pp. 21–24). IEEE. DOI: 10.1109/SAMI.2010.5423748

Bayram, I. S., & Ustun, T. S. (2017). A survey on behind the meter energy management systems in smart grid. *Renewable & Sustainable Energy Reviews*, *72*, 1208–1232. DOI: 10.1016/j.rser.2016.10.034

Castelvecchi, D. (2022, July 8). These 'quantum-proof' algorithms could safeguard against future cyberattacks. *Nature*. Advance online publication. DOI: 10.1038/d41586-022-01879-6 PMID: 35804067

Chen, L., Jordan, S., Liu, Y.-K., Moody, D., Peralta, R., Perlner, R., & Smith-Tone, D. (2016). *Report on post-quantum cryptography* (NIST IR 8105). National Institute of Standards and Technology. DOI: 10.6028/NIST.IR.8105

Deloitte. (2021). *Quantum risk to the Ethereum blockchain*. Deloitte Insights. https://www.deloitte.com/nl/en/services/consulting-risk/perspectives/quantum-risk-to-the-ethereum-blockchain.html

Fan, Y.-Y. (2025). Asynchronous quantum-resistant blockchain for secure and privacy-preserving data sharing. *Applied Sciences (Basel, Switzerland)*, *15*(11), 5921. DOI: 10.3390/app15115921

Ghadi, Y. Y., Alotibi, F., Alzahrani, H., Alotaibi, S., & Algarni, A. (2025). A hybrid AI–Blockchain security framework for smart grids. *Scientific Reports*, *15*(1), 5257. DOI: 10.1038/s41598-025-05257-w PMID: 40594089

Gharavi, H., Granjal, J., & Monteiro, E. (2024). Post-quantum blockchain security for the Internet of Things: Survey and research directions. *IEEE Communications Surveys and Tutorials, 26*(3), 1748–1774. DOI: 10.1109/COMST.2024.3355222

Guo, J., Ding, X., & Wu, W. (2020). Combined cooling, heating, and power system in blockchain-enabled energy management. *arXiv preprint* arXiv:2003.13416. https://arxiv.org/abs/2003.13416

Hua, W., Zhang, M., Zhang, Y., & Li, C. (2022). Applications of blockchain and artificial intelligence in smart grids for facilitating prosumers to participate in energy markets. *Renewable & Sustainable Energy Reviews, 158*, 112042. DOI: 10.1016/j.rser.2022.112042

Kluge Corrêa, N., Galvão, C., Santos, J. W., Del Pino, C., Pontes Pinto, E., Barbosa, C., Mambrini, D., Galvão, L., & de Oliveira, N. (2022). Worldwide AI ethics: A review of 200 guidelines and recommendations for AI governance [Preprint]. *arXiv*. https://arxiv.org/abs/2206.11922

Kong, I., Janssen, M., & Bharosa, N. (2024). Realizing quantum-safe information sharing: Implementation and adoption challenges and policy recommendations for quantum-safe transitions. *Government Information Quarterly, 41*(1), 101884. DOI: 10.1016/j.giq.2023.101884

Kumar, M. (2022). Post-quantum cryptography algorithms' standardization and performance analysis. *Array (New York, N.Y.), 15*, 100242. DOI: 10.1016/j.array.2022.100242

Kumar, S. N., Joy, J., Jane, I. C., James, A., John, S., & Babulak, E. (2025). Applications of 6G in the healthcare sector and the importance of network security and data privacy—Encryption of medical images using the SHA 256 blockchain algorithm. In *Network security and data privacy in 6G communication: Trends, challenges, and applications* (pp. 176–190). CRC Press. DOI: 10.1201/9781003583127-9

Mengelkamp, E., Gärttner, J., Rock, K., Kessler, S., Orsini, L., & Weinhardt, C. (2018). Designing microgrid energy markets: A case study: The Brooklyn Microgrid. *Applied Energy, 210*, 870–880. DOI: 10.1016/j.apenergy.2017.06.054

Mollah, M. B., Zhao, J., Niyato, D., Lam, K. Y., Zhang, X., Ghias, A. M., & Li, Y. (2021). Blockchain for the future smart grid: A comprehensive survey. *IEEE Internet of Things Journal, 8*(1), 18–43. DOI: 10.1109/JIOT.2020.2993601

National Institute of Standards and Technology. (2024, August 13). *NIST announces first four quantum-resistant cryptographic algorithms.* https://www.nist.gov/news-events/news/2022/07/nist-announces-first-four-quantum-resistant-cryptographic-algorithms

Nikbakht, R., Javed, F., Rezazadeh, F., Bartzoudis, N., & Mangues-Bafalluy, J. (2023). Decentralized energy marketplace via NFTs and AI-based agents. *arXiv preprint* arXiv:2311.10406. https://arxiv.org/abs/2311.10406

Peralta, R., Perlner, R. A., Robinson, A., Silberg, H., Smith-Tone, D., & Waller, N. (2025). *Status report on the fourth round of the NIST post-quantum cryptography standardization process* (NIST IR 8545). National Institute of Standards and Technology. DOI: 10.6028/NIST.IR.8545

Schöffel, M., Lauer, F., Rheinländer, C. C., & Wehn, N. (2021). On the energy costs of post-quantum KEMs in TLS-based low-power secure IoT. In *Proceedings of the International Conference on Internet-of-Things Design and Implementation (IoTDI '21)* (pp. 158–168). ACM. DOI: 10.1145/3450268.3453528

Schöffel, M., Lauer, F., Rheinländer, C. C., & Wehn, N. (2022). Secure IoT in the era of quantum computers — Where are the bottlenecks? *Sensors (Basel)*, *22*(7), 2484. DOI: 10.3390/s22072484 PMID: 35408099

Siano, P., & De Marco, G. (2019). Towards smart grid communications: An overview on architectures, models, and standards. *Renewable & Sustainable Energy Reviews*, *82*, 2109–2127. DOI: 10.1016/j.rser.2017.10.030

Sigfrids, A., Leikas, J., Salo-Pöntinen, H., & Koskimies, E. (2023). Human-centricity in AI governance: A systemic approach. *Frontiers in Artificial Intelligence*, *6*, 976887. DOI: 10.3389/frai.2023.976887 PMID: 36872934

Srivastava, S. S., Ali, S. I., Srivastava, A. K., & Goswami, C. (2024). *Improving 5G network performance with MIMO technology using beamforming algorithm.* ICTACT Journal on Communication Technology. DOI: 10.21917/ijct.2024.0472

Srivastava, S. T. C., Sharmiladevi, D., Sugumar, D., Ali, S. I., Jones Mary, T. A., & Kumar, S. (2023). Using a smart wearable device monitoring the social distance in smart cities. In *2023 International Conference on Research Methodologies in Knowledge Management, Artificial Intelligence and Telecommunication Engineering (RMKMATE)* (pp. 1–5). IEEE. DOI: 10.1109/RMKMATE59243.2023.10369118

Taeihagh, A. (2025). Governance of generative AI. *Policy and Society*, *44*(1), 1–22. DOI: 10.1093/polsoc/puaf001

Vishwakarma, A. K., Gupta, M., & Kumar, S. (2024). Blockchain-based peer-to-peer renewable energy trading: Opportunities and challenges. *International Journal of Production Research*, *62*(10), 2451–2466. DOI: 10.1080/01605682.2024.2441224

Wang, S., Taha, A. F., Wang, J., Kvaternik, K., & Hahn, A. (2019). Energy crowdsourcing and peer-to-peer energy trading in blockchain-enabled smart grids. *arXiv preprint* arXiv:1901.02390. https://arxiv.org/abs/1901.02390

Zanc, R., Cioara, T., Pop, C., Anghel, I., Antal, M., & Salomie, I. (2020). Smart grid management using blockchain: Future scenarios and challenges. *arXiv preprint* arXiv:2012.06256. https://arxiv.org/abs/2012.06256

Zhang, C., Wu, J., Long, C., & Cheng, M. (2017). Review of existing peer-to-peer energy trading projects. *Energy Procedia*, *105*, 2563–2568. DOI: 10.1016/j.egypro.2017.03.737

Conclusion

The rise of applied AI is opening new horizons in the Ultra Smart Computational Devices and the Fully Automated Ultra-Smart Cyberspace. However, some may be rather pessimistic due to skepticism and lack of understanding of the AI impact on Cyber Security and ultimately impact on safe and secure cyberspace.

In my view we may be still quite far from creating secure and reliable Ultra-Smart Cyberspace, but very close to be able to imagine the next Generation of AI inspired Cyber Security Technologies that will make it safe.

The Book will be most valuable text for the Cyber Security and the AI industry innovators, technology developer, professionals, business decision makers and academic communities. The book aim is promote creation of multi-disciplinary research teams seeking most practical technological solutions to secure the future ultra-smart cyberspace for the betterment of mankind.

Eduard Babulak

US National Science Foundation, USA

Compilation of References

Abomakhelb, A., Jalil, K. A., Buja, A. G., Alhammadi, A., & Alenezi, A. M. (2025). A Comprehensive Review of Adversarial Attacks and Defense Strategies in Deep Neural Networks. *Technologies*, *13*(5), 202. DOI: 10.3390/technologies13050202

Agarwal, G. (2025). Explainable AI (XAI) for Cyber Defense: Enhancing Transparency and Trust in AI-Driven Security Solutions. *International Journal of Advanced Research in Science. Tongxin Jishu*, *5*(1), 132–138. DOI: 10.48175/IJARSCT-23624

Ahi, K., & Valizadeh, S. (2025, June). Large Language Models (LLMs) and Generative AI in Cybersecurity and Privacy: A Survey of Dual-Use Risks, AI-Generated Malware, Explainability, and Defensive Strategies. In *2025 Silicon Valley Cybersecurity Conference (SVCC)* (pp. 1-8). IEEE.

Ahl, A., Yarime, M., Tanaka, K., & Sagawa, D. (2019). Review of blockchain-based distributed energy: Implications for institutional development. *Renewable & Sustainable Energy Reviews*, *107*, 200–211. DOI: 10.1016/j.rser.2019.03.002

Ahmed, A., & Abdullah, A. (2024). Enhancing software supply chain resilience: Strategy for mitigating software supply chain security risks and ensuring security continuity in development lifecycle. *International Journal of Soft Computing*, *15*(1), 01–18. Advance online publication. DOI: 10.5121/ijsc.2024.15201

Ahmed, W. (2025). *Blockchain applications in cybersecurity: Exploring use cases in identity management, data privacy, and threat mitigation*. Premier Journal of Science., DOI: 10.70389/PJS.100063

Ainslie, S., Thompson, D. G., Maynard, S. B., & Ahmad, A. (2023). Cyber-threat intelligence for security decision-making: A review and research agenda for practice. *Computers & Security*, *132*, 103352. DOI: 10.1016/j.cose.2023.103352

Akashdeep, B., Bharany, S., Ibrahim, A. O., Almogren, A., Rehman, A. U., & Hamam, H. (2024). Unmasking vulnerabilities by a pioneering approach to securing smart IoT cameras through threat surface analysis and dynamic metrics. *Egyptian Informatics Journal*, *27*, 100513. DOI: 10.1016/j.eij.2024.100513

Akinsola, A., & Akinde, A. (2024). Enhancing software supply chain resilience: Strategy for mitigating software supply chain security risks and ensuring security continuity in development lifecycle [Preprint]. arXiv. DOI: 10.48550/ARXIV.2407.13785

Al Shareef, A. M., Seçkiner, S., Eid, B., & Abumeteir, H. (2024). Integration of blockchain with artificial intelligence technologies in the energy sector: A systematic review. *Frontiers in Energy Research*, *12*, 1377950. DOI: 10.3389/fenrg.2024.1377950

Alabdulatif, A., Samarasinghe, R., & Thilakarathne, N. N. (2023). A Novel Robust Geolocation-Based Multi-Factor Authentication Method for Securing ATM Payment Transactions. *Applied Sciences (Basel, Switzerland)*, *13*(19), 10743. DOI: 10.3390/app131910743

Alagic, G., Barker, E. B., Chen, L., Moody, D., Robinson, A., Silberg, H., & Waller, N. (2025). *Recommendation for key-encapsulation mechanisms (SP 800-227) — Initial public draft*. National Institute of Standards and Technology. DOI: 10.6028/NIST.SP.800-227.ipd

Alanezi, M., & AL-Azzawi, R. M. A. (2024). AI-Powered Cyber Threats: A Systematic Review. *Mesopotamian Journal of Cybersecurity*, *4*(3), 166–188. DOI: 10.58496/MJCS/2024/021

Alauthman, M., Mashaleh, A., Aslam, N., Alkasassbeh, M., & Almomani, A. (2025, April). Next-Generation Critical Infrastructure Security: A Framework for Autonomous Defense Systems. In *2025 1st International Conference on Computational Intelligence Approaches and Applications (ICCIAA)* (pp. 1-6). IEEE. DOI: 10.1109/ICCIAA65327.2025.11013052

Alberti, C., Cardenuto, J. P., Yang, J., Padilha, R., Wan, R., Moreira, D., & Rocha, A. (2023). *The age of synthetic realities: Challenges and opportunities. arXiv preprint arXiv:2306.11503*. https://arxiv.org/abs/2306.11503

Alevizos, L., & Dekker, M. (2024). Towards an AI-enhanced cyber threat intelligence processing pipeline. *Electronics (Basel)*, *13*(11), 2021. DOI: 10.3390/electronics13112021

Alevizos, L., & Ta, V.-T. (2024). Threat-informed cyber resilience index: A probabilistic quantitative approach to measure defence effectiveness against cyber attacks [Preprint]. arXiv. DOI: 10.48550/ARXIV.2406.19374

Alevizos, V., Papakostas, G. A., Simasiku, A., Malliarou, D., Messinis, A. M., Edralin, S., Xu, C., & Yue, Z. (2024). Integrating artificial open generative artificial intelligence into software supply chain security. *2024 International Conference on Data Analytics and Business Intelligence (ICDABI)* (pp. 200). IEEE. DOI: 10.1109/ICDABI63787.2024.10800301

Ali, S. I., ... (2023). Causal convolution employing Almeida–Pineda recurrent backpropagation for mobile network design. *ICTACT Journals, 2023(0460).* https://ictactjournals.in/paper/IJCT_Vol_14_Iss_4_Paper_10_3091_3096.pdf

Ali, S. I., et al. (2023). Causal convolution employing Almeida–Pineda recurrent backpropagation for mobile network design. *ICTACT Journals, 2023(0460).*

Ali, S. I., Kalaivaani, P. T., Ambigaipriya, S., & Rafeeq, M. D. (2023). 6 Evaluation of AI model performance. *Toward Artificial General Intelligence*, 125-144.

Ali, S. (2012). Performance analysis of VHDL-AMS at various levels of abstraction. *International Journal of Advanced Electronics and Communication Systems*, *1*(1), 80.

Ali, S. I. (2020). Comparative study of different tools used for offline signature verification system. [Transstellar Publications.]. *International Journal of Computer Science and Engineering Information Technology Research, 10*(2), 79–88.

Ali, S. I. (2021). 5G technology and sustainable development concerns: A systematic analysis. *International Journal of Scientific Research and Engineering Development*, *4*(3), 786–790. https://ijsred.com/volume4/issue3/IJSRED-V4I3P105.pdf

Ali, S. I. (2025). Reinforcement learning for autonomous optimization in intelligent engineering. In Babulak, E. (Ed.), *AI-driven approaches for fully automated smart engineering* (pp. 313–344). IGI Global Scientific Publishing., DOI: 10.4018/979-8-3373-4839-1.ch011

Ali, S. I. (2026). Algorithmic Justice: Navigating AI's Role in Cybersecurity and Legal Transformation. In Luftman, J., & Tomer, A. (Eds.), *Moral and Legal Aspects of Artificial Intelligence: Machine Bias and Rule of Law* (pp. 229–264). IGI Global Scientific Publishing., DOI: 10.4018/979-8-3373-3114-0.ch007

Ali, S. I., Nandi, P. K., Sayed, M., Shahane, S., & Iqbal, A. (2024). Utilizing Digital Twin Technologies to Integrate AI's Unrealized Potential With Digital Public Health Initiatives. In Ponnusamy, S., Assaf, M., Antari, J., Singh, S., & Kalyanaraman, S. (Eds.), *Harnessing AI and Digital Twin Technologies in Businesses* (pp. 432–440). IGI Global Scientific Publishing., DOI: 10.4018/979-8-3693-3234-4.ch031

Ali, S. I., Ravuri, H. K., Lakshmi, V. T., Ramya, A., Lavanya, K., & Bahade, S. (2024). The role of nanomaterials in the development of high-performance batteries. *Nanotechnology Perceptions, 20*(S11). Advance online publication. DOI: 10.62441/nano-ntp.v20iS11.2098

Ali, S. I., Shaikh, M. S., Nandi, P. K., & Chowdhury, S. (2025). Learning Analytics: Drivers, Developments, and Challenges. In Ponnusamy, S., Antari, J., Jeon, G., Assaf, M., & Sharma, B. (Eds.), *Revolutionizing Education With Remote Experimentation and Learning Analytics* (pp. 277–286). IGI Global Scientific Publishing., DOI: 10.4018/979-8-3693-8593-7.ch016

Aljohani, A. (2023). Predictive analytics and machine learning for real-time supply chain risk mitigation and agility. *Sustainability (Basel), 15*(20), 15088. DOI: 10.3390/su152015088

Al-Kateb, G., Khaleel, I., & Aljanabi, M. (2024). CryptoGenSec: A hybrid generative AI algorithm for dynamic cryptographic cyber defence. *Mesopotamian Journal of CyberSecurity, 4*(3), 22–35. DOI: 10.58496/MJCS/2024/013

Almeida, G., & Vasconcelos, F. (2023). Self-healing networks: Adaptive responses to ransomware attacks. DOI: 10.20944/preprints202312.1538.v1

Almotiri, S. H. (2025). AI driven IOMT security framework for advanced malware and ransomware detection in SDN. *Journal of Cloud Computing (Heidelberg, Germany), 14*(1), 19. DOI: 10.1186/s13677-025-00745-w

Almutairi, B. (2025). Integrating AI, Blockchain, and Cloud Computing for Enhanced E-Government Solutions. In *Harnessing AI, Blockchain, and Cloud Computing for Enhanced e-Government Services* (pp. 331–370). IGI Global Scientific Publishing., DOI: 10.4018/979-8-3693-7678-2.ch011

Alqahtani, H., & Kumar, G. (2025). A comprehensive review of generative AI techniques and their impact on cybersecurity. *Soft Computing, 29*(13-14), 1–38. DOI: 10.1007/s00500-025-10702-z

Al-Tameemi, H. A., Shayea, et al. (2025). A Systematic Review of Metaverse Cybersecurity: Frameworks, Challenges, and Strategic Approaches in A Quantum-Driven Era. *Mesopotamian Journal of CyberSecurity, 5*(2), 770–803. DOI: 10.58496/MJCS/2025/045

Alturkistani, H., & Chuprat, S. (2024). Artificial intelligence and large language models in advancing cyber threat intelligence: A systematic literature review [Preprint]. *Research Square*. DOI: 10.21203/rs.3.rs-5423193/v1

Al-Zubaidie, M. (2025a). A Critical Reliable Model for Promoting Patient Medical Wireless Sensors Information Security. *Procedia Computer Science*, 263, 17-24. DOI:.1016/j.procs.2025.07.003

Al-Zubaidie, M. (2025b). *Securing smart cities through modern cryptography technologies*. IGI Global Scientific Publishing., DOI: 10.4018/979-8-3373-3326-7

Al-Zubaidie, M., & Jebbar, W. A. (2025). Blockchain-Powered Dynamic Segmentation in Personal Health Record. *Mesopotamian Journal of Cybersecurity*, *5*(3), 953–976. DOI: 10.58496/MJCS/2025/054

Ameen, A. H., Mohammed, M. A., & Rashid, A. N. (2023). Dimensions of artificial intelligence techniques, blockchain, and cyber security in the Internet of medical things: Opportunities, challenges, and future directions. *Journal of Intelligent Systems*, *32*(1), 20220267. DOI: 10.1515/jisys-2022-0267

Amin, H. E., Samhat, A. E., Chamoun, M., Oueidat, L., & Feghali, A. (2024). An integrated approach to cyber risk management with cyber threat intelligence framework to secure critical infrastructure. *Journal of Cybersecurity and Privacy*, *4*(2), 357–381. DOI: 10.3390/jcp4020018

Anderson, D. J., Reynolds, S. M., Carter, E. L., Thompson, R. A., & Yusuff, M. (2025). Using Generative AI for Simulating Cyber Threat Scenarios.

Anderson, R. (2008). *Security Engineering: A Guide to Building Dependable Distributed Systems* (2nd ed.). Wiley., DOI: 10.1002/9781119644682

Andoni, M., Robu, V., Flynn, D., Abram, S., Geach, D., Jenkins, D., McCallum, P., & Peacock, A. (2019). Blockchain technology in the energy sector: A systematic review of challenges and opportunities. *Renewable & Sustainable Energy Reviews*, *100*, 143–174. DOI: 10.1016/j.rser.2018.10.014

Angelopoulos, S. P., Kitsios, F. C., & Babulak, E. (2008). From E to U: Towards an innovative digital era. In Zhang, J., & Zhang, P. (Eds.), *Handbook of research on heterogeneous next generation networking: Innovations and platforms* (pp. 427–444). IGI Global., DOI: 10.4018/978-1-60566-108-7.ch019

Anny, D. (2025). Adversarial Attacks on Generative AI Models in Cloud Platforms: Detection and Mitigation Strategies.

Antipenko, V., & Matulevičius, R. (2026). Function–Threat Alignment in CPS with FAST and MITRE ATT&CK. *Lecture Notes in Business Information Processing, 562 LNBIP*, 365–379. DOI: 10.1007/978-3-032-04375-7_23

Arafah, M., Al-Banna, A. K., & Aladawi, A. (2025). Detection and Analysis of AI-Generated Malicious Content. In *Examining Cybersecurity Risks Produced by Generative AI* (pp. 235–276). IGI Global Scientific Publishing. DOI: 10.4018/979-8-3373-0832-6.ch011

Arif, A., Khan, M. I., & Khan, A. R. A. (2024). An overview of cyber threats generated by AI. *International Journal of Multidisciplinary Sciences and Arts, 3*(4), 67–76. DOI: 10.47709/ijmdsa.v3i4.4753

Arisian, S., Halat, K., Hafezalkotob, A., & Maskey, R. (2025). Coopetitive resilience: Integrating cyber threat intelligence platforms in critical supply chains. *Transportation Research Part E, Logistics and Transportation Review, 197*, 104043. DOI: 10.1016/j.tre.2025.104043

Ashitha, U., Amulya, A. H. L. S., Sushma, G., Irfana, S., & Saibaba, C. M. (2024, May). Strengthening Cloud Security through Multi-Factor Authentication: A Comprehensive Integration of Diverse Approaches. *In 2024 International Conference on Electronics, Computing, Communication and Control Technology* (ICECCC) (pp. 1-8). IEEE. DOI: DOI: 10.1109/ICECCC61767.2024.10593923

Axelsson, S. (2000). Intrusion detection systems: A survey and taxonomy. *Technical Report 99-15*, Department of Computer Engineering, Chalmers University of Technology.

Azgar, A., Nazir, M. I., Akter, A., Hossain, M. S., Wadud, M. A. H., & Islam, M. R. (2024). MNIST handwritten digit recognition using a deep learning-based modified dual input convolutional neural network (DICNN) model. In X.-S. Yang, S. Sherratt, N. Dey, & A. Joshi (Eds.), *Proceedings of ninth international congress on information and communication technology (ICICT 2024)* (Lecture Notes in Networks and Systems, Vol. 1014, pp. 467-478). Springer. DOI: 10.1007/978-981-97-3562-4_44

Babulak, E. (2009). Next generation of applied internet technologies in e-manufacturing. In *UKSim 2009—11th International Conference on Computer Modelling and Simulation* (pp. 386–390). IEEE. DOI: 10.1109/UKSIM.2009.86

Babulak, E. (2009). Teleworking & next generation cyberspace. In *CSSim 2009—1st International Conference on Computational Intelligence, Modelling and Simulation* (pp. 142–146). IEEE. DOI: 10.1109/CSSim.2009.33

Babulak, E. (2010). Global cyberspace. *AMS 2010: Asia Modelling Symposium 2010 – 4th International Conference on Mathematical Modelling and Computer Simulation* (pp. xxv–xxvi). IEEE. DOI: 10.1109/AMS.2010.12

Babulak, E. (2010). The 21st century cyberspace. *SAMI 2010 – 8th International Symposium on Applied Machine Intelligence and Informatics* (pp. 21–24). IEEE. DOI: 10.1109/SAMI.2010.5423748

Babulak, E. (2025). AI-Driven Approaches for Fully Automated Smart Engineering. In *AI-Driven Approaches for Fully Automated Smart Engineering*. DOI: 10.4018/979-8-3373-4839-1

Babulak, E. Al_Dabass, D., & Tomar, G. (2025). Editorial: Cyber security prevention, defenses driven by AI, and mathematical modelling and simulation tools. *Frontiers in Computer Science, Volume 7-*. https://www.frontiersin.org/journals/computer-science/articles/10.3389/fcomp.2025.1685873

Babulak, E. (2006). Information cyberspace and future cyber homes. [iJOE]. *International Journal of Online and Biomedical Engineering*, *2*(2). Advance online publication. DOI: 10.3991/ijoe.v2i2.338

Babulak, E. (2006). Interdisciplinarity and ubiquitous internet technologies in support of automation. [iJOE]. *International Journal of Online and Biomedical Engineering*, *2*(1). Advance online publication. DOI: 10.3991/ijoe.v2i1.304

Babulak, E. (2006). Quality of service provision assessment in the healthcare information and telecommunications infrastructures. *International Journal of Medical Informatics*, *75*(3–4), 246–252. DOI: 10.1016/j.ijmedinf.2005.07.019 PMID: 16137920

Babulak, E. (Ed.). (2023). *AI Tools for Protecting and Preventing Sophisticated Cyber Attacks*. IGI Global., DOI: 10.4018/978-1-6684-7110-4

Babulak, E. (Ed.). (2024). *Applied AI and humanoid robotics for the ultra-smart cyberspace*. IGI Global., DOI: 10.4018/979-8-3693-2399-1

Babulak, E. (Ed.). (2026). *The social impact of next-generation smart cyber technology*. IGI Global Scientific Publishing., DOI: 10.4018/979-8-3373-5656-3

Babulak, E., Al_Dabass, D., & Tomar, G. (2025). Cyber Security Prevention, Defenses Driven by AI and Mathematical Modelling and Simulation Tools. *Frontiers of Computer Science*, *7*, 1685873. DOI: 10.3389/fcomp.2025.1685873

Balasubramanian, P., Liyana, S., Sankaran, H., Sivaramakrishnan, S., Pusuluri, S., Pirttikangas, S., & Peltonen, E. (2025). Generative AI for cyber threat intelligence: Applications, challenges and analysis of real-world case studies. *Artificial Intelligence Review*, *58*(11), 336. Advance online publication. DOI: 10.1007/s10462-025-11338-z

Bamashmos, S., Chilamkurti, N., & Shahraki, A. S. (2024). Two-Layered Multi-Factor Authentication Using Decentralized Blockchain in an IoT Environment. *Sensors (Basel), 24*(11), 3575. DOI: 10.3390/s24113575 PMID: 38894368

Bartwal, U., Mukhopadhyay, S., Negi, R., & Shukla, S. (2022, June). Security orchestration, automation, and response engine for deployment of behavioral honeypots. In *2022 IEEE Conference on Dependable and Secure Computing (DSC)* (pp. 1-8). IEEE. DOI: 10.1109/DSC54232.2022.9888808

Batewela, S., Ranaweera, P., Liyanage, M., Zeydan, E., & Ylianttila, M. (2025). Addressing Security Orchestration Challenges in Next-Generation Networks: A Comprehensive Overview. *IEEE Open Journal of the Computer Society, 6*, 669–687. Advance online publication. DOI: 10.1109/OJCS.2025.3564788

Bayram, I. S., & Ustun, T. S. (2017). A survey on behind the meter energy management systems in smart grid. *Renewable & Sustainable Energy Reviews, 72*, 1208–1232. DOI: 10.1016/j.rser.2016.10.034

Bello, A. (2025, September). Ethical Risk Modeling for Trustworthy ML-Based Cyber Defense. In *2025 IEEE International Conference on eScience (eScience)* (pp. 333-334). IEEE. DOI: 10.1109/eScience65000.2025.00057

Beltrán-López, P., Pérez, M. G., & Nespoli, P. (2025). Cyber Deception: Taxonomy, State of the Art, Frameworks, Trends, and Open Challenges. *IEEE Communications Surveys and Tutorials*. Advance online publication. DOI: 10.1109/COMST.2025.3594788

Berbecaru, D. G. (2025). SAM-PAY: A Location-Based Authentication Method for Mobile Environments. *Electronics (Basel), 14*(3), 621. DOI: 10.3390/electronics14030621

Bhuiyan, T. M. A.-U.-H.. (2024). Brain tumor detection by image segmentation using customized UNet deep learning-based model. In *Proceedings of the 2024 6th International Conference on Electrical Engineering and Information & Communication Technology (ICEEICT)* (pp. 580–585). IEEE. DOI: 10.1109/ICEEICT62016.2024.10534553

Biggio, B., & Roli, F. (2018). Wild patterns: Ten years after the rise of adversarial machine learning. *Pattern Recognition, 84*, 317–331. DOI: 10.1016/j.patcog.2018.07.023

Billah, M. (2025). Developing an explainable AI system for digital forensics: Enhancing trust and transparency in flagging events for legal evidence. *Journal of Forensic & Scientific Research, 9*, 109–116. DOI: 10.29328/journal.jfsr.1001089

Bishwas, A. K., & Sen, M. (2024). Strategic Roadmap for Quantum-Resistant Security: A Framework for Preparing Industries for the Quantum Threat. *arXiv preprint arXiv:2411.09995.* /arXiv.2411.09995DOI: 10.48550

Boyens, J. M. (2020). *Key practices in cyber supply chain risk management: Observations from industry* (NIST IR 8276). National Institute of Standards and Technology. DOI: 10.6028/NIST.IR.8276-draft

Boyens, J. M., Smith, A., Bartol, N., Winkler, K., Holbrook, A., & Fallon, M. (2021). *Cybersecurity supply chain risk management practices for systems and organizations* (NIST SP 800-161r1). National Institute of Standards and Technology. DOI: 10.6028/NIST.SP.800-161r1-draft2

Brintrup, A., Kosasih, E. E., Schaffer, P., Ge, Z., Demirel, G., & MacCarthy, B. L. (2023). Digital supply chain surveillance using artificial intelligence: Definitions, opportunities and risks. *International Journal of Production Research, 62*(13), 4674–4694. DOI: 10.1080/00207543.2023.2270719

Buchanan, B. G., & Shortliffe, E. H. (1984). *Rule-Based Expert Systems: The MYCIN Experiments of the Stanford Heuristic Programming Project.* Addison-Wesley., DOI: 10.1016/0004-3702(85)90067-0

Bucur, C., & Babulak, E. (2019). Security validation testing environment in the cloud. In 2019 IEEE International Conference on Big Data (Big Data) (pp. 4240–4247). IEEE. DOI: 10.1109/BigData47090.2019.9006202

Burrell, D. N., Bhargava, N., Bradley-Swanson, O. T., Harmon, M., Wright, J. B., Springs, D., & Dawson, M. (2020). Supply chain and logistics management and an open door policy concerning cyber security introduction. *International Journal of Management and Sustainability, 9*(1), 1–15. DOI: 10.18488/journal.11.2020.91.1.10

Cabinet Office Japan. (2019). *Society 5.0: A Human-Centric Super-Smart Society.* Government of Japan.

Cao, Y., Chen, Y., Fan, X., Fu, H., & Xu, B. (2026). Advanced Design for High-Performance and AI Chips. *Nano-Micro Letters, 18*(1), 13. Advance online publication. DOI: 10.1007/s40820-025-01850-w PMID: 40728678

Castelvecchi, D. (2022, July 8). These 'quantum-proof' algorithms could safeguard against future cyberattacks. *Nature.* Advance online publication. DOI: 10.1038/d41586-022-01879-6 PMID: 35804067

CFG (Centre for Future Generations). (2025). *Strengthening AI trustworthiness: Strategic innovation for European security part 3.* https://cfg.eu/strengthening-ai-trustworthiness/

Chamola, V., Hassija, V., Sulthana, A. R., Ghosh, D., Dhingra, D., & Sikdar, B. (2023). A review of trustworthy and explainable artificial intelligence (xai). *IEEE Access : Practical Innovations, Open Solutions*, *11*, 78994–79015. DOI: 10.1109/ACCESS.2023.3294569

Chandola, V., Banerjee, A., & Kumar, V. (2009). Anomaly detection: A survey. *ACM Computing Surveys*, *41*(3), 1–58. DOI: 10.1145/1541880.1541882

Charmet, F., Tanuwidjaja, H. C., Ayoubi, S., Gimenez, P.-F., Han, Y., Jmila, H., Blanc, G., Takahashi, T., & Zhang, Z. (2022). Explainable artificial intelligence for cybersecurity: A literature survey. *Annales des Télécommunications*, *77*(11–12), 777–798. DOI: 10.1007/s12243-022-00926-7

Chawla, D. (2024, October). Security Analysis of Contemporary Password Storage Techniques: Strengths, Vulnerabilities, and Best Practices. *In International Conference on Data-Processing and Networking* (pp. 271-284). Singapore: Springer Nature Singapore. DOI: DOI: 10.1007/978-981-96-3102-5_20

Chen, L., Jordan, S., Liu, Y.-K., Moody, D., Peralta, R., Perlner, R., & Smith-Tone, D. (2016). *Report on post-quantum cryptography* (NIST IR 8105). National Institute of Standards and Technology. DOI: 10.6028/NIST.IR.8105

Chen, D., Wawrzynski, P., & Lv, Z. (2021). Cyber security in smart cities: A review of deep learning-based applications and case studies. *Sustainable Cities and Society*, *66*, 102655. DOI: 10.1016/j.scs.2020.102655

Chen, L., Dui, H., & Zhang, C. (2020). A resilience measure for supply chain systems considering the interruption with the cyber-physical systems. *Reliability Engineering & System Safety*, *199*, 106869. DOI: 10.1016/j.ress.2020.106869

Chennam, K. K., Mudrakola, S., Maheswari, V. U., Aluvalu, R., & Rao, K. G. (2022). Black box models for eXplainable artificial intelligence. In *Explainable AI: foundations, methodologies and applications* (pp. 1–24). Springer International Publishing., DOI: 10.1007/978-3-031-12807-3_1

Chennuri, M. R. C. (2024). Adaptive Multi-Factor Authentication Systems: A Comprehensive Analysis of Modern Security Approaches. [IJCET]. *International Journal of Computer Engineering and Technology*, *15*(6), 65–79. DOI: 10.5281/zenodo.14235976

Chen, Q., Li, D., & Wang, L. (2024). The Role of Artificial Intelligence in Predicting and Preventing Cyber Attacks. *Journal of Industrial Engineering and Applied Science*, *2*(4), 29–35. DOI: 10.5281/zenodo.12786734

Chen, S., & Wang, Y. (2025). Quantum optimization for logistics and supply chain management. *IEEE Transactions on Intelligent Transportation Systems*, *26*(1), 1–11.

Chergui, M., Nagano, A., & Ammoumou, A. (2025). Toward an adaptive learning system by managing pedagogical knowledge in a smart way. *Multimedia Tools and Applications*, *84*(24), 27777–27793. DOI: 10.1007/s11042-024-20207-w

Cheung, K.-F., Bell, M. G. H., & Bhattacharjya, J. (2021). Cybersecurity in logistics and supply chain management: An overview and future research directions. *Transportation Research Part E, Logistics and Transportation Review*, *146*, 102217. DOI: 10.1016/j.tre.2020.102217

Choi, J., Son, S., Kwon, D., & Park, Y. (2025). A PUF-Based Secure Authentication and Key Agreement Scheme for the Internet of Drones. *Sensors (Basel)*, *25*(3), 982. DOI: 10.3390/s25030982 PMID: 39943621

Clark, J., & Ruhwanya, Z. (2024, July). Investigating the Factors Influencing Individuals' Self-Sovereign Identity Adoption Intentions. *In International Symposium on Human Aspects of Information Security and Assurance* (pp. 61-78). Cham: Springer Nature Switzerland. DOI: DOI: 10.1007/978-3-031-72559-3_5

Coppolino, L., Carotenuto, D., D'Antonio, S., & Romano, L. (2025). The impact of generative AI on cybersecurity. *Journal of Network and Computer Applications*, *212*, 103571. DOI: 10.1016/j.jnca.2025.103571

Dakshinamurthi, V., Ali, S. I., Karthikeyan, T., & Kulkarni, N. S. (2023). Causal convolution employing Almeida–Pineda recurrent backpropagation for mobile network design. *ICTACT Journal on Communication Technology*, *14*(4), 3091–3096. DOI: 10.21917/ijct.2023.0460

Davis, M., & Taylor, J. (2025). Enhancing climate models with quantum computing. *IEEE Transactions on Geoscience and Remote Sensing*, *63*(1), 1–12.

DeepStrike. (2025). *AI Cybersecurity Threats 2025: How to Survive the AI Arms Race*. https://deepstrike.io/blog/ai-cybersecurity-threats-2025

Deloitte. (2021). *Quantum risk to the Ethereum blockchain*. Deloitte Insights. https://www.deloitte.com/nl/en/services/consulting-risk/perspectives/quantum-risk-to-the-ethereum-blockchain.html

Demertzi, V., Demertzis, S., & Demertzis, K. (2023). An overview of cyber threats, attacks and countermeasures on the primary domains of smart cities. *Applied Sciences (Basel, Switzerland)*, *13*(2), 790. DOI: 10.3390/app13020790

Denning, D. E. (1987). An intrusion-detection model. *IEEE Transactions on Software Engineering, SE-13*(2), 222–232. DOI: 10.1109/TSE.1987.232894

Devidas, S., Rekha, N. R., & Subba Rao, Y. V. (2023). Identity Verifiable Ring Signature Scheme for Privacy Protection in Blockchain. *International Journal of Information Technology : an Official Journal of Bharati Vidyapeeth's Institute of Computer Applications and Management, 15*(5), 2559–2568. DOI: 10.1007/s41870-023-01282-y

El Mimouni, S., & Bouhdadi, M. (2025). Fairness and bias in AI: A sociotechnical perspective. *Journal of Information, Communication and Ethics in Society*. Advance online publication. DOI: 10.1108/JICES-12-2024-0182

Emrouznejad, A., Abbasi, S., & Sıcakyüz, Ç. (2023). Supply chain risk management: A content analysis-based review of existing and emerging topics. *Supply Chain Analytics, 3*, 100031. DOI: 10.1016/j.sca.2023.100031

Ettiyan, R., & Geetha, V. (2023). A Hybrid Logistic DNA-Based Encryption System for Securing the Internet of Things Patient Monitoring Systems. *Healthcare Analytics, 3*, 100149. DOI: 10.1016/j.health.2023.100149

European Commission. (2025). *EU launches InvestAI initiative to mobilise €200 billion of investment in artificial intelligence.* https://ec.europa.eu/commission/presscorner/detail/en/ip_25_467

Eze, C. S., & Shamir, L. (2024). Analysis and prevention of AI-based phishing email attacks. *Electronics (Basel), 13*(10), 1839. DOI: 10.3390/electronics13101839

Fakhouri, H. N., Alhadidi, B., Omar, K., Makhadmeh, S. N., Hamad, F., & Halalsheh, N. Z. (2024, February). Ai-driven solutions for social engineering attacks: Detection, prevention, and response. In *2024 2nd international conference on cyber resilience (ICCR)* (pp. 1-8). IEEE. DOI: 10.1109/ICCR61006.2024.10533010

Fan, Y.-Y. (2025). Asynchronous quantum-resistant blockchain for secure and privacy-preserving data sharing. *Applied Sciences (Basel, Switzerland), 15*(11), 5921. DOI: 10.3390/app15115921

Fard, N. E., Selmic, R. R., & Khorasani, K. (2023). A review of techniques and policies on cybersecurity using artificial intelligence and reinforcement learning algorithms. *IEEE Technology and Society Magazine, 42*(3), 57–68. DOI: 10.1109/MTS.2023.3306540

Farooqi, S. A., Abd Rahman, A., & Saad, A. (2025, January). A theoretical comparison of federated learning with differential privacy and blockchain for security and privacy in iomt. In *2025 19th International Conference on Ubiquitous Information Management and Communication (IMCOM)* (pp. 1-8). IEEE. DOI: 10.1109/IMCOM64595.2025.10857505

Fei, Q., Rodríguez-Barroso, N., Luzón, M. V., Zhang, Z., & Herrera, F. (2026). Addressing data quality decompensation in federated learning via dynamic client selection. *Future Generation Computer Systems*, *176*, 108138. Advance online publication. DOI: 10.1016/j.future.2025.108138

Ferrag, M. A., Alwahedi, F., Battah, A., Cherif, B., Mechri, A., Tihányi, N., Bisztray, T., & Debbah, M. (2025). Generative AI in Cybersecurity: A Comprehensive Review of LLM Applications and Vulnerabilities. Internet of Things and Cyber–Physical Systems. arXiv+1DOI: 10.1016/j.iotcps.2025.01.001

Gani, A. B. D., Fernando, Y., Lan, S., Lim, M. K., & Tseng, M. (2022). Interplay between cyber supply chain risk management practices and cyber security performance. *Industrial Management & Data Systems*, *123*(3), 843–872. DOI: 10.1108/IMDS-05-2022-0313

George, A. S. (2024). Emerging Trends in AI-Driven Cybersecurity: An In-Depth Analysis. *Partners Universal Innovative Research Publication*, *2*(4), 15–28. DOI: 10.5281/zenodo.13333202

Ghadi, Y. Y., Alotibi, F., Alzahrani, H., Alotaibi, S., & Algarni, A. (2025). A hybrid AI–Blockchain security framework for smart grids. *Scientific Reports*, *15*(1), 5257. DOI: 10.1038/s41598-025-05257-w PMID: 40594089

Gharavi, H., Granjal, J., & Monteiro, E. (2024). Post-quantum blockchain security for the Internet of Things: Survey and research directions. *IEEE Communications Surveys and Tutorials*, *26*(3), 1748–1774. DOI: 10.1109/COMST.2024.3355222

Ghorashi, S. R., Zia, T., Bewong, M., & Jiang, Y. (2023). An analytical review of industrial privacy frameworks and regulations for organisational data sharing. *Applied Sciences (Basel, Switzerland)*, *13*(23), 12727. DOI: 10.3390/app132312727

Gilbert, C. (2024). *The impact of AI on cybersecurity defence mechanisms*. SSRN Electronic Journal. DOI: 10.2139/ssrn.5258783

Goodfellow, I., Pouget-Abadie, J., Mirza, M., Xu, B., Warde-Farley, D., Ozair, S., & Bengio, Y. (2014). Generative adversarial nets. *Advances in Neural Information Processing Systems*, *27*, 2672–2680. DOI: 10.48550/arXiv.1406.2661

Goodman, B., & Flaxman, S. (2017). European Union regulations on algorithmic decision-making and a "right to explanation". *AI Magazine*, *38*(3), 50–57. DOI: 10.1609/aimag.v38i3.2741

Gopireddy, R. R. (2022). Human-centric cybersecurity: Addressing the human element in cyber defense and ethical considerations in cybersecurity. *Journal of Artificial Intelligence & Cloud Computing*, *1*(4), 1–6. DOI: 10.47363/JAICC/2022(1)E118

Gorecki, A. (2020). Crafting an incident response plan. In *Cybersecurity Incident Response* (p. 143). Wiley., DOI: 10.1002/9781119679349.ch4

Greuter, K. O., & Sarmah, D. K. (2022). The baseline of global consumer cyber security standards for IoT: Quality evaluation. *Journal of Cyber Security Technology*, *6*(4), 175–194. DOI: 10.1080/23742917.2022.2105192

Grover, V., Jeong, S. R., & Segars, A. H. (1996). Information systems effectiveness: The construct space and patters of application. *Information & Management*, *31*(4), 177–191. DOI: 10.1016/S0378-7206(96)01079-8

Gunavathie, M. A., Sneha, P. D., Yuvarani, K., & Swathyshree, P. (2023, July). An Exploration of Real-Time Intrusion Detection and Prevention Systems for Next Generation Networks. In *2023 World Conference on Communication & Computing (WCONF)* (pp. 1-5). IEEE. DOI: 10.1109/WCONF58270.2023.10235147

Guo, J., Ding, X., & Wu, W. (2020). Combined cooling, heating, and power system in blockchain-enabled energy management. *arXiv preprint* arXiv:2003.13416. https://arxiv.org/abs/2003.13416

Hagen, R. A., Øverlier, L., & Helkala, K. (2025). Human factors in AI-driven cybersecurity: Cognitive biases and trust issues. *. *Digital Threats : Research and Practice*, *6*(4), 1–20. Advance online publication. DOI: 10.1145/3759260

Hakim, S. B., Adil, M., Velásquez, A., Xu, S., & Song, H. H. (2025). Neuro-Symbolic AI for Cybersecurity: State of the Art, Challenges and Opportunities. arXiv Preprint. arXiv:2509.06921. arXiv+1

Hamer, S., Bowen, J., Haque, M. N., Hines, R., Madden, C., & Williams, L. (2025). Closing the chain: How to reduce your risk of being SolarWinds, Log4j, or XZ Utils [Preprint]. arXiv. DOI: 10.48550/ARXIV.2503.12192

Hammi, B., Zeadally, S., & Nebhen, J. (2023). Security threats, countermeasures, and challenges of digital supply chains. *ACM Computing Surveys*, *55*(14s, 13s), 1–35. DOI: 10.1145/3588999

Han, S., & Park, S. (2022). A gap between blockchain and General Data Protection Regulation: A systematic review. *IEEE Access : Practical Innovations, Open Solutions, 10*, 103888–103908. DOI: 10.1109/ACCESS.2022.3210110

Hassan, A., Rauf, A., Shafqat, N., Latif, R., & Khan, H. (2025). ZenGuard a machine learning based zero trust framework for context aware threat mitigation using SIEM SOAR and UEBA. *Scientific Reports, 15*(1), 35871. Advance online publication. DOI: 10.1038/s41598-025-20998-4 PMID: 41087655

He, H., Vasilescu, B., & Kästner, C. (2025). Pinning is futile: You need more than local dependency versioning to defend against supply chain attacks. *Proceedings of the ACM on Software Engineering, 2*, 266. DOI: 10.1145/3715728

Helal, M. M., Abu-Elkheir, M., & Mashaly, M. (2025, May). A Generative AI Framework for Cloud Security: Automated Attack Simulation and Threat Detection. In *2025 International Conference on Innovation in Artificial Intelligence and Internet of Things (AIIT)* (pp. 1-8). IEEE. DOI: 10.1109/AIIT63112.2025.11082823

Herburger, M. (2022). *Supply chain resilience - A concept for coping with cyber risks*. Research Portal Denmark. https://local.forskningsportal.dk/local/dki-cgi/ws/cris-link?src=cbs&id=cbs-c28fb850-cb66-427a-...

Herburger, M., Wieland, A., & Hochstrasser, C. (2024). Building supply chain resilience to cyber risks: A dynamic capabilities perspective. *Supply Chain Management, 29*(7), 28–49. DOI: 10.1108/SCM-01-2023-0016

Hua, W., Zhang, M., Zhang, Y., & Li, C. (2022). Applications of blockchain and artificial intelligence in smart grids for facilitating prosumers to participate in energy markets. *Renewable & Sustainable Energy Reviews, 158*, 112042. DOI: 10.1016/j.rser.2022.112042

Hundeyin, W. O., Adegbenro, S. A., Rindap, Y. P., & Adaba, C. A. (2025). Integrating Privacy-Preserving AI Models into AI Governance Frameworks. DOI: 10.38124/ijisrt/25oct209

IBM Security. (2024). *Cost of a data breach report 2024*.

Ibrar, W., Mahmood, D., Al-Shamayleh, A. S., Ahmed, G., Alharthi, S. Z., & Akhunzada, A. (2025). Generative AI: A double-edged sword in the cyber threat landscape. *Artificial Intelligence Review, 58*(9), 285. DOI: 10.1007/s10462-025-11285-9

Ichetovkin, E., & Kotenko, I. (2025, March). A Technique for Protecting Machine Learning Components of Intrusion Detection Systems from Evasion Attacks. In *2025 International Russian Smart Industry Conference (SmartIndustryCon)* (pp. 735-740). IEEE. DOI: 10.1109/SmartIndustryCon65166.2025.10986131

Igwe, A. N., Ewim, C. P.-M., Ofodile, O. C., & Sam-Bulya, N. J.Abbey Ngochindo IgweChikezie Paul-Mikki EwimOnyeka Chrisanctus OfodileNgodoo Joy Sam-Bulya. (2024). Leveraging blockchain for sustainable supply chain management: A data privacy and security perspective. *International Journal of Frontline Research and Reviews, 3*(1), 61–72. DOI: 10.56355/ijfrr.2024.3.1.0030

Ilieva, R., & Stoilova, G. (2024, September). Challenges of AI-Driven Cybersecurity. In *2024 XXXIII International Scientific Conference Electronics (ET)* (pp. 1-4). IEEE. DOI: 10.1109/ET63133.2024.10721572

Intallura, P. (2024). *Preparing for a quantum future: What's next for quantum computing in financial services.* FinTech Futures.

Inter-American Development Bank. (2022, February 23). *Israel commits to IDB cybersecurity initiative in Latin America and the Caribbean.* https://www.iadb.org/en/news/israel-commits-idb-cybersecurity-initiative-latin-america-and-caribbean

Inter-American Development Bank. (2025, June 25). *Strengthening Sectoral Cybersecurity in Latin America and the Caribbean.* https://www.iadb.org/en/project/RG-T4577

Ishtaiwi, A., Aldweesh, A., & Al-Qerem, A. (2025). Adaptive Risk Mitigation Strategies for Generative AI-Driven Threats. In Examining Cybersecurity Risks Produced by Generative AI (pp. 487-520). IGI Global Scientific Publishing.

Islam, M. J., Pathan, M. N., Rahman, A., Islam, S., Sultana, A., & Das, S. C. (2024, December). Priority-based Traceability in Crude Oil Refined Products Supply Chain through Blockchain. *In 2024 6th International Conference on Sustainable Technologies for Industry 5.0 (STI)* (pp. 1-6). IEEE. DOI: DOI: 10.1109/STI64222.2024.10951058

Islam, M. R., Kabir, M. M., Mridha, M. F., Alfarhood, S., Safran, M., & Che, D. (2023). Deep learning-based IoT system for remote monitoring and early detection of health issues in real-time. *Sensors (Basel), 23*(11), 5204. DOI: 10.3390/s23115204 PMID: 37299933

Islam, M. R., Oliullah, K., Kabir, M. M., Alom, M., & Mridha, M. F. (2023). Machine learning enabled IoT system for soil nutrients monitoring and crop recommendation. *Journal of Agriculture and Food Research, 14*, 100880. DOI: 10.1016/j.jafr.2023.100880

Jebbar, W. A., & Al-Zubaidie, M. (2024). Transaction-Based Blockchain Systems Security Improvement Employing Micro-Segmentation Controlled By Smart Contracts and Detection of Saddle Goatfish. *SN Computer Science*, *5*(7), 898. DOI: 10.1007/s42979-024-03239-9

Kahya, I., Huschbeck, T., & Markovič, P. (2025). Predictive risk management in the supply chain. In *Studies in systems, decision and control* (p. 41). Springer., DOI: 10.1007/978-3-031-80935-4_3

Kalutharage, C. S., Liu, X., & Chrysoulas, C. (2025). *Neurosymbolic learning and domain knowledge-driven explainable AI for enhanced IoT network attack detection and response. Computers & Security*, 151, 104318. SpringerLink+1DOI: 10.1016/j.cose.2025.104318

Kampourakis, V., Kavallieratos, G., Gkioulos, V., & Katsikas, S. (2025). Cracks in the chain: A technical analysis of real-life supply chain security incidents. *Computers & Security, 148*, 104673. DOI: 10.1016/j.cose.2025.104673

Kamuangu, P. (2025). Exploring the Convergence of Cybersecurity, Fintech and Artificial General Intelligence: Innovations and Implications. *Abhigyan, 09702385251379163*(4), 362–384. Advance online publication. DOI: 10.1177/09702385251379163

Karamchand, G. (2025). Detecting the Abuse of Generative AI in Cybersecurity Contexts: Challenges, Frameworks, and Solutions. *Journal of Data Analysis and Critical Management, 1*(03), 1–12.

Kaur, H. SL, D. S., Paul, T., Thakur, R. K., Reddy, K. V. K., Mahato, J., & Naveen, K. (2024). Evolution of endpoint detection and response (EDR) in cyber security: A comprehensive review. In *E3S Web of Conferences* (Vol. 556, p. 01006). EDP Sciences. DOI: 10.1051/e3sconf/202455601006

Kaur, H., Gupta, M., & Singh, S. P. (2024). Integrated model to optimize supplier selection and investments for cyber resilience in digital supply chains. *International Journal of Production Economics, 275*, 109338. DOI: 10.1016/j.ijpe.2024.109338

Kayhan, H. (2022). Ensuring trust in pharmaceutical supply chains by data protection by design approach to blockchains. *Blockchain in Healthcare Today, 5*. Advance online publication. DOI: 10.30953/bhty.v5.232 PMID: 36779024

Kayode, B., Adebola, N. T., Akerele, S., Fagbohun, O., Agbo, C., Bantale, O., & Nwokocha, L. C. (2025). The State of AI-Driven Cybersecurity: Trends, Challenges, and Opportunities. *J Artif Intell Mach Learn & Data Sci, 3*(2), 2731–2739. DOI: 10.51219/JAIMLD/Bisola-Kayode/577

Khadka, K., & Ullah, A. B. (2025). Human factors in cybersecurity: An interdisciplinary review and framework proposal. *International Journal of Information Security*, *24*(3), 119. Advance online publication. DOI: 10.1007/s10207-025-01032-0

Khan, M. A., Alasiry, A., Marzougui, M., Bayhan, I., Kuna, S. S., Rao, G. S. N., Algamdi, S. A., & Aldossary, H. (2025). Securing Intelligent Transportation Systems: A Dual-Framework Approach for Privacy Protection and Cybersecurity Using Generative AI. *IEEE Transactions on Intelligent Transportation Systems*, 1–12. DOI: 10.1109/TITS.2025.3591007

Khatri, P., Duggal, H. K., Thomas, A., Corvello, V., Prałat, E., & Shiva, A. (2026). Development and validation of the generative artificial intelligence appropriation (GAIA) Scale: A comprehensive measurement tool for assessing user engagement and utilisation. *Technovation*, *150*, 103379. Advance online publication. DOI: 10.1016/j.technovation.2025.103379

Khondokar, O., Islam, M. R., Babar, J. I., Quraishi, M. A. N., Rahman, M. M., Mahbub-Or-Rashid, M., & Bhuiyan, T. M. A.-U.-H. (2025). FruVeg_MultiNet: A hybrid deep learning-enabled IoT system for fresh fruit and vegetable identification with web interface and customized blind glasses for visually impaired individuals. *Journal of Agriculture and Food Research*, *19*, 101623. DOI: 10.1016/j.jafr.2024.101623

Kinyua, J., & Awuah, L. (2021). AI/ML in Security Orchestration, Automation and Response: Future Research Directions. *Intelligent Automation & Soft Computing*, *28*(2), 527–545. Advance online publication. DOI: 10.32604/iasc.2021.016240

Kluge Corrêa, N., Galvão, C., Santos, J. W., Del Pino, C., Pontes Pinto, E., Barbosa, C., Mambrini, D., Galvão, L., & de Oliveira, N. (2022). Worldwide AI ethics: A review of 200 guidelines and recommendations for AI governance [Preprint]. *arXiv*. https://arxiv.org/abs/2206.11922

Kolhatin, A. O. (2025). From automation to augmentation: A human-centered framework for generative AI in adaptive educational content creation. *CEUR Workshop Proceedings*, *4060*, 143–195. https://www.scopus.com/inward/record.uri?eid=2-s2.0-105019297347&partnerID=40&md5=9984d27b9df38e2e4b15021498d4e68c

Kommers, P., & Babulak, E. (2025). Conceptual awareness for human navigation in A.I. In *Educational AI Humanoid Computing Devices for Cyber Nomads* (pp. 1–13). DOI: 10.4018/979-8-3693-8985-0.ch001

Kong, I., Janssen, M., & Bharosa, N. (2024). Realizing quantum-safe information sharing: Implementation and adoption challenges and policy recommendations for quantum-safe transitions. *Government Information Quarterly*, *41*(1), 101884. DOI: 10.1016/j.giq.2023.101884

Kotsias, J., Ahmad, A., & Scheepers, R. (2022). Adopting and integrating cyber-threat intelligence in a commercial organisation. *European Journal of Information Systems*, *32*(1), 35–52. DOI: 10.1080/0960085X.2022.2088414

Kumar, S. N., Joy, J., Jane, I. C., James, A., John, S., & Babulak, E. (2025). Applications of 6G in the healthcare sector and the importance of network security and data privacyencryption of medical images using the SHA 256 blockchain algorithm. In *Network Security and Data Privacy in 6G Communication: Trends, Challenges, and Applications* (pp. 176–190). DOI: 10.1201/9781003583127-9

Kumar, V., Gupta, S., & Gill, F. S. (2024). An overview on quantum computing for technology. In CRC Press eBooks (pp. 696–701). DOI: 10.1201/9781003559092-120

Kumar, M. (2022). Post-quantum cryptography algorithms' standardization and performance analysis. *Array (New York, N.Y.)*, *15*, 100242. DOI: 10.1016/j.array.2022.100242

Kumar, R., Jain, V., Ather, D., Kukreja, V., & Singhal, M. (2025). Network security and data privacy in 6G communication: Trends, challenges, and applications. In *Network Security and Data Privacy in 6G Communication*. Trends, Challenges, and Applications., DOI: 10.1201/9781003583127

Kumar, S. N., Zafar, S., Alam, M. A., Siddiqui, F., & Babulak, E. (2023). *Artificial intelligence in telemedicine: Processing of biosignals and medical images*. CRC Press., DOI: 10.1201/9781003307778

Kumar, S., & Mallipeddi, R. R. (2022). Impact of cybersecurity on operations and supply chain management: Emerging trends and future research directions. *Production and Operations Management*, *31*(12), 4488–4500. DOI: 10.1111/poms.13859

Labadie, C., & Legner, C. (2022). Building data management capabilities to address data protection regulations: Learnings from EU-GDPR. *Journal of Information Technology*, *38*(1), 16–38. DOI: 10.1177/02683962221141456

Lee, W., & Stolfo, S. J. (1998). Data mining approaches for intrusion detection. *Proceedings of the 7th USENIX Security Symposium*, 79–94.

Lee, Y., & Kim, S. (2025). Advancements in quantum machine learning for AI efficiency. *IEEE Transactions on Neural Networks and Learning Systems*, *30*(2), 1–10.

Li, J., Maiti, A., & Fei, J. (2023). Features and scope of regulatory technologies: Challenges and opportunities with industrial Internet of Things. *Future Internet*, *15*(8), 256. DOI: 10.3390/fi15080256

Liu, J., Sihes, A. J. B., & Lu, Y. (2025). How do generative artificial intelligence (AI) tools and large language models (LLMs) influence language learners' critical thinking in EFL education? A systematic review. *Smart Learning Environments*, *12*(1), 48. Advance online publication. DOI: 10.1186/s40561-025-00406-0

Li, Y., & Xu, L. (2020). Cybersecurity investments in a two-echelon supply chain with third-party risk propagation. *International Journal of Production Research*, *59*(4), 1216–1238. DOI: 10.1080/00207543.2020.1721591

Loevenich, J. F., Adler, E., Hürten, T., Spelter, F., Roncevic, D., & Lopes, R. R. F. (2025, May). Automating Cyber Threat Intelligence and Attack Chain Generation using Cyber Security Knowledge Graphs and Large Language Models. In *2025 International Conference on Military Communication and Information Systems (ICMCIS)* (pp. 1-10). IEEE. DOI: 10.1109/ICMCIS64378.2025.11047951

Lundberg, S. M., & Lee, S. I. (2017). A unified approach to interpreting model predictions. *Advances in Neural Information Processing Systems*, *30*, 4765–4774.

Lunt, T. F., Tamaru, A., Gilham, F., Jagannathan, R., Jalali, C., Neumann, P. G., . . . Tong, L. (1988). *A real-time intrusion-detection expert system (IDES)*. Technical Report SRI-CSL-88-05, SRI International.

Madiiarbekova, A. (2025). Cybersecurity in IoT devices: Vulnerabilities, risks, and mitigation strategies [Preprint]. *SSRN*. DOI: 10.2139/ssrn.5075016

Majgave, A. B., & Gavankar, N. L. (2024). Automatic phishing website detection and prevention model using transformer deep belief network. *Computers & Security*, *147*, 104071. DOI: 10.1016/j.cose.2024.104071

Malik, G., Brahmbhatt, R., & Prashasti, P. (2025). AI-driven security and inventory optimization: Automating vulnerability management and demand forecasting in CI/CD-powered retail systems. *International Journal of Computational and Experimental Science and Engineering*, *11*(3). Advance online publication. DOI: 10.22399/ijcesen.3855

Malik, V., Khanna, A., & Nalluri, S. (2024). *Blockchain technology in cybersecurity: Uses beyond cryptocurrencies*. PubPub., DOI: 10.21428/e90189c8.d37d59a9

Manda, J. K. (2024). AI-powered Threat Intelligence Platforms in Telecom: Leveraging AI for Real-time Threat Detection and Intelligence Gathering in Telecom Network Security Operations. Available at *SSRN* 5003638. http://dx.doi.org/DOI: 10.2139/ssrn.5003638

Masip-Bruin, X., Marín-Tordera, E., Ruiz, J. F., Jukan, A., Trakadas, P., Černivec, A., Lioy, A., López, D., Santos, H., Gonos, A., Silva, A., Soriano, J. A. A., & Kalogiannis, G. (2021). Cybersecurity in ICT supply chains: Key challenges and a relevant architecture. *Sensors (Basel), 21*(18), 6057. DOI: 10.3390/s21186057 PMID: 34577264

Massam, P., & Babulak, E. (2003). A decent service level. *Communications Engineer, 1*(3), 34–37. DOI: 10.1049/ce:20030313

Mathis, J., & Payne, B. (2023). *Quantum computing: Computing of the future made reality*. Proceedings on Cybersecurity Education, Research and Practice., DOI: 10.32727/28.2024.2

Matsubayashi, M., Shibahara, T., Koyama, T., & Tanaka, M. (2026). Reusability Evaluation of Reports in Security Operation Centers for IoT with Sentence ALBERT and Jaccard Similarity. *Lecture Notes of the Institute for Computer Sciences, Social-Informatics and Telecommunications Engineering, LNICST, 629 LNICST*, 51–72. DOI: 10.1007/978-3-031-94455-0_3

Mavikumbure, H. S., Cobilean, V., Wickramasinghe, C. S., Drake, D., & Manic, M. (2024, July). Generative AI in cyber security of cyber physical systems: Benefits and threats. In *2024 16th International Conference on Human System Interaction (HSI)* (pp. 1-8). IEEE. DOI: 10.1109/HSI61632.2024.10613562

Mazher, N., & Huma, Z. (2025). The Role of Generative AI in Offensive and Defensive Cyber Operations. *Baltic Journal of Multidisciplinary Research, 2*(4), 70–75.

Mbah, G. O., & Evelyn, A. N.Geraldine O MbahAchudume Nkechi Evelyn. (2024). AI-powered cybersecurity: Strategic approaches to mitigate risk and safeguard data privacy. *World Journal of Advanced Research and Reviews, 24*(3), 310–324. DOI: 10.30574/wjarr.2024.24.3.3695

Meduri, K., Gonaygunt, H., & Nadella, G. S. (2024). Evaluating the effectiveness of AI-Driven frameworks in predicting and preventing cyber-attacks. *International Journal of Research Publication and Reviews, 5*(3), 6591–6595. DOI: 10.55248/gengpi.5.0324.0875

Memon, Q. A., Ahmad, M. A., & Pecht, M. (2024). Quantum computing: Navigating the future of computation, challenges, and technological breakthroughs. *Quantum Reports, 6*(4), 627–663. DOI: 10.3390/quantum6040039

Mengelkamp, E., Gärttner, J., Rock, K., Kessler, S., Orsini, L., & Weinhardt, C. (2018). Designing microgrid energy markets: A case study: The Brooklyn Microgrid. *Applied Energy, 210*, 870–880. DOI: 10.1016/j.apenergy.2017.06.054

Ministry of Communications and Information Singapore. (2020). *Singapore Model AI Governance Framework* (2nd ed.).

Mmaduekwe, U. (2024). Bias and fairness issues in artificial intelligence-driven cybersecurity. *Current Journal of Applied Science and Technology*, *43*(6), 109-119. DOI: 10.9734/cjast/2024/v43i64391

Mohale, V. Z., & Obagbuwa, I. C. (2025). A systematic review on the integration of explainable artificial intelligence in intrusion detection systems to enhancing transparency and interpretability in cybersecurity. *Frontiers in Artificial Intelligence*, *8*, 1526221. DOI: 10.3389/frai.2025.1526221 PMID: 40040929

Mohamed, N. (2025). Artificial intelligence and machine learning in cybersecurity: Current advancements, challenges and future directions. *Knowledge and Information Systems*. Advance online publication. DOI: 10.1007/s10115-025-02429-y

Mohanty, R. K., Kumar, A. P., Padmaja, R., & Prashanthi, V. (2024). Deep Learning for Analyzing User and Entity Behaviors: Techniques and Applications. In *Consumer and Organizational Behavior in the Age of AI* (pp. 219-250). IGI Global. DOI: 10.4018/979-8-3693-6864-0.ch006

Mollah, M. B., Zhao, J., Niyato, D., Lam, K. Y., Zhang, X., Ghias, A. M., & Li, Y. (2021). Blockchain for the future smart grid: A comprehensive survey. *IEEE Internet of Things Journal*, *8*(1), 18–43. DOI: 10.1109/JIOT.2020.2993601

Moody's. (2025). Quantum computing's six most important trends for 2025.

Mounesan, M., Siadati, H., & Jafarikhah, S. (2023). Exploring the threat of software supply chain attacks on containerized applications. *2023 16th International Conference on Security of Information and Networks (SIN)*. IEEE. DOI: 10.1109/SIN60469.2023.10474901

Mozaffari, H., Choudhary, S., & Houmansadr, A. (2024). Fake or compromised? Making sense of malicious clients in federated learning. In *Lecture Notes in Computer Science* (p. 187). Springer. DOI: 10.1007/978-3-031-70879-4_10

Mulgund, P., Singh, R., Sharman, R., Gupta, M., & Pothukuchi, A. S. (2025). DEFENSE-IN-DEPTH MODEL OF COUNTERMEASURES AGAINST ADVERSARIAL AI ATTACKS: LITERATURE REVIEW AND CLASSIFICATION. *Journal of Information Systems Security*, *21*(1), 51–84. https://www.scopus.com/inward/record.uri?eid=2-s2.0-105008373545&partnerID=40&md5=79b1a6eb66ce8a5799d59838f4de4382

Mvula, P. K., Branco, P., Jourdan, G. V., & Viktor, H. L. (2024). A Survey on the Applications of Semi-supervised Learning to Cyber-security. *ACM Computing Surveys, 56*(10), 1–41. DOI: 10.1145/3657647

National Institute of Standards and Technology. (2024, August 13). *NIST announces first four quantum-resistant cryptographic algorithms*. https://www.nist.gov/news-events/news/2022/07/nist-announces-first-four-quantum-resistant-cryptographic-algorithms

Nguyen, V.-L., Lin, P., Cheng, B., Hwang, R., & Lin, Y. (2021). Security and privacy for 6G: A survey on prospective technologies and challenges. *IEEE Communications Surveys and Tutorials, 23*(4), 2384–2407. DOI: 10.1109/COMST.2021.3108618

Nia, M. A., Atani, R. E., Fabian, B., & Babulak, E. (2016). On detecting unidentified network traffic using pattern-based random walk. *Security and Communication Networks, 9*(16), 3509–3526. DOI: 10.1002/sec.1557

Nikbakht, R., Javed, F., Rezazadeh, F., Bartzoudis, N., & Mangues-Bafalluy, J. (2023). Decentralized energy marketplace via NFTs and AI-based agents. *arXiv preprint* arXiv:2311.10406. https://arxiv.org/abs/2311.10406

NIST. (2023). *Artificial Intelligence Risk Management Framework (AI RMF 1.0)*. https://doi.org/DOI: 10.6028/NIST.AI.100-1

Nott, C. (2025). Organizational Adaptation to Generative AI in Cybersecurity: A Systematic Review. arXiv. arXiv:2506.12060.

Nozari, H., Fallah, M., Szmelter-Jarosz, A., & Krzemiński, M. (2021). Analysis of security criteria for IoT-based supply chain: A case study of FMCG industries. *Central European Management Journal, 29*(4). Advance online publication. DOI: 10.7206/cemj.2658-0845.63

Nyangaresi, V. O., & Yenurkar, G. K. (2024). Anonymity Preserving Lightweight Authentication Protocol for Resource-Limited Wireless Sensor Networks. *High-Confidence Computing, 4*(2), 100178. DOI: 10.1016/j.hcc.2023.100178

Ofusori, L., Bokaba, T., & Mhlongo, S. (2025). Explainability and interpretability of artificial intelligence use in cybersecurity. *Discover Computing, 28*(1), 241. Advance online publication. DOI: 10.1007/s10791-025-09760-6

Ohm, M., Plate, H., Sykosch, A., & Meier, M. (2020). Backstabber's knife collection: A review of open source software supply chain attacks. In *Detection of Intrusions and Malware, and Vulnerability Assessment* (pp. 23–43). Lecture Notes in Computer Science. Springer., DOI: 10.1007/978-3-030-52683-2_2

Okafor, C., Schorlemmer, T. R., Torres-Arias, S., & Davis, J. C. (2022). SoK: Analysis of software supply chain security by establishing secure design properties. *Proceedings of the 2022 ACM SIGSAC Conference on Computer and Communications Security*. DOI: 10.1145/3560835.3564556

Okuno, M. J., & Okuno, H. G. (2025). Legal frameworks for AI service business participants: A comparative analysis of liability protection across jurisdictions. *AI & Society*, *40*(7), 5667–5683. DOI: 10.1007/s00146-025-02288-9

Olan, F., Spanaki, K., Ahmed, W., & Zhao, G. (2024). Enabling explainable artificial intelligence capabilities in supply chain decision support making. *Production Planning and Control*, •••, 1–18. DOI: 10.1080/09537287.2024.2313514

Otieno, D. O. (2020). Cyber security challenges: The case of developing countries. *Promoting Creativity, Innovation and Productivity for Sustainable Development Conference*. https://www.researchgate.net/publication/346485466_Cyber_security_challenges_The_Case_of_Developing_Countries

Pandey, S., Singh, R. K., Gunasekaran, A., & Kaushik, A. (2020). Cyber security risks in globalized supply chains: Conceptual framework. *Journal of Global Operations and Strategic Sourcing*, *13*(1), 103–128. DOI: 10.1108/JGOSS-05-2019-0042

Parag, Y., & Sovacool, B. K. (2016). Electricity market design for the prosumer era. *Nature Energy*, *1*(4), 16032. DOI: 10.1038/nenergy.2016.32

Patel, K. N., ... (2024). Cybersecurity risks and countermeasures in the threat landscape of IoT devices. In 2024 4th International Conference on Technological Advancements in Computational Sciences (ICTACS) (pp. 875–883). IEEE. DOI: 10.1109/ICTACS62700.2024.10841210

Patel, A., & Singh, R. (2025). Quantum simulations for accelerated drug discovery. *IEEE Transactions on Bio-Medical Engineering*, *72*(3), 1–9.

Patel, D. A.Devashish Ghanshyambhai Patel. (2025). Enhancing CI/CD security with provenance metadata and supply chain best practices. *World Journal of Advanced Engineering Technology and Sciences*, *16*(1), 19–27. DOI: 10.30574/wjaets.2025.16.1.1181

Patel, P., & Patel, R. (2025). Reinforcement Learning for Cyber Defense: AI Architectures for Securing US Critical Infrastructure. http://dx.doi.org/DOI: 10.2139/ssrn.5360107

Pattanaik, B., Kumari, S. S., Kumar, C. K., Pattnaik, M., Ali, S. I., & Kumarasamy, M. (2023). An innovation of algebraic mathematical-based statistical analysis model for complex number theory. In *Proceedings of the 2023 International Conference on Disruptive Technologies (ICDT)* (pp. 94–99). IEEE. https://doi.org/DOI: 10.1109/ICDT57929.2023.10151169

Peralta, R., Perlner, R. A., Robinson, A., Silberg, H., Smith-Tone, D., & Waller, N. (2025). *Status report on the fourth round of the NIST post-quantum cryptography standardization process* (NIST IR 8545). National Institute of Standards and Technology. DOI: 10.6028/NIST.IR.8545

Peréz-Morón, J. (2021). Eleven years of cyberattacks on Chinese supply chains in an era of cyber warfare, a review and future research agenda. *Journal of Asia Business Studies, 16*(2), 371–393. DOI: 10.1108/JABS-11-2020-0444

Perumal, R., & Aithal, P. S. (2024, December). Significance of Use of Generative AI in Cyber Security. In *Conference Proceedings of Emerging Trends in Information Technology* (Vol. 2, No. 1, pp. 181-191).

Pettersen, S., & Grøtan, T. O. (2023). Exploring the grounds for cyber resilience in the hyper-connected oil and gas industry. *Safety Science, 171*, 106384. DOI: 10.1016/j.ssci.2023.106384

Polampally, S. K., Nadella, G. S., Ragunayakula, S., Kumar, V. J., Kankala, S., & Babulak, E. (2025). AI-Driven Automation in Agile Software Development Teams Enhancing Efficiency and Collaboration. In *AI-Driven Approaches for Fully Automated Smart Engineering* (pp. 85–132). DOI: 10.4018/979-8-3373-4839-1.ch003

Pontorno, O., Guarnera, L., & Battiato, S. (2024). On the exploitation of DCT-traces in the generative-AI domain. arXiv preprint arXiv:2402.02209. https://arxiv.org/abs/2402.02209 DOI: 10.1109/ICIP51287.2024.10648013

Qi, Z., Li, H., Qin, H., Peng, K., He, S., & Qin, X. (2026). Harnessing large language models for virtual reality exploration testing: A case study. *Automated Software Engineering, 33*(1), 7. Advance online publication. DOI: 10.1007/s10515-025-00535-3

Qureca. (2025, April 11). Quantum computing applications in economics and finance conference.

Raaymann, S., & Spinler, S. (2024). Measuring supply chain resilience along the automotive value chain — A comparative research on literature and industry. *Transportation Research Part E, Logistics and Transportation Review, 192*, 103792. DOI: 10.1016/j.tre.2024.103792

Radanliev, P. (2025). *Generative AI cybersecurity and resilience. Frontiers in Artificial Intelligence*, Article 1568360. Frontiers Arifin, M. M., Ahmed, M. S., Ghosh, T. K., Akhand Udoy, I., Zhuang, J., & Yeh, J.-H. (2024, July 11). *A Survey on the Application of Generative Adversarial Networks in Cybersecurity: Prospective, Direction and Open Research Scopes*. arXiv. arXiv:2407.08839. arXivDOI: 10.3389/frai.2025.1568360

Radhakrishnan, I., Jadon, S., & Honnavalli, P. B. (2024). Efficiency and Security Evaluation of Lightweight Cryptographic Algorithms for Resource-Constrained IoT Devices. *Sensors (Basel)*, *24*(12), 4008. DOI: 10.3390/s24124008 PMID: 38931791

Rahman, S., Hossain, N. U. I., Govindan, K., Nur, F., & Bappy, M. M. (2021). Assessing cyber resilience of additive manufacturing supply chain leveraging data fusion technique: A model to generate cyber resilience index of a supply chain. *CIRP Journal of Manufacturing Science and Technology*, *35*, 911–928. DOI: 10.1016/j.cirpj.2021.09.008

Rajendran, R. K., & Tulasi, B. (2025). Natural Language Processing (NLP) for Threat Intelligence. In *Analyzing Privacy and Security Difficulties in Social Media: New Challenges and Solutions* (pp. 247-262). IGI Global Scientific Publishing. http://doi.org/DOI: 10.4018/979-8-3693-9491-5.ch011

Ramírez-Peña, M., Mayuet, P. F., Vázquez, J., & Batista, M. (2020). Sustainability in the aerospace, naval, and automotive supply chain 4.0: Descriptive review. *Materials (Basel)*, *13*(24), 5625. DOI: 10.3390/ma13245625 PMID: 33321743

Rana, S. K., Kim, H., Pani, S. K., Rana, S., Joo, M.-I., Rana, A. K., & Aich, S. (2021). Blockchain-based model to improve the performance of the next-generation digital supply chain. *Sustainability (Basel)*, *13*(18), 10008. DOI: 10.3390/su131810008

Razzaq, R. H., & Al-Zubaidie, M. (2024). Maintaining Security of Patient Data by Employing Private Blockchain and Fog Computing Technologies based on Internet of Medical Things. *Informatica (Vilnius)*, *48*(12), 12. Advance online publication. DOI: 10.31449/inf.v48i12.6047

Razzaq, R. H., Al-Zubaidie, M., & Atiyah, R. G. (2024). Intermediary Decentralized Computing and Private Blockchain Mechanisms for Privacy Preservation in the Internet of Medical Things. *Mesopotamian Journal of CyberSecurity*, *4*(3), 152–165. DOI: 10.58496/MJCS/2024/020

Razzaq, R. H., Tahayur, D. H., Jebbar, W. A., & Al-Zubaidie, M. (2025). Sturdy blockchain combined with e-apps repositories based on reliable camouflaging and integrating mechanisms. *Int. J. Comput. Netw. Inf. Secur*, *17*(3), 35–53. DOI: 10.5815/ijcnis.2025.03.03

Renero, J., Maestre, R., & Ochoa, I. (2026). REX: Causal discovery based on machine learning and explainability techniques. *Pattern Recognition, 172*, 112491. Advance online publication. DOI: 10.1016/j.patcog.2025.112491

Riad, M., Naïmi, M., & Okar, C. (2024). Enhancing supply chain resilience through artificial intelligence: Developing a comprehensive conceptual framework for AI implementation and supply chain optimization. *Logistics (Basel), 8*(4), 111. DOI: 10.3390/logistics8040111

Ribeiro, M. T., Singh, S., & Guestrin, C. (2016). "Why should I trust you?" Explaining the predictions of any classifier. In *Proceedings of the 22nd ACM SIGKDD International Conference on Knowledge Discovery and Data Mining* (pp. 1135–1144). https://doi.org/DOI: 10.1145/2939672.2939778

Rizky, A., Firli, M. Z., Lindzani, N. A., Audiah, S., & Pasha, L. (2024). Advanced cyber threat detection: Big data-driven ai solutions in complex networks. *Journal of Computer Science and Technology Application, 1*(2), 136–143. DOI: 10.33050/corisinta.v1i2.42

Roberts, H., Cowls, J., Morley, J., Taddeo, M., Wang, V., & Floridi, L. (2021). The Chinese approach to artificial intelligence: An analysis of policy, ethics, and regulation. *AI & Society, 36*(1), 59–77. DOI: 10.1007/s00146-020-00992-2

Rojas-Muñoz, L. F., Sánchez-Solano, S., Martínez-Rodríguez, M. C., Camacho-Ruiz, E., Navarro-Torrero, P., Karmakar, A., Fernández-García, C., Tena-Sánchez, E., Potestad-Ordóñez, F. E., Casado-Galán, A., Ortega-Castro, P., Acosta, A. J., Jiménez-Fernández, C. J., & Brox, P. (2024). Cryptographic security through a hardware root of trust. In *Lecture Notes in Computer Science* (p. 106). Springer. DOI: 10.1007/978-3-031-55673-9_8

Ronchini, A., Guida, M., Moretto, A., & Caniato, F. (2024). The role of artificial intelligence in the supply chain finance innovation process. *Operations Management Research*. DOI: 10.1007/s12063-024-00492-2

Roshanaei, M., Khan, M. R., & Sylvester, N. N. (2024). Enhancing cybersecurity through AI and ML: Strategies, challenges, and future directions. *Journal of Information Security, 15*(3), 320–348. DOI: 10.4236/jis.2024.153019

Saeed, S., Suayyid, S. A., Al-Ghamdi, M. S., Almuhaisen, H. A., & Almuhaideb, A. M. (2023). A systematic literature review on cyber threat intelligence for organizational cybersecurity resilience. *Sensors (Basel), 23*(16), 7273. DOI: 10.3390/s23167273 PMID: 37631808

Sahmi, I., & Abdellaoui, A. (2024, October). A Hybrid Lightweight Encryption Using SPECK and SIMON for E-Health Using IoT. *In 2024 10th International Conference on Optimization and Applications* (ICOA) (pp. 1-6). IEEE.

Saideh, M., Jamont, J. P., & Vercouter, L. (2024). Opportunistic Sensor-Based Authentication Factors in and for the Internet of Things. *Sensors (Basel), 24*(14), 4621. DOI: 10.3390/s24144621 PMID: 39066019

Sai, S., Yashvardhan, U., Chamola, V., & Sikdar, B. (2024). Generative AI for cyber security: Analyzing the potential of ChatGPT, DALL-E, and other models for enhancing the security space. *IEEE Access : Practical Innovations, Open Solutions, 12*, 53497–53516. DOI: 10.1109/ACCESS.2024.3385107

Saklani, P., Chauhan, S., & Tiwari, S. (2023). Unlocking the potential of quantum computing: A comprehensive review. *International Journal for Multidisciplinary Research*, *5*(6), 9440. Advance online publication. DOI: 10.36948/ijfmr.2023.v05i06.9440

Salayma, M. (2024). Risk and threat mitigation techniques in internet of things (IoT) environments: A survey. *Frontiers in the Internet of Things*, *2*, 1306018. Advance online publication. DOI: 10.3389/friot.2023.1306018

Salehi, A., Babaei, A., & Hamidi, H. (2026). AI-Driven Strategies for Supply Chain Resilience: A Review of Challenges and Solutions During Pandemics. *International Journal of Engineering, Transactions B: Applications, 39*(3), 585–605. DOI: 10.5829/ije.2026.39.03c.03

Salem, A. H., Azzam, S. M., Emam, O. E., & Abohany, A. A. (2024). Advancing cybersecurity: A comprehensive review of AI-driven detection techniques. *Journal of Big Data*, *11*(1), 105. DOI: 10.1186/s40537-024-00957-y

Sallam, K. M., Mohamed, M., & Mohamed, A. W. (2023). Internet of Things (IoT) in supply chain management: Challenges, opportunities, and best practices. *Sustainable Machine Intelligence Journal*, *2*. Advance online publication. DOI: 10.61185/SMIJ.2023.22103

Sanclemente, G. L. (2025). Digital tools: Safeguarding national security, cybersecurity, and AI bias. *CEBRI-Journal*, *4*(15), 137-155. https://doi.org/DOI: 10.54827/issn2764-7897.cebri2023.07.03.07.137-155.en

Sanjalawe, Y., ... 'mari, S., & Makhadmeh, S. (2025). Generative AI for Cybersecurity Applications in Threat Simulation and Defense. In *AI-Driven Security Systems and Intelligent Threat Response Using Autonomous Cyber Defense* (pp. 263-304). IGI Global Scientific Publishing.

Saravanamoorthi, P. (2023). A detailed review on quantum computing technologies. *Recent Research Reviews Journal*, *1*(1), 1–12. DOI: 10.36548/rrrj.2022.1.001

Sarker, I. H. (2024). *AI-driven cybersecurity and threat intelligence: cyber automation, intelligent decision-making and explainability*. Springer Nature., DOI: 10.1007/978-3-031-54497-2

Sarker, I. H., Janicke, H., Mohsin, A., Gill, A. Q., & Maglaras, L. (2024). Explainable AI for cybersecurity automation, intelligence and trustworthiness in digital twin: Methods, taxonomy, challenges and prospects. *ICT Express*, *10*(23), 935–958. DOI: 10.1016/j.icte.2024.05.007

Sayeed, S. A., Rahman, M. M., Alam, S., & Kshetri, N. (2025, April). FSCsec: Collaboration in Financial Sector Cybersecurity-Exploring the Impact of Resource Sharing on IT Security. In *2025 13th International Symposium on Digital Forensics and Security (ISDFS)* (pp. 1-6). IEEE. DOI: 10.1109/ISDFS65363.2025.11012024

Schneier, B. (2000). *Secrets and Lies: Digital Security in a Networked World*. Wiley.

Schöffel, M., Lauer, F., Rheinländer, C. C., & Wehn, N. (2021). On the energy costs of post-quantum KEMs in TLS-based low-power secure IoT. In *Proceedings of the International Conference on Internet-of-Things Design and Implementation (IoTDI '21)* (pp. 158–168). ACM. DOI: 10.1145/3450268.3453528

Schöffel, M., Lauer, F., Rheinländer, C. C., & Wehn, N. (2022). Secure IoT in the era of quantum computers — Where are the bottlenecks? *Sensors (Basel)*, *22*(7), 2484. DOI: 10.3390/s22072484 PMID: 35408099

Secretariat, B. R. I. C. S. (2025, April 10). *BRICS strengthens cooperation on cybersecurity*. https://brics.br/en/news/brics-strengthens-cooperation-on-cybersecurity

Segkoulis, T., & Limniotis, K. (2025). Enhancing Multi-Factor Authentication for Mobile Devices through Cryptographic Zero-Knowledge Protocols. *Electronics (Basel)*, *14*(9), 1846. DOI: 10.3390/electronics14091846

Sekti, B. A. (2025). Machine learning and artificial intelligence (AI) in manufacturing. In *Integrating Digital Innovation and Integrated Frameworks in Manufacturing* (pp. 255–292). DOI: 10.4018/979-8-3373-1082-4.ch011

Sewak, M., Sahay, S. K., & Rathore, H. (2023). Deep reinforcement learning in the advanced cybersecurity threat detection and protection. *Information Systems Frontiers*, *25*(2), 589–611. DOI: 10.1007/s10796-022-10333-x

Shahana, A., Hasan, R., Farabi, S. F., Akter, J., Mahmud, M. A. A., Johora, F. T., & Suzer, G. (2024). AI-driven cybersecurity: Balancing advancements and safeguards. *Journal of Computer Science and Technology Studies*, *6*(2), 76–85. DOI: 10.32996/jcsts.2024.6.2.9

Shaikh, M. S., Chauhan, P. S., Baig, I., & Ali, S. I. (2022). *Quantum computing for optimization problems: A review and future directions.* COMPUSOFT: An International Journal of Advanced Computer Technology, 11, 3995-3997. Retrieved from https://ijact.in/index.php/j/article/view/625

Shaikh, M. S., Chauhan, P. S., Baig, I., & Ali, S. I. (2023). Decentralized autonomous networks for secure data sharing: A theoretical framework and conceptual analysis. *COMPUSOFT: An International Journal of Advanced Computer Technology, 12*, 4007–4009. https://ijact.in/index.php/j/article/view/632

Shaked, A., Cherdantseva, Y., Burnap, P., & Maynard, P. (2023). Operations-informed incident response playbooks. *Computers & Security*, *134*, 103454. DOI: 10.1016/j.cose.2023.103454

Sharma, P., Homkar, A., Jha, S., Somasekar, J., Wbaid, S., & Dixit, K. K. (2026). Efficient Cybersecurity Threat Analysis Through Anomaly Detection and Graph Summarization. In *Synthesis Lectures on Computer Science: Vol. Part F729* (pp. 43–53). DOI: 10.1007/978-3-031-93802-3_4

Sharma, A. (2025). A comprehensive review of explainable AI in cybersecurity. *Computers & Security*, *141*, 102500. DOI: 10.1016/j.cose.2025.102500

Sharma, S. B., & Bairwa, A. K. (2025). *Leveraging AI for Intrusion Detection in IoT Ecosystems: A Comprehensive Study*. IEEE., DOI: 10.1109/ACCESS.2025.3550392

Shen, K. (2024). Research on the application of quantum computing in artificial intelligence. *Journal of Computing and Electronic Information Management*, *13*(1), 38–42. DOI: 10.54097/4cg2am4s

Sheoran, R. K., Verma, S., Sheoran, S. K., & Yadav, V. (2024). Quantum computing research. In Advances in computer and electrical engineering book series (pp. 236–263). DOI: 10.4018/979-8-3693-1168-4.ch012

Shrivastav, M. (2022). Barriers related to AI implementation in supply chain management. *Journal of Global Information Management*, *30*(8), 1–19. DOI: 10.4018/JGIM.296725

Siano, P., & De Marco, G. (2019). Towards smart grid communications: An overview on architectures, models, and standards. *Renewable & Sustainable Energy Reviews*, *82*, 2109–2127. DOI: 10.1016/j.rser.2017.10.030

Sigfrids, A., Leikas, J., Salo-Pöntinen, H., & Koskimies, E. (2023). Human-centricity in AI governance: A systemic approach. *Frontiers in Artificial Intelligence*, *6*, 976887. DOI: 10.3389/frai.2023.976887 PMID: 36872934

Singh, A., Singh, D., & Singh, R. (2024). Generative ai for cyberdefense. In Generative, A. I. (Ed.), *Current Trends and Applications* (pp. 121–145). Springer Nature Singapore. DOI: 10.1007/978-981-97-8460-8_7

Singh, H. (2025). Securing High-Stakes Digital Transactions: A Comprehensive Study on Cybersecurity and Data Privacy in Financial Institutions. *SSRN*, *5267850*, •••. https://ssrn.com/abstract=5267850. DOI: 10.2139/ssrn.5267850

Smith, J., & Johnson, M. (2025). Quantum computing for financial risk management. *IEEE Transactions on Computational Finance*, *10*(1), 1–8.

Sobhy, A., Amissah, J., Kinga, S., Mugerwa, G., Emmanuel, E., Mansour, D. E. A., & Prokop, L. (2024). Securing Modern Power Systems: Implementing Comprehensive Strategies to Enhance Resilience and Reliability against Cyber-Attacks. *Results in Engineering*, *23*, 102647. DOI: 10.1016/j.rineng.2024.102647

Sommer, R., & Paxson, V. (2010). Outside the closed world: On using machine learning for network intrusion detection. In *Proceedings of the 2010 IEEE Symposium on Security and Privacy* (pp. 305–316). https://doi.org/DOI: 10.1109/SP.2010.25

Sontan, A. D., & Samuel, S. V.Adewale Daniel SontanSegun Victor Samuel. (2024). The intersection of Artificial Intelligence and cybersecurity: Challenges and opportunities. *World Journal of Advanced Research and Reviews*, *21*(2), 1720–1736. DOI: 10.30574/wjarr.2024.21.2.0607

Sood, A. (2024). *Combating Cyberattacks Targeting the AI Ecosystem: Assessing Threats, Risks, and Vulnerabilities*. Walter de Gruyter GmbH & Co KG. DOI: 10.1515/9781501520549

Sood, S. K., & Pooja, N. (2023). Quantum computing review: A decade of research. *IEEE Transactions on Engineering Management*, *71*, 6662–6676. DOI: 10.1109/TEM.2023.3284689

Sowmya, R., & Konduri, B. (2025). Explainable and cognitive attention evoked learning framework for mitigating the large-scale real time cyber attacks. *Discover Computing*, *28*(1), 160. Advance online publication. DOI: 10.1007/s10791-025-09672-5

SpinQuanta. (2025). Top quantum computing applications in key industries. BlueQubit. (2025). Quantum computing software platforms of 2025.

Srivastava, S. S., Ali, S. I., Srivastava, A. K., & Goswami, C. (2024). Improving 5G network performance with MIMO technology using beamforming algorithm. *ICTACT Journal on Communication Technology*, *15*(2), 3173–3180. DOI: 10.21917/ijct.2024.0472

Srivastava, S. T. C., Sharmiladevi, D., Sugumar, D., Ali, S. I., Jones Mary, T. A., & Kumar, S. (2023). Using a smart wearable device monitoring the social distance in smart cities. In *2023 International Conference on Research Methodologies in Knowledge Management, Artificial Intelligence and Telecommunication Engineering (RMKMATE)* (pp. 1–5). IEEE. DOI: 10.1109/RMKMATE59243.2023.10369118

Stanford University. (2025). *Building Trustworthy AI: Navigating Security in the Agentic Era*. Stanford Online Conference Proceedings. https://almamater.at/conf/building-trustworthy-ai-navigating-security-in-the-agentic-era/

Sunkara, G. (2025). Multi-agent AI systems for coordinated cybersecurity in smart cities. *International Journal for Research Publication and Seminars*, *16*(3), 4–22. DOI: 10.36676/jrps.v16.i3.287

Sun, N., Ding, M., Jiang, J., Xu, W., Mo, X., Tai, Y., & Zhang, J. (2023). Cyber threat intelligence mining for proactive cybersecurity defense: A survey and new perspectives. *IEEE Communications Surveys and Tutorials*, *25*(3), 1748–1774. DOI: 10.1109/COMST.2023.3273282

Suryadi, A., & Rau, H. (2023). Considering region risks and mitigation strategies in the supplier selection process for improving supply chain resilience. *Computers & Industrial Engineering*, *181*, 109288. DOI: 10.1016/j.cie.2023.109288

Suthar, B. S., Ali, S. I., & Patel, K. (2025). Hand gesture sign language recognition embedded with Arduino. *IET Conference Proceedings, 7*(), Article 1565. DOI: 10.1049/icp.2025.1565

Suthar, B., & Ali, S. I. (2025). A survey on hand gesture sign language recognition with Arduino Leonardo. In *2025 International Conference on Computational, Communication and Information Technology (ICCCIT)* (pp. 111–115). IEEE. https://doi.org/DOI: 10.1109/ICCCIT62592.2025.10927994

Syahreen, M., Hafizah, N., Maarop, N., & Maslinan, M. (2024). A Systematic Review on Multi-Factor Authentication Framework. *International Journal of Advanced Computer Science and Applications*, *15*(5). Advance online publication. DOI: 10.14569/IJACSA.2024.01505105

Syed, S. A. (2025). Adversarial AI and cybersecurity: Defending against AI-powered cyber threats. *Iconic Research and Engineering Journals*, *8*(9), 1030–1041.

Taeihagh, A. (2025). Governance of generative AI. *Policy and Society*, *44*(1), 1–22. DOI: 10.1093/polsoc/puaf001

Taghizadeh, E., Venkatachalam, S., & Chinnam, R. B. (2024). A dynamic resilience management framework for deep-tier supply networks. *Cleaner Logistics and Supply Chain*, *13*, 100174. DOI: 10.1016/j.clscn.2024.100174

Tahayur, D. H., & Al-Zubaidie, M. (2025). Security Cooperation in the Protection Concerns of Agriculture Data Using Efficient Signatures and Artificial Bee Colony Manner. In *Sustainable Information Security in the Age of AI and Green Computing* (pp. 439–460). IGI Global Scientific Publishing., DOI: 10.4018/979-8-3693-8034-5.ch022

Tanikonda, A., Pandey, B. K., Peddinti, S. R., & Katragadda, S. R. (2022). Advanced AI-Driven Cybersecurity Solutions for Proactive Threat Detection and Response in Complex Ecosystems. *SSRN*, *3*(1). Advance online publication. DOI: 10.2139/ssrn.5102358

Tan, Z., Anagnostopoulos, C., & Singer, J. (2025). Distributed temporal graph learning with provenance for APT detection in supply chains [Preprint]. arXiv. DOI: 10.1109/ICDCSW63273.2025.00071

Tariq, M. U. (2025). Autonomous Data Orchestration With Generative AI: Re-defining Pipelines for Intelligent Analytics. In Elbaghazaoui, B., Amnai, M., & Gherabi, N. (Eds.), *Generative AI-Powered Data Architectures: From Governance to Autonomous Analytics* (pp. 165–192). IGI Global Scientific Publishing., DOI: 10.4018/979-8-3373-5616-7.ch007

Tariq, M. U. (2025). Defense Mechanisms Against Adversarial Attacks: Strengthening AI Security in Cybersecurity Applications. In Ul Rehman, S. (Ed.), *Challenges and Solutions for Cybersecurity and Adversarial Machine Learning* (pp. 199–226). IGI Global Scientific Publishing., DOI: 10.4018/979-8-3373-2200-1.ch007

Tariq, M. U. (2025). Enhancing Cyber-Physical System Resilience With Safe Data-Driven Control Strategies. In Arbi, A. (Ed.), *Safe Data-Driven Control for Cyber-Physical Systems* (pp. 103–128). IGI Global Scientific Publishing., DOI: 10.4018/979-8-3373-1832-5.ch004

Tariq, M. U. (2025). Ethical Implications of Collecting and Using Data to Power AI Tools. In Khan, S., & Pringuet, P. (Eds.), *Empowering Learners With AI: Strategies, Ethics, and Frameworks* (pp. 201–228). IGI Global Scientific Publishing., DOI: 10.4018/979-8-3373-7386-7.ch009

Tariq, M. U. (2025). Fraud Detection and Mitigation in Cybersecurity Insurance: AI-Driven Approaches and Best Practices. In Alawida, M., Almomani, A., & Al-authman, M. (Eds.), *AI-Driven Cybersecurity Insurance: Innovations in Risk, Governance, and Digital Resilience* (pp. 169–194). IGI Global Scientific Publishing., DOI: 10.4018/979-8-3373-5545-0.ch007

Thakur, A. (2023). Market trends and analysis of blockchain technology in supply chain. *Frontiers in Blockchain*, *6*, 1142599. Advance online publication. DOI: 10.3389/fbloc.2023.1142599

Thangamani, R., Vimaladevi, M., Kamalam, G. K., & Subramanian, K. M. (2025). Securing the Future: Quantum Computing in Cybersecurity. In *Quantum Computing, Cyber Security and Cryptography: Issues, Technologies, Algorithms, Programming and Strategies* (pp. 441-487). Singapore: Springer Nature Singapore. DOI: 10.1007/978-981-96-4948-8_17

Tikanmäki, I., Savolainen, J., & Ruoslahti, H. (2024). The role of standards in enhancing cybersecurity and business continuity management for organizations. *Information & Security: An International Journal*, *55*(1), 63–76. DOI: 10.11610/isij.5523

Topping, C., Dwyer, A. C., Michalec, O., Craggs, B., & Rashid, A. (2021). Beware suppliers bearing gifts!: Analysing coverage of supply chain cyber security in critical national infrastructure sectorial and cross-sectorial frameworks. *Computers & Security*, *108*, 102324. DOI: 10.1016/j.cose.2021.102324

Tran, N. K., Pallewatta, S., & Babar, M. A. (2024). An empirically grounded reference architecture for software supply chain metadata management. *Proceedings of the 28th International Conference on Evaluation and Assessment in Software Engineering*. DOI: 10.1145/3661167.3661212

Tregi, T. G., & Al-Zubaidie, M. (2025a). A Quantum Resilient Security System for Smart Power Grid Data: Combining Kyber, FALCON, and Zero-Knowledge Proofs Against Quantum Threats. *Applied Data Science and Analysis*, *2025*, 201–220. DOI: 10.58496/ADSA/2025/017

Tregi, T. G., & Al-Zubaidie, M. (2025b). Enhancing Traffic Data Security in Smart Cities Using Optimized Quantum-Based Digital Signatures and Privacy-Preserving Techniques. *Mesopotamian Journal of CyberSecurity*, *5*(1), 256–272. DOI: 10.58496/MJCS/2025/017

Triplett, W. J. (2022). Addressing human factors in cybersecurity leadership. *Journal of Cybersecurity and Privacy*, *2*(3), 573–587. DOI: 10.3390/jcp2030029

TVBRICS. (2025, October 7). *BRICS and cybersecurity: protecting shared digital space.* https://tvbrics.com/en/news/brics-and-cybersecurity-protecting-shared-digital-space/

Tzavara, V., & Vassiliadis, S. (2024). Tracing the evolution of cyber resilience: A historical and conceptual review. *International Journal of Information Security, 23*(3), 1695–1721. DOI: 10.1007/s10207-023-00811-x

Uddin, M., Irshad, M. S., Ali, I., Alanazi, F., Ahmed, F., Maaz, M., Hussain, S., & Ullah, S. S. (2025). Generative AI revolution in cybersecurity: A comprehensive review of threat intelligence and operations. [ResearchGate]. *Artificial Intelligence Review, 58*(8), 236. Advance online publication. DOI: 10.1007/s10462-025-11219-5

Vadisetty, R., & Polamarasetti, A. (2024, November). Generative AI for Cyber Threat Simulation and Defense. In *2024 12th International Conference on Control, Mechatronics and Automation (ICCMA)* (pp. 272-279). IEEE. DOI: 10.1109/ICCMA63715.2024.10843938

Vast, R., Sawant, S., Thorbole, A., & Badgujar, V. (2021, April). Artificial intelligence-based security orchestration, automation and response system. In *2021 6th International Conference for Convergence in Technology (I2CT)* (pp. 1-5). IEEE DOI: 10.1109/I2CT51068.2021.9418109

Venables, A. (2021). Modelling cyberspace to determine cybersecurity training requirements. *Frontiers in Education, 6*, 768037. Advance online publication. DOI: 10.3389/feduc.2021.768037

Verma, D. (2024). Enhancing Cybersecurity Through Adaptive Anomaly Detection Using Modern AI. https://urn.fi/URN:NBN:fi:jyu-202405273981

Vikram, A., Shnain, A. H., Jeet, R., Vennila, C., Sahu, P., & Krishnakumar, K. (2024, September). AI-Powered Network Intrusion Detection Systems. In *2024 IEEE International Conference on Communication, Computing and Signal Processing (IICCCS)* (pp. 1-6). IEEE. DOI: 10.1109/IICCCS61609.2024.10763627

Vishwakarma, A. K., Gupta, M., & Kumar, S. (2024). Blockchain-based peer-to-peer renewable energy trading: Opportunities and challenges. *International Journal of Production Research, 62*(10), 2451–2466. DOI: 10.1080/01605682.2024.2441224

Wairagade, A., & Ranjan, S. (2025, April). User Behavior Analysis for Cyber Threat Detection: A Comparative Study of Machine Learning Algorithms. In *2025 13th International Symposium on Digital Forensics and Security (ISDFS)* (pp. 1-6). IEEE. DOI: 10.1109/ISDFS65363.2025.11011949

Wallis, T., & Dorey, P. (2023). Implementing partnerships in energy supply chain cybersecurity resilience. *Energies, 16*(4), 1868. DOI: 10.3390/en16041868

Wallis, T., & Dorey, P. (2024). Collaboration practices for the cybersecurity of supply chains to critical infrastructure. *Applied Sciences (Basel, Switzerland), 14*(13), 5805. DOI: 10.3390/app14135805

Wang, S., Taha, A. F., Wang, J., Kvaternik, K., & Hahn, A. (2019). Energy crowdsourcing and peer-to-peer energy trading in blockchain-enabled smart grids. *arXiv preprint* arXiv:1901.02390. https://arxiv.org/abs/1901.02390

Wang, S., Yin, J., Wang, X., & Khan, R. U. (2026). Mitigating Typhoon Disruptions and Enhancing Port Infrastructure Performance: A Risk Assessment Approach. *ASCE-ASME Journal of Risk and Uncertainty in Engineering Systems. Part A, Civil Engineering, 12*(1), 04025090. Advance online publication. DOI: 10.1061/AJRUA6.RUENG-1670

Weisman, M. J., Kott, A., Ellis, J. E., Murphy, B., Parker, T., Smith, S. C., & Vandekerckhove, J. (2024). *Quantitative measurement of cyber resilience: Modeling and experimentation.* ACM Transactions on Cyber-Physical Systems., DOI: 10.1145/3703159

Williams, L., Benedetti, G., Hamer, S., Paramitha, R., Rahman, I., Tamanna, M., Tystahl, G., Zahan, N., Morrison, P., Acar, Y., Cukier, M., Kästner, C., Kapravelos, A., Wermke, D., & Enck, W. (2025). Research directions in software supply chain security. *ACM Transactions on Software Engineering and Methodology, 34*(5), 1–38. Advance online publication. DOI: 10.1145/3714464

Wu, M., Su, H., & Majd, M. (2026). Can We Change Two-Semester Academic year to Trimester Semester System? ~ meeting Competitive World with Effective Educational Policy Upgrade~. *Lecture Notes in Computer Science, 15914 LNCS*, 129–138. DOI: 10.1007/978-3-031-98197-5_15

Wu, Y., Pang, M., Ma, J., Ou, W., Yue, Q., & Han, W. (2025). An Identity Management Scheme Based on Multi-Factor Authentication and Dynamic Trust Evaluation for Telemedicine. *Sensors (Basel), 25*(7), 2118. DOI: 10.3390/s25072118 PMID: 40218645

Xie, S., Qiao, T., Li, S., Zhang, X., Zhou, J., & Feng, G. (2026). DeepFake detection in the AIGC era: A survey, benchmarks, and future perspectives. *Information Fusion, 127*, 103740. Advance online publication. DOI: 10.1016/j.inffus.2025.103740

Xue, M. (2023). Research on quantum computers characteristic. *Theoretical and Natural Science, 5*(1), 355–359. DOI: 10.54254/2753-8818/5/20230582

Xu, L., AlMahri, S., Mak, S., & Brintrup, A. (2024). Multi-agent systems and foundation models enable autonomous supply chains: Opportunities and challenges. *IFAC-PapersOnLine*, *58*(19), 795–800. DOI: 10.1016/j.ifacol.2024.09.200

Yeboah-Ofori, A., Islam, S., Lee, S. W., Shamszaman, Z. U., Muhammad, K., Altaf, M., & Al-Rakhami, M. (2021). Cyber threat predictive analytics for improving cyber supply chain security. *IEEE Access : Practical Innovations, Open Solutions*, *9*, 94318–94337. DOI: 10.1109/ACCESS.2021.3087109

Yekeen, A. O., Ewim, C. P.-M., & Sam-Bulya, N. J.Adeoluwa Omoyemi YekeenChikezie Paul-Mikki EwimNgodoo Joy Sam-Bulya. (2024). Enhancing supply chain security and transparency with AI and blockchain integration for future-proof solutions. *International Journal of Frontline Research in Science and Technology*, *4*(1), 43–57. DOI: 10.56355/ijfrst.2024.4.1.0052

Zanc, R., Cioara, T., Pop, C., Anghel, I., Antal, M., & Salomie, I. (2020). Smart grid management using blockchain: Future scenarios and challenges. *arXiv preprint* arXiv:2012.06256. https://arxiv.org/abs/2012.06256

Zdrojewski, K. (2025). AI-Powered Cyberattacks: A Comprehensive Review and Analysis of Emerging Threats. *Advances in IT and Electrical Engineering*, *31*, 55–70.

Zhang, C., Wu, J., Long, C., & Cheng, M. (2017). Review of existing peer-to-peer energy trading projects. *Energy Procedia*, *105*, 2563–2568. DOI: 10.1016/j.egypro.2017.03.737

Zhang, Q., Mohammed, A. Z., Wan, Z., Cho, J.-H., & Moore, T. J. (2021). Diversity-by-design for dependable and secure cyber-physical systems: A survey. *IEEE Transactions on Network and Service Management*, *19*(1), 706–729. DOI: 10.1109/TNSM.2021.3091391

Zhang, X. (2024). The impact of digital technologies on supply chain resilience: A framework analysis. *Advances in Economics Management and Political Sciences*, *140*(1), 155–164. DOI: 10.54254/2754-1169/2024.GA18772

Zhang, Y., Behnia, R., Yavuz, A. A., Ebrahimi, R., & Bertino, E. (2024). Uncovering attacks and defenses in secure aggregation for federated deep learning. *2022 IEEE International Conference on Data Mining Workshops (ICDMW)* (pp. 650). IEEE. DOI: 10.1109/ICDMW65004.2024.00090

Zhang, Z., Ning, H., Shi, F., Farha, F., Xu, Y., Xu, J., Zhang, F., & Choo, K. K. R. (2022). Artificial intelligence in cyber security: Research advances, challenges, and opportunities. *Artificial Intelligence Review*, *55*(2), 1–25. DOI: 10.1007/s10462-021-09976-0

About the Contributors

Eduard Babulak is an accomplished international scholar, researcher, consultant, educator, professional engineer, and polyglot. He successfully published his research which has been cited by scholars from all over the world. He is a Fellow of Royal Society RSA and Chartered Fellow, Mentor, and Elite Group Member of the British Computer Society in the UK.

***

Syed Ibad Ali holds a distinguished academic background with a Bachelor of Engineering in Electronics and Communication Engineering (ECE), a Master of Technology in VLSI Design, and a Ph.D. in Electronics and Communication Engineering. With over 14 years of rich academic and research experience, Dr. Ali has been at the forefront of interdisciplinary innovation, merging traditional ECE principles with cutting-edge advancements in artificial intelligence and data science. Currently serving as an associate professor in the Department of Artificial Intelligence and Data Science at Parul Institute of Engineering and Technology, Parul University, Gujarat, he is recognized for his commitment to fostering analytical thinking and research-led pedagogy. His work often bridges theory with impactful applications, inspiring the next generation of engineers and AI specialists. Dr. Ali's passion lies in advancing transparent and ethical AI systems, a vision that is deeply embedded in the themes of this book.

Mishall Al-Zubaidie received the bachelor's degree in computer science from Basrah University, Iraq, in 2004 the master's degree in the security of the wireless network from Basrah University, Iraq, in 2010 and the PhD degree with the School of Agricultural, Computational and Environmental Sciences, Faculty of Health, Engineering, and Sciences, University of Southern Queensland, Toowoomba, QLD, Australia in 2020. His current research interests are - Network communications - Authorising and authenticating users in Electronic Medical Record (EMR) - Authorising and authenticating users in Electronic Health Record (EHR) - Incorporating security and privacy into Health Wireless Sensor Network (HWSN) - Public-Key cryptography - Lightweight hash functions - Anonymity and pseudonymity techniques - XML/XACML policies and authorisation - Keys exchange and session keys - WSN performance - Protection of MAC address - Routing protocols (LEACH/SPIN) - Keys exchange/agreement algorithm in the health system, security, and privacy challenges in smart cities, security and forensics, blockchain and integrity techniques, quantum cryptography keys and signatures, multi factors authentication for modern applications. He has published many research papers in the field of security and privacy, in addition to reviewing more than 1296 research papers for different journals (more than *5 journals) and publishers (such as IEEE, Springer, ELSEVIER, MDPI, Sage, Willy, etc.). Also, he worked in an editor role for over 66 assignments.

Farzeen Basith is a dedicated academic and researcher specializing in Artificial Intelligence, Machine Learning, and Cyber Security. She has contributed several book chapters to reputed international publishers such as IGI Global and Emerald Publishing, focusing on topics like AI-powered cybersecurity, cognitive IoT, behavioral threat analysis, and ethical AI in data-driven management. Her research extends beyond academia, with conference publications on AI-based forecasting and deep learning applications for accessibility. She also holds a design patent for a Sensory-Based Smart Sandal for the Blind, reflecting her commitment to inclusive technological innovation.

Apurbo Biswas is an undergraduate student in the Department of Computer Science at the American International University-Bangladesh (AIUB). His research interests include machine learning, deep learning, natural language processing, computer vision, image processing, Industry 5.0, and CVPR-related domains. He has contributed to multiple research initiatives and has served as a peer reviewer for international journals. His work spans practical machine learning applications, ethical AI, and sustainable technology solutions.

Amal Khaleel Hamad received her bachelor's degree in Computer Science from the College of Sciences, University of Thi-Qar, Iraq, in 2011. The theme of her bachelor's research focused on information security and encryption techniques. She is currently pursuing her master's degree in the Department of Computer Science, Education College for Pure Science, University of Thi-Qar, Iraq. Her research interests focus on cybersecurity and the protection of digital transactions, particularly within industrial and oil-sector environments. Email: amal_khaleel@utq.edu.iq

Muhammad Virga Mulia is a Software Engineer specializing in the development of reliable, efficient, and scalable software solutions. He possesses strong technical expertise in Java, JavaFX, Laravel, MySQL, and Node-RED, with practical experience in IoT-based systems and data warehouse design. His work emphasizes secure communication, system optimization, and architectural precision. With a commitment to continuous learning and innovation, he aims to contribute to the advancement of technology through high-quality engineering and data-driven development

Owafeeuzzaman Patwary widely known as Owafee, is an enthusiastic researcher and a Student of B.Sc. in CSE at American International University-Bangladesh (AIUB). His academic interests include Artificial Intelligence (AI), Machine Learning (ML), Internet of Things (IoT), and Cybersecurity. Owafee is Passionate about innovation, he explores emerging technologies and interdisciplinary research. For any queries, Owafee can be reached by email: 22-49885-3@student.aiub.edu

Binastya Anggara Sekti has been a lecturer at the Faculty of Computer Science, Esa Unggul University, Jakarta, since 2016. He is actively involved in the Artificial Intelligence and Information Security Study Group. He holds a Bachelor's degree in Informatics Engineering from the Bandung Institute of Technology and a Master's degree in Information Systems Management from Trisakti University, Jakarta. Prior to entering academia, he accumulated over 25 years of professional experience as an IT practitioner in various companies across Jakarta. His work focused on developing data centers for internet service providers and delivering IT solutions for the manufacturing and oil & gas sectors. His research interests include artificial intelligence, cybersecurity, and the development of IT infrastructure.

Anisah Sri Utami is an undergraduate student majoring in Information Technology with a strong interest in digital innovation and system development. Throughout her studies, she has actively participated in various academic and project based activities focused on utilizing technology to improve efficiency and information security. Driven by curiosity and a passion for continuous learning, she is dedicated to expanding her expertise in programming, cybersecurity, and artificial intelligence (AI). Anisah believes that technology plays a vital role in creating sustainable solutions to the challenges of the digital era.

Muhammad Usman Tariq is a strategic higher education leader and scholar with more than 17 years of international experience across academia, research, and industry. He holds dual doctorates, a PhD in Artificial Intelligence and a Doctorate in Business Administration and has published extensively as the author of research articles, case studies, book chapters, and academic texts. His contributions also include several patents, reflecting his applied research in technology, business, and education. He is the Founder and CEO of TheCaseHQ.com, a global hub for professional certification programmes, narrative and video case studies, and digital learning innovation. In addition, he serves as President of the Gulf Higher Education Network (Gulf HE), an initiative dedicated to advancing academic practice, faculty development, and institutional collaboration across the region. He is a Principal Fellow of Advance HE (UK), Chartered Fellow of the CIPD (UK), Senior Fellow of SEDA (UK), and a Senior Member of IEEE, reflecting his standing as both an academic innovator and a global professional leader.

Index

A

Adversarial AI 62, 63, 66, 218
Adversarial Machine Learning 24, 30, 32, 48, 191, 219
AI in Cybersecurity 4, 59, 73, 76, 77, 81, 83, 100, 160, 161, 163, 165, 166, 169, 170, 171, 182, 185, 189, 217, 218
Artificial Intelligence 2, 3, 7, 31, 33, 34, 35, 38, 40, 41, 42, 46, 49, 50, 51, 52, 56, 57, 62, 65, 66, 67, 69, 73, 74, 86, 87, 97, 98, 99, 100, 101, 109, 140, 143, 146, 157, 158, 161, 162, 172, 189, 191, 192, 193, 217, 219, 246, 250, 260, 262, 263, 267, 268, 269, 274, 275, 276, 278, 283, 299, 307, 308, 313, 314, 315, 317, 318, 320, 321, 322, 323, 324, 326, 327, 329, 330
Autonomous Threat Response 188

B

Biometric Data 109, 130
Blockchain-Based Governance 301

C

Cognitive Adversarial Security 139, 140, 143, 144, 150, 151, 154, 157, 159
Cross-cultural Implementation 171, 179
Cryptography 38, 101, 102, 103, 108, 109, 117, 128, 131, 133, 137, 187, 259, 273, 274, 275, 276, 278, 279, 283, 288, 290, 301, 302, 303, 304, 305, 306, 307, 310, 312, 313, 314, 315, 316, 317, 318, 319, 321, 324, 328, 329, 330
Cyber Resilience 35, 39, 45, 72, 139, 140, 142, 143, 144, 145, 146, 149, 150, 152, 157, 158, 159, 227, 231, 232, 233, 234, 241, 257, 260, 265, 268, 270, 271
Cybersecurity 2, 4, 5, 6, 7, 8, 9, 21, 26, 29, 31, 32, 33, 35, 37, 38, 39, 40, 41, 42, 45, 46, 49, 50, 51, 54, 56, 57, 59, 61, 62, 63, 64, 67, 69, 70, 71, 72, 73, 74, 75, 76, 77, 80, 81, 82, 83, 84, 85, 86, 87, 88, 89, 91, 92, 93, 94, 95, 96, 97, 98, 99, 100, 101, 103, 104, 112, 118, 120, 121, 122, 125, 127, 131, 133, 135, 136, 140, 141, 142, 143, 145, 146, 147, 148, 149, 150, 151, 156, 157, 158, 159, 160, 161, 162, 163, 164, 165, 166, 167, 168, 169, 170, 171, 172, 173, 174, 175, 176, 177, 178, 179, 180, 182, 183, 184, 185, 186, 187, 188, 189, 191, 192, 193, 196, 197, 200, 201, 210, 215, 216, 217, 218, 219, 221, 222, 223, 227, 228, 229, 231, 232, 233, 235, 236, 237, 241, 242, 245, 246, 247, 250, 251, 255, 257, 258, 260, 261, 262, 263, 265, 266, 269, 270, 271, 273, 277, 278, 279, 280, 281, 288, 290, 295, 296, 299, 301, 307, 308, 310, 312, 314, 315, 318, 320, 323, 324, 326
Cyber Threat Intelligence (CTI) 36, 72, 98, 247, 248, 249, 250, 260, 261, 269
Cyber Transactions 101, 104, 117, 131

D

Data Privacy 1, 24, 37, 57, 66, 87, 99, 131, 161, 171, 236, 247, 253, 255, 258, 260, 264, 265, 266, 298, 329
Deepfake Detection 53, 62, 68
Defense Systems 1, 2, 7, 8, 11, 21, 24, 28, 31, 33, 39, 41, 44, 51, 59, 91, 140, 157, 158
Digital Forensics 1, 17, 19, 37, 38, 69, 71, 75, 78, 79, 83, 85, 86, 87, 91, 93, 98

E

Explainable Artificial Intelligence (XAI) 30, 33, 34, 39, 40, 41, 42, 45, 46, 50, 52, 55, 58, 60, 62, 63, 64, 69, 70, 71, 72, 73, 74, 77, 86, 89, 92, 93, 98, 99, 100, 101, 102, 103, 109, 137, 146, 150, 161, 164, 169, 172, 175, 178, 183, 258, 267

F

Financial Institutions 26, 29, 37, 49, 61, 273, 274, 277, 278, 279, 281, 282, 291, 295, 296, 297

G

Generative Adversarial Networks (GANs) 48, 51, 58, 69, 70, 75, 78, 88, 140, 161, 168, 177
Generative AI 36, 39, 40, 42, 43, 61, 63, 64, 66, 69, 70, 71, 72, 73, 74, 75, 77, 80, 81, 82, 83, 84, 85, 87, 91, 93, 95, 96, 98, 99, 103, 104, 117, 118, 120, 121, 122, 125, 127, 131, 139, 140, 141, 142, 143, 144, 145, 146, 147, 148, 149, 150, 151, 160, 161, 162, 163, 165, 169, 170, 175, 177, 178, 185, 195, 200, 217, 218, 219, 258, 301, 303, 306, 307, 309, 310, 311, 312, 314, 316, 317, 323, 324, 326, 330
Generative Artificial Intelligence (GenAI) 36, 39, 40, 42, 43, 56, 61, 63, 64, 65, 66, 69, 70, 71, 72, 73, 74, 75, 77, 80, 81, 82, 83, 84, 85, 87, 91, 93, 95, 96, 98, 99, 103, 104, 117, 118, 120, 121, 122, 125, 127, 131, 139, 140, 141, 142, 143, 144, 145, 146, 147, 148, 149, 150, 151, 157, 160, 161, 162, 163, 165, 169, 170, 175, 177, 178, 185, 195, 200, 217, 218, 219, 258, 260, 301, 303, 306, 307, 309, 310, 311, 312, 314, 316, 317, 321, 322, 323, 324, 326, 330

I

IDPS 1, 18, 22
Incident Response 2, 3, 4, 5, 7, 17, 18, 23, 27, 56, 164, 173, 180, 225, 233, 237, 245, 246, 249, 250, 252, 255, 257, 258, 263, 269, 305

L

Lightweight Cryptography 101

M

Machine Learning 1, 2, 3, 4, 5, 8, 17, 18, 19, 23, 24, 26, 30, 31, 32, 35, 38, 40, 44, 48, 51, 56, 60, 67, 74, 99, 106, 140, 165, 167, 168, 172, 176, 182, 183, 186, 187, 188, 191, 193, 219, 233, 246, 250, 255, 260, 263, 264, 271, 274, 275, 277, 281, 283, 291, 292, 298, 310
Malware Evolution 75

N

Neuro-Symbolic AI 140, 143, 146, 149, 150, 160

P

Post Quantum Cryptography 276

Q

Quantum Computing 38, 100, 186, 187, 234, 273, 274, 275, 276, 277, 279, 280, 281, 282, 283, 284, 286, 287, 288, 289, 291, 292, 293, 294, 295, 296, 297, 298, 299, 300, 308, 313, 314, 321, 323, 324, 326
Quantum Key Distribution 273, 282, 283, 296
Quantum-Resilient Cybersecurity 323

R

Reinforcement Learning for Cyber Defense 37

S

Security Models 31, 49, 73, 129
Self-Evolving Cyber Resilience 139, 143, 145, 149
Smart Cyber Defense 1, 2, 7, 21, 24, 30, 31
SOAR 1, 4, 5, 17, 18, 21, 22, 23, 24, 25, 26, 27, 28, 29, 31, 263
Supply Chain 3, 13, 67, 106, 135, 222, 223,

224, 225, 226, 227, 228, 229, 230, 231, 232, 233, 234, 235, 236, 237, 238, 241, 242, 243, 244, 245, 246, 247, 248, 249, 250, 251, 252, 253, 254, 255, 256, 257, 258, 259, 260, 261, 262, 263, 264, 265, 266, 267, 268, 269, 270, 271, 272, 277, 292, 298

Z

Zero Trust Architecture 20, 35, 234

www.ingramcontent.com/pod-product-compliance
Lightning Source LLC
LaVergne TN
LVHW081538300926
849161LV00006B/1480